A Violent God-Image

To John Wingate,
With gratitude for
setting up the book
signing at Drew.
My best wishes!

[signature]

Drew University, March 1, 2005

A Violent God-Image

An Introduction to the Work of Eugen Drewermann

MATTHIAS BEIER

continuum
NEW YORK • LONDON

2004

The Continuum International Publishing Group Inc
15 East 26 Street, New York, NY 10010

The Continuum International Publishing Group Ltd
The Tower Building, 11 York Road, London SE1 7NX

Printed in the United States of America

Library of Congress Cataloging-in-Publication Data

Beier, Matthias.
    A violent God-image : an introduction to the work of Eugen Drewermann /
Matthias Beier.
        p.   cm.
    Includes bibliographical references and index.
    ISBN 0-8264-1584-9 (hardcover : alk. paper)
    1. Drewermann, Eugen. 2. Violence – Religious aspects – Christianity.
3. Psychoanalysis and religion. 4. Drewermann, Eugen. Kleriker. 5. Catholic
Church – Clergy – Psychology. 6. Catholic Church and psychoanalysis.   I. Title.
BT736.15.B45 2004
230′.2′092 – dc22
                                                                        2003027590

To Those of My Patients
Who Wrestle with a
Violent God-Image

Drewermann attempts to think nonviolently —
something which has little tradition
in the European history of theology
with its obsession with obedience and self-sacrifice
of especially those who have never learned to live their own life.

—Dorothee Sölle, "Heilung und Befreiung"

Contents

ACKNOWLEDGMENTS xi

INTRODUCTION 3

Nazi Germany and a Violent God-Image   3

Spiritual *and* Psychological Nonviolence   10

Eugen Drewermann — Glimpse of the Public Figure   13

The Work of Eugen Drewermann — A Trojan Horse   19

Chapter 1
FEAR, EVIL, AND THE ORIGINS OF A VIOLENT
GOD-IMAGE 23

Historical Context: The Banality of Evil and the Impotence
of Christianity   23

Fear and the Origin of a Violent God-Image   33

Results of the Exegetical Analysis of Genesis 3 and 4:1–16   34

The Serpent / 37

From Harmony with God to a Heteronomous God-Image / 38

The Deadly Effects of Human Sacrifice for the Divine:
Genesis 4:1–16 / 45

Results of the Psychoanalytic Analysis of Genesis 3
and 4:1–16   47

Universal Images of the Psyche? / 47

Sin as a Neurosis Before God / 51

A Bird's-eye View of the Psychoanalytic Interpretation of
Genesis 2–11 / 55

Genesis 3 in Psychoanalytic Perspective / 59

Genesis 4:1–16 in Psychoanalytic Perspective / 87

Results of the Philosophical and Theological Interpretation
of Genesis 3 and 4:1–16   90

   *Philosophical Analysis of the Structure of "Sin" as Universal
and the Result of Free Choice / 91*

   The Fall in an Analysis of Dasein / 96

   Genesis 4:1–16 in Existential-philosophical Perspective / 106

   Theological Interpretation of Genesis 3 and 4:1–16 / 108

   Faith as Trust: The Alternative to Sin as Fear / 119

   *An Existential Proof of God and the Reality of Psychic
Images / 124*

Conclusion   127

**Chapter 2
WAR, CHRISTIANITY, AND THE DESTRUCTION
OF INNER AND OUTER NATURE: EFFECTS OF
A VIOLENT GOD-IMAGE** 131

Fear, Trust, and the Importance of Psychic Images   131

Fear, War, and God   135

   *Roots of War — from Struggle for Survival to Fears of
the Spirit / 137*

   The Confusion of Religion with Ethics / 145

   *War and Christianity, Or: Belligerent Consequences of a
Violent God-Image / 152*

   A Religious Solution for the Problem of War / 186

**Chapter 3
RECOVERING THE NONVIOLENT GOD-IMAGE OF
JESUS: WORKING THROUGH A SADOMASOCHISTIC
INTERPRETATION OF THE CROSS** 209

Violent God-Image and Sacrificial Religion   212

The Death and Resurrection of Jesus Christ and the
Redemption from a Violent God-Image   219

Jesus Facing the Cross: The End of Fear / 220

The Historical Jesus and a Typological Reading of History / 226

The Symbol of the Cross and the Redemption from a Violent God-Image / 244

Chapter 4
ANALYZING THE CLERGY-IDEAL OF THE ROMAN CATHOLIC CHURCH 273

Diagnosis   280

Etiology   292

Development Through Psychological Stages, Or:
Psychogenesis of the Evangelical Counsels   300

Poverty and Oral Conflicts / 302

Obedience and Anal Conflicts / 304

Chastity and Oedipal Conflicts / 311

Therapeutic Treatment Suggestions   320

The Spiritual Value of the Evangelical Counsels / 323

Religious Reorientation and Reform of the Education of the Clergy / 325

CONCLUSION 327

Appendix 1
DREWERMANN IN AMERICA 335

Appendix 2
A NOTE ON TRANSLATION 339

WORKS CITED 343

INDEX 377

Acknowledgments

Thanks first to Dr. Eugen Drewermann for granting me extensive personal interviews that helped in identifying more clearly key tenets of his complex and multifaceted work. To his siblings, Helmut Drewermann and Else Schaub, and friends for the valuable interviews and online responses that brought into sharper relief the historical context within which his work grew.

I am grateful to Dr. Bernhard Lang, a European expert on Dr. Drewermann's work, for his enthusiastic support of this project. Gratitude to Drs. Robert Corrington, Bill Elkins, Art Pressley, and Dorothy Austin for their encouragement during the process of writing. Above all to the many friends who urged me to introduce Drewermann's innovative, spiritually and emotionally nonviolent interpretation of the Christian message to a wider English-speaking audience. And, finally, thanks to my wonderful editor at Continuum International, Frank Oveis, a visionary who for many years agonized over the challenges of publishing Drewermann in the English-speaking world. May this be a good start!

A Violent God-Image

Introduction

Drewermann's contribution is indispensable for two reasons: because he takes mental/spiritual [*seelisch*] suffering seriously and works for the liberation of those who "all their life long, crippled and cramped by fear, were prevented from risking themselves in life." Secondly, because he does something for the worldwide Church which Latin American liberation theologians cannot achieve but need: he challenges the mega-institution's attempt to stabilize power by means of fear and names authoritarian religion "a form of violence."

— Dorothee Sölle[1]

Nazi Germany and a Violent God-Image

Biblical religion teaches that history is the place of God's revelation. I have never been able to believe this without reservation. Certainly there are great revelations of the human spirit in history, stages of human development, which really cannot be completely disavowed. But is this God's providence? Is world history world judgment? Auschwitz and Dachau as parts of a divine order of salvation? Even if human history harbors [*birgt*] a vast treasure of possibilities of development, it still resembles an indiscriminate slaughter house with countless sacrifices more than a temple of meditation or a place where pilgrims give thanks. ... Where then does God live? A history which to this day is not able to do without wars hides [*verbirgt*] rather than reveals God. (Drewermann 1989d, 40–41)

This statement by German theologian Eugen Drewermann introduces us to the historical context for his sweeping reinterpretation of the Christian faith: in light of twentieth-century history he critically as-

---

1. Sölle 1990, 30.

3

sesses Christian theology for the *way* it tends to interpret its historical
nature. If external (physical, biological, social, political) events or
structures are rashly interpreted as manifestations of an all-knowing
and all-powerful God who has a firm grip on history, then humans
cannot but put God on trial in Nuremberg for his all-knowing, all-
passive, and all-condoning silence in the face of the most inhumane
atrocities of Nazi Germany. If God needs Auschwitz and Dachau
as part of a divine order, Drewermann's whole work wants to say,
then God has an infinitely more genocidal mind than Hitler. God
would then be behind the inhumane imperialism and terror of human
authorities. How can one put an end to the inadvertent theological
propagation of such a tyrannical God-image that legitimates all sorts
of inhumanities? That is one of the key questions Drewermann tries
to answer explicitly and implicitly in his "therapeutic theology of
liberation" (Eicher 1992a, 495). I will quote two passages at length
from Drewermann's writings which serve well to introduce central
themes of his work and life.

> "After Auschwitz one can no longer believe in God." Thirty
> years ago this statement was the core of the so-called God-is-
> dead theology. Faced with the orgies of the organized eradication
> of humans in the twentieth century, one thought the end of
> "monotheism" had arrived. Indeed, the notion of a God who sits
> on his throne beyond the human world and judges the deeds of
> mortals is not consistent with the monstrous crimes which hu-
> mans can and do inflict upon other humans again and again.
> No, this notion certainly belies the way in which the God of the
> Bible apparently deals with his "own" people above all.
>
> During the days of the Babylonian exile, in the middle of
> the sixth century B.C.E., Second Isaiah echoed the lament of the
> people with whom he lived as an "educational measure" of their
> God for those who are obstinate: "So he poured upon him the
> heat of his anger and the fury of war," he wrote. "He set him
> (i.e., Israel) on fire all around, but he does not understand it;
> He burns him, but he did not take it to heart" (Isa. 42:25).[2]
> Two thousand five hundred years ago Second Isaiah believed
> even the Babylonian king Nebuchadnezzar to be a tool of di-
> vine judgment. All the misery which this triumphal ruler of the

---

2. Direct translation from Drewermann's rendition of the biblical passage.

new Babylonian kingdom brought upon a small people at the margins of his rule was understood by the prophet as a lesson of divine punishment. This explanation is and has remained a possibility for the pious among Jews as well as Christians. This is what one is supposed to think.

But now: Hitler...! "He set him on fire all around...; He burns him...."?

No, once and for all: no! One can, one *may* no longer think this way. Even and especially as a theologian. Once and for all such a God "does not exist"; he is — thanks be to God! — finally and forever completely "dead"!

But what then is the status of the faith of the man from Nazareth in *his* "heavenly father," whom he wanted to teach through his word and his person as the one place of hope for the people of his time and probably of all times?

The answer sounds paradoxical. Nothing that humans do can prove the God which Jesus wanted to bring to us to be contradictory or superfluous. On the contrary, the worse the actions of humans to each other the more they can be explained in the eyes of Jesus by the *absence* of God, not because God is not "there," but because humans are "far" from him — far from the land which is their home, from the Garden of Eden as the biblical myth of Genesis puts it. We live "far" from God, if we take the myth seriously, when we accustom ourselves, as did Cain in Genesis 4:16, to settle in the land of Nod, the land of flight. (Drewermann 1996a, 140–51)....

It is therefore not the God of Jesus who is in a state of crisis in the face of the horrors of the twentieth century, but rather that which we usually call theology: the whole scholarly *talk* of God which cannot but paralyze, even pervert into its opposite the central therapeutic concern of Jesus.... [T]he whole perspective of Jesus' thought is projectively displaced [in the scholarly talk of God]: the dismay over humans, the shock about ourselves is turned into a helpless guessing game about the incomprehensibleness of God; the task of making comprehensible the misery of human existence in its abysmal depths and monstrosities and of thinking of ways to change it is then turned into ritual lamentation about the seeming passivity of God; instead of taking issue with the excesses of the human will for justice like the retaliatory wars of the Nazis and the "moral lessons" of the Americans in Hiroshima and Nagasaki, the theological effort gets lost in questions such as what *God* may have thought when he, seemingly unmoved, allowed the horrors of human history — or at least stood passive in their presence.

If we really want to comprehend and seize the original concern of Jesus in our time, then the entire manner of the theological inquiry about God and of the talk of God in the face of humans has finally to be made plain as a flight from oneself, as an escape from the burden of one's own responsibility. The attitude of Jesus was to ask *the human being* what she has gotten into. Here was a prophet who stood up against the machinations of godless rulers as well as the ritual wheels of a god-obsessed priestly caste. Not the Godhead seemed doubtful to Jesus, but rather we who are still the way we have always been: scared children of Adam and Eve, the daughters and sons and heirs of Cain, not children of God, not daughters and sons of light.

The task of theology today is foremost a psychological or anthropological one. To bring light into the darkness of human existence — how else can this be possible at the end of the twentieth century than by reversing the projections into the divine of human fears and aggressions? One hundred fifty years after Feuerbach religion may no longer be abused for the purpose of the humanization of God and the dehumanization of humans, but must finally serve the divinity of God and the humanity of humans. What was going on in God during the "hell of Verdun" and the madness of all the other "battles" and slaughters of humans in the twentieth century is not the real question, but rather what is going on in humans when they, for whatever reason, let go of all kindness, all reason, and all humanity — most often in the name of special duties and heroic virtues! Theology in particular has no choice other than to uncover all possible reasons in humans that prevent us from living the "simple" message of Jesus. A "theology" has to be created which, together with all the anthropological sciences available today, is able, following the message of Jesus, to shed light on the reasons for human deformations and to overcome them as *he* taught us with concrete alternatives through an attitude of deeper trust....

Any religion, deeply enough perceived, wants to bring together and unite humans of all times and territories nonviolently in the core of their humanity [*Menschlichkeit*]. It is only dogma, only the absolute claim of each culturally and historically conditioned form of interpretation of religious experience that turns even the question of God into an object of conflict, of a divine know-it-all attitude and of relentless claims of exclusivity.

Nonetheless there exists a "specific nature" of the religious attitude of Jesus, but it does not lie at the level of doctrine and dogma. God as a means of healing for the sickness of human existence, God as a comfort against the sadness of death, God as a foundation of kindness against the manic love of ever greater violence, God as a medication against the madness of creating value for oneself by means of money — religion as a *therapy* for all the pain it costs to be a human being, — *that* indeed is what is decisively new and essential in Jesus' talk of God as the "father"; that shake-up of everything is indeed what he brought into the world. And therefore it is never exclusive. . . .

In view of human history the religious question in Jesus' sense does not go from humans to God but goes from God to humans. Only in this reversal of theology is the "turn around" which the man of Nazareth proclaimed (Mark 1:15) seriously possible. Not to lecture about God — but to really perceive [*wahrzunehmen*] him and to make him come true [*wahrzumachen*] is all that is important. God in his existence is the redeemer, the "savior," the "helper"; he does not intervene, he does not need to do anything, it is enough that he exists, that he gives himself. More is not necessary and more is not possible in order to reconcile humans with themselves based on the message of Jesus. (Drewermann 1998b, 18–23)

But does it really take Auschwitz to ask whether there may be something wrong with the world or with an omnipotent God-image? No, says Drewermann. He asks: What about the constant suffering in the world? What about the "uncanny" fact that in nature killing is "not only a secondary symptom but its core." Is all this suffering, this "permanent war," this "established terror in nature" not a theological problem? "What theology can withstand this? That is what I would like to know" (ibid.).

Drewermann has recently dedicated a book to the question of the relation between modern biology and the question of God (1999a). Yet he raises the question of suffering not in terms of God but in terms of human beings. His work has not been preoccupied with the question of theodicy, that is, Leibniz's famous question how God can be justified in the face of a world of suffering (Leibniz 1951; Drewermann 1999a, 123–51, 691–92), but rather with the question of *anthropodicy*, of how humans can be justified in the face of the evil they inflict upon each other. It is here that the horror of Auschwitz epitomizes the basic question of why humans inflict evil and which God-image may consciously or unconsciously support rather than prevent such evil. In view of the Holocaust, Drewermann stresses, we cannot simply ask what drives an individual to commit evil. We are faced rather with the question how an entire people can commit evil.

> No theologian will say "Auschwitz was inevitable." To the contrary, we say: "Auschwitz is a crime." . . . [A]t the same time it is said that the Nazis were insane. If insane people commit crimes then they are morally no longer responsible. The question is then: How can entire peoples, cultures, get into this state which is beyond doubt insanity, murderous insanity? How can one separate insanity and crime? Or does one have to identify them? But if they were identical, how could one make a moral judgment about it? (Drewermann 1999d)

Drewermann asks these questions as a German struggling to understand why the generation of his parents was not only unable to prevent but also for the most part willing to support the rise of the dictatorship of the Third Reich. He asks these questions, moreover, as a German *Catholic theologian* trying to come to grips with his own Church's screaming silence during the Nazi terror regime. He sees a close connection between the sacrificial mentality fostered in Christianity against the happiness of the individual and the mentality required by fascism. After he spoke to a packed hall at the nationwide twenty-fifth German Protestant Church Day in June 1993, he reported the following incident to listeners at his next speaking engagement in Austria.

> Just as I said farewell a few hours ago at the Protestant Church Day, where I preached courageously: "People, trust yourself

to become happy!," the speaker after me said: "Christianity does not want happiness but salvation." Great! I was tempted to shout into the room: "In Germany the word 'salvation [Heil[3]]' has been corrupted by the idea of sacrifice in fascism." (Drewermann 1993b, 116)

How is it possible that sacrifice in the name of God, in the name of morality, in the name of Christianity supports rather than prevents fascism? What kind of God-image lends itself to rouse the masses in support of an authoritarian leader? What has to happen in humans that they become swept away by the wave of mass hysteria, in the midst of one of the oldest Christian nations? We need to bear these questions in mind if we want to understand rather than misunderstand Drewermann's theology which sets the dynamic between fear and trust and the relation between the collective human psyche and the individual, historical ego in the center of a comprehensive reinterpretation of Christian theology.

Drewermann, along with feminist and liberation theologians, exemplifies a breakthrough in the Western view of God. In light of the unprecedented atrocities of the twentieth century, Drewermann came to question traditional views of God as an omnipotent ruler and as guarantor of moral law. Drewermann's critique of the notion of a crudely omnipotent God, which I presented above, has striking resemblance to Hans Jonas's subjectively engaged philosophical reflections in "The Concept of God after Auschwitz: A Jewish Voice" (Jonas 1996). While Drewermann developed his views first within the Roman Catholic Church, the significance of his work extends far beyond denominational borders and aims to discern criteria for distinguishing healthy from neurotic spirituality and religion. His work has received attention not only from Catholics, but from people of diverse traditions, such as Protestants, Buddhists, and Muslims — even atheists (see Drewermann and Dalai Lama 1993, Jeziorowski 1992).

Having so far situated Drewermann's work in the context of twentieth-century violence, we can recast his task within the context of the general question whether religion necessarily implies internal, psychological violence against a person.

---

3. Cf. the use of the word in *Heil Hitler!*

Spiritual *and* Psychological Nonviolence

> It is my conviction that the root of evil is want of a living faith
> in a living God. It is a first-class human tragedy that peoples of
> the earth who claim to believe in the message of Jesus whom
> they describe as the Prince of Peace show little of that belief in
> actual practice.
> — Mahatma Gandhi[4]

Erik Erikson, while writing his psychohistorical narrative of the great
Indian leader Mahatma Gandhi, reached a point halfway through
where he almost "felt unable to continue writing *this* book because I
seemed to sense the presence of a kind of untruth in the very protes-
tation of truth; of something unclean when all the words spelled out
an unreal purity; and above all, of displaced violence where nonviolence was the professed issue" (1970, 230–31). The subtitle of
Erikson's study read "On the Origins of Militant Nonviolence." Erikson decided to place a "personal word" (ibid., 229–54) addressed to
Gandhi in the center of the book, revealing to the man who strove
with utmost rigor to implement the principle of nonviolence that
there remained a vestige of violence in the manner in which he attempted to implement *ahimsa*. The principle of nonviolence could
inadvertently become harmful if achieved at the cost of "moralistic repression," the great American psychoanalyst observed. Erikson
enumerates instances where Gandhi seemed unaware of violating the
freedom of those who were closest to him, such as his wife Kas-
turba or his son Harilal, when he put moralistic pressure on them
to follow his own example — in the name of the "spiritual truth"
of nonviolence. The task Erikson set himself in *Gandhi's Truth* was
to confront Gandhi's "spiritual truth" (*Satyagraha*) with "the psychological truth" of psychoanalysis as formulated by Sigmund Freud
and elaborated by his followers. Erikson explains: "I believe that the
psychoanalytic method itself, by dint of always being a self-analysis
with an attempt to understand another man's inner conflicts, is a
counterpart to your Satyagraha, because it confronts the *inner* enemy
nonviolently" (ibid., 244). Here Gandhi, Erikson suggested, should
be complemented by the insights of his Western contemporary, Freud.

Freud himself had confronted the spiritual tradition in the West
in no uncertain terms. Though he acknowledged that psychoanalytic
reason shares the same aims as proclaimed by religion in the name of

---

4. *Truth is God* (1955, 145).

God, namely, "love of man and the decrease of suffering," and though he could conclude from this that "we may tell ourselves that our antagonism is only a temporary one and not irreconcilable" (Freud 1927a, 53–54), Freud for the most part saw the actual practice of religion to be opposed to the kind of self-knowledge psychoanalysis envisioned. He viewed religious practices and doctrines as obstacles to psychological truth. Religion, as he knew it, was harmful to mental health. He considered religion a necessary step in the development of civilization, but a step to be surpassed by reason. At best, religion could be regarded as a "universal obsessional neurosis of humanity" which spared most individuals the development of individual neurosis (ibid., 43). Freud questioned whether there was any truth at all to be found in religion. Addressing his imaginary religious protagonist in *The Future of an Illusion,* Freud was able to exclaim: "your religious doctrines will have to be discarded.... You know why: in the long run nothing can withstand reason and experience" (ibid., 54).

Freud's friendship with the Swiss Protestant pastor and famous lay analyst Oskar Pfister could evoke on rare occasions a more conciliatory tone toward religion. Pfister's work and that of other clergy who came to value psychoanalysis as complementary to the Christian faith led Freud to acknowledge — in the very year he published *The Future of an Illusion* (1927a), his staunchest critique of religion — that Protestant as well as Catholic clergy could employ psychoanalysis in the service of religion. These clergy, Freud learned, had begun to foster faith in their congregants *after* they had freed them through analytic enlightenment from inhibitions that thwarted their lives (1927b, 251–58).

Many books have since addressed whether and how the psychological truth of psychoanalysis can be reconciled with the spiritual truth of religious traditions (especially of the Judeo-Christian tradition).[5] The authors of these titles are variously trained either in psychoanalysis or in theology, or in both.

Does religious practice need to be opposed to the psychological truth of psychoanalysis? Does religion need to have neurotic effects? Does it inevitably lead to moralistic repression? And, to ask more specifically in view of the dominant Western religion, Christianity,

---

5. Among them are classics such as: Erikson 1958, 1970; Fromm 1950; Homans 1970; Jung 1931, 1932, 1933, 1938, 1948, 1954; Küng 1979; Meissner 1984; Pfister 1948; Pruyser 1968; Reik 1951; Rizzuto 1979; Tillich 1957, 1958; Ulanov and Ulanov 1975.

does religion need to do violence to the self in the name of self-renunciation and sanctify suffering in the name of bearing the Cross of Christ? Is the God of Christianity categorically opposed to human desires and to human self-realization? Does this same God sanctify the killings of millions of people in wars declared to be "just" by the Churches? Does this God legitimize the violent exploitation of nonhuman nature and the aggressive, economic exploitation of non-Christian cultures and countries in the name of a secularized religious ideal of "Be fruitful and multiply, and fill the earth and subdue it: and have dominion...over every living thing that moves upon the earth" (Gen. 1:28 NRSV)? And, above all, is the Christian God of love and grace also a God of violent justice? If all these questions are answered in the negative, then one central question remains unanswered: how can religion, especially the Christian religion, become violent internally as well as externally?

Drewermann argues that Christianity has inadvertently been doing violence to people by using *fear* as one of its prime motivators for faith: fear of hell, fear of being excluded from the (dominant) social group, fear of losing one's status, and most of all, fear of God — all have been and are being instrumentalized to keep people in line with the interpretations of Christian beliefs formulated by a hierarchy of Church officials. If religion is based on fear it inevitably not only becomes violent but will sooner or later bring about its own demise, Drewermann predicts. Therefore, in the center of his nonviolent interpretation of key Christian articles of faith stands an analysis of the ambivalent God-image that characterizes traditional interpretations of sin and of the Cross.

Drewermann diligently presents every possible evidence to support his claim that a Christianity based on fear is contrary to the very message of Jesus, whose religion is based on trust. One who healed by means of trust, Jesus accepted those marginalized by the religious and theological elite of his time and challenged *any* system of religious power that is based on fear and intimidation. Christianity, according to Drewermann, soon abandoned the message of faith as trust and replaced it with a message of faith as belief in a certain set of doctrines which must be accepted as historical facts or else one goes to hell. Early Christianity thus adopted the very principle of religious violence that the one it calls its founder fought to his death. Drewermann suggests that Christianity can best rediscover its own spiritual truth, namely, faith as trust, if it learns from the art of psychoanalysis how to confront "the inner enemy nonviolently." In his first trilogy (*Strukturen des Bösen* 1986a, 1985a, 1986b), he implicitly identifies the "inner enemy" of Christianity with the seductive force that leads humans in the biblical story of the fall to follow the voice of the serpent. Just what this "inner enemy" in Christianity is, is one of the surprises Drewermann presents his readers.

But, who is Eugen Drewermann?

Eugen Drewermann — Glimpse of the Public Figure

> If Archbishop Dyba [of Fulda] calls Eugen Drewermann a professional dreamer, then he himself can only be described as a professional boaster. While Dyba believes that the birth of Jesus by the Virgin Mary took place with a closed uterus, Drewermann is honest and interprets it symbolically. That cost him his license to teach. — Gerd Lüdemann, *Focus* magazine, 14 April 1997

Even his fiercest critics had to acknowledge that "Eugen Drewermann has for years been the most widely read and at the same time the most controversial theological author in the German language" (Lauter 1988b, 5). The purpose of this book is to introduce key ideas of Eugen Drewermann in the English-speaking world. It hopes to build a bridge across the Atlantic with the aim of stimulating discussion of Drewermann's far-reaching ideas in the theological and psychological discourse of English-speaking countries.

Drewermann's voice emerged in the late 1970s and grew over the next two decades to become *the* symbol in Europe for attempts to reform Christianity by therapeutic means. A Renaissance man with immense creative output — more than sixty books to date — Drewermann, an ordained Roman Catholic priest, developed from within the Church a critique of Christianity as it actually exists with the aim not of discarding (as Freud had suggested) but of therapeutically reinterpreting its beliefs from the ground up. Drewermann's analysis focuses particularly on the inadvertent psychological violence of Christianity, with the purpose of working through the unresolved psychological and philosophical conflicts that underlie that violence. What makes his work so appealing to many spiritual seekers, Christians and non-Christians alike, is that he does not disavow the validity of a single doctrine of Christianity — or of other religions — but instead attempts to recover in the very beliefs of Christianity the liberating potential that strengthens and builds up the individual against any authority, including the Church, which claims to know better than the individual what is good and what is bad for her or his existence. His work has received such broad resonance that the national news magazine *Der Spiegel* (15 June 1992, 36) concluded "Goliath Church trembles before David Drewermann."

Eugen Drewermann is the most ardent advocate today for the integration of depth psychology into Christian theology. Far from being merely an abstract methodological goal, this is for Drewermann basically a matter of freeing "subjugated knowledges" (Foucault 1980, 78–92) on a psychological and spiritual level in order to empower people to become integrated persons capable of resisting the pull of the collective. Depth psychology serves him as a tool to allow people to become personally and experientially competent in matters of religion and spirituality, a means to safeguard against the infringement of freedom of thought, feeling, and speech within Christianity. As the *Boston Globe* quoted exiled French Bishop Jacques Gaillot, a personal friend of Drewermann: "He allows people who are disappointed with the church, or are far away from it, to be free to speak" (Rosenblum 1996). No cleric before Drewermann has made such extensive efforts to restore psychological health to the interpretation of Christian faith.

Drewermann's most daring attempt to reform the Roman Catholic Church from within came in 1989. "On the very day that the Berlin Wall fell [November 9, 1989] a book appeared from the midst of the Catholic clergy which raised hopes that the high walls between a hierarchy grown powerful and the women and men of God's people grown powerless could fall one day as well: Eugen Drewermann's *Kleriker*" (Eicher 1990b, 14).[6] *Kleriker* (Drewermann 1990a) analyzes the official Church's current clergy-ideal, portrays the mental violence the ideal imposes on its clergy, and makes far-reaching suggestions for reforms toward a more humane ideal. Based on his own

---

6. Cf. Drewermann's comparison of the repressive system of the former East German Communist government with the psychological structure of the Roman Catholic Church. While the former had a law which made it the duty of any soldier at the border to shoot anyone attempting to flee the country and threatened to punish severely any soldier who did not obey this law, the Catholic Church, according to Drewermann, required her priests to treat in essentially the same way those who once were validly married, then divorced, and subsequently wanted to remarry: she requires her clergy to exclude those Catholics from receiving the sacraments, hence from communion with Christ and life in his community, and none of the officials of the Church is permitted on threat of punishment to speak out on their behalf (Drewermann 1990d, 290–93).

psychotherapeutic work with the clergy and on literature on the subject, Drewermann's psychological assessment revealed in depth the neuroticizing structures within the hierarchy of the Roman Catholic Church as it currently exists and questioned the metaphysical ideology of power at its core which supports these structures.[7] The result of Drewermann's wide-ranging attempts at reform came to many as a shock: in 1991 he was silenced as a theologian (as were Leonardo Boff and Matthew Fox) (Fox 1998), and in 1992 suspended as a priest by Archbishop Johannes J. Degenhardt of Paderborn. *Time International* reported that during the height of the controversy, the Roman Catholic Church in Germany lost a record number of more than 300,000 congregants (Johnson 1992).

To convey to the English-speaking reader the cultural-historical significance of Drewermann, I should perhaps present him as most people know him in Europe: as a public figure through the eyes of the media. In 1991 and 1992 the German, French, and Dutch media closely followed the conflict between Drewermann and the official Roman Catholic Church with prime-time TV and front-page news coverage.[8] He "has become a phenomenon in our time of spiritual/intellectual [*geistigen*] change. People are either for or against him" (Schönborn 1993, 7). He has been and is a frequent guest on major radio and TV stations in German-speaking countries as well as in France, Italy, the Netherlands, and other European countries. Contested areas between him and the Roman Catholic leadership on the moral plane include issues such as war, divorce, and abortion. On the dogmatic plane, controversy surrounds the meaning of core Christian beliefs such as the virgin birth, resurrection, crucifixion, miracles, and the role of the Church. In addition to *Kleriker,* his most widely read book, many of Drewermann's books have been national bestsellers in German-speaking countries. His psychotherapeutically oriented interpretations of biblical texts have reached millions of readers, radio listeners, and TV viewers and have inspired clergy throughout the denominational spectrum. Besides members of the Christian churches who support his calls for contemporary reforms within the churches, Drewermann's audiences include a large number of people who do not identify themselves as believers, people who are at the margins of

---

7. A book review of *Kleriker* appeared in *Time International,* 8 January 1990.
8. For a sample of newspaper articles, see *Der Fall Drewermann: Ausgewählte Presse-stimmen* (Walter-Verlag 1991).

the Church, and people who have turned their back to organized religion. While his work has been most influential in German-speaking countries, it has also stirred passionate public debates in France, the Netherlands, Italy, and other European countries. In addition, hundreds of thousands have heard him speak in person during the more than one hundred lectures he gives annually in Europe and beyond. In 1995 French Bishop Jacques Gaillot was suspended from his duties specifically for engaging in a TV discussion with Drewermann on the cultural channel *arte* in April 1994 where the bishop had shown agreement with Drewermann on the need for reforms in the Church (*Der Spiegel*, 23 January 1995).

Drewermann's popularity is indicative of the cultural resonance he has as a public figure. At the peak of the debate around him, polls conducted in Germany indicated strong support for his views. For instance, a poll[9] conducted in 1992 by Emnid, a major German opinion-research institute, found among West Germans that on a scale ranging from +5 to -5 Drewermann had a 2 point lead in popularity over Pope John Paul II. Drewermann had an average rating of +1.8, while the pope received a negative rating of -0.2. Seventy percent of those polled supported Drewermann's right to voice critique of official interpretations of key articles of faith, while only 22 percent agreed with his archbishop, Johannes J. Degenhardt, that as a priest Drewermann had no right to express criticism.

The case of Drewermann is in many respects comparable to the controversy around the Swiss-born Roman Catholic theologian Hans Küng[10] in the 1970s. Küng had taught Catholic theology in Tübingen, Germany, and was silenced by the Vatican in 1979 for his open critique of the doctrine of papal infallibility (Swidler 1981, 384–89). The Vatican's proceedings against Küng mobilized early on, in 1970, no less than 1,360 Catholic theologians from 53 countries to sign a general declaration addressed to the Vatican in support of "freedom of theology" (ibid., 27–30). Among Küng's colleagues at the Catholic Theology Faculty of Tübingen who protested his silencing in 1979 in a public statement (ibid., 392–93) were two men, Gerhard Lohfink and Walter Kasper — the latter a bishop himself at the time of Drewermann's silencing — who in the case of Drewermann sided with the Catholic hierarchy's position and three men, Norbert Greinacher,

---

9. Reported in the German magazine *Der Spiegel*, 15 June 1992, 36–57.
10. For the Küng controversy, see Swidler 1981, Jens 1978, and Häring 1998.

Bernhard Lang, and Herbert Haag, who supported Drewermann's right to free speech within the Church. In an effort to avoid the negative worldwide attention that disciplinary procedures by the Vatican against Küng, Schillebeeckx, Pohier, Boff, and others received, the Vatican began to adopt a strategy of regionalizing conflicts (Walf 1990, 322–23).

In Drewermann's case, the Vatican's Sacred Congregation for the Doctrine of the Faith (hereafter referred to as the CDF), though deeply concerned, did not want to get directly involved. A letter from Joseph Cardinal Ratzinger, Prefect of the CDF, dated 7 May 1986, to Archbishop Degenhardt, Drewermann's local bishop, noted that "after careful study, the publications of Dr. Drewermann caused deep worry" in the Vatican and instructed the bishop to "take appropriate initiatives" (Rick 1992, 348–49).[11] Degenhardt followed suit. He imposed the most severe disciplinary measures ever on a priest-theologian in Germany during the twentieth century. Not only was Drewermann silenced as a theologian — as Küng had been — he was also suspended as a priest — unlike Küng. The "deep worry" about Drewermann extended beyond his influence on the academic discussion of theology. The Church feared his influence as a priest of international recognition who speaks of God in ways which aim to empower the individual, thus challenging the exclusive authority of the teaching office of the Church in matters of personal faith. Like Luther, Drewermann asserts the basic freedom of conscience of each individual in matters of faith.

The Vatican's attempt to regionalize the conflict with Drewermann succeeded only partly. While the case did not get the sustained worldwide attention the Küng case had received a decade earlier, in

---

11. Note that Cardinal Ratzinger ten years later affirmed Drewermann's argument that historical-critical exegesis is limited. In the widely circulated 1996 speech at a meeting in Guadalajara, Mexico, of the CDF with the presidents of the Doctrinal Commissions of the Bishops Conferences of Latin America, in May 1996, Ratzinger said: "This is the point on which Drewermann rightly criticized historical-critical exegesis to the extent that it presumes to be self-sufficient. Such exegesis, by definition, expresses reality, not today's or mine, but yesterday's, another's reality. Therefore, it can never show the Christ of today, tomorrow and always, but only — if it remains faithful to itself — the Christ of yesterday" (Ratzinger 1996). Drewermann's comment: "up to that point he [Ratzinger] has understood [me] correctly." But, Drewermann continued, the difference between himself and Rome would be: "In reality, I take the historical-critical method very seriously. The key difference between me and Paderborn and Rome actually revolves around the issue that while I presuppose historical-critical results in my reading of the Bible they hollow them out dogmatically. I accept the fact that the historical-critical approach to the Bible provides genuine results which the theologian has to accept. If, in addition, one wants to provide [anthropological] reasons for faith, one needs, however, a new method" (Drewermann 1999b).

continental Europe it received no less, in Germany perhaps even more publicity. A statement from 28 September 1989, prepared by Drewermann's colleagues at the Catholic Faculty at Paderborn and signed by 140 professors of theology and more than 26,000 lay people from many countries, called for a fair process and condemned the Kafkaesque procedure the Church hierarchy had adopted in dealing with Dr. Drewermann (Eicher 1990a, 241–42). All over Germany, peaceful demonstrations in favor of Drewermann's views were held, thousands of signatures collected in support of his right to freedom of thought and speech within the Church, hundreds of articles for and against Drewermann's views appeared in the daily press, in denominational magazines, and in academic journals, and heated discussions occurred on all levels of society.[12]

As a person, Drewermann was described by the media as a "soft rebel" (Rudolf Augstein, editor of the magazine *Der Spiegel*), as a man known for his simple, ecologically minded lifestyle, living without car, phone, and refrigerator, "the man always wearing a sweater" (even on TV), and as a vegetarian and passionate pacifist. His voice is soft but determined, but can become passionate yet still restrained when he speaks emphatically of the oppressive effects of religious power. Known for his eloquence, many of his extemporaneous sermons or talks on a wide variety of subjects soon find their way into print. He possesses a phenomenal memory for details. "Without ever making a mistake, the well-read [Drewermann] recites from memory lengthy passages from plays, fairy tales or mythological texts — as though he were a TV anchor person reading texts that are invisible for viewers" (Schönborn 1993, 11). It is said that his readers, reviewers, and critics cannot keep up with his creative output.

The worldwide implications of Drewermann's work are poignant at a time when the psychological violence of certain types of religious attitudes have entered the spotlight in two major areas: the use of God-talk as justification for terrorism and for retaliation against terrorism, and the abuse of religious power in the case of the Church's handling of pedophile priests. As we will see, Drewermann argues that understanding the unique aspects of pedophilia in priests requires an analysis of the overall context of the repressive attitude toward sexuality in the Roman Catholic Church (Drewermann 2002a).

---

12. For a comprehensive bibliography — spanning more than a hundred pages — of the literature by and around Drewermann up to 1993, see Sobel 1993.

The Work of Eugen Drewermann—A Trojan Horse

During one of the interviews conducted by the author, Eugen Drewermann described his life's work as a project "to change the doctrinal system of the Catholic Church in three concentric circles from the outside to the inside" (1999b). His goal is to reinstate the authority of the individual in each circle starting first with moral theology, moving next to biblical interpretation, and arriving finally at the interpretation of Christian doctrine. Drewermann often applies the metaphor of the Trojan horse or Trojan troika to his attempts to revamp Christian theology by means of depth psychology (e.g., 1984a, 18). Depth psychology serves him as a tool that can analyze the "resistances" the Christian Church has against a nonambivalent, nonviolent God-image, and the rationalistic defense mechanisms which keep theological discourse removed from the powerful emotions in the human psyche in which the healing images of Jesus of Nazareth are rooted.

In the area of moral theology Drewermann realized that he had to make a basic choice between his conscience and official interpretations of Christian faith. A burning question of his youth in the 1950s—as for many Germans during that era—centered around the question of postwar German rearmament. A devout Catholic and believer in the Christian message of peace, he was suddenly faced with the unimaginable: Pope Pius XII declared in his Christmas address of 1956 that "under current circumstances" no Catholic called upon by an elected government had the right to conscientious objection to military service—a statement fueled by fears of an invasion of Western Europe by the atheist Communist Soviet Union (Pius XII 1956, 178). Drewermann was fifteen years old at the time. For more than five years he wrestled with a choice between allegiance to the Church's teaching and allegiance to his own conscience. A few years later, one of the pope's closest advisors, the German Jesuit priest Gustav Gundlach, claimed that Pius XII considered even the use of nuclear bombs justified to protect the divine order from Communist atheism (Gundlach 1959).[13] As was the case with the majority of Germans who grew up during the war and postwar years, Drewermann's conscience emphatically rejected the idea of participating in military training,

---

13. For the debate over Pope Pius XII's view on rearmament and the use of nuclear weapons, see also Hirschmann 1958, 1984; Böckenförde and Spaemann 1960, Dirks 1958, Doering-Manteuffel 1981, Stratmann 1960.

that is, in "training to kill on command." The lack of support and outright disapproval he received from the official Catholic Church in his decision to be a conscientious objector severely disillusioned him. The Church tried to override the individual's right to follow his conscience.

This represents a core conflict in religion addressed in Drewermann's work: a conflict between the individual's right to follow her own conscience and the Church's (or any religious institution's) claims to know and to dictate with divine certainty the real duties of the individual. In light of Nazi absolutism where the notion of the sacrifice of the individual and of everything human for the sake of the group was carried to its most painful and cruel extreme, Drewermann came to question the group psychology of the Church with its call for suffering in the name of the Cross.

Any study of the multifaceted and diverse nature of Drewermann's work is inevitably selective and fragmentary. Still evolving, his work has in the past decade arrived at the innermost concentric circle: a reinterpretation of the doctrine of creation in light of modern anthropology, biology, physics, and cosmology (Drewermann 1998b, 1999a, 2002b). This book will focus mostly on works published prior to the disciplinary measures against him in 1992. These titles revolve essentially around the integration of depth psychology into moral theology, biblical interpretation, and ecclesiology — although Drewermann, who received his doctorate in dogmatic theology, always writes with an eye on the implications for doctrinal theology.

Drewermann wants to redefine the role of the Church from a judgmental agency, imposing all kinds of restrictions on people and keeping them in spiritual immaturity, to an agency where people find understanding for their moral dilemmas and a place of unconditional acceptance that empowers them therapeutically and that fosters spiritual maturity. His premise is that a healthy group exists only to the extent it has healthy individuals capable of healthy relationships. The group psychology of the Church is analyzed by Drewermann, and experienced by countless clergy, listeners, and viewers to whom his work speaks, as a psychology aimed at keeping people in infantile emotional and spiritual positions while at the same time idealizing a few select group members into quasi-omnipotent (i.e., psychologically archaically narcissistic, see Kohut 1971) parental and divine positions. Drewermann has become a spokesperson for the victims of such a group psychology: for those who have been marginalized or excluded by the Church for moral reasons (for instance, Catholic women who have had abortions, divorcees who remarry, gays and lesbians, clergy who question the humaneness of obligatory celibacy) and for those who seek a poetic language of faith that goes beyond a superstitious repetition of biblical or doctrinal phrases, a language that touches the heart while not sacrificing reason in the name of religion. Drewermann's analysis finds that the Church's central psychological and spiritual instrument for keeping people psychologically and spiritually immature revolves around an ambivalent God-image that is born of fear. An ambivalent God-image involves the fear-based confusion of ambivalent parental introjects with the divine.

This book will present the following key aspects of Drewermann's work: Chapter 1 portrays Drewermann's nonmoralistic reinterpretation of the biblical story of the fall and its consequences for human relationships and introduces us to his use of a unique combination of exegetical, psychoanalytic, and philosophical-theological methods. The central importance of the dynamics of fear versus trust for the emergence of a violent God-image will be fleshed out. We will learn how Drewermann develops the thesis that in a field of fear sacrifice and moral striving inadvertently become caught up in a sadomasochistic dynamic and usually turn into results opposite to those consciously intended. Chapter 2 embarks on a journey through Drewermann's application of the analysis of the dynamics that invoke a violent God-image to an analysis of the psychospiritual dynamics underlying ecological exploitation and the spiral of violence in war and terror. It centers on Drewermann's thesis that Christianity in spite of itself promoted violence against nature and peoples because of its own unresolved ambivalent and violent God-image. Chapter 3 outlines Drewermann's reading of the message of Jesus as an antidote to the spell of fear by means of images of trust which recover a nonviolent God-image. Here we see Drewermann attempting to work through pervasive sadomasochistic interpretations of the Cross in Christianity, especially as manifested in fear-based notions of self-sacrifice. Chapter 4 presents Drewermann's widely known analysis of power dynamics built on fear and self-sacrifice in the Roman Catholic Church's treatment of its clergy, together with his proposal for a more humane reinterpretation of the clergy-ideal based on trust and self-acceptance. A Conclusion recapitulates and ties together the preceding chapters.

As we shall see, Drewermann proposes a therapeutic theology of individual and communal healing that aims at working through the spiritual fears that transform universal and developmentally normal (oral-)sadistic impulses in humans into absolute aggression against self and others in the name of a violent God-image. By paying attention to the *anthropological* dynamics involved in the creation of a violent or nonviolent God-image, Drewermann tries to redeem Christianity from historicizing interpretations which too easily lead to anti-semitism, racism, sexism, and cultural imperialism. He reinterprets the historical nature of Christianity through an emphasis on the *personal-attitudinal* dimension rather than the external-historical-factual dimension, thus arriving at a typological reading of age-old texts which perceives in those texts spiritual and emotional dynamics found across times and spaces of human history.

Chapter 1

Fear, Evil, and the
Origins of a Violent God-Image

Historical Context: The Banality of Evil
and the Impotence of Christianity

The trial of Adolf Eichmann in Jerusalem in 1961 revealed to the world the shocking "banality of evil" of Nazi Germany (Arendt 1965). The world witnessed how the functionaries of the Nazi machinery of death had performed their administrative tasks in the name of moral values such as "duty [*Pflicht*]" to the fatherland or "obedience [*Gehorsam*]" to superiors. These values combined with technological reason to create the infrastructure required for the "final solution," the attempt to eradicate the "Other" who was perceived as an ultimate threat. Eichmann's answers to questions from the prosecutor and the panel of three judges show how well-intentioned allegiance to authority, fearful lack of an inner sense of self, and remove from human feelings[1] can produce a mentality capable of the creation and sanction of extermination camps. Presiding Judge Moshe Landau's question was on the mind of "nearly everyone who followed the trial — whether the accused had a conscience" (ibid., 95). Reviewing the material of the trial, Arendt concluded: "yes, he had a conscience, and his conscience functioned in the expected way for about four weeks, whereupon it began to function the other way around" (ibid.). The "four weeks" refer to a time when Eichmann "took initiative contrary to orders" in September of 1941 (ibid., 94). Instead of sending the first transport of Jews as ordered to Riga or Minsk where he knew they would be immediately shot to death, he directed the transport to the ghetto of

---

1. "...he lost the need to feel anything at all. This was the way things were, this was the new law of the land, based on the Führer's order; whatever he did he did, as far as he could see, as a law-abiding citizen. He did his *duty*...; he not only obeyed *orders*, he also obeyed the *law*" (Arendt 1965, 135). For details of Eichmann's understanding of duty, see chap. 8, "Duties of a Law-Abiding Citizen," of Arendt's report (ibid., 135–50).

Lódz where no preparations for exterminations had been made. When complaints reached his superiors, he was forgiven and from then on slavishly obeyed and executed all orders. Eichmann portrays himself as someone who gave up his freedom (of conscience) at a time when he felt that his "own projects" were futile. These projects included deporting all Jews of the Reich to a Jewish area in the annexed territories in Poland after the war had begun in 1939 (ibid., 73–76). At the trial he said: "I emphasize that I was bitterly disappointed that this project also failed. So I said to myself: 'What's the point in working out my own projects? I'm too weak and powerless. From now on — it was wartime — I'll simply obey orders. I am a soldier.' I couldn't get away. I tried to get away from it as has been established. I had to obey. I recognized my powerlessness with regard to my own proposals or ideas because they were crushed by superior forces" (Sivan and Brauman 1999). Eichmann described his attitude plastically as *Kadavergehorsam,* that is, blind obedience[2] (Arendt 1965, 135). After his superior, Reinhardt Heydrich, chief of the Head Office for Reich Security, a branch of the SS, told him in August of 1941 that Hitler had ordered "the physical extermination of the Jews," the final solution, Eichmann was sent to several extermination locations to observe and report back to Heydrich or to Heinrich Müller, his immediate superior. Eichmann did as ordered. Upon returning from the horrendous sight of the killings, Eichmann told Müller that he "was not 'tough enough' for these sights, that he had never been a soldier . . . that he could not sleep and had nightmares" (ibid., 89). "After I made my report to Müller, I asked him for the first time to transfer me to other duties, saying I was not the right man for this task. Müller answered that a soldier at the front had no choice where he was posted and had to do his duty" (Sivan and Brauman 1999). Eichmann obeyed and continued to do his duty.

The tragedy of Eichmann seems to be that on some level he "personally thought that this violent solution was not justified. . . . Even at that time, [he] considered it to be a monstrous act" but that a certain ideal of duty and obedience made him the henchman of death. Eichmann had hidden his life behind laws and orders. The following statement in regard to the Wannsee Conference in January 1942 expresses the religious quality these "virtues" had for him and the attempts by which he tried to rid himself of any guilt feelings: "At that moment I felt the kind

---

2. *Kadavergehorsam* literally connotes that one has killed one's self and that one treats oneself as a "corpse" devoid of any choice. One has sacrificed oneself completely for the ideal of obedience.

of satisfaction Pontius Pilate must have felt because I felt devoid of any guilt. The prominent figures of the Reich spoke at the Wannsee Conference. The Popes had given their orders. I had to obey. I kept this in mind throughout the following years . . . I told myself that I did all I could. I was an instrument in the hands of superior powers. . . . I had to wash my hands in innocence for my inner self." The words of his superiors were words of gods or of "Popes" to him: absolute truth. By identifying with them so completely, by sacrificing his self to them, he felt absolved. At the trial, he maintained that legally he was not guilty. He felt he had "not acted willingly." But when pressed by the prosecutor whether he was guilty, Eichmann finally admitted, yet without "remorse" and with a desperate flight into "doing" something to prevent such atrocities from happening again: "In human terms, yes! Because I am guilty of organizing the deportations. Remorse changes nothing, it won't bring anyone back to life. Remorse is pointless. Remorse is for little children. What is more important is to find a way to prevent those things happening in future" (ibid., cf. Arendt 1965, 115). How could Eichmann's conscience be "silenced" during the various crises of conscience which he evidently had (Arendt 1965, 137, 139)? What needs to take place in a person before he or she comes to believe that following duty, orders, and laws obediently, even where they kill, is absolutely required?

Against this background, Eugen Drewermann's therapeutic theology represents an attempt to understand how Christianity not only failed to prevent the Third Reich and other systematic atrocities in the twentieth century but inadvertently fostered over the centuries a God-image that could drive masses into blind obedience to a dictator who played the role of godlike savior. Drewermann's nonviolent reinterpretation of Christianity must be read as a response to the silencing of conscience during the Nazi regime in the name of duty and obedience, and his conscientious objection to the violence of Church and state represents in the area of religion the postwar sentiment of "Never again!" Drewermann's work essentially tries to understand how a sacrificial theology could lead people to obey in the name of duty rather than to rebel in the name of humanity. A passage from his article "The Church in the Second Half of Our Century: Transmission and Problems of Religious Life in Germany" (1981) provides essential components of the backdrop for the themes at the center of Drewermann's work: anxiety, the threat to the individual by the collective, the failure of morality and politics, and the failure of the Church to address the truly religious questions of people:

To tell the truth: even during the years between 1925 and 1933, the Church should have prevented National Socialism if it wanted to rise in 1945 as the spiritual [*geistig*] force of integration and guidance. The causes for its powerlessness before 1933 were not resolved but rather repeated during the time of the new beginning.

National Socialism has been called a mass hysteria and a collective madness. This is correct if it means that Nazism represented the German people's desperate attempt at self-healing from abysmal fear as they staggered forward aimlessly in the midst of unemployment, civil-war-like disunity, national shame, and dark uncertainty about the rise of the technological mass age. The Church — this is a fact — was unable to still with its teachings and symbols this cauldron of fear of a whole nation. By means of moral appeals for moderation and humaneness it tried to calm the storm. In its role as the political "Center Party," however, it did not have any language to make itself intelligible in the very center of the whirlwind. In the midst of the feeling of extreme threat, fascism with its total centralism and absolute nationalism remained the only power that kept things together and pushed fear aside. It was itself nothing but the desperate will of the German people to unite against the threatening danger of falling apart, of fear and of impotence, possibly against a whole world of enemies. The symbols of unification and of the channeling of fear did not come from Christianity. They had to be artificially created according to Germanic models. One may give the Church credit for the fact that overall it did not let its teaching be put in the service of National Socialism.[3] But its best efforts and even the power of its honorableness could not prevent the collective fear of the German people from passing it by and drifting into National Socialism.

To that extent National Socialism was tantamount to a final revelation of the spiritual and religious impotence of the Church [in Germany]. To that extent the filled churches and the increase of public interest in the Church during the postwar years were deceptive. They led the Church to believe it had a power which

---

3. Drewermann revised his view on this score after more research showed that the Church had actually sanctioned and sanctified Hitler's wars in the name of God in many of its official Pastoral Letters at the time.

in reality was no greater than in the days of the explosive collective fear during National Socialism — an impotent power whose strength lay in legal and institutional safeguards and whose weakness lay in the distance from the powers of fear and despair and from hope and confidence in the human psyche.

... Just as the Church of the 1930s had been unable to counterbalance the great fear of the German people through a deepened form of faith, so it was now unable to correct by means of a deepened experience of human happiness the great need of Germans to make up [for the deprivations of war]. The inner isolation of religion from the deep layers of sensation and of experience condemned the Church to an impotent moralizing or to a heaping up of useless guilt feelings in "those loyal to the Church" across the country. If national pride and faithful self-humiliation opposed each other before the war, so now did "joy of life" and "theology of sacrifice." One could not overlook the paradox of the Church closely aligning itself precisely with those political groups [i.e., the Christian Democratic Union and the Christian Social Union] that favored most extensively and most successfully the striving for material consolidation and material protection on the inside and against the outside. While the Church seemed institutionally, politically, and in terms of spiritual continuity to represent stability, in reality it existed in a vacuum of spiritual superficiality. Less than a decade went by until the signs of instability became evident. (1981, 238–40)

In his doctoral dissertation and *Habilitation, Strukturen des Bösen* [Structures of Evil] (3 volumes, 1,977 pages: 1986a, 1985a, 1986b), Drewermann advances the argument that it is fear which leads humans to become evil. The basic thesis of the work is that in an attempt to calm existential fear through their own efforts humans structure their spirit, their psyche, their societies, and their material resources in ways harmful to themselves and to others. The word "structures" refers first of all to a certain projection [*Entwurf* in Heidegger's sense] of the human spirit under the spell of fear. Through an analysis of the story of the fall and its consequences in Genesis 3–11, Drewermann elucidates the spiritual structures at the heart of human evil and their manifestation in mental and social structures. The foundation upon which all his later writings are built, *Strukturen des Bösen* is fundamentally a study of how religion turns unhealthy and feeds a spiral of fear and violence. Analyzing the disastrous effects of a violent God-image, Drewermann employs modern exegesis, depth psychology, and philosophy to interpret texts at the heart of the Judeo-Christian notion of sin in Genesis 2–11.

> Only those who are not used to tracing mistakes of human behavior to mistakes in the relationship of a person to herself and to God will find discussions of this sort purely academic. In reality, there are enough examples, especially from the recent past, which show how a false view of religion directly brings about worldwide catastrophes. We have already shown in the case of A. Hitler how all moral appeals go unheard if an entire nation sinks into the cauldron of its collective fear without being anchored by the bonds of religion deep in the layers of the unconscious (Drewermann 1985a, 495–503): it then inevitably has to project the archetype of the God-human onto some kind of redeemer-figure dragging itself and its neighboring nations through idolatry of the state and through mass ecstasy to destruction. (Drewermann 1986b, 528)

At the root of human evil Drewermann sees above all a God-image poisoned by fear, whether present in the form of religion or secularized in the form of morality. The kind of fear Drewermann has in mind is not identical with fear as affect, although it can produce such affects and may be ontogenetically first experienced affectively. The kind of fear that makes us evil, Drewermann writes, is "more immediate, more enslaving, and less perceptible than all affects and passions" (ibid., XVIII). This kind of fear is a basic attitude toward life which a person may subjectively have no awareness of at all. It is an *existenzialer Entwurf* (existential project) in Heidegger's sense of the word (Heidegger 1972, 260; Heidegger 1996, 240). In the following three passages from *Strukturen des Bösen* Drewermann addresses this type of fear.

> The crews of the B-52 planes, for instance, who bombed North Vietnam coming from Thailand, did not need to fear much that the enemy would shoot them down. They could calmly drink a cup of coffee while they used ingenious devices to set huge areas underneath them on fire with napalm bombs or precision bombs aimed at bridges and truck depots. But they greatly feared refusing to do their job: they feared to be degraded, to be thrown

out of the army, to be despised as dishonorable by their wives, and to look like losers at their clubs. As a rule they did not have a clue for what reason, against whom, and to what extent they let suffering and destruction rain from the sky. But the fears we just mentioned naturally determined their behavior. No intense forces of drives made them become henchmen of death, rather very banal everyday fears. Their "aggressions" during the bombardment were lower than that of a driver of a car passing on a highway. Their sexuality awakened again only at night in the bars of Bangkok. But fears which did not increase their pulse rate by a single beat — because they did not need to waste a single thought on them as long as everything was functioning — allowed them to observe their dashboards with the neutral matter-of-factness of a technician while they were subjectively completely unaware that they were compulsively guided, down to every detail, by certain fears and, as a consequence of these fears, caused unspeakable suffering. (Drewermann 1986b, XVII)

The fear Drewermann is concerned with theologically is a fear that liquidates the individual's freedom and makes him simply a function of the collective. This kind of fear produces the type of follower mentality that made the Nazi regime possible and was the motor behind the individual and collective expressions of evil during the Third Reich. Discussing the question of guilt in the Third Reich, Drewermann emphasizes that the rule of the collective is the *result* and not the cause of the liquidation of individual freedom due to existential fear.

The collective context of evil, to exemplify this question in Germany in our century, has never become so compellingly and terribly evident as during the time of the Third Reich. If any concrete historical situation could show how the deeds of all prequalify the freedom of the individual and force him into evil, and how vice versa the individual through his freedom participates culpably in the perfidious malice of the entire system simply by the fact that he eats, drinks, marries, begets children, works or goes on vacation to the Baltic Sea, it is this period. . . . [O]ne could see how individual freedom became alienated from itself within the collectivity of evil and hit the individual back as a counter-finality[4] — for instance, when a worker in a ball-bearing factory

---

4. Drewermann borrows this term from Sartre 1991 (see Drewermann 1986b, 333–40).

in Schweinfurt or Regensburg in August of 1943 drew a carpet
of RAF bombs down upon himself (cf. A. Speer 1970, 284–
86). The twelve-year period of National Socialist horror rule
in Germany is certainly the most forceful lesson in our century,
which in any case has no want of horrors, of this counter-
finality. The clearer and more concretely one faces the dialectical
back-and-forth between individual freedom, group behavior,
and re-internalized unfreedom during that time the clearer we
see that even then no universal law existed of, in a way, *having
to* become *guilty* (a *contradictio in adjecto*). Even back then one
could have emigrated, gone to a concentration camp, or joined
the resistance. And because one could as such have done this one
became guilty by simply continuing, obeying, and fulfilling one's
duty as a citizen. One became a criminal through the modest
will for normality and ordinariness. Although, then, an entire
nation, more or less against its will, became guilty in history in
a monstrous way, one cannot speak of a wholesale universality
of guilt, of a universal complicity. Seen from the outside, every
individual as such could also have acted differently. That she
acted as she did was her guilt. (Drewermann 1986b, 365)

Drewermann identifies the underlying fear as an attitude driven by
the *Entwurf* of a person simply wanting to be a "good citizen" and
following societal roles. Arguing against the thesis of Piet Schoonenberg (1967; 1965, 124–91) that "sin" could be understood as the
"being situated" of humans, Drewermann presents an example of a
physician which shows how even passivity and best intentions may
well contribute to evil.

The situation of Nazi fascism does not at all explain why,
for instance, in 1940, in a Polish village, a good internist and
father of three children participates in separating "Aryan" genetic material from "Slavic subhumans." The situation of the
Third Reich: ideological manipulation, intimidations, threats of
reprisals against family members — these are all external facts.
As such, if they were to explain anything, then one would actually have to affirm the conviction that external force is all
powerful and to fall back on the assumption of fatalistic de-
termination. But even without such an absurd determinism one
understands very well why this ... capable physician and loyal
father of a family necessarily becomes a henchman of fascism:

he must become it simply because he has projected [*entworfen*] himself in his freedom only and exclusively as citizen and father of a family. Within this projection [*Entwurf*] he really cannot but give in to the pressure of some Nazi lackey and himself become a lackey. In order to understand the seeming inevitability with which he adopts the preexisting malice of another person into his own behavior one first of all has to understand his own projection of his freedom with which he himself first constitutes the omnipotence of circumstances....

Of course, this physician does not have to be active as a National Socialist in the internment camp for Polish children, it is enough that he is one passively. But his passivity, his anxious compliance exists only if set up by his freedom. His lack of resistance is his personally active attitude — what else?

One might say he himself does not want the evil of National Socialism; he only wants his career or security for his family. And this will of his, in itself good, is turned into something criminal through preexisting [collective] structures. That is true but only shows once more that the discussion of evil has to begin at a deeper level than that of certain moral facts. What forces, in this hypothetical example, the physician into moral evil, what lets him become necessarily guilty is — prior to any single morally accountable act — the manner of his self-projection [*Selbstentwurf*] which basically consists of him having no self.... To understand the seeming inevitability of the development of guilt means above all to understand that the constitution of outside malice [of the collective] as a determining force for an individual's freedom is the result of a prior projection of the individual. Through this projection, the individual determines to miss herself and to liquidate herself as an independent personality. Only when we understand the interest which any individual freedom has in escaping from itself into a state of not-really-existing [*Uneigentlichkeit*] can we make the universality of sin comprehensible. Theologically one therefore has to start with the individual and with his relationship to himself in order to understand the culpable dependency [of his acting] on the action of others in certain factual situations. (Drewermann 1986b, 368)

How people liquidate their freedom prior to any behavior that can be qualified as morally evil is Drewermann's concern in *Strukturen des Bösen.* In particular, Drewermann wants to show the central role which a certain God-image plays either explicitly or implicitly in any self-projection that liquidates its own freedom. He tries to unfold the existential structures of fear that lead to the rise of an ambivalent and violent God-image and to the reactive delusional human feelings of "being like God" and/or of elevating others to the level of "gods." At the same time, Drewermann attempts to help us understand why appeals to morality and reason come too late at a time when the structures of fear have the individual — including her morality and reason — already firmly in their grip. Moral evil is a secondary, often nonintended symptom of an existential attitude that precedes all questions of ethics. Hence evil can only be prevented and overcome if due attention is given to existential attitudes.

When Drewermann wrote *Strukturen des Bösen,* he explicitly wanted to free the notion of sin from the moralistic misinterpretation with which it is commonly identified. Drewermann did retain the term "sin" even though he often set it in quotation marks. To understand "sin" properly, the perspective of the ethical has to be suspended. Moralizing a person's existential attitude will only increase fear and be counterproductive. In fact, Drewermann finds that in a field of fear any moral efforts to do good inevitably lead to opposite consequences from those consciously intended. Borrowing from Sartre, Drewermann calls this dynamic the counter-finality of aim and result (*Gegenfinalität von Ziel und Ergebnis*) (1986b, 333–40). Only a theological perspective that tries to understand rather than judge people will contribute to an end of the cycle of fear and violence. In *Strukturen des Bösen* Drewermann implies what he will later explicate: that a theology which reduces God practically to a moral watchdog and considers sin to be an act of "disobedience" or the result of "pride" is itself the victim of a God-image distorted by fear. The serpent of Genesis 3 and the Grand Inquisitor in Dostoevsky's *The Brothers Karamazov* (Dostoevsky 1976) are of the same mind. In view of failed human efforts to recreate the lost paradise after the fall, Drewermann can write that "sin can be understood as an attempt to restore the order of God without and against God. This creates the qualitatively inverse structure in the deeds of humans as well as the mirror image of the resemblance of the aims of sin with the original destiny of humans" (1985a, 314).

Drewermann thus wants to implement the "old Kierkegaardian concern" to "free theology finally from the tyranny of the Kantian reduction of religion to morality by showing that sin is not the opposite of virtue but of faith and that it is one thing to relate to the common moral good [*dem ethisch Allgemeinen*] and another thing to relate to God" (1986a, XIII–XIV). Based on Genesis 2–11, the key theological alternative of human life is not one between moral good or evil, virtue or vice, but between fear or trust, despair or faith. Far from relativizing the human experience of guilt — as some have charged him — Drewermann wants to restore credence to the religious dimension of this experience and thus remove the moralistic interpretations of sin which provide a caste of theological experts with a pretentious amount of power over so-called lay people.

In *Strukturen des Bösen* Drewermann intends to defend one of the core beliefs of Christianity, the doctrine of original sin, by bridging experience and dogma (Drewermann 1999b, see also Drewermann 1986d, 1986e [= Ricoeur 1986]). If theology is not committed to the level of human existence as such in relation to God, it tends to idolize parts of human existence, preferably moral values such as duty, loyalty, and obedience, to use them against humans and to inadvertently legitimize all sorts of evil in the name of a morally misunderstood God. As early as 1977, Drewermann explicitly thought of his work strategically. "We want to build here a sort of Trojan horse which can be smuggled behind the walls of [existential] noncommitment in theological ivory towers" (1986a, XIII).

Fear and the Origin of a Violent God-Image

> I will not and cannot continue to conduct services in praise and worship of this angry petulant old man in whom you believe. You turn your backs on the God of love and compassion and invented for yourself this cruel senile delinquent who blames the world and all that he created for his own faults.
> — Tennessee Williams, *The Night of the Iguana*

Drewermann bases his study of the structures of evil on the Yahwist's account in Genesis 2–11. He chooses this literary-critical construct not only because of the tremendous influence these stories have had in world history but also because the biblical author himself claims to make principal statements on the relationship between God and humans, intending to portray how "evil" takes possession of all humans (1986a, XV). Drewermann views his analysis as an attempt "to understand humans in all areas of their existence, that is, by

utilizing scientifically all anthropologically relevant methods" (ibid.,
XIII). The resulting understanding of humans has to be so legitimate
that "it would remain valid even if one day the entire literary-critical
construction of a Yahwistic primordial history became dated due to
further progress of exegetical knowledge" (ibid., XIII).

The "relevant anthropological methods" for a theological interpretation of the Yahwist's texts include historical-critical exegesis,
depth psychology, ethnology, ethology, and philosophy. Following
roughly the breakdown of the three volumes of *Strukturen des Bösen*,
Drewermann's interpretation is presented in three steps. Methodological considerations will be addressed at the beginning of each section.
Though Drewermann has analyzed all the Yahwistic stories in Genesis 2–11 in depth, we will focus mainly on the so-called story of the
fall proper (Gen. 3:1–7) to understand Drewermann's etiology of sin
from fear and on the story of Cain and Abel (Gen. 4:1–16) to show
how humans, situated in the field of fear, are compelled to sacrifice
the best to a "God" whom they perceive as in need of sacrifices and
how such a God-image is the origin of humans killing other humans.
For our purposes, Drewermann's detailed motif-historical, tradition-
historical, literary-critical, or redaction-historical analyses need not
be presented. Rather I will provide conclusions of his exegetical analysis, with particular attention to the distortion of the God-image by
human fear. Of central importance to Drewermann is the imagery in
the texts. I will select the key motifs of serpent and tree to illustrate
his argument that religious language lives from mythic imagery to
convey truths affectively that cannot be conveyed in abstract prose.
All subsequent references to the biblical texts in Genesis 2–11 are to
the Yahwist tradition unless otherwise indicated.

Results of the Exegetical Analysis of Genesis 3 and 4:1–16

Drewermann's exegetical analysis is firmly grounded in traditional
historical criticism. He expands historical criticism, however, by
structuralist observations and, most importantly, by a reading of the
emotions, moods, and motives "between the lines" (1986a, 53). Following the Yahwist's own intention, the exegetical analysis clearly
distinguishes between the mythical motifs employed in the narrative
and the theological, demythologized interpretation which the Yahwist
gives the material through his redaction (ibid., 45–53). In determining

the meaning of the text, Drewermann follows the Yahwist's theological intention. For instance, while Genesis 2–11 contains many stories which originally functioned as etiologies of cultural accomplishments and progress, Drewermann argues, particularly against Westermann, that the Yahwist sees such "progress" in theological perspective not positively but negatively as compensations for a loss of God (e.g., the making of loincloths from fig leaves in Genesis 3:7 is not seen as cultural progress by the Yahwist but as compensation for the sense of shame over being naked). On the whole, the structure of Genesis 2–11 falls into two broad blocks with parallel development: Genesis 2–8 describes the divisive effects which the separation from God has on being human (*Menschsein*), while Genesis 9–11 shows its social effects on humans in the arena of human history (*Menschheit*) (ibid., 294; Drewermann 1986b, 330, 400–6).

Drewermann's translation of Genesis 3:1–7 from the original Hebrew is for the most part in agreement with Martin Buber's excellent German translation (Buber 1976). Since it is of importance for the subsequent psychoanalytic and theological interpretation, we should note the literary-critical finding that originally Genesis 3:1–5 (the actual story of the temptation) existed relatively independent and was only later expanded by Genesis 3:6–7 (the woman's sharing of the fruit with the man and the knowledge of being naked) (Drewermann 1986a, 42). The following text is my English rendition of Drewermann's German translation.

[1]*Now the serpent was more cunning than any living being of the field that Yahweh, the God, had made. The serpent said to the woman: "Did God really say 'Do not eat from any of the trees of the garden'?"* [2–3]*The woman said to the serpent: "We may eat from the fruit of the trees in the garden, but of the fruit of the tree which stands in the middle of the garden God has said: 'Do not eat from it nor touch it, otherwise you must die.'"* [4]*The serpent said to the woman: "No, no, you will not die.* [5]*Rather, God knows that the day you eat from it, your eyes will be opened and you will be like God, knowing good and evil."* [6]*The woman saw that the tree was good to eat from and that it was a lust to the eyes and that the tree was to be desired for grasping.*[5] *She took from its fruit and ate, and she*

---

5. The German *begreifen* (trans. as "grasping") means both to grasp in the sense of touching and to grasp in the sense of understanding.

gave her husband who was with her as well, and he ate. [7]*The eyes of both were opened and they became aware that they were naked. They sewed fig leaves together and made loincloths for themselves.*

Drewermann stresses the Yahwist's understanding of primordial history as a story of beginnings. Based on a comparison of the dynamic quality of Hebrew thinking and the more static quality of Greek thought, Drewermann explains that the Yahwist does not want to describe a historical beginning of humans in the sense of modern historiography but instead equates beginning with how humans have always been. "Stories of beginnings in Hebrew are to be understood as stories about the nature [*Wesen*]" of humans. They describe the essential character of humans instead of supplying us with historical origins, an element they share with all mythological texts. "*In principio* should not mean 'in the beginning' but 'principally,' *a principio,* fundamentally, essentially." There is, however, a key difference from mythological thinking in the theological interpretation which the Yahwist puts on these stories about the essential nature of humans: the Yahwist combines them with "a genuine historiography" and interprets the mythic material "nonmythically." How? For the Yahwist the "nature [*Wesen* or *Natur*]" of things is not immutable, ever the same, as Western thinking "in Plato's sense" may suggest. "The Yahwist does not think philosophically in the Greek sense of the word, but 'theologically'; he describes not how humans are in themselves but how they are before God and in relation to God. This theological reality of humans is understood by the Yahwist in his primordial history, however, prior to any concrete history and to the life of the individual as a universal reality which cannot be changed by humans, a basic, hence 'essential' reality." In other words, the Yahwist portrays in Genesis 3–11 how humans always relate to God, but that they, as the story of Abra(ha)m in Genesis 12 shows, would not have to relate in this fashion. Hence, "[w]hen the Yahwist describes in Genesis 3 how humans sinned against God, then he does so not in order to say that humans sinned back then but to say that humans are from the beginning [*vom Ursprung her*] sinners, that they sin in this manner and that it is part of their character to act toward God like that" (Drewermann 1986a, XXI–XXII, cf. XVIII–XXX).

The Serpent

Drewermann takes issue with the traditional historical hypothesis which traces the symbol of the serpent in Genesis 3 to the presence of serpents in other ancient oriental religions such as the Canaanite cult of Baal or religious traditions of Babylon or Egypt. Such an interpretation has suggested that the temptation to fall from God lies in human sexuality as exemplified in the fertility cult of Baal. Drewermann shows that although it seems certain that the Yahwist picks up mythical traditions of the serpent and temptation which had clear sexual connotations (e.g., in the Gilgamesh epic), the Yahwist in Genesis 3 consciously uses the motif of the serpent as other than a fertility motif (1986a, 27–42). The Yahwist's concern in Genesis 3 is not the struggle between Yahweh and Baal or between Israel and Canaan. The theme of the fertility cult is first introduced — except for the allusion to it in the "marriage of angels" in Genesis 6:1–4 — "in Genesis 9:20–27 in the context of Ham's 'sin.'" Israel is introduced only in Genesis 10 in form of the figure of Eber, one of its forefather's (ibid., LXVII). The Yahwist's genealogy is not only historically reasonable but

> prevents us from reading the conflict between Israel and Canaan, between Yahweh and Baal already into Genesis 3. In Genesis 2–3, the Yahwist speaks of "Adam," *the* human being, and of "Chawwa," the "mother of all who live" (Gen. 3:20; cf. ibid., 97). What is said here is in *no* way nationally bound. It has to be understood completely as a statement about *all of humanity.* The serpent in Genesis 3:1–5 is thus certainly not to be understood as the representative of a specific cult or of a specific people . . . ; it is rather a power which speaks to *every* human and ties her down in opposition to God at the root of human existence. Correspondingly "Yahweh, the God" in Genesis 2–3, too, is no national tribal God but the creator and sustainer of the whole world and of all humans. It takes a long development of misery in the Yahwist's primordial history before one can *no* longer see in this God the God of all humans but the God of a human tribe in opposition to other peoples (Gen. 9:20–27). (ibid., LXVII)

If the Yahwist uses the motif of the serpent to say something not only about one group of people but about all humans then,

Drewermann concludes, a proper interpretation has to move beyond the historical-critical question of the derivation of the symbol of the serpent in this text and make it intelligible in its "universally human character" (ibid., LXVIII). This perspective paves the way for Drewermann's depth-psychological and philosophical interpretation of the symbol of the serpent which follows below.

From Harmony with God to a Heteronomous God-Image

Besides historical-critical scholarship and structural analysis Drewermann's exegetical analysis of Genesis 3:1–7 (1986a, 53–78) relies on an empathic verbalization of the feelings and motives between the lines, because "we can understand the present text only if we read it with 'the inner eye,' feel it, apply it to ourselves and let it affect us deeply" (ibid., 53–54). To this end, he particularly employs the method of client-centered psychotherapy (*Gesprächspsychotherapie;* see Tausch 1970), which reflects on what the statements of one person mean to another person, "which feelings, wishes, hopes, worries, etc." they imply (Drewermann 1986a, LXXXI).

The passage of Genesis 3 is preceded by Genesis 2 where humans live in harmony with God, with the earth, and with themselves. They are naked and not ashamed of it. They work and do not experience it as a burden. They love without one dominating the other (ibid., 9–26). Genesis 2 in relation to Genesis 3–11 shows that humans, in order to live truly as humans, have to "rely completely" on God (ibid., 156).

Genesis 3:1–7 starts with the introduction of the serpent, expressly said to be created by God. The serpent's question first paints a tyrannical God-image. It incorrectly suggests that God forbade humans to eat from *any* of the trees in the garden (v. 1). God's original words had been "You may freely eat of every tree of the garden; but of the tree of the knowledge of good and evil do not eat, for on the day you shall eat from it you shall die" (Gen. 2:16–7). Later the serpent will continue to distort the God-image by proposing that God gave the commandment out of jealousy in order to prevent humans from becoming like God (v. 4).

The woman tries to defend God by correcting the serpent (v. 2). She does not want to fall from God but explicitly wants to hold onto God. This is of central importance for Drewermann's argument, since it shows that the original motive for sin is something other than pride, hubris, or undue self-assertion.

The woman's reply betrays the motive. After the question of the serpent, she herself can no longer clearly remember the words of God and cannot but distort them herself through an important addition to the original commandment: the tabu of touching (v. 3). This reveals several things, Drewermann suggests. It shows that, against her will, the woman's trust in the goodness of God has already been shattered at this early stage of the story by the image of prohibition which the serpent has painted of God. She can recall the words of God only within a feeling of fear. Making a prohibition more severe than it is by adding a tabu to it points, on the other hand, to the fact that in response to the serpent's image of God, desire has been aroused in the woman to eat from the fruit of the tree of the knowledge of good and evil. At the same time that desire has been resisted because the woman does not want to lose God. The question of the serpent has stirred for the first time the fear that she could lose God.

The added tabu indicates that, after the God-image has become distorted by fear through the question of the serpent, the threat of death attached to the eating (and, in the woman's mind, now also to the touching) of the forbidden fruit is for the first time a source of anxiety. The main success of the serpent has been to distort the image of God so completely by fear that God no longer can be counted on as a help against the fear but rather appears as its source and cause. "That is the most important point" (ibid., 62).

With God lost in a fantasy of fear, the serpent can easily pose as savior to the woman. The serpent cunningly reassures the woman that her fear of death is unfounded (v. 4). After the question of the serpent has submerged the image of God into a sea of fear, the woman's main motive to follow the commandment became the fear that God would otherwise punish her with death. What was stated in the original commandment as a simple consequence, receives in the exchange between serpent and woman the quality of anticipated "punishment" from God. By promising that she will not die as a result of eating from the fruit, the serpent cleverly calms the woman's fear of death. The serpent has identified God with the threat of death and poses as the giver of life to the woman.

While the serpent poses as savior, God is portrayed by it as powerless: as someone who gave the commandment only as protection against human usurpers. The heteronomous image of God is now complete: God appears in the serpent's perspective as jealous of the power of humans, who therefore need to be suppressed. The serpent's picture of God does not leave any room for the possibility that God set up the commandment to genuinely protect humans from unforeseeable misery, from the "sickness unto death" (Kierkegaard).

The serpent's rhetoric in which God is reduced to a jealous competitor indeed gives humans a feeling of equality with God. It is on that background that the feeling "to be like God" becomes persuasive (v. 5). The woman's fear of God is cunningly answered by the serpent's insinuation not that "humans have to fear God, but, to the contrary, God has reason to fear humans. Based on that argument, now all reasons hindering the woman from taking the pernicious step [of eating the forbidden fruit] are dropped" (ibid., 67).

After all barriers of the fear of God have disappeared, the "tabooed" tree appears as the epitome of what is desirable (v. 6). The tree has not changed as such, but through the exchange with the serpent and the dynamic of fear it has become the most desirable thing in the world, something that the woman can no longer resist. The act of taking and eating the forbidden fruit now seems like an inevitable consequence of the feeling of mistrust toward God. "Everything has really already happened before the woman takes [the fruit]. . . . Never has she been more powerless than in the moment she imagines herself to be like God" (ibid., 70).

That the woman shares the forbidden fruit with the man who is with her and that he too eats is portrayed simply as a matter of fact, as if the man would need no other motivation than to "be with her" (v. 6). The mutuality of humans created by God which was originally a source of joy now turns into a mutuality of guilt and to a separation of man and woman by mutual shame (v. 7). "The attempt to reestablish the mutuality which had been broken through the guilt of one partner, by having the other partner participate in the guilt, leads to the fact that the mutuality has separating effects" (ibid., 72).

The knowledge of good and evil, so far hidden from humans, is "that they are naked" (v. 7). Drewermann highlights the fact that the Hebrew words for "being naked" and for the description of the serpent as "cunning" (also: wise) have the same root: 'rwm. "To become wise in this manner means to get to know oneself in a way that one is ashamed of oneself" (ibid., 72). Humans discover a way of knowing that is "evil." Being naked, which they were already in Genesis 2:25

and which they "were not ashamed" of then, now is experienced as evil. "Humans become aware of their nakedness. In contradiction to God they fall back on what they are without God and they begin to be ashamed of themselves. They have not become anything else than they were before. But now, in contradiction to God, they begin to be embarrassed by what they are. And that changes everything" (ibid., 72). When the relationship with God has been poisoned by the cunning words of the serpent, humans inevitably become ashamed of being simply human. Their initial fear to lose God turns into a fear of God and only then into the compensatory desire to become like God. Once they have lost sight of who God really is, they are ashamed of being human and consequently need to be like God.

Drewermann stresses that "the content of the knowledge of good and evil according to Genesis 3:7 is nothing outside of humans that could be managed but is in humanity itself. What is good or evil for humans is nothing inherent in the things of the world, which they make practical use of; but humans are good or evil to themselves, whether they live with or far from God" (ibid., 72–73). The knowledge of good and evil is not a moral category as in knowing what is morally right or wrong, but strictly a theological category as in knowing how life turns bad without God, the creative source of life, and how good it was with God.

Only under the spell of fear does all of existence appear to humans more and more evil (see Drewermann 1990d, 27). Nowhere, Drewermann emphasizes against any positive interpretations of this passage by philosophers (e.g., Kant and Hegel) or exegetes (e.g., Westermann), does the Yahwist consider the knowledge of good and evil in the story as positive progress. Rather, the knowledge of good and evil here means to find the world turning evil, that being merely human feels like a "lack" to be ashamed of and to be hidden, when and only when humans are separated from the creative ground of their existence in whose company their nakedness was by no means a "lack" (Drewermann 1986a, 73).

Against usual interpretations of the fall as motivated by pride or by a desire for autonomy (e.g., G. von Rad and O. H. Steck), Drewermann points out that in the text "the polarity of heteronomy and autonomy" is a secondary consequence of the "abyss of fear and mistrust" that has been opened between humans and God. "Humans separate from God not because they want to be autonomous, but they experience God as 'heteronomous' because they have, without directly wanting it (!), alienated themselves from God" (ibid., 75; cf. Drewermann 1986b, 137).

Nor does sin consist in an act of "disobedience" against God (Drewermann 1986a, 77; cf. Drewermann 1990d, 12–13). Sin is instead committed in a desperate attempt to be obedient to the commandment as evidenced by the woman's attempt to defend God against the distortions of the serpent. "The tragedy of what the Yahwist portrays in Genesis 3 and in Genesis 4 is rather that humans do evil exactly by trying to do good in their own way" (Drewermann 1986a, 131). It is against their best will that humans fall into sin and slip into evil. With reference to the story of the fall, Drewermann succinctly addresses this dynamic in his commentary on the Gospel of Mark (1990d) in light of Pope John Paul II's reiteration that the deepest core of sin lies in *"disobedience against God"*:

> One confuses the symptom with the cause if with reference to... Genesis 3:1–7... one asserts that *the* sin of *the* human being consists of "disobedience" against God.... * Nothing could be further from the picture that the Yahwist paints with extraordinary empathic ability as the portrait of *the* human being in the scene of the temptation. The problem of the *condition humaine* is not that humans want to *"disobey"* God, rather, if we look closer, we see the opposite: the woman in Genesis 3:3 tries most meticulously to recall the instructions [*Weisungen*] of God against the suspicions and doubts of "the serpent." ... But she can repeat the commandment of God only with the feeling and through the intensification of *fear*.... Words of God which were originally meant as freedom of and as protection for humans turn now under the spell of fear into words of an alien demand and of despotic confinement. The origin of life now turns into the threatening origin of death and the instructions of divine permission into a demand to prove oneself morally. This shows that a human being *with his best will* cannot live if the sources of his life become poisoned with deadly fear. A "religion" whose relationship to God is shaped only by fear must make it seem in the end as if God and the human being stand opposed to each other like absolute combatants — "God" because of the suspicion she would humiliate and degrade the human being and the human being because he has to remove such a

"God" by trying to set himself up as an absolute being. . . . Only fear turns words of God into "commandments."

*So still (and again) John Paul II: Reconciliatio et Paenitentia. *Verlautbarungen des Apostolischen Stuhls* 60, 2. December 1984 (Bonn), 26: "In the story of the Garden of Eden the darkest and most inner core of sin becomes visible in all its seriousness and drama: *disobedience against God,* against his law, against the moral norm which he has written into the heart of humans and has confirmed and perfected through his revelation."

(Drewermann 1990d, 12–13)

Sin is not the act of transgression but precedes any act. "The actual guilt of the woman lies in the fact that she does not go back to God after a shadow of mistrust and fear has fallen on God's image through the serpent's doubt, that her fear is stronger than her trust" (Drewermann 1986a, 78). Though the fall from God under the spell of fear seems psychologically inevitable, it will be the task of the philosophical and theological interpretations to show in which sense it has to be recognized as the guilt of humans. *Why* human fear is stronger than human trust is a question which the story does not answer. According to Drewermann, the Yahwist does not "explain" [*Er-Klärung*] why humans give into the fear and fall from God but rather clarifies [*Klärung*] what "typically" happens "inside humans when they sin" (ibid., 86).

Genesis 3:8–24 portrays the consequences of the fall. Though God walks with humans as ever in the Garden, humans from now on are able to see God only in the twilight of ambivalence. They now need to hide from God's view. They are now ashamed of their nakedness in front of God. God's question "Where are you?" is meant as an opening for humans to repair the relationship with God, but the "tragedy of fear" does not only lead to guilt but makes it now also impossible to trust God, to admit responsibility for the fall, and to turn again toward God as the source of life. Instead of reestablishing the trusting relationship with God which could disentangle them from the fangs of their fear, humans begin to defensively point to who is guilty, which is eventually directed at God: the woman *you* gave me made me eat from the tree.

Drewermann highlights the fact that the "punishments" do not consist in a change of the world nor in a change of God, but in a change in the human experience of the world and of God. Both the world and God appear in a world "without God" as adversarial. It was knowledge of how harsh the world would be without God, without the creative source of life, which God wanted to spare humans. Only with this in mind does it make sense that God wanted to withhold the knowledge of good and evil from humans. After humans have lost sight of God in their fear, they subsequently will experience God as adversary, as someone who punishes them. "Protection and annihilation, salvation and doom, security and deadly threat — these lie in God; how God will appear to them depends on what humans do" (ibid., 219). The God who speaks to humans in Genesis 3:14–19 and in all subsequent stories of the Yahwist's primordial history is the image of an ambivalent God as it appears under the spell of fear. The God-image has been "demonized" (ibid., 136).

That the punishments are the result of a different way of the human experience of the world is confirmed by the fact that they consist in nothing but a complete reversal of the quality of all existing structures of human life (ibid., 87). Nothing has changed externally in the world: humans are still naked, they still live together, they still will work to obtain food. All of these elements were present in Genesis 2 and were good then. But the inner human experience of everything has changed. Everything appears in a different light after humans have gained knowledge of good and evil, after they feel separated from God (ibid., 47–50). Though humans do not die physically at the moment they eat from the forbidden fruit, their entire life changes its quality and turns into a "being unto death" (ibid., 107). The kind of knowledge of good and evil they gain turns the fact of nakedness into a source of shame. It makes life seem like a never-ending battle marked by pain: life now becomes a constant struggle with evil (in form of the serpent); human love turns into domination and subordination; procreation now becomes a painful burden; human labor for subsistence, miserable toil. If dust was the stuff for the creative formation of humans, now dust becomes the symbol of death.

Ironically the adversarial experience of the nature of the world as a punishment from God contains in itself also the other side of the ambivalence: by seeing the adversity of nature as a punishment from God, the Yahwist highlights that, although this experience "draws the consequence from the behavior of humans," although "it is the guilt which contains the punishment in itself," it does so not "due to a causal automatism, but through a deed of God" (ibid., 139). This leaves room for the possibility that even though humans cannot break the cycle of fear and its adversarial consequences, God can —

for instance, by making a new beginning with humans after the Great Flood in Genesis 8:21–22. Though humans distance themselves ever further from God, though God seems to them more and more as a greedy, jealous, and unjust God, humans also retain a sense that God wants to save them from the ever increasing spiral of fear, evil, and violence. The human contradiction of God introduces into the God-image a deep contradiction. Though humans know that God wants to protect them from the spiral of fear and violence, God, despite all efforts and measures, "*cannot* (!) prevent" humans from moving step by step further away from the ground of their existence (ibid., 211). At the same time, the Yahwist portrays God as one who does not leave people alone in their misery but tries as much as possible, often without success, to contain the effects of sin (ibid., 89, 99–106, 128, 143, 164–66, 188–89, 211, 229).

The Deadly Effects of Human Sacrifice for the Divine: Genesis 4:1–16

The story of Cain and Abel, the first children of Adam and Eve, shows Drewermann above all how religion situated in fear and distance from God becomes the cause of jealous and eventually deadly dissension among people. Again I cannot convey every detail of the sensitive interpretation by Drewermann of this story (ibid., 111–47) and will concentrate on his interpretation of the sacrificial mentality of the characters as a result of the fall from God. Only when humans feel far from God do they feel that the "Other," the "brother," becomes a competitor for the blessing from God. It is not God who needs sacrifice. Humans need sacrifice, so they think, in an attempt to recover a merciful God who has been lost due to the experience of ambivalence (ibid., 121). Sacrifice is an attempt to gain the lost absolute recognition by God which once, before the God-image became ambivalent, was taken for granted. It is true, Drewermann acknowledges, sacrifices are part of all religions. But this does not mean that they are "an unsuspicious testimony of human piety." For the Yahwist it means rather that the sacrificial "attitude" is created through the dynamic portrayed in Genesis 3 (ibid., 121).

After Genesis 3 humans are no longer sure of God. Outside of Eden God is experienced as one who dispenses blessings arbitrarily. The success of Abel becomes the occasion for Cain's feelings of rejection, envy, and eventually deadly rage that cannot be suppressed even when Cain tries to prevent it by talking to Abel.[6] The tragedy of this story is, Drewermann writes, that in the very process of sacrificing the best for God, by doing the best they can, humans become murderous (ibid., 131). The rivalry between Cain and Abel for the absolute attention of a lost God is, in Drewermann's analysis, the prototype of all deadly human conflict. Genesis 4 shows that when "humans kill each other they actually do not fight for possessions or similar things but for God and God's blessing, and that it is precisely the separation from God" which lets God's blessing be misunderstood and even effect misery in a miserable world. "Outside of Eden God appears to humans . . . where God blesses as unjust and confusing, as capricious and unpredictable" (ibid., 133).

Cain's failed attempt to gain God's absolute recognition through an effort of the will by means of sacrifice has as a consequence that Cain permanently "settles" in the "land of Nod," which means literally "land of flight." An existence characterized by flight from God cannot but settle in a land of "groundlessness" (ibid., 143, 147).

The story of Cain and Abel is only the first in a series of stories which portray how humans desperately try on their own to regain the absolute ground lost under the spell of fear: they displace their need for this absolute hold (*Halt*)[7] onto technological advances, onto their own power to scare others (Gen. 4:23–24), onto their generative abilities (Gen. 6:1–4; 9:20–23), onto political leaders and powerplays (Gen. 10:8–12), and onto the human collectivity (Gen. 11:1–9) (see the table in ibid., 316–18). Because they are haunted by fear, their best moral efforts and deeds, including those aimed at building a peaceful society, fail. Drewermann concludes that the Yahwist's picture of human relationships and human history enveloped in fear attempts to show "that in everything which humans do [after losing sight of God] they are really concerned with God and that they seek and have to seek God even where they leave God behind. 'God' is the goal and the topic of human sin" and evil. "Sin is characterized by seeking God, but by missing God because it attempts to do what only God

---

6. Leaning on Buber's translation of Genesis 4:8, Drewermann translates differently than the NRSV which translates "Cain said to his brother Abel, 'Let us go out to the field.' And when they were in the field, Cain rose up against his brother Abel, and killed him." Drewermann translates: "Cain talked with Abel, his brother. But then as they were in the field Cain rose up against Abel, his brother, and killed him." See Drewermann 1986a, 131, for a discussion of the translation.

7. See Appendix 2 for the psychospiritual connotations of this term.

can do" for humans: to provide an absolute ground and justification for one's existence (Drewermann 1986b, 136, cf. 530–31).

Results of the Psychoanalytic Analysis of Genesis 3 and 4:1–16

> ...my sick soul, as sin's true nature is...
> —*Hamlet*, Act IV, Scene V

Universal Images of the Psyche?

Drewermann's exegetical analysis found that the motif of the serpent is employed by the Yahwist not only to say something about one group of people but also to express something *universally* human. This implies that a historical-critical perspective is insufficient for the interpretation of Genesis 3 and needs to be supplemented by anthropological methods which may shed light on the universal significance of the concrete imagery of the mythic material of the story. Drewermann hence turns to the comparative study of mythology and ethnology to research whether the motifs of serpent and tree show similar meanings in different cultures, preferably in cultures which are historically unrelated, and to depth psychology for an interpretation of the anthropological meaning of these motifs. Since the claim to universal symbols may raise methodological suspicions, I will present in some detail Drewermann's rationale for his choice of method.

Drewermann notes the historical circumstance that many myths — including the mythic material the Yahwist uses in Genesis 2–11 — which originally had both a social and a psychical function are available to us today only "completely divested of their social context." They are "handed down only in written form and...have received their shape completely due to their literary and not their social context....The function which they may once have had for the interpretation of a rite or for the representation of certain basic tasks and institutions of life can at most be deduced hypothetically from an analysis of the texts, but can in no case be used for the interpretation of the existing texts" (1986a, XXXII). If such myths continue to exert significant influence although they have been stripped of their social context, Drewermann reasons, we must seek their enduring significance not on the social but on the psychological, that is, "emotional" level. Therefore he chooses to interpret the mythic material in the Yahwist's account not along the lines of the "functionalist" school (e.g., Malinowski) but of the "symbolistic" school (e.g., Freud, Jung) of myth interpretation.

If myths now stripped of their social context once had the psychosocial function "to connect in their symbolism powerful psychological drives [*Antriebe*] — which could otherwise become chaotic — with social institutions and thus help integrate the individual into the life of the tribe" (ibid., XXXIV), they currently "gain a universal breadth of meaning" where they no longer characterize a particular group of people but "the fundamental reality of being human." Myths isolated in the course of history from their social function "hence have actually lost their mythic meaning, as is the case with the stories of the Yahwist's primordial history." They are thus "to be read like fairy tales and dreams" (ibid., XXXIV).

"This circumstance makes it possible and necessary to take a step which is ethnologically irresponsible but which is 'anthropologically,' in the sense of the Yahwist, required: namely, to relegate the functionalist method of interpretation to second place and to seek refuge in the symbolistic procedure of interpretation" (ibid., XXXII–XXXIII). In order to understand the transhistorical meaning of myths, the question is thus not which function a myth had in a past society by connecting certain psychological drives with certain social institutions, but which "emotional value the mythic images have," in other words, "which drives, wishes, hopes, defense mechanisms, etc. are connected with them" (ibid., XXXIV–XXXV).

Drewermann's psychoanalytic interpretation thus asks what a certain myth symbolizes in the human psyche. It focuses above all on the affective, emotional level. The enduring affective meaning of myths is the reason for "the possibility and necessity of a depth-psychological interpretation of the Yahwist's primordial history" (ibid., XXXV). Even a structuralist interpretation, though useful for ascertaining certain logical structures within myths, cannot do justice to the meaning which the motifs of myths have *in themselves*. A depth-psychological interpretation is necessary in order to understand the *emotional* significance of the concrete imagery of a symbol and to show how religious symbols respond to fundamental, concrete experiences of human existence, which the rationally oriented structuralist interpretation could not do (ibid., XLVI–LIV).

By being isolated from its social function, the meaning of a myth does not necessarily decrease but can gain tremendously. It may transform itself into a fairy tale or may turn into a motif of artistic creation in theater, poetry, music, and the performing arts and thus survive the life of the tribe from which it originated by thousands of years. It is evidently able "to evoke as always the strong affects of pleasure and dread, terror and joy, enthusiasm and disgust . . . in people from very different cultures and very different periods" (ibid., XXXIII).

How should mythic imagery from the past be able to evoke strong affective reactions in the present? Drewermann answers that "beyond historical mediation common constants of experiencing are found *in the human psyche*" (ibid., LXXII). In volumes 1 and 2 of *Strukturen des Bösen* Drewermann has gathered a vast store of nature myths with motifs of serpent and tree culled from all corners and periods of the world. That this mytholological material displays such surprising similarities only makes sense if one presupposes "certain regularities of experiencing in the human psyche which, under similar circumstances, bring forth again and again a similar symbolic language and which one needs to know in order to understand the meaning of the respective symbols" (ibid., LXIX). Drewermann compares these psychical presuppositions for affectively understanding the concrete imagery of myths to the "a priori ideas and categories" of reason in the philosophy of German Idealism which are necessary postulates for thought (1985a, XXVI–XXVII; cf. Drewermann 1984, 58–71).

Psychologically, Drewermann thinks of these a priori forms of imagining along the lines of Sigmund Freud's assumption of the phylogenetic roots of the symbolism of the unconscious and of Jung's assumption of the evolutionary roots of the collective unconscious[8] (Drewermann 1986a, XXXV–XL). He employs the schools of Freud and Jung, supplemented by findings from the works of A. Adler, L. Szondi, and H. Schultz-Hencke, pragmatically and not dogmatically (ibid., XLV). In addition, in the philosophical analysis he turns to existential psychology (especially Sartre) to connect the drive-psychological and archetypal dynamics to existential structures of the human spirit. Trained in the neopsychoanalytic tradition of Harald Schultz-Hencke,[9] who tried to bring all analytic schools "through a

---

8. Drewermann cites passages from lectures 10 and 13 of Freud's *Introductory Lectures to Psycho-Analysis* (Freud 1916–7) and from *Moses and Monotheism* (Freud 1939); and from C. G. Jung's *General Problems of Psychotherapy* (1966a), *The Structure of the Psyche* (1972a), *On the Psychology of the Unconscious* (1966b), and *On the Nature of the Psyche* (1972b).

9. For the work of Harald Schultz-Hencke (1927, 1940), with special focus on Freud's tragic opposition during the Third Reich to Schultz-Hencke's inclusive approach, see the collection of articles in *The Psychoanalytic Review: Psychiatry, Psychotherapy, and Psychoanalysis in the Third Reich* (Lothane 2001a), especially Lothane 2001b, 205, 210–22; Cocks 2001, 236;

reduction of their theoretical claims to one table," Drewermann employs either of the classic depth-psychological schools wherever it is helpful for an interpretation of "any detail" of the Yahwist's primordial history (1986a, XLV). Similar to Fred Pine, Drewermann holds that psychic "phenomena" can be addressed from a number of theoretical perspectives, each shedding light on a particular aspect of the mental experience (Pine 1985, 54–72).

After 1945 fear of a return to the biologistic anthropology of the Third Reich led to a preference for the *tabula rasa* theory according to which one finds in the human psyche only that which has been introduced to it socially from outside (cf. the Frankfurt School, Kardiner) (Drewermann 1985a, XXXV). While Drewermann does not doubt the value of the social-psychological perspective, he considers it insufficient to explain the humanity-wide [*menschheitliche*] themes present in the mythic material in the Yahwist's primordial history. For Drewermann, depth psychology shows that the nature of human beings is "precisely not an ensemble of societal circumstances, but to the contrary: societal circumstances have to be seen as arrangements of the human psyche which are, to be sure, sociohistorically *conditioned* [*bedingt*] but never sociohistorically *established* [*begründet*]" (ibid., XLIII). Each culture is a socially conditioned variation of "biologically given basic needs of humans" (ibid., XLIV–XLV).

Drewermann seems to emphasize that humans cannot be reduced to social circumstances precisely because in Nazi Germany the rule of the social collectivity was idolized and used every possible pseudo-science, most prominently its biological race ideologies, to justify itself. Drewermann's dual assumptions of biological roots of psychological phenomena and of the freedom of the human spirit gain him a view of the individual beyond either biological or social determinism. By emphasizing *universal* constants of the human psyche and by stressing that the human spirit needs archetypal images of the psyche to perceive the existential meaning that finds expression in religious

---

Goggin and Goggin 2001, 184–91. This collection presents evidence that Freud, in an effort to keep the Berlin Psychoanalytic Institute alive under Nazi rule, was willing to make concessions to the Nazis in regard to the leadership of the Institute (Matthias Heinrich Göring, the cousin of the Reichsmarschall Hermann Göring) for fear that otherwise the views of H. Schultz-Hencke, who was married to a Jewish woman (Lothane 2001b, 211) and "made no secret within the Göring Institute of his anti-Nazi views" (Cocks 2001, 236), could dilute "the purity of psychoanalysis" (Goggin and Goggin 2001, 185). Besides calling for the pragmatic use of the various analytic schools which responds to the needs of the patient, Schultz-Hencke elaborated S. Freud's notion of inhibition, questioned Freud's libido theory, and stressed the importance of sociocultural factors of adult life in health and illness (Lothane 2001b, 205).

imagery across space and time, Drewermann wants to say that the individual finds ultimate meaning, that is, meaning in relation to the divine, not essentially in society but by being guided from within. His anthropology thus strengthens the individual's power vis-à-vis social manipulation. It is an attempt "to get a step away from the predilection of the 'human makers' in Skinner's *Walden Two* [1948] 'to play God' " (ibid., XLVIII).

Drewermann holds that the evolutionary heritage of the human psyche can be instrumentalized to act out horrors such as we have witnessed in the twentieth century only when the human spirit is lost in absolute *fear*. On the ontogenetic level of experience archetypal images evoke either positive or negative effects *depending* on whether a person's ego experiences these images in relation to another person within an atmosphere of trust or of fear. Hence the *relational* and *personal* dynamic within which psychic and mythic imagery (and through it all reality!) is experienced is psychologically and theologically of critical importance for the interpretation of religious and quasi-religious texts. Archetypal imagery can thus heal or destroy depending on whether it drowns the ego or whether it is integrated in an ego-strengthening manner that is possible only in an atmosphere of trust. The philosophical-theological section below will present Drewermann's argument that existential fear can be calmed only if psychic images of healing are not mere images.

Sin as a Neurosis Before God

Drewermann's exegetical analysis found that the Yahwist draws on transmitted mythic imagery to show how all structures of existence turn evil and become sources of misery if humans lose God as the creative source and foundation of their life. Consequently, his depth-psychological analysis of Genesis 3 and 4 focuses on the ontogenetic dynamics of human development in the stories, particularly on the dynamics of fear, guilt, and the emergence of defense mechanisms in relation to the primary caregivers. Although the second volume of *Strukturen des Bösen* draws on "*all* classic schools of depth psychology" (ibid., XLVIII), the Freudian psychoanalytic perspective best matches the Yahwist's focus on the "sickening" effects of "sin" in the life of the individual and of society (Drewermann 1986a, XLII–XLIII). While the mythic motifs present in Genesis 2–11 could in themselves be seen as "symbols of life," Drewermann follows the

Yahwist's theological intention by interpreting these motifs to describe the disastrous mental and spiritual "symptoms of the human turn away from God" (ibid., XLIII).

Drewermann points out that Freud's psychology of religion, which was developed in a culture characterized by "patriarchal conditions," is especially suitable for the analysis of the ambivalent traits of the patriarchal image of God in Genesis 2–11. Only after the ambivalence has been worked through, is it possible to see beyond Freud's psychological notion of God as identified with the human father-image to a theological notion of God which needs to be absolutely differentiated from the human father-image (Drewermann 1985a, 6).

Drewermann uses Freudian psychoanalysis as a phenomenology of anxiety and guilt in the biblical texts, shedding light on the way various characters experience God, themselves, and the world. Psychoanalysis, in conjunction with existential psychology, helps the exegete to understand ambivalent elements in the God-image in religious texts as the result of human anxiety and is a major diagnostic tool for assessing how the loss of God necessarily must distort human existence empirically. In other words, psychoanalysis serves Drewermann as a "phenomenology of sin" or "as a phenomenology of the basic attitudes which can destroy or heal humans mentally [*seelisch*]" (1986b, 468; Drewermann 1985a, XX; cf. Drewermann 1986a, LXXXIX).

In fact, Drewermann understands sin "as a neurosis before God" (1985a, 556). By calling sin a neurosis before God, Drewermann does not propose "the absurd thesis...that all mental illnesses would be consequences of a false spiritual attitude, a projection of life [*Lebensentwurf*] which passes God by: as if all mental activity did not also have its external side, which can in itself be damaged by biological, chemical, or physical noxae, and as if mental behavior were not also, beyond all possibility for personal decision and guilt, to a large extent a learned behavior which has been adopted from outside" (ibid., XVI). Nor does he mean by it that all "sinners" — which means, according to the Yahwist, all humans — are clinically neurotic in the sense of psychoanalysis, which would "simply be absurd" (ibid., 555).

What the notion of sin as a neurosis before God instead tries to convey is first "that the developmental history of sin in the Yahwist's primordial history is presented in the [same] stages on which the development of neurosis is based as well; and that the psychoanalytic theory of neurosis presents a useful, even indispensable way for understanding the reality of sin as portrayed by the Yahwist; furthermore, that which we call 'neurosis' psychoanalytically the Yahwist understands as a symbol [*Bild*] of sin" (ibid., 556).

For Drewermann, the prime symptom of a neurosis before God is the desperate attempt to be like God. The term "neurotic" is used by Drewermann not in terms of whether a human being is "normal" or not in comparison to social norms and behaviors but whether a human being is "sick" due to fear at the ground of his existence in relation to God, as the Yahwist considers all human beings to be. The overcompensations of having to "be like God" most often have little to do with the overt grandiosity we may associate with the phrase. Because human existence feels — often without conscious awareness — ultimately groundless without God, "sin is the mental illness per se" (ibid., XIV). The German term "mental illness" is *Geisteskrankheit*, which means literally "sickness of the spirit" and allows Drewermann to emphasize that spiritual despair, that is, a projection of human existence without ultimate ground, "God," inevitably leads to mental illnesses across the spectrum.

The clinical notion of neurosis in psychoanalysis and the spiritual notion of neurosis in Drewermann's theology are differentiated in terms of the objects in relation to which neurosis develops. If the conflicts in the Yahwist's primordial history should be read as images of a ubiquitous, humanity-wide development which has the character of a sickness, then

> we have to leave the psychological category of neurosis behind and introduce the theological concept of sin, that is, we have to take seriously that the Yahwist does not want to describe a mental developmental failure in the relationship between child and parents [in Freudian psychoanalysis] or ego and self [in Jungian psychology] but a theological developmental failure in the relationship between the human being and God. Since he chooses for this, however, the picture of a developmental progression which is known to us psychoanalytically in terms of ontogenesis and whose order completely coincides [with the Yahwist's developmental progression], we can succinctly formulate the findings simply ... [by saying]: the Yahwist's primordial history describes *sin as a neurosis before God.* (ibid., 556)

The object in relation to which the existential neurosis develops is hence God. Tracing human despair to a spiritual neurosis before God has important implications for the power of healing which Drewermann attributes to the trusting relationship with God. He argues that working the spiritual neurosis through in relation to the divine, while using the affective language of the human psyche as expressed in religious texts, is necessary as a condition for the possibility of transcending rather than repeating the clinically neurotic structures which humans develop in relation to their parents and live out in relationship to all subsequent authority figures.

Drewermann uses *daseinsanalytic* (i.e., existential-psychological) analysis to detail how basic spiritual attitudes may find expression in mental illness. If a human being "wants to be 'like God,' all forms of neurosis follow in *daseinsanalytic* perspective" (ibid., XIII). Drewermann hence asks "to what extent certain mental illnesses express basic spiritual attitudes, to what extent a certain psychology stands in function of a certain projection of life [*Lebensentwurf*] and [how far] the mental constitution changes depending on whether someone finds faith or not" (ibid., XVI). "What makes sin a 'neurosis before God' (ibid., 556) is precisely the fact that in all forms in which they miss themselves [*Selbstverfehlung*] humans actually do not repress certain areas of drives but God. And in the fear which befalls them then, in the substitute formations in which they then must seek refuge, they fall ever deeper into compulsions and bonds. The paradigm of neurosis offers itself for the description of the external aspect" of compulsions and bonds (Drewermann 1986b, XXX). In the philosophical and theological analysis, Drewermann hence relates certain types of existential anxiety, explicated by Kierkegaard, such as despair of infinity, of finitude, of possibility, and of necessity, to psychodynamic forms of anxiety in depressive, schizoid, hysterical, and obsessive compulsive disorder (ibid., 469–79). In *Strukturen des Bösen* Drewermann outlines "a radically theocentric psychology, an understanding of the human psyche [*Seele*] in which nothing can be understood without God or — even better — in which everything becomes understandable in view of the nothingness and the fear of having to exist without being held by and firmly grounded in God" (ibid., XXXI).

Such "missing oneself," such spiritual neurosis, however, need not take the form of clinical neurosis in the psychoanalytic sense of the word (since this would be "simply absurd") but can find expression instead in socially highly rewarded and "normal" behaviors such as doing one's duty, being obedient, living a life of self-sacrifice, supporting war, destroying the environment — all possibly done in the name of "God." This is of utmost importance for an understanding of the challenge Drewermann's theology poses to any state or Church system which claims to legitimize its power and authority with reference to God.

Drewermann qualifies the use of the term "neurosis" as a symbol for the spiritual dynamics of Genesis 3–11 in one central aspect. The key element of neurosis involves the permanent "repression" or "inhibition" of forbidden drives. But in Genesis 3–11 humans act out precisely what in the neurotic remains repressed: "(cannibalistic) eating (Gen. 3), murder (Gen. 4:1–16), incest (Gen. 6:1–4), homosexuality (Gen. 9:18–27). It seems more correct to speak of perversion instead of neurosis" (Drewermann 1985a, 557–58). Passages which evidence clear "traits of a mad identification of consciousness with the contents of the unconscious (Gen. 3:5, 6:1–4, 11:1–9)" would even warrant the use of the "concept of psychosis." Despite psychotic elements and "perverse" acting out, Drewermann prefers the concept of "neurosis before God" because Genesis 3–11 does not portray a fixation on a single partial drive, as would be the case in what psychoanalysis calls "perversion," and because the developmental picture of Genesis 3–11 also shows that humans actively attempt to take defensive measures against their perverse strivings and to make up for past failures of their inhibition. "We prefer to describe such a mixture of perverse strivings and of (partly failing) defensive measures as neurosis" (ibid., 558).

A Bird's-eye View of the Psychoanalytic Interpretation of Genesis 2–11

With these clarifications and qualifications in mind, before turning to the close reading of the story of the fall in Genesis 3 and of the story of the first human murder in Genesis 4, I will outline Drewermann's analysis of the Yahwist's primordial history as a developmental story following the ontogenetic structure of human development from infancy to adolescence. The Yahwist portrays this primordial history not as a success but as a failure. That the structure of the text resembles the psychogenesis of the individual becomes especially evident in that both "histories" are divided into two sections: just as the primordial history is interrupted by the catastrophe of the Great Flood

(Gen. 6–8), so the development of psychogenesis is interrupted by the latency period. And

> [j]ust as the conflict with the parents is in the foreground during mental development up to the latency period, so the Yahwist's primordial history portrays the human conflict with and failure before God up to the Great Flood. And just as — based on the background of what has so far been introjected — the development toward individual social action outside the family begins after the latency period, . . . a further unfolding [of development] in the direction of the forms of historical and social community begins . . . after the Great Flood. (ibid., 545–46)

The affinity between the developmental stages of the human psyche and the developmental structure of the themes in Genesis 2–11 leads Drewermann to treat the stories first "as if the relationship between God and humans could be read without difficulty like a relationship of father and child or mother and child or of consciousness and the unconscious" (ibid., 555). This allows for an understanding of the affective significance of the spiritual relationship with God. Drewermann's philosophical analysis will later show how psychological dynamics can express existential attitudes on the spiritual plane.

A brief summary of the developmental structure of Genesis 2–11 can be found in volume 2 of *Strukturen des Bösen* (ibid., 540–52), including a table which utilizes psychoanalytic tables provided by K. Abraham, E. Bohm, and E. H. Erikson (ibid., 546–48). I will list the major themes, the psychological developmental stage and approximate age, the particular type of neurosis which is etiologically related to the stage (NB: the etiological stages for types of neurosis come to an end with the Oedipal stage), and the major characteristics which Drewermann finds expressed in the stories of the Yahwist's primordial history. In parentheses I will add — where provided by Drewermann — for each story the subjective-level, Jungian interpretation (Jung 1966b, 84), and selectively the social dynamic which springs from the unresolved mental conflicts. Psychoanalytically, the stories of Genesis 2–11 are structured as follows:

Genesis 2:4b–25: the image of paradise with its theme of the primordial unity of humans with God represents the early oral stage; Klein's "schizoid position," age 0–½; pre- and postnatal experience of the symbiotic mother-child dyad; preambivalent; neurosis associated: schizoid disorder, schizophrenia. (On a subjective level: represents undifferentiated unity of consciousness and the unconscious, which corresponds phylogenetically to the lack of individual awareness where the individual is prereflexively identified with the tribe.)

Genesis 3: the story of the fall into sin through eating and expulsion, with its themes of separation, fear, guilt feelings, and shame, represents the later, oral-sadistic stage; Klein's "depressive position," age ½–1; desire to incorporate object totally, conflicts around teething; ambivalent (as all subsequent stages!); dynamic of basic trust versus basic mistrust; neurosis associated: depression, melancholy. The story of the fall has phallic connotations addressed in a detailed analysis below. (On a subjective level: the separation from God represents the differentiation through which consciousness separates from the "mother" as an archetype of the unconscious and the growth of individual existence; in contrast to dragon-slaying myths of solar and lunar heroes, the Yahwist sees the story of Genesis 3:1–7 as a failed attempt of healthy separation and subsequent integration and views it instead as a "symbol for being devoured by the forces of the unconscious, as the outbreak of a sick, insane state of consciousness" [ibid., 542]. At this juncture Drewermann's work locates the vulnerability of the individual to the rule of the collective: if a healthy separation from the parents externally and a healthy differentiation from the unconscious internally do not take place, then the individual is easily devoured by the unconscious, falls victim to a godlike inflation of the ego, sinks societally, as in the Third Reich, into the collective and projects in insane fashion the archetypes on her own ego and collectively on society and the "hero" who represents the society [see ibid., 151]. See also the interpretation of Genesis 11:1–11.)

Genesis 4:1–16: the story of Cain and Abel, with its themes of sacrifice, rivalry, murder, and stubbornness, represents the anal-sadistic stage; age 1–3; it is characterized by conflicts around sharing and keeping, around the wish to dominate the object, the annihilation of the object; dynamic of autonomy verses heteronomy; neurosis associated: obsessional neurosis. (On a subjective level: represents the fight of consciousness with its shadow; in contrast to solar and lunar myths, the victory of the darkness [of the unconscious] does not serve the rejuvenation of consciousness but leads to forms of self-suppression, repression and the dissociation of consciousness and the unconscious.)

Genesis 4:23–4 and Genesis 6:1–4[10] represent the Oedipal stage in its masculine and feminine version respectively.

Genesis 4:23–4: the story of Lamech and his song of the sword, with its themes of the exhibition of aggressive masculinity, of fear of vulnerability, and of revenge represents the Oedipal stage in the development of the boy; age 3–5; it is characterized by active object love (of the mother), exhibition, ambivalence of love and hate simultaneously, and of competition with the father; associated neurosis: hysteria. (No interpretation on a subjective level provided.)

Genesis 6:1–4: the story of the sons of God marrying the daughters of humans (in short: the marriage of angels), with its themes of the desire of the girl for unification with the divine and for the birth of strong children, represents the Oedipal stage in the development of the girl; age 3–5; it is characterized by active object love (of the father), change of object (father instead of mother), exhibition, ambivalence of love and hate; associated neurosis: hysteria. (On a subjective level: theme of merging of contents of consciousness with opposite contents of the unconscious as in myth of *hieros gamos;* but the Yahwist's redaction sees in this story not an image of successful merger but a symbol of the "rape" of consciousness by forces of the unconscious which leads to an "insanely distorted" form of the self [Drewermann 1985a, 543].)

Genesis 6:5–Genesis 8: the story of the Great Flood, with its theme of the end of the world as a punishment, represents the latency period; age 5–10; it is characterized by the dissolution of the Oedipus complex and the introjection of the parental images in the form of the superego. (On a subjective level: attempt at a rebirth of consciousness, of a more encompassing personality out of the unconscious; Yahwist portrays it, however, as the quasi-psychotic drowning of consciousness in the chaos of the unconscious.)

---

10. In the Foreword to the second edition of volume 1 of *Strukturen des Bösen,* published in 1979, Drewermann adds that further exegetical research has seriously questioned whether Genesis 6:1–4 belongs to the Yahwist's primordial history (1986a, LXXXIX–XC). But even if it is not from the Yahwist, Drewermann finds it remarkable that the later addition of this particular story was placed precisely at the point of the primordial history where it would be psychoanalytically expected in terms of ontogenetic development. What may not belong to the Yahwist's primordial history by the standards of literary criticism, can nonetheless thematically belong to it. Thus what appears exegetically as a mistake confirms to Drewermann the validity of the psychoanalytic analysis of the Yahwist's primordial history and the hypothesis that the reason why certain motifs appear in stories, even as they continue to grow over long historical periods, is, for the most part, due to unconscious associations.

Genesis 9:20–28: the story of Ham's crime, with its themes of voyeurism, castration fears, homosexuality, and shame as a reaction formation represents early puberty; age 10–12; it is characterized by the resuming of sexual development and by object love that includes the genital sphere. (On a subjective level: as image of the destruction of the introjected father-image and hence a step toward greater independence; the homosexual strivings are understood as longings for masculinity; the Yahwist portrays the "return of the father," however, as a curse which takes on a life dominated by guilt feelings and self-suppression.)

Genesis 10:8–12: the story of Nimrod, the hero, the first mighty warrior and hunter, with its themes of conquest, the rule of violence, and of exhibitionism of phallic masculinity, represents the stage of puberty; age 12–18; it is characterized by identity conflicts which attempt to solve latent (castrative) self-doubts, show repressed homosexuality, and overcompensations of inferiority feelings. Drewermann exemplifies in an analysis of the lives of Alexander the Great and of Adolf Hitler how the "Nimrod complex" characterizes something typical in all politically "great" people (ibid., 488–503). (No interpretation on a subjective level provided.)

Genesis 11:1–11: the story of the building of Babel and its tower, with its themes of joining together against the sense of isolation, of unity through a common goal, and of diligence and achievement, represents the stage of adolescence; from around age 18; it is characterized by idealism, self-confidence, single-mindedness and social joining together, with latent Oedipal tendencies. (On a subjective level: attempt of an artificial self-integration which employs mandala symbolism in order to violently force a connection between the isolated consciousness and the unconscious which is experienced as chaotic and threatening; the artificial attempt inevitably ends in a catastrophe; the "external-magical handling of the contents of the unconscious leads to ego-inflation, to an insanity in individual as well as collective life" [ibid., 545].)

Genesis 3 in Psychoanalytic Perspective

As we follow Drewermann interpreting the mythic motifs of the story of Genesis 3 in terms of ontogenetic stages and conflicts, we bear in mind that he will later read the psychoanalytic interpretation as a *symbol* in his theological interpretation. Many of the motifs in Genesis 3 are first introduced in Genesis 2. The progression from paradisal harmony in Genesis 2 to alienation in Genesis 3 is essential to the interpretation, which we find reflected in the fact that Drewermann's psychoanalytic analysis treats Genesis 2 and 3 as a unity. Although the following summary of his interpretation will focus on Genesis 3, Genesis 2 is always in the background as a reference point.

In accordance with the notion that myths which have been stripped of their social context are best interpreted with the same rules that apply to fairy tales and dreams, Drewermann's primary tool for the psychoanalytic interpretation of the mythic material in Genesis 2–11 is "dream analysis."

> [W]e must, as is the case in dream analysis, trace the manifest content of the transmitted mythic material back to latent contents. That will allow us to understand the path through displacements, condensations, symbolizations, etc. to the current formulation of these contents. Based on the "defense mechanisms" found in that dream work we will also receive important clues in terms of neurotic structures. After that we can pick up the question of the (associative) bridges which lead to the secondary enrichments of the motifs and arrangements of the transmitted material. We will always supplement the reductive-analytic method of psychoanalysis by asking from C. G. Jung's perspective which meaning finds expression in the mythic images of the Yahwist's stories, that is, for which purpose (not merely: for what reasons) are they arranged in this and not in another way. (1985a, 11)

On the other hand, Drewermann stresses that the value of dream analysis for the texts in Genesis 2–11 is clearly limited. The "methods of dream psychology of the unconscious" cannot be employed when one wants to understand the "conscious (!) redaction" of the mythic material which the Yahwist provides, the understanding of which requires knowledge of the exegetical results (ibid., 11). The Yahwist gives the material a theological interpretation which builds on but cannot be reduced to the meaning of the mythic material in itself. The theological interpretation which the Yahwist gives the material is adopted in Drewermann's own theological interpretation.

Drewermann's psychoanalytic interpretation of the story of Genesis 3 notes that the central symbols of the mythic material: tree, fruits, and serpent are clearly polyvalent. The story portrays ontogenetically conflicts on both the oral-sadistic and the phallic (Oedipal) level. By assuming the principle that "in myths almost all essential symbols have bisexual character" (ibid., 104), Drewermann presupposes R. Waelder's classic article on "the principle of multiple function" and overdetermination although he does not explicitly refer to it (Waelder 1936).

Our explication will basically follow the development of Drewermann's own psychoanalytic argument: first, Drewermann addresses the manifest oral theme of tree and fruit and relates it to oral-sadistic conflicts the infant experiences during the period of teething in relation to the mother figure; second follows the interpretation of the story on the genital-sexual (phallic) level (hereafter referred to as "sexual" unless otherwise indicated), with both serpent and tree as sexual symbols, the clarification of the nature of the relation between sexual and oral levels, and the argument that the story refers both to female and male ontogenetic development; third is an analysis of the dynamic of fear, of the defense mechanisms employed in the story to contain the fear, and of the meaning of the feeling of "being like God" in light of the fear; fourth is an analysis of the origin of the guilt feeling on the oral-sadistic level; the psychoanalytic analysis concludes with Drewermann's interpretation of the "punishments of God" in light of five basic paleoanthropological forms of fear.

The Symbol of the Forbidden Tree and Fruits: Oral-sadistic Dynamics

In this section we will focus on the interpretation of the oral dynamic, which centers around the motif of forbidden tree and its fruits (Drewermann 1985a, 52–68). Through an analysis of mythical literature, Drewermann finds that the motif of the tree is present in myths of religions throughout the world (ibid., 52–55). He provides ample evidence of "myth, fairy tales, and dreams" in which tree and fruits are associated with "woman (mother) and the female breast" (ibid., 60). While he considers interpreting the symbol of the tree as an archetype using Jung's method, he opts instead first for an objective-level interpretation which explores "the ontogenetic origin of this symbolism" (ibid., 56). Drewermann uses L. Szondi's work, which attempts to connect archetypal imagery with drive components, to argue (in 1977!) that as long as the Jung school would not take note of the basic connections between "drives and archetypes" (Szondi 1977, 25), it would remain speculative and would tend to interpret concrete symbols such as the motif of the tree in Genesis 3 speculatively "as fixed images for something as general as 'the unconscious'" (Drewermann 1985a, 56).

In addition to the connection between archetypal structures and drive components, archetypal theory needs to be grounded in the ethological theory of innate release mechanisms if it wants to escape the biological speculations to which Freud's psychoanalysis or Jung's analytic psychology are vulnerable (ibid., 60–68). Drewermann therefore reads the depth-psychological findings in light of ethological research, that is, the comparative study of the behavior and character of animals and humans, and of paleoanthropology (e.g., Bilz 1971, Lorenz 2002, Eibl-Eibesfeldt 1973). Only if one clarifies step by step by means of ethology "which biological determinants from the evolutionary heritage of all of humankind preform the drive-psychological themes of orality, anality, and genitality" can one, on the one hand, avoid claiming biological status for phenomena which are clearly social variations (e.g., Freud's Oedipus complex), and show that many of the findings of psychoanalysis are correct on the other hand (ibid., XLV). At the same time, Jung's theory of archetypes and symbol interpretation "can receive its real justification only on the background of ethology" (ibid., XLVI).

To understand the reasons why the imagery of garden, tree, and fruit in Genesis 2 and 3 can become symbols for the infant's early experiences with the mother and to comprehend their full affective quality, Drewermann grounds psychoanalytic theory in the study of ethology by relating R. A. Spitz's notion of "'primary narcissism' [S. Freud] of the infant" in the "mother-child-dyad" and S. Freud's notion of "anaclitic object choice" (ibid., 23, 45) to L. Szondi's "'primordial drive to cling'" (Szondi 1977, 419). Based on ethological research, Szondi relates human instinctual [*Instinkt*][11] life to the drive theory of psychoanalysis. He connects the archetypal symbol of the tree and fruit with ethological findings (Drewermann 1985a, 61)

---

11. The German word *Instinkt* here refers to one of the meanings of the English word "instinct," namely: a "complex and specific response on the part of an organism to environmental stimuli that is largely hereditary and unalterable though the pattern of behavior through which it is expressed may be modified by learning, that does not involve reason, and that has as its goal the removal of a somatic tension or excitation" (Merriam-Webster 1986, 1171). Szondi uses the terms *Instinkt* (instinct) and *Trieb* (drive) at times interchangeably, namely, as follows: drives are seen as "imperfect instincts [*unvollkommene Instinkte*]" in which "the instinctive behavior pattern is only partly inherited and the organism needs in individual life personally acquired practice in order to execute the behavior perfectly" (Szondi 1977, 39).

and Freud's stage of oral development with the evolutionary primordial "drive to cling"[12] (Szondi 1977, 89). Drewermann cites a passage from Szondi which sums up the connections between orality and the drive to cling, the tree and the mother, and the religious significance of these connections. The infant's drive to cling is an

> urge to hold on tightly with mouth and hand to breast and body of the mother and to hang oneself almost inseparably from it — as if from a tree of life — and to *cling to* it in order to *secure* the mother and all her subsequent substitute objects eternally just for oneself, the urge to hide oneself away in the womb of the mother and to eternalize oneself in the security of the womb, *the urge to be unconditionally accepted by the mother within a basic trust, just as one is,* to have all characteristics — whether good or evil — completely affirmed by her, the urge of lovers to grasp with hands and mouth for each other, . . . all of these tremendous demands originate in the tendency of clinging. (Drewermann 1985a, 60, quoted from Szondi 1960, 182; again quoted in Drewermann 1992a, 331–32, n. 61)

Primate studies by I. Hermann (1923, 1924, 1926a, 1926b, 1933, all quoted in Szondi 1977, 419–20) and studies of biological anthropology by A. Portmann (1962, 1964, 1969) confirm that humans share a drive to cling even after the dual union of mother and child has been dissolved (Drewermann, 1985a, 61). The mother is the "first tree" (Portmann) of the young primate. Drewermann thus can see the urge of "clinging-oneself-to [*Sich-Anklammern*]" as "a phylogenetically acquired instinct," which "is activated ontogenetically first in relation to the mother and is subsequently transferred onto objects which substitute for the mother. The symbolism of the tree as a maternal symbol has then its foundation in the fact that due to the instinct to cling experiences can be repeated on trees which were first made with the mother" (ibid., 61–62). The drive to cling finds expression in human needs for hold (*Halt*) and security and is the phylogenetic root for the religious needs of hold and security in one's existence. The word "fall" in English and *Fall* in German thus refer to the sense of loss of hold and security portrayed in Genesis 3. The experiences

---

12. When in the following "drive" and "instinct" are used interchangeably, "drive" is equivalent to "imperfect instinct."

of finding hold, protection, food, and security which the (primate) infant first makes with the mother can later be projected onto trees and other objects which resemble the mother experientially, for example, houses, caves, and so on.

The catalytic process in which drives and innate release mechanisms and the corresponding affects are activated in relation to the primary "objects" is central to Drewermann's thinking. It provides the basis for the profound affective quality of religious experiences which encompasses human nature as a whole. This catalytic process allows for the possibility that the central archetypal images of father and mother, while first activated and experienced in relation to primary caregivers, can become the key building blocks for the religious experience of the divine as a person.

Referring to R. A. Spitz's work, Drewermann notes that the link between the drive to cling and the oral stage can be established through the observation of certain "innate release mechanisms [angeborene auslösende Mechanismen (AAM)]." Such innate release mechanisms have been found at work as the neonate typically rotates her head and performs a snapping motion of the mouth in response to stimulation of the snout/mouth region, and are coordinated in the first month of life with the closing of the fingers (Klammerreflex, i.e., clinging reflex) in response to palmar stimulation (Drewermann 1985a, 62; Spitz 1957, 19–22). This inherited coordination of innate release mechanisms in the oral sphere of the "primal cavity" and in the palmar sphere of the hand (Spitz 1955, 1965) establishes the connection between the primal needs of nurture and of hold which find symbolic expression in the taking and eating of the forbidden fruit in the story of Genesis 3.

In the case of the tree symbol, the phylogenetically inherited drive to cling and the oral snapping motion are for Drewermann the bridge for an understanding of the universal significance of the motif of the tree. The image of the tree itself is not innate. Rather "the instinct to cling [and the oral snapping reflex] and the corresponding... release mechanisms" are innate. Hence "we understand that the 'tree' can be an 'archetypal' image of the mother or of woman as such" (Drewermann 1985a, 62).

Having connected the psychosocial stage of orality with the phylogenetic drive to cling and the symbol of the tree with the mother, Drewermann turns to E. H. Erikson and K. Abraham to show "how and when in the course of psychical ontogeny a prohibition to eat appears" which carries a deadly threat if transgressed (ibid., 56). He quotes a well-known passage from Erikson's *Childhood and Society* that seeks "the ontogenetic contribution to the biblical saga of paradise, where the first people on earth forfeited forever the right to pluck without effort what had been put at their disposal" in the second oral stage, that is, in K. Abraham's oral-sadistic stage, which is characterized by teething (Erikson 1993). Erikson attributes "universality" to the experience symbolically expressed in the story of the fall. Part of the cited portion reads: "Our clinical work indicates that this point in the individual's early history can be the origin of an evil dividedness, where anger against the gnawing teeth, and anger against the withdrawing mother, and anger with one's impotent anger all lead to a forceful experience of sadistic and masochistic confusion leaving the general impression that once upon a time one destroyed one's unity with a maternal matrix.... [T]hey bit into the forbidden apple, and made God angry" (Drewermann 1985a, 63; quoted from Erikson 1993, 79). Teething ontogenetically creates a crisis experience which disrupts the basic trust between mother and child. Following K. Abraham, Drewermann sees in this crisis of the oral-sadistic stage the "beginning of the conflict of ambivalence" by means of which the mother (and later substitutes) is both loved and hated (1985a, 63–64). Drewermann speaks of this loss of original unity with the mother as an experience "in which the child comes in conflict over having to destroy what he loves and what he lives from" (ibid., 236, cf. 190–91). The expulsion from paradise relates symbolically to the weaning of the child during the teething period. Drewermann locates in this early conflict, following M. Klein, psychoanalytically the origin of guilt feelings.

I already alluded to the core theological assumption that allows Drewermann to connect the ethologically grounded psychoanalytic interpretation to the theological interpretation, namely, that certain needs and expectations which humans originally relate to their mother and father are transferred onto God in religion. The connection between empirical research and theology is of great significance to Drewermann: "For the theological interpretation of Genesis 3 it is not of little significance to see that where the Yahwist speaks of God and the tree in paradise, psychoanalytically speaking, longings and fears appear which relate 'actually' to mother and father" (ibid., 66). By tapping through mythic material into such "vital drives," the Yahwist wants "to express that God is everything for humans:

their father, their mother, their entire life. God — and not the father or the mother, the Yahwist thinks — means for humans from
the first day of their lives everything they wish for 'orally' in the
form of clinging-oneself-to, of seeking food, life, protection, security, acceptance, justification (cf. Ps. 27:10; Isa. 66:5–13)" (ibid.).
The tree can be a symbol ontogenetically for the security experienced
in the mother, on a subjective level for the unity with oneself, and
theologically for the security experienced in God "because it was
phylogenetically a real place of security for existence and because
the corresponding inherited coordinations [*Erbkoordinationen*] still
exist today" (ibid., 68). Following the paleoanthropologist Rudolf
Bilz, Drewermann wonders whether the notion of "God above" may
be partly a mental reaction to the loss our early ancestors experienced when they went into the steppe, thus losing the protection of
the forests where they could escape from danger by climbing up into
trees (ibid., 66–68).

Serpent and Tree as Bisexual Symbols: Oedipal Dynamics and Regression to Oral Dynamics

So far I have paraphrased Drewermann's psychoanalytic interpretation of the story of the fall in Genesis 3 in light of ambivalent impulses
during the oral-sadistic stage. The interpretation focused on the symbol of the tree, emphasized its maternal aspect, and located the fears
involved in the fall in terms of a basic human need to cling, that is, to
find hold, and, as related, to the basic need for nurture. The concept
of sin was connected to the guilt feelings the infant experiences in
response to the perceived withdrawing mother as a consequence of
internalized anger.

The reading on an oral-sadistic level of development can, Drewermann says, only provide insight into one aspect of Genesis 3:1–7.
Not only is it unable to shed light on the other prominent motif, the
serpent, but also on the sexual implications of the symbol of the tree
itself. In this section I will present Drewermann's interpretation of
serpent and tree as sexual symbols, his understanding of the relation
between the phallic and oral levels, and the argument that the story
addresses the ontogenetic development of both boy and girl.

An analysis of the nature mythological texts from around the
world (Drewermann 1985a, 69–152) reveals that mythic serpents
are closely connected to "the phenomena of rain, to cloud formation,
thunderstorms, rivers and lakes, and to the darkness of clouds and

of the night" (ibid., 70). As such, the serpent embodies "fertility in the vegetation," often has phallic meaning in which rain symbolizes the sperm that fertilizes the earth, and is frequently seen as a god of fertility (ibid., 72). The association of the serpent with the darkness of night, and therefore with the moon, sets it mythologically in eternal enmity to the light of the sun, to the "solar hero, the sun god" (ibid., 75). Later mythic interpretations in Egypt, for instance, can identify the serpent as the "darkness of the yawning nothingness." Such "identifications of the serpent with nothingness [*Nichtsein*], with chaotic primordial matter, with winter, droughts or with the darkening wind of a storm are probably already secondary meanings" (ibid., 77). The Great Goddess can produce a serpent which serves as the "creative-phallic principle for the self-copulation of the Great Goddess" and stands for the fertility of all of the earth. The serpent often has "male-female traits" (ibid., 81). The serpent can be associated with having healing wisdom and harboring the ability for self-regeneration (ibid., 85).

Drewermann notes the historical development from the matriarchal view of the serpent as creativity and fertility to the more and more negative patriarchal view (ibid., 81–82, 87). "The more, however, the male, spiritual [*geistige*] element develops with its will for the eternal and the immortal beyond the cycle of nature, the more the serpent appears as temptress to just such higher striving and is condensed into an image of what is low, evil, secret, and demonic, which no longer brings life but the death of the natural, always mortal life" (ibid., 87).

Psychoanalytically, the mythic imagery with its description of external processes of nature functions at the same time as a symbol for mental processes. "Without knowing it, through myth humans see in external nature their own internal life, that is, in their relation to nature they actually relate to themselves" (ibid., 89). The nature mythological analysis showed that the serpent is a "principal of natural fertility from which death and life, becoming and perishing, birth and dying derive" (ibid., 90) and that it can be a symbol for both masculine and feminine sexuality. It noted that the shape of the serpent seems to be often the associative bridge for the choice of symbolism: winding rivers, falling rain, the waning and waxing moon, the shedding of the skin, the phallus. Drewermann states that such resemblance with external nature, however, would most likely not lead to the creation of myths were it not for the resemblance of the serpent and nature symbols with the human body itself. "Without such a contribution of the projective transference of the human body pattern into nature, the serpent probably would not have advanced to its overarching significance in myth, despite all of its resemblance to winding river beds, pillars of clouds, twitching lightnings" (ibid., 90). The symbol of the serpent may also harbor phylogenetically inherited "realistic anxieties" based on the real danger serpents pose to humans (ibid., 101). As we proceed to recapitulate Drewermann's interpretation of Genesis 3:1–7 on the phallic level, we need to keep in mind that he clearly distinguishes between the original mythic motifs present in the story and the demythologized use of the mythical material in the redaction by the Yahwist.

While translating the manifest content of the story of the fall psychoanalytically into its latent thoughts, Drewermann finds that psychoanalytic writers (e.g., K. Abraham and O. Rank) have advanced interpretations of the mythic motifs of both tree and serpent in terms of the Oedipal stage as phallic symbols. While the nature mythological analysis clearly supports this interpretation, Drewermann cautions that a premature interpretation of the story of the fall on the phallic level would neglect the fact, however, that the original literary unit of Genesis 3:1–5 manifestly portrays the prohibition and the fall not as a sexual-genital one, but as an oral one. Hence, Drewermann says, the first question must be: which "associative bridge" exists in the unconscious between oral and genital motifs? The story connects the fall with the motif of knowing. Sexual curiosity is, in the beginning, intimately bound up with the question where babies come from (Freud 1905, 195; quoted in Drewermann 1985a, 103), in accordance with Freud's well-known observation that "intellectual activity" during the phallic age (between 3 and 5) stands in the "service of sexual exploration" (Drewermann 1985a, 103, quoting Freud 1940). Among the typical infantile sexual theories is the idea "that children came into the womb of the mother through eating, that is, through oral conception" (Drewermann 1985a, 108), an idea often found in myths as well (ibid., 104).

If eating from the tree as "oral conception" symbolizes sexual intercourse, then the tree would have to represent, in addition to the maternal meaning, a "male, phallic symbol," made possible through the polyvalence of key mythic symbols (ibid., 104). Within the sexual theory of an oral conception, the prohibition of the eating of the fruit from the tree and the threatened consequence of dying in Genesis 3 becomes plausible. If the tree represents the male genitals and the young child thinks that children are conceived through an act of eating, then it is possible "that the child identifies himself... with the fruits of the tree, and he would kill himself if he ate from the fruits of the tree" (ibid., 110). "The tree would hence be tabooed as a source of food, because it embodies and guarantees the life of the child himself through totemistic identification.... To die has its meaning and foundation in the context of this cannibalistic thinking of being eaten" (ibid., 111).

This interpretation gives rise to two questions. First, why does the story cast the serpent's words to aim "at a seemingly nonsexual deed which appears far more childlike and harmless than that expressed by the serpent itself as a symbol. The eating from the tree looks like a mere 'nibbling' (Gunkel)." Drewermann thinks that it is precisely this playing down of the sexual-genital aspect by symbolizing it as "eating of the fruits" which has purpose in the story (ibid., 112). But what is the reason for replacing the sexual-genital theme by the oral theme? Drewermann sees a defensive maneuver at work. The oral symbol of the eating from the tree is understood "as a defensive process and a regression from the genital area of sexual development to the oral level" (ibid., 113).

The second question which the interpretation of the tree as a phallic symbol raises is why the story should need two phallic symbols: serpent and tree. The two symbols have two different functions in the story. While the symbol of the serpent represents for the woman the tempting sexual wish for intercourse which arises as she is tempted by "male desire," the symbol of the tree represents the phallic symbol defended against by oral regression (ibid., 114–15, 173). Both serpent and tree stand for the phallus, the one expressing the temptation, the other the defense against the temptation by means of a revival of oral imagery.

Drewermann turns to ethological research to ground this interpretation of the regressive revival of oral imagery as a defense against male sexuality by showing how oral imagery, which is intimately related to experiences of the maternal, can be linked to male sexuality (ibid., 113–15). Ethological studies by R. Bilz and I. Eibl-Eibesfeldt show, in fact, that courtship behavior among animals and humans displays gestures of feeding and role play in which one partner feeds the other as if they were parent and child. Kissing is a remnant of such playful nurturing during courtship. The role of the nurturing party in the relationship is not restricted to the female. The man, too, takes "the role of the covering [*Bergenden*], hold-providing, nutrition-giving one during the courtship in order to gain the favor of his loved one." "The regression of the sexual drive onto the oral developmental level" need not only be "a superfluous step backward, but we perceive in it the precursor of a progression which already anticipates in courtly play the later care of the young." Drewermann concludes that oral regression in the fall story evidently "could not take place unless a certain archaic functional readiness exists in humans which steers the courtship of man and woman into oral paths from the start" (ibid., 115).

Thus the latent thoughts of Genesis 3:1–5 are:

> Desymbolized we can say that this story deals with a sexual temptation stirred up in a woman by male desire (the serpent). As we have already shown in the exegetical investigation, the woman reacts to the temptation with fear. This fear is symbolically expressed by substitution of the genital theme through the oral one. Originally the eating from the tree has to do with a notion of infantile sexual exploration, and, even more fundamentally, with a regression of sexuality to the stage of the oral conception phantasy. For fear of male sexuality orality is regressively revived. Thus we understand the serpent, the tree, the fruits, the standing side by side of serpent and tree, the eating of the fruits as well as the motif of knowledge or of knowing: all of these motifs show themselves as sexual symbols which revive infantile sexual ideas along paleoanthropological lines during a process of regression charged with anxiety. The only motif that is still missing is the "to-be-like-God." (ibid., 115)

While Drewermann related the prohibition on the oral-sadistic level to the child's fears of killing the very person from whom she lives, the interpretation of the prohibition and fear on a sexual-genital level requires a different explanation. In particular, the question is: "Whence comes the fear which forces the oral regression?" (ibid., 115).

Two elements in the story provide Drewermann clues as to the source of the fear on the sexual-genital level. The first is the idea that humans compete with God. Psychoanalytically, "God" represents one of the parental figures, which raises the question with which parent the child competes. The second clue stems from the particular type of defensive regression, namely, from genital sexuality toward oral dynamics. Developmentally such a regression must be assumed to occur during the period in which genital sexuality first emerges as a focus for the child. That means that "Genesis 3:1–5 [describes] a conflict of the Oedipal (phallic) phase" (ibid., 116). It is during this phase that children target both parents and particularly one of them with sexual wishes while the other is turned into a rival (ibid., quoting A. Freud), which sheds light on the idea that humans compete with God. "The prohibition which 'God' has imposed is, understood this way, an Oedipal incest prohibition" (ibid.).

In the exegetical analysis, Drewermann had indicated that literary criticism has shown that Genesis 3:1–5 was the original narrative fragment and that the expansion of this passage by Genesis 3:6–7 is the work of the Yahwist. The latter two verses portray how the man shares in the guilt through an act of eating mediated by the woman. Drewermann points out that culturally Genesis 3:1–7 in its current form, which attributes all responsibility to the woman, is probably the work of patriarchal redaction in defense against matriarchy, while Genesis 3:1–5 may originally have been told as a story in matriarchally organized groups (ibid., 123). The purely passive role which the text manifestly attributes to the man would thus be due to a "certain social-psychological interest" (ibid.). Through a psychoanalytic interpretation of the latent thoughts, Drewermann can show that "the fate of the woman is the same as that of the man" and thus avoid the patriarchal finger-pointing to which a historical reading of the story has been vulnerable (ibid.). A psychoanalytic interpretation shows that the story speaks of the Oedipal dynamics of the girl and of the boy.

If we assume that mythic material in Genesis 3:1–5 is originally "dreamed from the perspective of the girl, then [the story] deals with the strong but forbidden wish of the little girl to get a child from the father and to be equal to the mother. Due to this prohibition the relationship between child and parents breaks. She has to separate from them as original libidinal objects. Prohibition and exile thus find their explanation. Both are inevitable. Thus the phallic symbol of serpent and tree would finally have to be identified with the father.... The temptation of the woman by the serpent would thus consist in the invitation to incestuous intercourse with the father. It would represent the wishful impulse" in the girl for such a union (ibid., 116).

This interpretation raises, of course, the question whether Drewermann does not assume S. Freud's theory of the Oedipus complex. Although Drewermann rejects the idea of a "biological foundation of the 'Oedipus complex,'" he nonetheless finds that the theme of the Oedipus complex is universally present *psychologically* in the fact that the "incest tendency itself, that is, the tendency to be fixated on the parent of the opposite sex, does and probably has to meet everywhere [i.e., in all societies] (with privileged exceptions) with the strongest disapproval" (ibid., 117). In addition, the love of a woman for a man *psychologically* leads to the regressive reactivation of early childhood experiences with one's father during the various developmental stages (and vice versa in the case of the love of a man for a woman), including the stage in which genital sexuality first becomes a psychological focus and is experienced in a particular way in relation to the parent of the opposite sex.[13] For these reasons it makes sense why in this story — which in its current form comes from a patriarchal culture clearly shaped by Oedipal dynamics — "a *symbol* of Oedipal prohibition of a drive can serve the Yahwist to express the universality of the human experience of guilt" (ibid., 116–17, italics added).

Drewermann's psychoanalytic interpretation of the eating from the forbidden tree as a symbol for the boy's ontogenetic development can connect with the fact that the dialogue with the serpent in Genesis 3:1–7 uses the plural forms of "you" and "we," thus aiming from the beginning not only at the woman but also at the man (ibid., 117). We already noted that in mythology the tree can be both a maternal symbol (oral level) and a phallic symbol (sexual-genital level). Further examples from mythic literature where the serpent appears as a feminine symbol (ibid., 118) allow a psychoanalytic interpretation of the story on the phallic level from the perspective of a boy in relation to the mother. For the boy the serpent stands Oedipally for the desire for the mother while the tree represents the desired mother. Oedipally, the God-image represents the mother as rival for the girl and the father as rival for the boy.

---

13. Since the story of Adam and Eve assumes heterosexual dynamics, Drewermann here does not address the question of an "incest tendency" that may be "fixated" on the same-sex parent. For his criticism of the Roman Catholic Church's condemnation of homosexuality and his calls for understanding and inclusiveness, see Drewermann 1991b, 171–78, 291–96; Drewermann 1990d, 293.

Drewermann sums up the psychoanalytic interpretation of Genesis 3:1–7 on both the oral and the Oedipal level with the following statements: "What the serpent points to for man and woman is the tree, which stands in the sexual symbolism Oedipally as mother for the man and as father for the woman and for both (orally) as the maternal tree of life" (ibid.). And: "both fail through the temptation of the same force of drive (the serpent) and the same aim of drive (the tree)" (ibid., 123). On the Oedipal level, the fear which leads to regression from the genital-sexual level to the oral level thus has its source in "the wishful impulse" for union with the parent of the opposite sex, an impulse which the child has to defend against. But what is the specific nature of this fear and why and how is it defended against in Genesis 3:1–7?

Fear, Defenses, and "Being-like-God"

Drewermann (1985a, 153–60) connects the fear at play in Genesis 3:1–7 with the notion of anxiety advanced by Freud in *Inhibitions, Symptoms and Anxiety* (1926) and in *New Introductory Lectures* (1933). Fear is seen as a function of the ego in the service of self-preservation. Neurotic anxiety is a signal by means of which the ego, in anticipation of certain external danger situations, activates the pleasure-unpleasure principle through which the ego can exert influence on the id by, for instance, repressing an impulse that is perceived as causing external danger. Drewermann adopts Freud's idea that the *condition* for the anxiety is the experienced (and subsequently anticipated) external danger situation of separation from the mother (loss of the object), which could mean death for the infant in his biological and psychological helplessness (Freud 1926, 138). This is the reason why separation anxiety can be experienced as "death anxiety" (Freud 1923, 65–66). Although the infant does not subjectively experience it as such, birth is in that sense "a precursor of anxiety because it 'objectively speaking...is a separation from the mother' (Freud 1926, 130).... Separation from the mother thus becomes the basic experience of anxiety; separation from the breast and separation from the excrements" are the conditions for the emergence of anxiety at the oral stage and at the anal stage (Drewermann 1985a, 155). Castration fear at the next stage, the phallic, too, is basically a separation fear and bound to the same condition: the danger of losing the loved object. "Whereas the genital guarantees the possibility for union with the mother, castration is equal to the final separation

from the mother" (ibid.). Psychodynamically the danger of separation, that is, of "object loss," is the *condition* for the anxiety, while
"the *real reason* which triggers the anxiety consists in the area of
the drives (or wishes)" (ibid.; italics added). Drewermann clarifies a
point psychoanalytically which is important for his theological interpretation, namely, that originally, that is, on the oral level, the
fear is not really one of "losing the object," but rather one of falling
out of the symbiotic primordial unity with the mother which exists
intra- or extra-utero during the first months of life, which can also be
conceptualized as the stage of "primordial narcissism" (ibid., 158).
Drewermann stresses that although his use of terms such as "primordial narcissism" leans on the terminology of "Freud's libido theory"
he is not concerned with "the reception of this theory but with an
analysis of the reality which it describes" (ibid., 158, cf. 168). Theologically, the parallel fear consists not only in losing God, but in
"falling out of a unity with God where God does not 'stand over
against' humans but completely encompasses and contains humans"
(ibid., 158).

Drewermann recognizes that from a psychoanalytic perspective
Genesis 3:1–7 locates the conflict at a time in ontogenetic development when the superego has not yet been formed. Hence the
fear of separation in the story cannot be considered moral anxiety
[*Gewissensangst*] although it evidently constitutes the immediate precursor of the latter (ibid., 156–57). Freud (1923, 65–66) suggested
that "death anxiety" would have to be thought of as a dynamic "between the ego and the superego." The story instead portrays how
"the experience of guilt is experienced for the first time," that is,
prior to the existence of a superego (Drewermann 1985a, 156). On
the other hand, the story contains a "central prohibition" which is a
"superego-precursor" (ibid.). The oral situation in which this prohibition is first experienced is one of "total dependency and helplessness."
Therefore: "It is precisely because the parents are everything the child
needs in order to live that separation anxiety amounts in its final consequence to death anxiety, not as such, however, but in connection
with a prohibition against a (necessary) drive impulse and threatening an ultimate separation (Freud's 'castration')" (ibid., 156). The
anxiety in Genesis 3:1–7 is thus "not an anxiety between ego and superego but between the ego and the central object of love (God; the
parents). Since this [i.e., the love object] not only guarantees the fulfillment of wishes but also represents reality, the origin [of 'neurotic'

anxiety] in 'realistic anxiety' becomes apparent without difficulty: the fear of separation from God is not an imagined one but is grounded realistically in the [spiritual] helplessness of humans" (ibid., 157).

Just as the prohibition of biting into the breast on the oral level and of incest wishes on the phallic level is necessary for healthy psychological development, so the prohibition of eating from the tree of knowledge of good and evil is theologically necessary for healthy spiritual development. Drewermann highlights that the picture the Yahwist paints in Genesis 2–3 is ontogenetically fully warranted when it "shows that God places humans first into 'paradise,' then issues a prohibition, which provokes contradiction in humans only later": in the early oral stage (paradise) a prohibition existed which is resisted only in the later, oral-sadistic stage; the expectations of love for the parents result in a conflict between prohibition and longing only once the desire has reached its phallic character (ibid.).

After characterizing the fear in Genesis 3:1–7 psychologically as separation anxiety in relation to the parents due to forbidden oral-sadistic impulses and theologically in relation to God, Drewermann next turns to an analysis of the defense mechanisms that manage this anxiety (ibid., 159–78). Neither repression nor sublimation are used during the defensive maneuver. This is in accord with ontogenetic development: according to A. Freud, repression requires a certain level of differentiation between ego and id while sublimation presupposes the formation of a superego — neither condition is fulfilled in Genesis 3:1–7 (ibid., 159; quoting A. Freud 1937, 52; S. Freud 1915). Drewermann observes the following defense mechanisms in the story and discusses them in light of the theories of A. Freud, S. Freud, and L. Szondi: "identification (introjection), tabooing, denial of reality, isolation, counter-cathexis, projection, and regression" (Drewermann 1985a, 160). In our summary of Drewermann's analysis of these mechanisms we will pay special attention to the motif of "being-like-God."

The psychoanalytic interpretation saw in the words of the serpent "the awakening of drive impulses which deeply threaten unity with the parents (orally: the dual union; phallically: the libido cathexis of the parents)" (ibid.). The child reacts with an equally great fear of loss of the loved object which is experienced ultimately as death anxiety in view of the prohibition and the threat of death. It is this fear which submerges the prohibition of Genesis 2 into the twilight of ambivalence in Genesis 3 (ibid., 165). Drewermann continues to describe the defensive dynamic from the perspective of the woman. In an effort to overcome both the threatening loss of object and the ambivalence that arose in response to the disappointment which the question of the serpent evoked in her, the woman *identifies* with God by repeating the prohibition, but she does so under the spell of her ambivalent feelings, that is, she introjects not the original, purely loving and caring image of God which had existed in Genesis 2 but instead an "image of God...that now bears the character of her own ambivalence which the woman turns against herself" (ibid., 162). On both the oral and the sexual-genital level the ambivalence is basically an "oral ambivalence," although on the sexual level "we have to assume a *regression* to the stage of oral sadism, that is, we have to interpret the introjection as it is typical for melancholia: as a 'regression from one type of object choice to the original narcissism...the oral or cannibalistic phase of libidinal development' (S. F[reud] 1917b, 249 [GW X, 436]), which does not necessarily belong to [every] introjection but which we have to assume here simply as a result of the purely oral problem.... [B]oth [an interpretation on the oral level or on the sexual level] lead us to the same result, namely, that the God-image which the woman introjects bears the character of oral ambivalence. The God of the woman now carries for the first time not only loving and caring but also envious and cruel traits" (Drewermann 1985a, 162, italics added).

By introjecting the prohibition, the woman has transformed an external privation into an internal one. Psychodynamically this means that "the conflict between God and the woman has become basically a conflict between id-drives and ego-drives. At the same time a *fixation* takes place on the forbidden object to which the libido is attached but which one has to deny oneself for self-preservative reasons" (ibid., 163). This explains the fixation on the tree after the serpent's question, which goes hand in hand with the *tabooing* of the tree that is expressed in the prohibition of touching added by the woman to the original prohibition. Tabooing points to the fact that a strong wish exists for the touching of the tree. Since the interpretation has located the primary conflicts in the story on the oral and phallic level, tabooing is not the result of a repression (which would require the existence of a superego that is formed at a later stage), but rather of a *counter-cathexis* which has the character of a "momentary" reaction-formation in the ego: the ego now fears and despises what the serpent's question made her unconsciously desire.

The reaction-formation does not hold: the woman wants to repress the wish but does not succeed (ibid., 164). The serpent continues to speak.

The defensive regression to the stage of oral sadism revives the "narcissism of the libido organization" which leads to the emergence of a sense of "immortality." It is "the narcissistic cathexis of the id-impulses which lead one to consider one's ego immortal" (ibid., 166). Apart from God, however, such narcissism tends to *deny the reality* of death by means of fantasy (ibid., 173; quoting A. Freud 1937, 73). The result is a magical feeling of omnipotence, of believing one can be like God, and in this feeling the tree, too, becomes endowed with magic, divine powers: by eating from it one becomes like God (Drewermann 1985a, 168).

The feeling of omnipotence due to secondary narcissism now requires the eradication of the introjected ambivalence. The ambivalence is precisely the result of the inner conflict between the ego's efforts to follow the prohibition for fear of separation and death and the id-impulse to eat from the tree. The ambivalence, expressed in the tabooing of the tree, threatens the sense of omnipotence. In order to relieve herself of the ambivalence, the woman unconsciously *projects* the instinctual wish onto God. With her own wish to transgress the prohibition thus externalized the wish now seems to approach her from outside. "It is not she who desires to interfere in the rights of God by eating from the tree, but rather God who wants to interfere in the rights of humans by reserving the tree" for herself (ibid., 171). While the woman "is not allowed to have anything, God wants everything" (ibid., 172). This projection creates a sense of entitlement to transgress against God. After the ambivalence has been removed only uninhibited narcissism remains. Only at this point in the story can we observe for the first time something like pride — but as a consequence of the original dynamic of fear (ibid., 171).

Drewermann compares the structure of sin in this story with the structure of psychosis. In a somewhat paranoid fashion "we see the woman, who in her fear is totally thrown back upon herself, indeed become mad by declaring herself to be God after she feels separated from God" (ibid., 173). For belief in one's immortality apart from God is certainly a "wishful delusion," which, as the symbol of the serpent signifies, stems from wishes in the id (ibid.). "In sin as in psychosis a human person to all appearances falls completely in upon himself. With the belief of one's own omnipotence infantile helplessness and lack of freedom return — which the person, however, does not notice. One cannot come closer to the mystery of evil by means of psychoanalysis...: a human person becomes mad with fear if he does not know himself to be secured in God" (ibid., 174). Being completely thrown back upon one's own narcissism also creates a deep sense of *isolation.* Drewermann observes that "the border between madness and religion seems to lie only in the difference between narcissism and object love" (ibid., 173). To this complex of "the sinner as a child who wants to be God," Drewermann sees a redemptive answer in the Christian Scriptures with their "new 'myth' of the God who wants to be human" (ibid., 174).

The final element in the series of defensive maneuvers is the *actual introjection* of the forbidden fruit which completes a cycle of defenses that began with the initial identification with the prohibition. "The woman has to eat [the forbidden fruit] in order to become God" and to become omnipotent (ibid., 177). "The introjection is basically an oral process" and aims at realizing the promise of the serpent: to become like God. "The introjection takes the place of the preceding phase of projection during which all wishes of having power [*Habmachtswünsche,* a term borrowed from Szondi] had been placed into the forbidden object" (ibid.). The tree now seems to represent everything desirable and needed in life. In that sense it stands as a symbol for the mother. "If we keep in mind that the mother which the child 'eats' during the introjection, represents the entire world of the child, then it is completely correct to interpret the eating from the forbidden tree as an introjection of 'all,' as a striving 'to have all' " (ibid.). Drewermann compares the function of the introjection in the story to a totem meal which serves as an oral identification with what has once been feared (ibid., 178). By appearing to bestow omnipotence the tree plays the role "of stopping up all sources of anxiety." It is supposed to prevent the breakout of death anxiety (ibid., 177).

The Inevitability of the Guilt Feeling

The similarity of the introjection in Genesis 3:1–7 with a totem meal suggests an understanding of the guilt feeling ensuing from the act of eating the forbidden fruit in terms of Freud's scientific myth of the origin of guilt feelings in the killing of the primal father and subsequent cannibalistic identification with him. While acknowledging certain similarities between Freud's story of the root of guilt in the

Oedipus complex as advanced in *Totem and Taboo* (Freud 1913), Drewermann concludes that the story of the fall differs substantially from Freud's scientific myth: in Genesis 3 nothing points to a violent act of communal killing of the father; the totemistic character of the tree is not due to a repression of an original killing but the result of a long process of trying to deal with fear. "Unless one already believes in the killing of the primordial father as the primordial form of original sin, it is impossible to find it in Genesis 3" (Drewermann 1985a, 186). Instead of seeing the connection between the guilt feeling and the fear of death under the aspect of an Oedipal regression to orality, Drewermann sees it as an original phenomenon on the oral level.

Drewermann's interpretation of the ontogenetic inevitability of guilt feelings as a symbol for the rise of such feelings in Genesis 3:1–7 follows post-Freudian developments in psychoanalysis (e.g., Abraham, Klein, Erikson) which locate the origin of guilt feelings prior to the Oedipal stage in the oral-sadistic stage. We already noted Drewermann's interpretation of the symbolism of the forbidden fruit in light of Erikson's description of the ontogenetic effects of teething. Now Drewermann turns to K. Abraham and M. Klein — without adopting their metapsychology — to make the emergence of guilt feelings plausible based on oral-sadistic strivings while, in Abraham's case, also elucidating their later link to the Oedipal phase. For Abraham, "biting" represents the "original form taken by the sadistic impulses" (Abraham 1924, 451, quoted in Drewermann 1985a, 188). "The narcissistic identification and the sadistic destruction hence form an ambivalence during the oral phase which necessarily goes hand in hand with the emergence of tremendous guilt feelings. This happens because, due to the introjection of the mother, the 'sadistic thirst for vengeance now finds its satisfaction in tormenting the ego — an activity, which is in part pleasurable' (Abraham 1924, 464), that leads to masochistic self-punishment under the pressure of vivid reproaches for the cannibalistic annihilation of the loved object" (Drewermann 1985a, 189). Abraham also argued that if the oral-sadistic urges had not ceased with the passing of the oral phase then " 'a permanent association will be established between his Oedipus complex and the cannibalistic stage of his libido' (Abraham 1924, 459)" (Drewermann 1985a, 189). This would explain why in melancholia the castration complex of male patients centers predominantly around the mother (ibid.).

Abraham's insights lead Drewermann to M. Klein's notion that the superego stems from the oral stage rather than from the Oedipal, in which it only receives its final shape. Drewermann emphasizes particularly Klein's notion of the interplay between projection and introjection in the dynamic of guilt feelings. "She saw the origin of the guilt feeling established through an interplay of projection and introjection of oral-sadistic strivings in which the child projects her wish to devour the breast onto the breast itself; she thus feels threatened and fears being devoured by the breast of the mother; on the other hand, she longs for the breast and by 'eating' it takes the whole ambivalence of hate and love into herself for which she has to feel guilty." The guilt feeling is thus closely related to the idea of "devouring breasts" (ibid., 190). Drewermann notes the ubiquitous presence of the fears of devouring creatures in myths, fairy tales, and monster stories as evidence for this idea, although he acknowledges that for some of his theological readers this idea might be "something too monstrous" (ibid., 190). In Klein's " 'depressive position' "[14] the child grieves for losing the breast of the mother and the "love, goodness, and security" which it represented in the child's psyche. " 'All these are felt by the baby to be lost, and lost as a result of his own uncontrollable greedy and destructive phantasies and impulses against his mother's breasts' " (Klein 1975a, 345; quoted in Drewermann 1985a, 191). "The child experiences the withdrawal of the breast as punishment of his own doing, for which he has to feel guilty; he only has himself to blame for the mother's rejection of him" (Drewermann 1985a, 191). Drewermann notes that Klein's observations are based on phenomena in infants as well as in psychotic patients, which led her to the "hypothesis that anxieties of a psychotic nature are ubiquitous in infancy" (M. Klein 1975c, 137 n. 1; quoted in Drewermann 1985a, 191).

As always, Drewermann seeks to ground his results "biologically." Findings in psychosomatic medicine and ethology seem to suggest a biological relation between orality, aggression, and guilt feelings (Drewermann 1985a, 195). Drewermann refers to studies

---

14. Drewermann is aware that Klein saw the ambivalent interplay of projection and introjection already present in the dynamics of the earliest ontogenetic fears during the "schizoid position." But since Genesis 2–3 does not present "reminiscences of schizoid fears and issues" and since Klein herself noted that guilt feelings are connected with a special form of anxiety, namely, "depressive anxiety" (M. Klein 1975b, 34–38; quoted in Drewermann 1985a, 195), Drewermann's interpretation of the Yahwist's story of the fall does not seek the key conflicts of the story during the period of the schizoid position.

by W. B. Cannon and R. Bilz which show a correlation between the increase of aggression and a rise in appetite. He cites psychosomatic studies by H. Glatzel which suggest that acute episodes of stomach ulcers occur " 'only if the disposed human gets into certain conflictual situations.... [T]he specific conflictual situation of the ulcer patient lies in rebellion against a chronic inhibition by the environment' (Glatzel 1959, 440)" (Drewermann 1985a, 196). Paleoanthropological studies (especially by R. Bilz) point to the fact that the origin of the experience of guilt lies in the scruples, the oral ambivalence the early hunters had in eating the prey they had killed, as seen in the bear cults of Siberia (ibid., 196–202, 236). Basically, then, human guilt feelings stem from the experience of "having to kill what gave us life" (ibid., 201).

The value of the neo-Freudian analysis of the origin of guilt feelings in the oral stage resonates widely for Drewermann: "The Yahwist's story contains, indeed, in symbolic disguise the processes of the earliest development of guilt feelings. The theme itself turns out to be an anthropologically inevitable conflict.... In other words: the biblical text employs a myth which portrays the process of how every human necessarily gets involved in the feeling of guilt, how she is exiled from a primordial unity because of oral greed and how she cannot but experience this as punishment for her guilt" (ibid., 192). The theological notion of sin thus builds on the universal ontogenetic experience of guilt feelings.

Drewermann's analysis confirms Freud's intuition that the origin of guilt feelings has roots in oral dynamics, but he corrects Freud's "reprojection" of Oedipal dynamics into past millennia by means of ethological and paleoanthropological research (ibid., 197). While Freud's theory of the origin of guilt feelings in the Oedipus complex cannot be universal, since the Oedipus complex is not a biological constant, the "assumption of an oral-sadistic conflict of ambivalence can claim universality and indeed the character of biological constancy" (ibid., 192). Drewermann is aware, though, that the particular shape this oral-sadistic conflict takes and is dealt with varies from culture to culture (ibid., 192–93., quoting Erikson 1993, 135–37 on Sioux Child Training).

Drewermann alludes to what he considers the only possibility of avoiding the oral guilt feeling during adult life: "the absolute prohibition to kill (*ahimsa*) of the Indian Jainas" (1985a, 201). And, looking forward, he notes that it is the age-old experience of oral guilt in the culture of the hunters which also seems "to represent the background of the Christian notion that one has to kill the God in order to live from him" (ibid.). We will see below in Chapter 3 how Drewermann elaborates this connection in his interpretation of the doctrine of the death and resurrection of Christ.

In an excursus, Drewermann finds that the clinical picture of anorexia nervosa exemplifies the interweaving of oral and genital-sexual psychic conflicts which are at play psychoanalytically in the story of Genesis 3. In summary, Drewermann writes: "If we keep in mind that anorexia — as any neurotic illness — is a kind of attempt to heal oneself, one may at this point say in regard to Genesis 3 that here sin is described as a path on which humans, after they have fallen and are separated from God, attempt to live from their own capital [*von der eigenen Substanz leben*]: self-sufficient, narcissistic, filled with guilt feelings, beset by anxiety, carriers of disgust and shame... without hope and future, burdened with the feeling of inner worthlessness and emptiness, in a hide-and-seek game of external compliance and everlasting flight... an existence whose basic feeling is shaped... by guilt for the mere fact of one's existence" (ibid., 246–47).

Shame, the Threat of Death, and the "Punishments of God" in Light of Five Basic Paleoanthropological Forms of Anxiety

Genesis 3:7–13 connects guilt feeling with a sense of shame and an image of God as a judge. After the fall, God has traits of a "judgmental agency" and must be recognized as the God-image which humans, analogous to the mother-image of ontogenetic development, create in response to the loss of God under the spell of fear: "the image of God serves on the objective level as projective background for the [self-]reproaches which have been split off by consciousness; on the subjective level as representative of an introjected yet repressed reproach which [now] approaches humans [in paranoid fashion] from outside" (Drewermann 1985a, 207). But this interpretation does not suffice to explain the concrete content of the sense of shame as "being naked" which clearly suggests a sexual connotation. The shame of "being naked," expresses in Freudian language the issue of the castration complex: the fear of castration (in the boy) or of having been castrated (in the girl); the shame expresses — in the neopsychoanalytic language of H. Schultz-Hencke — fears of "giving oneself and of inhibited aggressions" (Dührssen 1967, 270; quoted in Drewermann 1985a, 208). Psychoanalytically, the shame in Genesis 3 describes the child's experience "of the central loss and lack: the castration" (Drewermann 1985a, 209). The loss of object which interpretation at the oral-sadistic stage saw in the separation from the breast is experienced later on the phallic level as separation from the penis, as castration, and leads to the reaction-formation of shame (ibid., 208–10). Psychoanalytically, an experience of sexuality as something shameful or "bad" is thus the result of ambivalent psychical images of father and mother. Theologically, the Yahwist portrays the experience of shame as a result of an introjected and projected ambivalent God-image due to fear of separation.

The punishment of the threat of death in Genesis 3:19 "is not an additional punishment for the deed of humans but represents merely the central aspect of separation from God, the expulsion from paradise." Life has become a "being-unto-death" (ibid., 211).

Drewermann refrains from an elaborate psychoanalytic interpretation of the remaining punishments in Genesis 3:8–24, because of the Yahwist's massive editing of the material appropriated for these passages and because they address partly real "biological (hence not intrapsychic)" and social descriptions of human misery (ibid., 213–21). Drewermann considers these passages valuable because of their "associative explanations" for the dynamics in the preceding passage of Genesis 3:1–7. The mood after the fall is one of "depression" in which everything lies under the "cloud of guilt" (ibid., 217). "We cannot understand by means of psychoanalysis alone what the Yahwist actually means by Genesis 3:8–24, namely, that all 'punishments' represent a characterization of the basic sense [*Grundbefindlichkeit*] of the merely natural life of humans, who are left to their own devices without God. We understand even less why the 'punishments' represent an exact reversal of Genesis 2 (Drewermann 1986a, 47, 107)" (Drewermann 1985a, 222).

All punishments share in common the aspect of fear. To that end "[w]e only have to remove the analysis of fear from the frame of ontogenesis — and with that from psychoanalysis — and establish it where it belongs according to the intention of the Yahwist. We have to read the 'punishments' in Genesis 3 as descriptions of primordial fears which belong to human existence itself" (ibid.). Phylogenetic fears fundamentally characterize human fears. Drawing on the work of Rudolf Bilz (1971), whose research studied analogies and homologies of human and animal behavior in situations of fear and in view of the fight-or-flight reaction in the sense of W. B. Cannon, Drewermann "shows the relation of ontogeny to phylogeny by means of precise observations rather than through speculation" (1985a, 223).

Bilz (1971, 427–65) proposed that the philosophical notion of "existential anxiety [*Daseinsangst*]" can be traced to five empirically proven "primordial fears [*Urängste*]." He connects certain "behavior patterns of humans with certain primordial situational scenes and thus attributes to them a fixed functional symbolic meaning [*festgelegte funktionale Sinngestalt*]" (Drewermann 1985a, 222). Each punishment represents one of the five primordial fears: fear of guilt, fear of hunger and of impoverishment, hypochondriacal fear, segregation fear, and fear of no-way-out (ibid., 223–32).

Genesis 3:8–10 portrays how humans hide after the fall from the "face of God," because they feel ashamed of being naked. Drewermann relates this passage to the phenomenon of fear of guilt [*Schuldangst*], precursors of which have been observed in animals in "the situation of giving offense or taking offense." In seagulls or crows, for instance, any deviation from "normal" plumage (e.g., if feathers are glued by oil or lost due to disease) in one bird gives offense to the others and leads to deadly attacks on the bird who is out of line. "The one who gives offense . . . and the mob which takes offense . . . combine in an archetypal scene of guilt (i.e., illness, deviation) and atonement (i.e., culling) whose biological-selective meaning seems to lie in the annihilation by the group of what is sick" (ibid., 224). "That the lynch justice usually takes optical triggers as occasions for the offense seems to have a certain analogy in the urgency with which humans after 'the fall,' in an attempt to avoid exposition, seek to withdraw from the sight of God and try to cope with their 'fear of guilt' in terms of the issue of clothing" (ibid., 225). At the same time, another "archaic functional readiness" is activated which, too, can be observed in animals, for instance, among wolves: the avoidance of the glance of the other (God) is an admission of one's inferior role, while God appears as the superior who has the right to control glances. Related is the fear of being exposed publicly, as is common in criminal justice systems. The "oral-depressive mood" of being unsightly and of fearing to be guilty and exposed by the highest authority are the first consequence of the fall.

In Genesis 3:17–19a, where punishment turns the search for food and subsistence into miserable toil, Drewermann observes primordial fears of hunger and impoverishment at play (ibid., 226–28). As a consequence of the fall, God is portrayed as the one in the highest role and humans are lower in status. The fear of starvation is connected to status issues, for instance, in the way feeding is strictly regulated among animals along the order of roles which each animal has within its group. The "miserable toil" associated with "cultivating" land is understood in terms of the fact that domesticated, cultural work does not belong "to the original functional repertoire of humans" (ibid., 227). The depressive mood of the story is evident: "Part of the depressive form of self-perception is the constant fear of impoverishment ... and of loss. . . . The fear of impoverishment of one's emotional budget finds its counterpart in the fear of impoverishment of one's economic livelihood. Bilz accurately notes that the melancholic's fear of impoverishment repeats psychically the constant fear of archaic forms of a life of starvation" (ibid., 226–7).

The threat of death by God in 3:19 expresses a primordial hypochondriacal fear. "The fear of impoverishment, expressed in terms of the body, results in the picture of melancholia in hypochondriacal fear, which excessively exaggerates the reality of progressive bodily disintegration and experiences the threat of death at any moment" (ibid., 228). Studies of funeral rites during the mesolithic period show that the question of death was of central importance for the thinking of archaic humans. "With the discovery of death begins the human life we know" (ibid., 229). The feeling of the inevitability of death which finds expression in Genesis 3:19, "although in sick distortion," expresses a concern which "distinguishes humans from animals from time immemorial. The question about death is the most certain indicator that a living being has to solve problems of a nonbiological nature with nonbiological, basically, religious means" (ibid., 228).

Genesis 3:23–24 connects to the "paleoanthropological scene of herd or horde loss," which meant certain death for our ancient ancestors. The expulsion from paradise is grounded paleoanthropologically in segregation fear. "Being abandoned is, according to this primordial scene, identical with being lost." "If it is correct that fear triggers a reflexive movement of clinging, as we said during the analysis of the symbolism of the tree, then we understand the dreadfulness of the experience of being abandoned: segregation fear is a fear which literally triggers one to grasp at nothing." Segregation fear is at play, for instance, in the fear of the depressed person "to be abandoned and alone" and in his complaints that no one really understands or is interested in him (ibid., 229). The situation of humans after the fall from unity with God is thus portrayed by the Yahwist as a "situation of segregation, of being lost, of the primordial fear of radical isolation" (ibid., 230).

Genesis 3:19 also portrays life characterized by the experience of the inevitability of death. Drewermann finds that this verse, together with 3:24 which bars the entrance back into paradise, relates to the paleoanthropological "fear of no-way-out [*Angst der Ausweglosigkeit*]." He notes that the "primordial scene of no-way-out" consists, according to Bilz, of the situation in which an enemy, hunter, or animal of prey has power over the subject. Bilz pointed out that in situations of no-way-out animals have "an archaic reactional readiness" which creates an "emergency exit" through "a suicidal mechanism": "vagus death" due to a drastic vagovasal slowing of the heart rate. Bilz (1971) referred to the cruel experiment by C. P. Richter (1957) in which wild rats were thrown into a glass container of water with no exit. They died within a few minutes. When, however, Richter provided the wild rats just once with a possibility of escape, the rats swam — like the laboratory rats — for their life for up to 80 hours until they had reached their physical limits. The experience of "no-way-out had been visibly substituted by means of a precursor of hope, born from a single experience of rescue. There was no need for the mercy of the vagus death" (Drewermann 1985a, 231). The Yahwist portrays the life of humans after the fall as an existence without any way out. Everything which humans do in the situation of no-way-out, the situation without God, is characterized by a "longing for death." Only if there is some hope in the face of death can humans avoid a life that is nothing but a "sickness unto death" (ibid., 231–32).

As Drewermann sums it up, the "common content of all listed fears is the fear of being annihilated, of death. . . . All fears have in common that they belong to the depressive experiential readiness. This confirms our earlier observation that the experience of fear (in the theory of Freud) is triggered by certain forms of object loss, since depression is characterized by nothing more than by the loss of libidinal objects which were once narcissistically cathected and without whose presence the ego thinks it cannot live" (ibid., 232). Thus fear not only is decisive in what tempts humans to fall from God but also "shapes the entire existence of humans when they have turned away from God" into an existence of "misery [*Elend*, also: poverty, distress]" (ibid., 233). The "real 'punishment' for the 'fall' consists psychoanalytically in the transformation of all of existence into fear, in the final instance into a depressive fear of death and — in reaction to it — into longing for death" (ibid., 237). Genesis 3 presents "the picture of an existence which is characterized by the basic experience of feeling guilty merely because one exists and of becoming continuously and inevitably guilty through the basic processes of preserving one's life (by eating)" (ibid., 247).

Genesis 4:1–16 in Psychoanalytic Perspective

Drewermann's review of nature myths containing the widespread motif of hostile brothers, which is the heart of the story of Cain and Abel, finds that this motif usually represents the change between "day and night, sun and moon," light and darkness. Human conflicts are projected into this natural phenomenon. The worldview which sees in the change between day and night a representation of human conflicts "gains its real meaning...only if in the human psyche a lightness exists which is hostile to the night-aspect, that is, if humans themselves feel torn inside between opposing powers" (ibid., 256). The story of Cain and Abel, however, differs from most mythological stories of the struggle between sun and moon in that it does not contain a story of "resurrection" after the "killing" of one of the "brothers." It is thus clearly no story of salvation but of doom (ibid.).

Through an analysis of the story of Cain and Abel by means of L. Szondi's dialectical theory of drives and of C. G. Jung's psychology, Drewermann finds in "Cain the image of a way of being human which has bought its consciousness at the price of the destruction of the healing powers of the unconscious, which has repressed what is natural inside by means of its stony world of reason and transformed it into a desert" (ibid., 262). Drewermann critically adds, however, that Szondi's theory, especially, which sees in Cain and Abel representations of the "ambitendent" nature of a paroxysmal drive, creates a difficulty because "in it [i.e., Szondi's theory] what is anthropologically significant appears as some biological condition and something psychologically necessary. But it is precisely this view which is essentially inconsistent with the message of the Yahwist's primordial history, which, though it deals with essential traits of being human and of human history, does so in a way that does not accept these essential traits as necessary conditions but as deriving from the relationship of humans to God" (ibid., 261–62). Szondi's biological drive dialectics, moreover, neglects the ontogenetic developmental analysis which, Drewermann says, would first help us understand why it is the

Cain aspect that prevails over the Abel aspect in the story and why the motif of "sacrifice" is so prominent. A psychodynamic analysis is required that locates the conflict between Cain and Abel within the developmental frame of ontogenetic development (ibid., 263).

Earlier in this chapter, the exegetical analysis found that Cain and Abel attempt to reestablish the lost relationship with God by means of sacrificing their best, but their need for absolute recognition "outside of Eden" leads them inevitably to deadly conflict. Drewermann's psychoanalytic study of the psychodynamics of this story takes its departure from insights of K. Horney and A. Adler, along with an evaluation of John Steinbeck's novel *East of Eden* (1952), and sees the following dynamic at play in the story of Cain and Abel: after the expulsion from paradise humans harbor a "feeling of hostility" (Horney 1937) against God (the parents). This feeling of hostility creates further anxiety of rejection and has to be suppressed due to a sense of dependency, fear, and guilt feelings. The relationship of humans to God (the parents) is thus pervaded by a "basic anxiety" (ibid.). This evokes in reaction the attempt to regain through obsequiousness the favor of God. In this attempt — which Drewermann interprets in terms of Szondi's subjective-level theory — the "good" Abel aspect finds acceptance while the "bad," hostile Cain aspect feels rejected and thus follows the path of self-sufficient power and isolation. "Cain and Abel would thus be representatives of the ambivalence in the relationship of humans to God" (Drewermann 1985a, 270). This ambivalence is unbearable and hence results in the good Abel aspect being overpowered by the reactively heightened hostile Cain aspect.

Of central importance is that the story presupposes from the start a basic rivalry between the two brothers. The story is characterized by an "all-or-nothing" mentality in which God completely accepts the one and completely rejects the other. The God of this story appears in the relation between Cain and Abel only within the "categories of competition and rivalry" (ibid., 271). By presenting their sacrifices, Cain and Abel from the beginning basically ask who of the two will be favored and who will be rejected, who will be superior and who will be inferior in the eyes of God. "The problem of competition and of rivalry then has to be considered from the start as an original one. It is not first kindled with respect to the 'sacrifice,' but finds in the latter only its concrete intensification" (ibid.). At the heart of the competitive conflict between Cain and Abel is an attempt to "compensate" for the "feeling of inferiority" (Adler 1927,

1972) which humans feel after the loss of God (the parents). "In the attempt to gain recognition from God, the pair of brothers must from the start have been concerned with an either-or, with an all-or-nothing, so that the fundamental question was one of being worth more or less before God, namely, in such a way that everything depended on ousting the other. Only if such a dramatic issue of rivalry is already connected with the sacrifice does it become understandable psychologically why the rejection of Cain leads to murder. Only if the question of acceptance before God has the value of existing or not existing does the deed of Cain appear as a psychically understandable reaction to his nonacceptance" (Drewermann 1985a, 272–73). Cain's feeling of being neglected must be "understood by him as an annihilating confirmation of his inferiority. That explains Cain's inability to pay attention to the admonishing words of God" (ibid., 273). "The consequence of his absolute fight for recognition is in the end that no one at all recognizes him, except that he himself can feel like something special, as marked, and that with 'masculine protest' he can transform, on the other hand, the obvious disadvantage of the construction of his life into an advantage" (ibid., 275).

Anchoring the psychodynamic analysis of Horney and Adler in ontogenetic development, Drewermann turns to Freud (1913), Rank (1919, 1952), Spitz (1965), and other (Neo)-Freudians to identify in the story of Cain and Abel at the "core . . . anal-sadistic conflicts" (Drewermann 1985a, 284). Drewermann finds that psychoanalytically the rivalry between the brothers is not first on the Oedipal, but on the pre-Oedipal, anal level. The story then describes, Drewermann writes, the universal human experience of wanting undivided attention from the mother (God), which is (classically) radically questioned by the arrival of a younger sibling (or any other person distracting from the mother's undivided attention). The rivalry of the brothers is thus actually an attempt to regain the lost mother (Rank) (ibid., 277).

Locating the sibling rivalry in the competition between the older sibling and the new, younger sibling, who arrives and is given all the privileges which the older sibling now has to dispense, corresponds with all details of the story of Cain and Abel: the older Cain hates the younger Abel; the unfairness and injustice Cain experiences over the preferential treatment Abel receives; the tragic reactive and absolute character of the hostility Cain turns against Abel; the maternal character of God in the story (which is later transferred onto the father as an almighty and all-benevolent, but also punishing God) (Rank) (ibid., 311); the universal character of the motif of deadly sibling rivalry; the trust of humans toward God (of the child to the mother) is in doubt already at the start of the story through the previous experience of mistrust and guilt in paradise (on the oral-sadistic level) (ibid., 280–82).

The sacrifice, too, can be understood in terms of the dynamics of anal-sadistic conflicts. Unlike in depression, which springs from an identification where oral sadism is directed against the ego and later leads to an identification of the ego with the superego, the character of Cain is shaped by an "obsessional-neurotic ambivalence of the anal phase" expressed in the rebellion of the ego against the guilt feeling. Excrements are at first experienced by the child as gifts (Freud 1917a, 130–31; Abraham 1921–25, 377). They are the first sacrifice. Whether they are accepted or not decides for the first time for the child whether to adopt a "narcissistic or an object-loving attitude" (Freud 1917a, 130). If rejected, the child reacts with defiance (*Trotz*) and anal sadism (Drewermann 1985a, 285). The experiences of acceptance or rejection made with the caregivers, especially with the mother, in view of the first sacrificial act of humans during the anal dynamic of retaining or giving, "remain valid for later life. The theological demand that in sacrifice one should not give something but oneself is realized in classic fashion on the anal level and psychoanalytically has its origin there. For the excrements are for the infant not a sacrifice of something but of a piece of her own ego" (ibid., 285). While Drewermann considers the psychoanalytic view of the anal phase as a stage marked by the first decisive power struggle between the will of the child and that of the parents to be the result of specific Western European cultural conditions, he also takes note of ethological findings that give credence to psychoanalytic observations by establishing a link between defecation and self-assertion in terms of marking one's territory and power sphere (ibid., 286–88).

Results of the Philosophical and Theological Interpretation of Genesis 3 and 4:1–16

We learned in the psychoanalytic interpretation that Drewermann speaks of sin as a "neurosis before God." I clarified his distinction between the clinical notion of neurosis and the existential-spiritual notion of neurosis. Drewermann can use the psychoanalytic interpretation *symbolically* for the philosophical and theological interpretation because he discovers in Genesis 3–11 a developmental structure which corresponds to human ontogenetic development and because the Yahwist portrays the development of sin as deeply characterized by fear and defenses against fear which closely resembles dynamics in the development of neurosis. In this section we will summarize how Drewermann relates the psychoanalytic analysis of the emotional dynamics in Genesis 3 and 4 to existential and theological analyses of the spiritual dynamics in relation to the divine.

Philosophical Analysis of the Structure of "Sin" as Universal and the Result of Free Choice

The central philosophical question of the third volume of *Strukturen des Bösen* is: if the Yahwist portrays "sin" as a universal dynamic motivated by fear into which all human beings fall how can it be that he also portrays it as the result of a free decision and hence as guilt? "[H]ow can the necessity of guilt (a *contradictio in adjecto*) be comprehended; because guilt needs to be necessary otherwise not all people would be guilty, but it also needs to be a free choice otherwise it would not be guilt?" (Drewermann 1986a, LV). To tackle this question, Drewermann embarks on a *tour de force* through modern philosophy, with an emphasis on the works of Kant, Hegel, Sartre, and Kierkegaard. The philosophies of Kant, Hegel, and Sartre view evil as the inevitable consequence of the process of self-awareness, a view theologically untenable because it must lead to fatalism. Despite that central criticism, Drewermann nonetheless finds important reflections on the nature of the human spirit and of freedom in these philosophies which provide him with the basic philosophical building blocks for a theological interpretation of sin as both universal and guilt. Sartre's philosophy serves Drewermann as a particularly valuable tool for the existential interpretation of the concrete imagery of the biblical stories.

Drewermann begins with Kant's notion that humans are part of two spheres: the sphere of *noumena* and *phenomena* (Kant 1927), the sphere of the thing in itself which is not subject to causality and the sphere of how the thing appears in the world of causality, the world of spirit and the world of matter, of freedom and necessity (Drewermann 1986b, 1–59). Humans can use their freedom either to follow the moral law, which belongs to the sphere of *noumena,* or instead to follow the laws of nature. Freedom can choose to subject itself to causality and necessity. Based on this distinction, it is possible to conceive that something which *appears* to be subject to causality and necessity is actually the result of an original free choice, hence as guilt. To conceive of humans as beings who are more than nature allows us "to think that what appears as necessity functions in the service of an act of freedom [*in Funktion einer Setzung aus Freiheit steht*]" (ibid., 9). Kant sees evil in this perspective as freedom choosing unfreedom, as freedom adopting the law of the external, empirical world. This allows Drewermann to clarify the statement that sin is a neurosis before God: "sin *appears* in Genesis 2–11 (Y[hawist]) as a neurosis. Its appearance possesses empirically the structure of causal necessity" (ibid., 14; emphasis added).

In "Conjectural Beginning of Human History" (Kant 1963), Kant interprets the fall and the expulsion from paradise in Genesis 3 as a decisive moral step forward by means of which human freedom was discovered and broke through mere instinctual life. Kant understands evil, among other things, as the process in which humans adopt the principles of external nature as maxims of their freedom (Drewermann 1986b, 30–36). Evaluating Kant's interpretation of Genesis 3, Drewermann notes that while Kant, in contrast to the Yahwist, sees the fall as a necessary part of the process of the emergence of human freedom, he does not locate the origin of evil in the inner reality of freedom itself but in the demands of the external, empirical world of the natural drives which lead an originally "weak" human reason to give in to them (ibid., 39–42). Both views are theologically untenable, because in the one case the fall is necessary and thus cannot be the guilt of humans, while in the other case external nature, especially the human passions, becomes inevitably demonized. Furthermore, Kant's notion of freedom does not allow us to conceive of sin as something universal because freedom is the opposite of necessity, which makes it impossible to explain why every human would choose evil (ibid., 16–17).

Here Hegel's dialectic becomes useful, although Drewermann naturally does not agree with Hegel's metaphysics of the spirit (ibid., 60–197). Hegel's philosophy of the spirit makes it possible to understand both good and evil as springing from the spiritual process of freedom (ibid., 68). Hegel portrays the act of becoming conscious as a process in which the human spirit (thought of as thesis; *An-Sich*) becomes aware of itself as "being other" (anti-thesis; *Für-Sich*) (Hegel

1969, 1977). It thus introduces a difference within itself which it then aims to overcome. It does so by negating its otherness and by recognizing that it is identical with what it viewed as "being other" (synthesis; *An-und-Für-Sich-Sein*). In this scheme, evil consists in the falling out of the original unity of the spirit which enters a negation into itself, that is, in the establishment of the anti-thesis, and in the wish to perpetuate that anti-thesis.

Hegel reads evil ultimately as a necessary development of the human spirit's becoming conscious of itself as part of the larger movement of the divine spirit (1953, 1988). Drewermann's main critique of Hegel's view is that it does not allow for a real possibility of redemption from evil. Inadvertently Hegel's philosophy denies the existence of radical evil and, in the end, sees all evil only as an appearance which aims at higher good — an unbearable rationalization of evil. Without Hegel's metaphysics, however, he can help us conceive of evil as something that stems not from the fact that humans are part of external nature, as in Kant, but as something that arises from within the human spirit, from freedom itself. The universality of evil cannot, as in Hegel's philosophy, be explained by thinking of everything that happens as a necessary part of the process of spirit. Otherwise, Drewermann cautions, theology would condemn itself to the gnostic view in which evil belongs necessarily to the world and to God (Drewermann 1986b, 58, 63, 130–31). Theologically, the unity between God and humans is thought of not on an ontological level but on a personal level (ibid., 114, 136, 146). Ontologically God and humans are not one. The act of becoming conscious of oneself is hence not connected as such with a falling away from God. Becoming conscious is not identical with sin (ibid. 123). Instead of conceiving of "becoming conscious of oneself [*Bewußtwerdung*]" in itself as the fall, Drewermann stresses that the fall is a particular *kind* or *way* of becoming conscious of oneself. He sees the Hegelian dialectic as the logic of the infinite "self-movement of the spirit in the field of anxiety," in a world without God. It is the description of a kind of "consciousness which, left alone to its fear, does not know of a God who exists beyond the immanent contradictions [*Gegensätzlichkeiten*] of nature and of the human psyche and through whom it could relativize the contradictions of life and, through that relativization, could come to a unity with itself" (ibid., LII, cf. 185, 188).

Sartre helps Drewermann to understand that the *kind* of becoming conscious of oneself which leads to a fall from God is one experienced under the spell of fear (ibid., 198–435). Drewermann's exegetical analysis of Genesis 3–11 found that fear plays a key role in the birth of evil. To interpret this finding philosophically, he turns to Sartre's analysis which sees human existence characterized fundamentally by fear [*Angst*] and lack [*Mangel*] of being. In *Being and Nothingness* (Sartre 1956), Sartre leans on Hegel's description of the process of becoming conscious but removes it from Hegel's metaphysics of the spirit. In becoming conscious, consciousness falls from being-in-itself (*l'être-en-soi, An-sich-Sein*) into being-for-itself (*l'être-pour-soi, Für-sich-Sein*). Ontically, being-for-itself is identical with the being of being-in-itself. Being-for-itself does not have its own being and is thus its own "nothingness." It is characterized by freedom which consists in the ability to annihilate being-in-itself. Unlike Hegel, Sartre does not believe that a synthesis of being-in-itself-for-itself (*An-und-Für-sich-Sein*) is possible. The jump from being-in-itself to being-for-itself, the jump into nothingness is purely contingent and not part of a progressive development of a divine spirit. Sartre rejects the notion of the existence of God, because he could imagine God only as consciousness which would imply that God, too, could only bring forth nothingness but not being. Lacking a bridge between being-in-itself and being-for-itself, human consciousness and existence is and remains characterized by nothingness. It is a "lack of being" that cannot be abolished.

For Sartre, the emergence of consciousness through the jump from being-in-itself to being-for-itself constitutes freedom. Freedom is the possibility to bring forth nothingness. Freedom is experienced as fear [*Angst*], because to bring forth nothingness means to separate oneself from being-in-itself without having a ground of being in oneself. Fear is the feeling which accompanies the fall of freedom from itself and the opening of nothingness. "Freedom is thus a 'nothingness of being [*Nichts an Sein*]' " (Drewermann 1986b, 214). Fear is the expression of the lack of hold given with the nothingness that characterizes freedom. Fear indicates the radical "contingency and lack of justification of all our choices" (ibid., 215). It is this fear of a lack of being which propels humans to gain by all means the lost unity of being-in-itself and being-for-itself, but forever to no avail. Humans forever attempt to undo their radical contingency and to fill up the "hole" (*das Loch*) in their existence. They feel forever compelled to try to go beyond their own lack and become like God, to become the foundation of their own being.

Sartre thus provides Drewermann with a description of the process of becoming conscious of oneself as inevitably connected with the emergence of the fear of the spirit. This allows Drewermann to understand the fall as a particular way of becoming conscious of oneself, namely, under the spell of fear. He objects, however, theologically to Sartre's view that becoming conscious of self necessarily leads to an existence under the spell of fear. Drewermann agrees that the process of becoming conscious is necessarily accompanied by fear, but he stresses that fear does not necessarily need to dominate one's existence and lead to a fall from oneself and, theologically, to a fall from God (ibid., 545). Fear of nothingness, the experience of the lack of being, does not need to lead to self-alienation. Only when the inevitable fear of the human spirit is not calmed by an absolute spirit; in theological terms: only if a person does not live in unity with God who is the source of being, is existence as a whole experienced as a lack and falls prey to a vicious cycle of fear. "If humans fall [in the Yahwist's primordial history] from God because of a fear that they *could* fall from him, for Sartre there is no fall due to fear of freedom but only a fall that is freedom and is experienced as anxiety....What belongs *factually* together for the Yahwist, namely, fear and fall, is for Sartre *ontologically* one" (ibid., 237). Drewermann thus differentiates an ontological misunderstanding of the fall as something necessary for human self-awareness from the biblical view of the fall as an event on a personal level, between a human person and the person of God (ibid., 261). Only the personal fall from God transforms the fall from being-in-itself into "the torture of nonnecessity, of the graceless nonjustification, of the eternal lack of recognition in the look of the Other" (ibid., 261).

Drewermann's philosophical preparation for an understanding of sin as both universal and an act of freedom and as stemming from a specific kind of experience of the freedom of the human spirit can be summed up as follows. With Kant it is possible to conceive of the fall as due to an originally free choice, hence as guilt, although it *appears* to be subject to causality and necessity. With Hegel it is possible to conceive of evil as something springing from certain dynamics within the human spirit and within freedom itself. And with Sartre it is possible to conceive of the fall as a specific way of becoming conscious of oneself under the spell of fear. Both Hegel and Sartre portray the emergence of evil as a universal phenomenon of the process of the spirit becoming aware of itself and relate this experience to the experience of freedom and nothingness.

The Fall in an Analysis of Dasein

Before we explicate Drewermann's theological analysis in detail, we will show how he employs Sartre's existential psychoanalysis, which he subsumes under the concept of *daseinsanalysis*[15] (see Drewermann 1986b, 328 passim), in relation to psychoanalysis to interpret key elements of the symbolism of the story in Genesis 3. In this section we will begin to clarify how Drewermann differentiates the theological interpretation of the symbol of the serpent from nature-mythological, psychoanalytical, and philosophical interpretations. We will quote central passages from the third volume of *Strukturen des Bösen* which succinctly summarize his interpretation.

In Genesis 2, in paradise, humans are naked but are not ashamed of being naked. Being naked is read existential-philosophically as being contingent. Only after humans have lost sight of God in Genesis 3 do they feel ashamed of their nakedness, of their contingency, and feel a need to hide it (ibid., 253–63). Only then they begin to focus existentially primarily on *anxiety* and on all the desperate attempts to calm it on their own. Drewermann takes this to mean that in unity with God, one's existence has a ground, is justified, is held, which in turn allows humans to feel content as they are. This is expressed in the Yahwist's primordial history, particularly in the different attitude which humans display in regard to their nakedness before and after the fall.

In the exegetical analysis Drewermann pointed to the etymological relationship between the Hebrew words for serpent and for nakedness. The theological interpretation again discerns a relationship between the two symbols. In mythological analysis the serpent represents the natural process of fertility which encompasses both becoming and perishing. Psychoanalytic analysis saw the serpent as a symbol on the objective level of forbidden drive strivings and on the subjective level of the inner desire of the psyche for unity with itself and of the power of the unconscious which can devour consciousness (Drewermann 1986a, LXXII–LXXIII). Philosophically, Drewermann

---

15. In *Strukturen des Bösen*, Drewermann relies, in addition to Sartre, on G. Condrau's application of Medard Boss's *daseinsanalytic* psychology to psychotherapy (Condrau 1962, 1963; Boss 1963).

sees in the symbol of the serpent not "the chaos of the drives but...the possible chaos which lies in human freedom and in the radical contingency of existing as a human itself, in the awareness of the *nothing* [*Nichts*] which humans discover in their spiritual nature [*Geistigkeit*]. The cosmic serpent of myths lies in philosophical perspective at the foundation of each human existence, simply because it [i.e., human existence] is free and because it is not 'like God,' but radically contingent" (Drewermann 1986b, XXV). More generally, the serpent can stand philosophically for the contradiction in the material world between formation and destruction. It "thus symbolizes as the principle of the undifferentiated and unformed something akin to what Aristotle [1966] describes in his *Metaphysics* as *materia prima*.... The serpent...can be philosophically understood as principle of materiality, as embodiment of the material world with its dialectic of formation and destruction, of blooming and withering, of life and death.... It is thus a symbol of the utterly natural world [*ganz naturhaften Welt*].... While the serpent appears *psychologically* as symbol of the dominance of the drives, it expresses *philosophically* the primordial metaphysical opposition between spirit and matter, of transitoriness and eternity" (Drewermann 1986a, LXXIII–LXXIV).

But, Drewermann cautions, one should not confuse the theological meaning of a symbol either with its psychological or philosophical meaning. For instance, that the serpent possesses psychologically sexual connotations does not allow us to conclude "that in Genesis 3:1–5 'sexuality' would be described as something sinful.... *It would be a grave professional error to confuse the psychic meaning of a symbol with the theological meaning of its use*" (ibid., LXXII). Nor is the subjective-level psychological interpretation to be confused with the theological one. "[A]s psychologically true and profound as it is, [it] by no means accords with the *theological* meaning of the symbolism of the serpent. It...would set as metaphysically absolute the psychic problem of contradiction in humans if we were to confuse the psychological level of interpretation with the theological one. In gnostic fashion one would then have to identify the dialectic of the human psyche with God's spirit as happened most clearly in Hegel's philosophy (Drewermann 1986b, 157–63). The Yahwist's statement which emphasizes precisely the difference between humans and God would be utterly falsified with such theorems" (Drewermann 1986a, LXXIII). Similarly the philosophical interpretation of the serpent should not be confused with the theological meaning of the symbol. If they were identified, one "would in the last instance consider matter as something hostile to God in the sense of neo-Platonism," which would misunderstand the Yahwist just as much as Hegel's Promethean interpretation (ibid., LXXIV).

"Everything depends on carrying out a separate, purely *theological* interpretation of the symbolism of the serpent which does not contradict the previous historical, mythological, psychological, and philosophical interpretations, but traces them back to an even deeper level of contradiction. The other levels of interpretation can then be understood within the frame of the Yahwist's conception as manifestations of a more original conflict of human existence before God" (ibid., LXXIV). The point of departure for a theological interpretation is the fact that according to the Yahwist the serpent belongs to God's creation (Gen. 3:1) and can thus not stand in metaphysical opposition to God. The serpent appears as a force which drives humans into "culpable" opposition to God and gives rise to the inner contradiction and disunity of human existence. In a theological interpretation the serpent is not dialectically part of the immanent process of dying and rebirth or a contradiction within God or the human spirit. Rather "it is now important to understand this 'darkness' in all creation as the absolute *opposite of God*" (ibid., LXXV). The deepest contradiction in the symbol of the serpent thus "does not consist in the contradiction between spirit and matter, drive and consciousness, becoming and perishing, but in the *opposition between nonexistence* [*Nichtsein*] *and being* [*Sein*], between nothingness [*Nichts*] and Creator, between earthly emptiness [*Nichtigkeit*] and divine omnipotence. Only nonexistence is in itself the pure opposite of the divine and it belongs nonetheless, as Genesis 3:1 explicitly says, to the world which God has created. In *theological* perspective the serpent in Genesis 3:1–5 is hence to be understood as a symbol of the nothingness in all of creation, as expression of the radical *contingency* of all that is created, which pulls humans away from God through the suction of *fear* [*Angst*] that it creates in human consciousness" (ibid., LXXV).

With the theological meaning of the symbol of the serpent clarified as the human spirit's experience of radical contingency, we can now follow Drewermann's existential-philosophical interpretation of the other key aspects of the symbolism of the story of the fall. Drewermann interprets the "eating of the fruit" from the tree of the knowledge of good and evil as the first attempt of humans to calm on their own the anxiety that inevitably arises from the experience of nothingness. Drewermann employs notions from Sartre's existential psychoanalysis such as the "lack [*Mangel*]" or "hole [*Loch*]" of existence, "craving for being [*Seinsbegierde*]," and "being-for-others [*Sein-für-Andere*]" to show how humans are led to desperate attempts to fill up their nothingness by using their body symbolically. The following passages provide existential-philosophical interpretations of some key aspects of the story in Genesis 3 as well as some general considerations on how Drewermann interprets the psychoanalytic results existential-philosophically.

> The decisive question cannot be what certain objects or drives [*Antriebe*] are "in themselves" in the sense of Kant's epistemology [*Erkenntnistheorie*]. Rather all objects and drives receive their meaning only through a preceding [*vorgängigen*] projection [*Entwurf*] of existence which uncovers them in their objective qualities.
>
> Let us clarify this issue in terms of a central example from psychoanalysis: Freud's entire psychoanalysis with its theory of the drives is tied to certain organ-specific locations of lack [*Mangelstellen*] of the body. Early Freudian drive theory presupposes "libido" as a primordial striving [*Urstreben*] and then notices how this striving runs by degrees through certain bodily zero locations [*Nullstellen*], gaping physical openings, and aims to close them up: as orality the opening of the mouth, as anality the opening of the anus, as sexuality the vagina (the penis functions in the "male protest" as proof for noncastration). It always is concerned with closing up a lack, a hole [*Loch*]. But if existence itself were not already a fundamental lack, if it were not ontologically already from the start and from the ground up a perforated [*durchlöchertes*] being, then there would be no understanding of what a "hole" is. No "hole" as such would "exist [*gegeben*]," no invitational character could be attached to it unless existence itself were this boundless longing for the closing up of its own lack. All drives which psychoanalysis perceives empirically are merely functions of the single infinite craving for being which existence itself is and which appears in being-for-others. Before one can speak of "sexuality" or "striving for power" one needs to notice the preceding striving by existence for the elimination of its contingency which is in the background of all its striving.

The hole which calls to be filled is therefore a symbol for human existence itself. The stuffing of the mouth with the finger, the act of eating, which uses food as putty for the sealing of the mouth — all that points to the *pre*-sexual experience which understands everything gaping as a cry for being. (Drewermann 1986b, 221)

Existentially, human strivings are understood not in terms of "(biological) sexuality and aggression, but in terms of the craving for being of human existence [*Dasein*], in terms of a striving for the abolition of the fundamental lack of *Dasein*" (ibid., 328). In this perspective "the central categories of psychoanalysis (anxiety, shame, guilt feeling, longing for complete self-sufficiency, overcompensation, castration complex, Oedipus complex, vicious cycle of neurosis) receive an existential foundation and thus become liberated from the narrow perspective of Freud's libido theory and the sociocultural conditions of the Oedipus complex" (ibid., 328). Of central importance is that Drewermann holds the infinite fear of the human spirit responsible for the fact that "normal drive impulses and needs" increase to levels of neurotic quantity (ibid., 329). Neurotic conflicts are thus due to an existential projection under the spell of fear.

Just as psychoanalysis assumes that neurotic illness unconsciously provides the promise of some key advantage, namely, to reduce psychological fear, Drewermann finds that philosophically the key advantage of the fall is that it promises to "abolish [existential] fear through the creation of one-sided tensions in one's existence [*Vereinseitigung der Daseinsspannungen*], through destruction of one's freedom, and through annihilation of one's own and then of other people's existence" (ibid., XXIV). The invitation of the serpent to eat from the forbidden tree means existential-philosophically "to close the nothingness of being, radical contingency by means of orality and sexuality. The temptation by the serpent would then have to be understood as the inclination which, out of the experience of the nothingness characterizing all creation, automatically begins to speak to humans: they might want to stop up their own contingency with the things and the people they find in the world. The human being who is under the influence of the all-devouring serpent of nothingness has to devour the whole world into herself in order to escape her own nothingness" (ibid., 236). Eating from the tree is an expression of the absolute longing to "bestow upon life as a whole in its basic functions — eating and procreation, hunger and love — the character of a necessity of being" (ibid., 259).

Humans' discovery of the knowledge of good and evil, that is, of their own nakedness as something to be ashamed of, after the eating of the forbidden fruit is the discovery that they are unable to fill their own lack, that humans are incapable of calming the fear that springs from the nothingness of their existence on their own. This is the *kind* of awareness of one's existence without God, that is, without ultimate foundation. Drewermann finds in Sartre's notion of "disgust [*Ekel*]" an apt description of the way nakedness is experienced after the fall. Being-for-itself is experienced as groundless, as obscene, because it is "lacking" of being, and so are all the "things" of the world (ibid., 238–45). Wanting to "be-like-God" expresses existential-philosophically being-for-itself's "effort to gain on one's own an *absolute necessity* and density of being [*Seinsdichte*], to become the ground [*Grund*] of one's own existence and to reject any foundation [*Begründung*] or justification of one's existence from outside" (ibid., 240). What may be psychoanalytically interpreted along the lines of the clinical picture of anorexia nervosa as an attempt to live as completely self-sufficient, from one's own substance, can be existential-philosophically interpreted as a "projection...in which existence attempts to make itself the *origin of itself*" (ibid.).

Distinct from Sartre, Drewermann emphasizes that this is not the only way existence can be experienced, but that it rather is the kind of experience which does not find a calming of the anxiety which inevitably belongs to human self-awareness. "Coming from Genesis 3:1–7 we have to stress against Sartre that anxiety itself is not yet identical with 'the fall,' that before the structuring of the Sartrean being-for-itself another development takes place which we cannot sufficiently comprehend with Sartrean categories" (ibid., 241).

The experience of death as punishment in Genesis 3:19 is related to Sartre's view of death as something that can never be appropriated by existence. Contrary to Heidegger's view that philosophically death could be seen as the focal point for a projection of life-as-a-whole, Drewermann agrees with Sartre that death cannot be tamed in that manner. "To think death means to think nonthinking. To project oneself toward death means to project nonprojection — which is an impossibility. Death is an ultimate *alienum* which I can never make my own, an accident from outside" (ibid., 247).

The experience of shame found in Genesis 3 is related existential-philosophically to Sartre's reflections on the existence of "the Other." The Other appears to being-for-itself (a subject) as a simply given subject which looks at it and transforms it back, in the form of being-for-others, into a being-in-itself, an object. Existence takes on the form of "being-for-others" (ibid., 251–53). By looking at me, the Other thus alienates 'me' from myself, evokes "*shame*" in me, and measures me in alienating ways which first make me feel guilty. "I therefore stand before the alternative whether I consent to my being-as-object, ready to see myself with the eyes of the Other as guilty and willing to accept the contradiction to turn my own freedom into unfreedom, or whether I restore my own being-for-itself again out of the alienation: that is, to transform the subject-other through my look into an object and to confirm my freedom by employing my transcendence for the purpose of transcending his transcendence. From here we arrive at the *sadomasochistic* polarity in the structure of inter-subjectivity" (ibid., 252–53). "God's look [*Blick*]" is for Sartre "the formalization of being-looked-at . . . God is by definition the one who always sees without being seen . . . the ultimate subject . . . which can never become object" (ibid., 255). Drewermann emphasizes that in Genesis 2 the look of God did not originally make humans feel shame. It does so only after humans have lost, metaphorically speaking, sight of God. God's look "reveals to them, after their sin, the nakedness which they are ashamed of. In addition, they fear God *because* they are naked" (ibid., 254). According to the Yahwist "humans are at first ashamed before God not because of their guilt . . . but because of their nakedness. . . . [H]umans are ashamed not so much because of a certain deed but rather because of their being. But that they are ashamed of their being is based on what they have done" (ibid., 257). The fear in the story is evoked in response to the voice of contingency (the serpent) in one's existence which makes humans aware of their "radical nonnecessity" and tempts them to flee into the world and to use it "for the purpose of creating a foundation, a necessity" for oneself (ibid., 258). The efforts of the fear are completely aimed at creating oneself "as an *ens a se*, as a being which finds sufficient reason in itself" (ibid.). That is the "decisive leap": "humans no longer seek support and justification of their [existence] in God, their Creator, but *want to be like God* through themselves because in fear they are unable to bear their own createdness" (ibid.). Drewermann stresses that originally, before the fall, God is not experienced as the Other in Sartre's sense but as the one who gives humans the key recognition [*Ansehen;* lit., being-seen] and dignity they need in order to live a human life. The story of 'paradise' and many passages from the Psalms attest to that. 'God' reemerges as the "wholly Other" (K. Barth) "only when under the spell of fear one has completely lost sight of God." God then appears "as adversary, as competitor, as a being which allows only the polarity of autonomy and heteronomy (Kant) and sado-masochism (Sartre) and as one who throws humans relentlessly back upon their nothingness. Because now God's look necessarily equals the collapse of the self-fabricated world of godlikeness, of dreams of metaphysical self-sufficiency, of measures to calm anxiety which we had to seek psychoanalytically in the vicinity of psychosis" (ibid., 259–60). When God is perceived by humans as their ultimate enemy, "atheism becomes the guarantor for freedom. . . . Because humans are in the eyes of their God a 'nothing,' there can be 'nothing' with God for humans" (ibid., 262). The psychically violent God-image which is completely opposed to anything human is thus the result of an original fall from God due to the fear of one's own nothingness, one's own existential contingency. That fear does not have to lead to this alienation from God, self, fellow-human, and creation is a theological thesis of Drewermann which we will consider shortly.

Before proceeding to that thesis, two summary passages that draw together the philosophical and theological interpretation of the psychoanalytic analysis of the story of the fall in Genesis 3 and the story of Cain and Abel in Genesis 4 follow. With regard to the interpretation of the fear, Drewermann, leaning on Sartre in vocabulary, writes:

We recognized that needs of orality, anality, and genitality have to be understood as *symbols* of the "obscene perforation [*Durchlöchertheit*]" of *Dasein*, of the infinite craving for being of consciousness in the face of its own nothingness. From the start, organ-specific needs that seem biologically based are thus driven [*hereingepeitscht;* lit., whipped] into the infinite, into the boundlessness of anxiety and of the flight from oneself. The reason is not certain anxiety-producing factors of the early childhood milieu — which could simply lead to purely factual, accidental difficulties of individual development — but is in the truest sense of the word "endogenous": a fear which arises from the depths of being human itself. *This* fear is not simply

drive-, real-, or superego-fear. It is not simply a fear of separation at birth [a reference to Rank's theory of the trauma of
birth which Drewermann appropriates critically as a symbol in
the psychoanalytic interpretation], of weaning (orally), of defecation (anally), and of castration (phallically), but a fear born
from the experience of nothingness which consciousness is and
which forces one to lose sight of God. The disaster, however,
is that from one stage to another, the further the distance from
God grows, the more the fear increases, so much so that in the
end it completely fuses phenomenologically with *Dasein* itself.
Fear then appears as the necessary mode in which existence must
experience itself and everything surrounding it in the fall from
God. This fear forces one to increase all desires: to be, to possess, to be valued — comprehensible by means of the concepts
of orality, anality, and genitality only in their external aspect —
into desires for absolute being, absolute possession, and absolute
value. It forces one to waste oneself in endlessness and boundlessness, in never ending frustrations and in ever new reactive
overcompensations. (ibid., 404–5)

Drewermann's existential interpretation of the guilt feelings critically relates the "wish to be like God" to the psychoanalytic notion of
the Oedipus complex. He differentiates the psychoanalytic notion of
God and the theological notion of God in view of the discussion of the
Oedipus complex and concludes that humans feel existentially castrated in a world without God and try by all means (especially in form
of reactive exhibitionistic tendencies) to compensate for the final separation from God (Drewermann 1985a, 208–10). Existentially, the
guilt feeling accompanying the fall is not

merely a product of the ambivalence of drive impulses on the
oral (cannibalistic), anal (sadistic), or Oedipal level of psychic
development. It consists not merely in the conflict between introjected societal values, concretized in one's parents, and the drive
strivings that necessarily oppose them. We see instead that *Dasein* itself, in alienation from God, must be ashamed of its
unjustified nothingness — upon which *Dasein* must radically fall
back without God — in the face of the Other and be judged
guilty [*schuldig*] by the Other. Under the burden of fear, *Dasein* deforms with seeming necessity into a pure contradiction
of itself. It thus owes [*schuldig*] itself everything because neither

in the "circle of self absorption [*Zirkel der Selbstheit*]" nor in its "being-for-the-Other" can it come to accept itself and escape the alienation of its being and behavior.

Where psychoanalysis sees the central pathogenic conflict in the fear of castration (Freud) or, in reaction to it, in "over-compensation" (Adler), existential psychoanalysis perceives the curse of existence as the nothing [*Nichts*], the lack of being at the foundation [*Untergrund*] of *Dasein* which has fallen from God and is radically left to its own contingency. Hence existential psychoanalysis interprets the desperate striving of humans to be "like God" in the Yahwist's primordial history as an answer of existence to its radical nothingness of being [*Seinsnichtigkeit*] without God. The "Oedipus complex" of psychoanalysis, this "core complex" of all neuroses, thus gains a deeper *gestalt* of meaning [*Sinngestalt*] that is independent from all socially dependent variables.... [A]bove the abyss of each existence [*Existenz*] without God there exists indeed the one all-dominating "sickness" of wanting to replace one's own "father" for the love of the "mother." Expressed in the language of existential philosophy: without God the infinite longing exists to become one's own creator, the foundation of oneself, and the origin of one's own being so that finally one gains a feeling of justification in *Dasein* and of a sense of security in the very "homelessness [*Unbehaustheit*]" of this world. In *psycho-analytic* perspective, humans reconstruct the entire world as a substitute for their lost mother and become sick over the fact that in all things they nevertheless can never find her completely. *Existential-philosophically,* humans long for a lost density of being [*Seinsdichte*] which they can never attain as conscious beings — whatever else they may achieve. Unless they know themselves wanted and accepted by an absolute "motherly" love in the depth of their existence, beyond the "adverse [*Widrig-keit*]" and "gaping nature [*Sperrigkeit*]" of the existing world, humans must forever ruin themselves. The faith of the Yahwist in God, to be sure, does not develop out of the Oedipus complex but puts an end to it. Without faith in a God who is the creator of all humans, all humans have to create themselves anew or have to take absolute refuge in other people, accompanied by all forms of self-humiliation and submission. One way or another they remain stuck in their total existential projection in the "Oedipus complex" — if one understands by that the urge of having to become one's own father (and creator) in order to gain through this at least the illusion of a certain justification of being [*Seinsberechtigung*]. (Drewermann 1986b, 405–6)

Genesis 4:1–16 in Existential-philosophical Perspective

Beyond Sartre's philosophy of the individual, Drewermann finds Sartre's social philosophy helpful for an understanding of how the subjectively experienced lack of being and the internalized opposition between God and humans becomes the driving force for deadly social division. In the field of fear and lack of being, the Other radically questions the recognition [*Ansehen*] and value of my being by objectifying me, by reminding me of my nothingness. The result is conflict which leads to a sadomasochistic interrelationship that tries to dissolve the tension between self and Other by either subjugating the Other as if I were God, that is, "the principle of necessity," and treating her as nothing or by idolizing the Other, by making her into a God and hoping that thereby my own lack can be closed (ibid., 263–78). Neither attempt succeeds, however, since this would require that either self or Other lose its subjectivity. Cain's killing of Abel is precisely this: Cain's attempt to kill the person who seemingly is in the way of him finding divine recognition and thus firm ground under his feet (ibid., 270–78). "Only if my own existence would have absolute justification could I bear the look of the Other. The Yahwist thinks that such a justification exists in 'recognition' by *God*. If it has been lost then humans have to become absolute enemies in the fight for their absolute justification" (ibid., 270–71). When humans kill each other under the spell of fear they desperately try to regain the lost experience of absolute recognition from God. In the story, murder is the result of Cain's subjective experience that God does not recognize him. The Other becomes the deadly enemy, the competitor for absolute recognition, and the target for the unique expression of human aggression that aims at the eradication of the Other. Killing the Other is done in hope of drawing the absolute recognition by God back upon oneself (ibid., 271). "Without God the other human being is the absolute measure of my self-worth. His 'being better' [in comparison to me] becomes the annihilation of me" (ibid., 273). Drewermann emphasizes that human aggressiveness cannot be sufficiently explained with reference to "the destructive power of a drive of aggression" (ibid., 274). The human "drive of aggression" only takes on the absolute and murderous forms we know from history because humans are desperately in need of absolute recognition and seek it where they will never be able to find it: through their own efforts. Only when humans do not feel absolutely accepted and loved (by God) do they need to gain such a feeling of absolute acceptance and love through their own best efforts (sacrifice to God) and eliminate the Other (Abel), be it physically or mentally (ibid., 273–74).

The story of Cain and Abel points to the inner division of humans outside of Eden and their desperate attempts to perfect themselves. "In this lies the tragedy of the figure of Cain: outside of Eden one cannot be good enough. Within the field of rejection, of being outcast, of the loss of God, of the relentless nonacceptance of existence one is forced to become flawless. This compulsion [to be ever better] separates the existence of humans into two isolated parts [i.e., the permitted perfect part and the repressed flawed part] which fight each other. In the end, it is this attempt [to attain] one's own purity and impeccably exemplary behavior which leads to murder and [existentially] to suicide. The wisdom of redemption would be to let weeds stand together with wheat on the same field (Matt. 13:29). But the fear of nonjustification does not know the patience of waiting for things to ripen" (ibid., 297). The being unto death (Gen. 3:19) turns through the experience of shame — due to a sense of one's own nothingness without God — into a being that kills (Gen. 4:8) (ibid., 299).

The fear that springs from the experience of the fundamental lack of being also colors all human dealings with the material world. Just as the self feels alienated from itself, so the material world (e.g., the machine) is perceived as characterized by lack and hence becomes the ground on which humans play out their own fear and their attempts to fill up the lack of being by material means. The collective becomes the "social mode of alienation" (ibid., 339) and its aim is to do away with the alienation and powerlessness experienced by individuals. Drewermann employs Sartre's social philosophy, plays, and other masterpieces of world literature to shed light on the interpersonal and social consequences of the fall (ibid., 331–400). According to Sartre, attempts to overcome social alienation work through the creation of groups that create a new unity bringing forth planned actions by means of which members of the group free themselves for a moment from their alienation and their feeling of powerlessness. In the group the individual can feel like a "special embodiment of the communal person" (ibid., 341) and the Other no longer must be experienced as a threat who simply objectifies one's subjectivity. But the group can never maintain its unity. It inevitably will fall apart. New groups will form and a cycle of unity and division is created which never ends (ibid.). Drewermann sees in Sartre's social philosophy a perfect model for describing the deterioration *after* the fall which leads from the killing of one individual by another (Cain and Abel, Genesis 4) all the way to the human project of creating unity among all, which inevitably fails (Tower of Babel, Genesis 11).

Genesis 3–11 raises the question why God is apparently unable to redeem humans from their misery and their "evil ways." Drewermann points out that the image of God as impotent in the face of human evil is itself a consequence of the fall. Humans try to redeem themselves. But "the human being in the state of sin cannot redeem himself. This correct statement leads in Sartre's work — and in the existentialist period of his time — to the thesis that even God has no possibility of redemption at all for humans. That is correct only within sin" (ibid., 274). The meaning of Sartre's atheism was not so much that God did not exist "but that God even if he or she existed cannot help us (ibid., 223). God is powerless" (ibid., 274). In line with the psychoanalytic picture that humans try to strive for complete self-sufficiency in the Yahwist's story, Drewermann pointedly formulates: "being-for-itself cannot be helped because as long as it is . . . mere being-for-itself it will not let itself be helped. And it has, as we now see, good reasons to reject such help because the acceptance of such external help, even the admission of the possibility of an external source of help, would necessitate a total break with and overturning of one's existence. The being-for-itself would cease to be its own God and Creator" (ibid., 275).

Theological Interpretation of Genesis 3 and 4:1–16

To show, in contrast to Sartre, that the fear which springs from human awareness of the radical contingency of its existence does not necessarily lead philosophically to disunity within oneself, to deadly, sadomasochistic competition with the Other, and theologically to a fall from God, Drewermann in a final step of his analysis of the Yahwist's primordial story turns to Kierkegaard's thought. Quoting from *The Concept of Anxiety* (Kierkegaard 1980a), Drewermann stresses that for Kierkegaard evil, the fall, is not inevitably a "reality [*Wirklichkeit*]" in the process of becoming conscious of oneself, as it is in Hegel and Sartre, but a "possibility" (1986b, 438; cf. ibid., XXIV, 136–37). Freedom is the "possibility of *being able*" and as open possibility implies the experience of the nothingness that lies within oneself (ibid., 438, referring to Kierkegaard 1980a, 44, 49). But that the possibility of evil, which springs from freedom, does develop into a reality of evil is, according to Kierkegaard, not necessary theologically — although theology always sees sin *factually* as becoming reality in existence. In other words, "sin as a decision of human existence" must not be identified with human existence. In Kierkegaard, as in Sartre, anxiety is the experience of one's own nothingness, but that one's freedom falls into this nothingness is not necessary but an original deed of freedom itself. Kierkegaard acknowledges, however, that in the aftermath of sin "the *impression* appears that human existence is identical with sin" (Drewermann 1986b, 438).

Kierkegaard's distinction between the possibility and the reality of evil, in conjunction with Kant's notion that what appears necessary functions in the service of an original choice of freedom, allows Drewermann now to answer the question of how we can think of sin both as the guilt of humans, and thus due to a free choice, and as universal, meaning that all humans fall into it. Drewermann argues that evil, which seems philosophically necessary, according to Hegel and Sartre, as part of the human process of becoming conscious of oneself and psychologically necessary, according to Freudian and Jungian interpretations of the development of the human psyche, is theologically not necessary. How so? In a sense, Drewermann is bringing a Trojan horse within the walls of the very philosophies and psychologies he has used to describe in modern terms the fall and its disastrous consequences leading up to the Tower of Babel. Drewermann agrees that what the philosophies and psychologies of modernity describe as universal characteristics of the human spirit and of human development can be theologically accepted as descriptions of universal elements of what *factually* all humans experience. It is these factual, universal experiences described by philosophy and psychology which Drewermann sees as confirmation that the phenomena which the Yahwist describes as sin in Genesis 3–11 are universal. "We now know that if someone says 'freedom,' she says at the same time 'anxiety,' and we comprehend that perishing due to the fear of oneself is the seemingly necessary reaction of freedom to the dizziness of anxiety.

Psychologically and philosophically this reaction appears to be absolutely necessary. Only theologically (dogmatically) is the category of guilt asserted" in regard to this reaction (ibid., 447). That — now the Trojan horse! — the existential fear which characterizes the human spirit leads all humans *factually* to alienation from self and from God, hence to evil, does not preclude that humans could *possibly* deal differently with this fear when it first arises. The universality of a phenomenon does not mean that no alternative possibility exists which could lead to a different reality. What appears within philosophical and psychological immanence as a necessity stands theologically in service of an original decision of freedom to liquidate itself. And this is where the fall becomes sin, the guilt of humans. It is very important, however, to highlight that Drewermann stresses again and again that the responsibility for unfreedom can only be recognized from the experience of faith and grace. Any moralizing of the theological guilt of humans is itself working by means of fear and thus reinforces sin. Only the experience of trust and unconditional acceptance can melt the icy structures of fear and evil. For a theological analysis of an "alternative possibility," Drewermann turns mainly to Kierkegaard's *The Concept of Anxiety* (1980a), *The Sickness Unto Death* (1980b), and *Fear and Trembling* (1983) (Drewermann 1986b, 436–562).

Kierkegaard understands humans as a synthesis of soul and body. Therein lie two polar axial systems between which freedom is stretched: the polarity between the infinite and the finite on the one hand and the polarity between possibility and necessity on the other. The synthesis between the polarities is established by the spirit. In the human spirit lies the freedom of humans and also the experience of nothingness which creates anxiety. It is this anxiety which drives humans into sin. Kierkegaard compares the process of falling into sin due to fear with the experience of dizziness. Drewermann quotes the following passage from Kierkegaard's description of "subjective anxiety."

> Anxiety may be compared with dizziness. He whose eye happens to look down into the yawning abyss becomes dizzy. But what is the reason for this? It is just as much in his own eye as in the abyss, for suppose he had not looked down. Hence anxiety is the dizziness of freedom, which emerges when the spirit wants to posit the synthesis and freedom looks down into its own possibility, laying hold of finiteness to support itself. Freedom

succumbs in this dizziness.... In that very moment everything is changed, and freedom, when it again rises, sees that it is guilty. (Kierkegaard 1980a, 61; see Dostoevsky's description of anxiety [Dostoevsky 1945] in Drewermann 1986b, 288). (Drewermann 1986b, 438–39)

Differentiating the Kierkegaardian view of evil from the psychoanalytic view, Drewermann emphasizes that evil as a consequence of the fall of freedom is the "guilt of existence" and cannot be explained either through external danger situations nor through the "causality of drive-based 'necessities'" (ibid., XXVII). That one experiences one's own existence only in terms of causally determining drive-based necessities and external constraints is itself a result of the "fear of freedom" of the human spirit (ibid.). Only under the spell of existential anxiety does the psychoanalytic view seem inevitably to see "fear only as a reflex of *external* danger situations" (ibid., XX). But such a "causal explanation of evil locks humans eventually and inevitably into a completely pessimistic anthropology" (ibid.).

It is not enough to describe evil psychoanalytically as a "sickness." Not only because the decisive element: the freedom and responsibility of human behavior, would be left out of the process but above all because the totality by means of which evil seizes humans in the Yahwist's primordial history would then have to appear as the mere consequence of a flawed natural order. In that view, humans would remain sick animals for whom there would ultimately be no rescue.... Just as neurotics have an interest to relieve themselves constantly by referring to certain factors of their present or early childhood environment, so a purely genetic-causal thinking, as in psychoanalysis, would need to lead to a general amnesty of humans and to a general indictment of nature or of God as its creator. With that any possibility of therapy would, of course, ultimately have become pure illusion. (ibid., XXI–XXII)

A real possibility of change must transcend causal-genetic thinking and take seriously the human spirit's capacity for freedom. Drewermann wants

to get away from the psychoanalytic naivete that fear would basically (in the sense of early childhood object loss) be introduced to the ego from outside. Rather, the ego is the "seat of anxiety" because as ego it is reflexivity, spirit, and freedom. According to Kierkegaard, freedom itself is a synthesis of body and soul (time and eternity). In this lies the terrible possibility of infinitely missing oneself and of infinite guilt of existence. This comes about when due to sheer anxiety the synthesis of the finite and the infinite is not really implemented as synthesis, and freedom binds itself absolutely for its seeming security to either of the poles that should be unified. With infinite effort freedom clamps itself, driven by anxiety, to the finite (or to the infinite) and, through this one-sidedness, to nothingness. Psychologically this process seems very understandable, and yet this does not mitigate that it is nonetheless guilt. "For suppose he had not looked down!" One then should not have refused the synthesis of one's actual existence. (ibid., 439)

Kierkegaard described sin as despair. Despair is the result of human anxiety getting lost in staring down the abyss of nothingness and leads humans to lose sight of the divine. The other, theological possibility — the possibility which opens the world up beyond the confines of philosophical and psychological thought of immanence — is, instead of trying to deal with the fear on one's own and thus being consumed by it, instead of "keep-staring-upon-oneself," to reach for help to an absolute freedom, "God," which calms the fear stirred by the experience of the possibility of one's own nothingness. Thus we are made to feel absolutely "held and carried" in existence and helped to discover that we are from the ground up absolutely affirmed, wanted, and justified in our existence (ibid., XXIX, 546). This does not make humans "necessary" as such. The key point is not whether we are absolutely necessary but whether we feel absolutely wanted. "Humans, the Yahwist says in Genesis 2, do not possess any necessity to exist other than that God — out of free choice — means and wills them. Humans are not 'necessary' because of that. But God wants them to exist. Before God they have a right to exist. They do not need to exist, but they may exist from the perspective of God [von Gott her leben]" (ibid., 260).

Connecting with Sartre's notion of freedom as the opening up of nothingness, Drewermann explicates why belief in an absolute God is necessary if the evil which springs from the fear of nothingness and of freedom can ever be overcome.

Kierkegaard does not consider the movement of transcendence, this anxiety-producing step beyond anything finite, as a grasping into infinite emptiness, as a movement of escape from nothingness into nothingness, as an eternal fleeing from shame and disgust which never arrives at itself, but as humans' encountering in infinity another freedom [i.e., God] who is not identical with them but from whose perspective they can understand themselves and can comprehend themselves as "derived," "put forth," "created." In becoming aware in fear of their infinite destiny, it is possible that humans see the finite things of the world not simply vanish and feel that therein lies no ground, no necessity, no justification of their existence, but that in infinity they find God. There is in *anxiety an opportunity* for humans to encounter God. At the moment, when everything to which they are immediately attached in finitude falls in anxiety out of their hands, they have the possibility to discover the true source of their life. This is the step of *faith:* that I discover myself, my contingent, nonnecessary, superfluous existence as created and as affirmed, wanted, justified by infinity and that this discovery enables me to accept myself, to give up the desperate escape from (or into) myself and to affirm myself. . . . Henceforth I am able to accept my limitations, my finite characteristics without having to hide myself for being this way. . . . This, Kierkegaard thought, was *Abraham's* faith: a faith by means of infinity into the finite. It is thus possible that the fear which belongs necessarily to humans does *not* lead to despair but instead to faith. But this presupposes that the fear is not left to itself but grounds itself in God. (ibid., 546–47)

It is "sin" to try to escape from one's freedom; it appears as the exceedingly obvious, even psychologically and phenomenologically necessary attempt of the freedom of humans to liquidate itself through a self-created necessity. Once entered, sin can hence no longer be dissolved. The energy of freedom, the destiny for infinity now consumes itself infinitely in the maintenance of its self-created unfreedom. Desperately humans now seek to prevent the return of fear, and the more the fear of their empty freedom threatens them the more they dig themselves into the slavery of sin, into this compulsion to create themselves as their own ground and to thus gain the status of a God, of an *"ens a se."* (ibid., 547)

Sin as despair then is a mis-relation to God as the source of one's existence and then to oneself. With Kierkegaard, Drewermann agrees that "if in relating to themselves, in their reflectivity, humans at the same time do not relate to God, they indeed get caught necessarily in a mis-relation to themselves and are forced into desperate existence" (ibid., 462). If humans see themselves all alone, without God, then they are condemned to a desperate and futile show of self-redemption (ibid.).

Drewermann tries to make the four major forms of neurosis: depression, schizoid disorder, obsessive compulsive disorder, and hysteria — where not due to organic reasons — transparent as external expressions of Kierkegaard's four types of despair of human freedom (ibid., 460–86; cf. Drewermann 1991d, 128–62; Drewermann 1990d, 39–40), as expressions of a *"lack of God"* (Drewermann 1986b, 463). " 'Neurosis' and 'being-for-itself' make up the inner and outer sides of an existence that despairs without God in the whirlpool of anxiety" (ibid., 464). Psychoanalysis serves Drewermann in order to "deepen the existential hermeneutics in the direction of an anthropologically grounded understanding of the concreteness of the symbolism of religious speech" (1990d, 39, n. 21). Kierkegaard distinguished between conscious and unconscious forms of despair (Drewermann 1986b, 467). One may not at all be aware of one's despair. The following paragraph sums up how Drewermann applies Kierkegaard's "forms of despair" to an elucidation of nonorganic mental illness.

All derivatives from the particular forms of despair which Kierkegaard developed serve, then, a kind of theological psychology. They show that humans have to become *sick* even in the psychological sense if they attempt to become masters of the fear of their existence without God. Thus Kierkegaard's position relates to psychology *dialectically.* He confirms the correctness of psychological descriptions of forms of mental illness. But to stop at psychological categories would be identical with the very self-incarceration of existence that consists in despair. Hence psychology has to perish due to itself and open itself up to theology. The Kierkegaardian development of the forms of human despair expands and confirms therefore the psychology of neurosis as a theological phenomenology of sin. (ibid., 468)

Referring frequently to other existentially oriented writers in the field of psychology such as Riemann (1961), Schultz (1955), von Gebsattel (1959a, 1959b), and V. E. Frankl (1975, 1986), Drewermann proposes that Kierkegaard's four forms of despair correspond to the four main forms of neurosis described by psychoanalysis in the sense that in each form of despair one pole of existence is repressed, leading to a deformation of existence that expresses itself psychologically in specific forms of neurosis (Drewermann 1990d, 39). Within the first polarity of human existence between finitude and infinity, Kierkegaard perceives two forms of despair in which the attempt is made to solve the anxiety-producing tension within the synthesis of existence "through exclusion of either of the poles: there exists a despair which consists in disavowing finitude and in fleeing into infinity, and a despair which tries to cling to finitude by disavowing infinity" (Drewermann 1986b, 469).

The first form of despair disavows finitude and "sets all human strife, hopes, and duties into infinity and necessarily creates the infinite boundlessness, disappointments, and guilt feelings which are characteristic of the neurosis of *depression*." The depressive has "oral mega-expectations" which are a sign of the despair of infinity. She feels responsible for the whole world and hence carries an infinite amount of guilt feelings. Instead of deriving depression causal-genetically from the area of oral drives, as in psychoanalysis, Kierkegaard derives "the sheer infinite 'longing' from a *spiritual* movement of transcendence which in its flight from itself flees from unbearable finitude into infinity." A depressive person tends to join religions which preach self-annihilation and the surrender of the ego. He cannot stand finite existence and in relation to God tries to make himself infinite. Any thought of contingency is a source of deep fear of oneself. The depressive feels like humans in Genesis 3 after the fall from God: their entire existence is transformed "into fear and guilt, into a constant feeling of lacking justification and of having to hide." By trying to take responsibility for the whole world, by fleeing into infinity, depression is a "basic coloration of existence" after the fall. The depressive person feels she has to be as perfect as only God could be in order to be allowed to live as a human being. "What Sartre identified as infinite craving for being with the perforated being of consciousness shows itself now as the despair of a life which must strive into infinity because it has lost God as a person, as support, as mercy and grace in a merciless world" (ibid., 469–71). In depression "the ego goes to extremes to accommodate and to submit in order to offer itself to the Other as lovable.... [T]he Other is put in the place of one's own ego. The fear of the threat to one's own person has thus vanished. But the constant guilt feeling that one may not be able to do justice to the gigantic expectations of others is answered by making one's ego completely dependent on the judgment of others and thereby liquidating responsibility for one's own decisions" (ibid., 473–74).

The opposite form of despair is the "despair of finitude" which corresponds in psychoanalysis to the *schizoid* character structure (ibid., 471–75). This is an attitude which loses itself in finite reality, often accompanied by a particular efficiency in life and hence most of the time not noticed. From the outside, the schizoid person may be very successful, may do everything as expected, but "participate basically in a way that does not include any inner investment." Internally there is a cautious distance from all others who threaten the total loss of one's ego. Religiously, schizoids are usually skeptical and cynical and tend to worship themselves rather than God. "The schizoid is constantly concerned with herself, but Kierkegaard notes accurately of those who despair of the lack of infinity: 'They use their capacities, amass money, carry on secular enterprises, calculate shrewdly, etc., perhaps make a name in history, but they are not themselves; spiritually speaking, they have no self, no self for whose sake they could venture everything, no self before God — however self-seeking they are otherwise' (Kierkegaard 1980b, 35). In this respect one may well say that the Kierkegaardian form of despair of finitude corresponds to the neurotic form of schizoid disorder so that existentially the schizoid is basically a *person in despair* who does not find a self in finitude because she lacks a hold in infinity" (Drewermann 1986b, 472). The schizoid desperately tries to "set her own ego in the place of the world and of the Other" (ibid., 474). Drewermann finds that no single story in the Yahwist's account of primordial history corresponds exclusively to the schizoid disorder and its underlying despair of finitude. Instead "it offers in a sense the background of all other stories of the Yahwist's primordial history but is represented in no single story." In the continuation of the neurotic structure of the schizoid lies the psychotic experience of the schizophrenic. "[S]chizophrenia [where not due to organic factors] is with its central symptoms of self-divination and self-demonization of the ego, with its contrast of an absolute, insane freedom hand in hand with an objectively absolute unfreedom, clinically the purest form of a self-presentation of human existence in the midst of a world completely devoid of God" (ibid., 486).

> The threat and danger of the environment, and the resulting mistrust, lead the *schizoid* either to turn his attention completely away from the environment onto one's own ego or to undo the mistrusting separation from the environment by means of identification: since one cannot believe that a God exists or a human being who would love and protect one, the schizophrenic declares himself to be God. Since he is God he is no longer dependent on any God and the uncertainty of the not-being-loved and of mistrust disappear. The world loses its hostility since one has created it oneself and can let it perish at any time. The schizophrenic insanity is the psychotically ultimate end of the problem that is given with the schizoid neurosis: the problem of a self which is none and which desperately tries to embrace itself in order to put itself finally in the place of the whole world. (ibid., 473)

Drewermann, along with Kierkegaard, believes faith can overcome despair. In depression and schizoid disorder, Drewermann sees expressions of the two forms of Kierkegaardian despair which become sin if not overcome by faith. Depression corresponds to the attempt *"before God, or with the conception of God, in despair not to want to be oneself,"* also referred to as "despair in *weakness*," while schizoid disorder is the attempt *"in despair to want to be oneself"* also referred to as the despair in *"defiance"* (Drewermann 1986b, 474, 487–92, quoting from Kierkegaard 1980b, 49,67, 77).

The second Kierkegaardian polarity of human existence, between possibility and necessity, offers another perspective on the basic polarity of finitude and infinity. Because "mere finitude would at the same time be the field of mere necessity and mere infinity would be mere possibility and self-determination" (Drewermann 1986b, 475), the despair of possibility is due to the lack of necessity and the despair of necessity is due to the lack of possibility. For Drewermann the despair of possibility corresponds to hysteria and the despair of necessity to obsessive compulsive disorder.

The key problem of hysteria is that any kind of necessity is experienced as a constraining affront. The hysteric is afraid of anything that is definite or inevitable and prefers the play of possibilities and of appearances. Existentially, hysteria corresponds to Kierkegaard's "despair of possibility" as the "lack of necessity."

> The exclusion of necessity shows itself as the existential meaning of hysteria. It appears as a despair of oneself, as an escape from external enslavement by necessity into inner arbitrariness. That does not prevent but is reason for the endless search of the hysteric for a godlike hold which he, of course, seeks neither in God nor in himself but in the other human person. What *appears* in psychoanalytic perspective as incest-flight from the Oedipus complex, is understood daseinsanalytically as longing for and fear of necessity. Without God human freedom flees into lack of commitment which represents only the counterpart to the desperate search for a human being who could substitute for God (Drewermann 1986b, 314–16). We observed the complete obedience and submissiveness into which the hysterical disorder can grow (Fenichel 1945) in the motif of the marriage of angels [Genesis 6:1–4] (cf. Drewermann 1985a, 349). (Drewermann 1986b, 476)

Finally, Drewermann associates obsessive compulsive disorder with Kierkegaard's notion of the "despair of necessity" which is a "lack of possibility" (ibid., 476–79). The obsessive is afraid of anything that "could be," "of possibility and of freedom." Possibility is experienced as a total threat to her existence. The obsessive tries to flee into perfectionism and hopes to find necessity in it. "The self of someone desperate in this manner in a sense suffocates under the compulsion of always having to breathe only what is necessary and of having no space for her own unfolding" (ibid., 477). Kierkegaard distinguishes two subgroups: a "spiritless" position and a "spirited" position. Quoting Kierkegaard, Drewermann defines the spiritless form of despair of necessity as the mentality of "petit bourgeois conformism, . . . a lack of fantasy . . . which spares itself the excitement of existence, of fearing and hoping, by accepting everything as given and *necessarily* given, completely unable even to imagine that it could be different. The *spiritual* form of despair is the conviction of the fatalist or determinist for whom life exhausts itself in the recognition of an unchangeable necessity and a dead lawfulness" (ibid., 477–78). Without faith in God, nothing else remains for the obsessive than "to worship necessity either with or without spirit and in so doing to destroy herself as a human being, as a self" (ibid., 478). Eichmann's story is a case in point.

The story of Cain and Abel (Gen. 4:1–16) exemplifies this mentality. There "the obsessive compulsive seeks an absolute justification for existence, but since he feels rejected from the ground up, he believes that he has to force and fight for this justification — with a murder of everything that is human" (ibid., 477). That the existential despair of necessity, finding psychological expression in the *"anal-sadistic con-flicts"* of Genesis 4:1–16, has to aim at murder was made intelligible by Drewermann by means of Sartre's existential philosophy. "But from Kierkegaard we can learn how the self, one's own ego, is suffocated and killed if it clings desperately to the idea of a (godless) necessity in order to justify itself before itself and to reconcile itself with its fate. It is then only logical that this existential self-destruction through the desperate flight into necessity must externally lead to the destruction of the Other" (ibid., 484–85). To the obsessive, one would have to stress that God is not a fatalistic cipher of necessity but instead, to paraphrase Kierkegaard, God is that everything is possible, "even if within the frame of existing circumstances no rescue is in sight. 'The *believer* sees and understands his downfall, humanly speaking, ... but he believes. For this reason he does not collapse' " (ibid., 478, quoting Kierkegaard 1980b, 39). Hence: "If humans lack a firm hold in the person of God facing them, then they are unable to bear the fear of existence in its tensions. The bridge collapses which humans build within their existence between time and eternity (in the moment), finitude and infinity (as created spirit), possibility and necessity (in reality), in order to find themselves" (Drewermann 1986b, 481).

Faith as Trust: The Alternative to Sin as Fear

A spiritual neurosis can appear as the result of an existentially projected mis-relation to God and to oneself only when a person in "treatment" learns and "chooses" to react differently than before. As in psychoanalysis, this change in self-projection is only possible within a climate of acceptance by and of trust in another person, the "therapist." Since the decisive issue of the "sickness" of the spirit revolves around the fear that one's existence is not ultimately and absolutely justified, only an absolute trust and acceptance can enable a change of the spiritual self-projection. Only then can defenses which crippled the ego be accepted as choices and slowly undone. The experience that trust evokes a radical spiritual change implies existentially that there was *virtually* always the possibility not to give in to fear but to trust oneself in the presence of God. It is this experience which Drewermann sees as the experience of faith. Faith

> is the power which, beyond weakness and obstinacy, calms the nothingness of human existence, the anxiety, the lack of hold of the possibility and of one's own freedom, ... in view of God through a new attitude of trust [*Vertrauens*]. What causes fear, namely, possibility, now becomes the principle of faith. What once gave reason for despair, namely, one's own nothingness, now becomes the occasion for a relationship characterized by a new sense of security. . . . [I]n existence, a predisposed alternative to the experience of being lost in anxiety exists and, at least retrospectively, ... always existed. From the perspective of faith we realize that it was in no way necessary for humans to retreat into themselves in the fear of their own freedom and to incarcerate their existence into the self-created necessities of sin. Hence we do not have to retract any of the insights gained from Sartre and Freud in the Yahwist's primordial history. We only have to and are able to confirm now that in the moment of anxiety as a fundamental phenomenon of human existence faith was at least virtually just as much a predisposition as despair. . . . [T]he step leading from anxiety not to faith but to despair is *viewed from the perspective of faith as guilt.* Evidently a necessity of the development of anxiety exists which leads to despair and which is discovered as nonnecessity only from the perspective of faith, while it seems imperative independently from the perspective of faith. Only faith recognizes as *guilt* the seeming necessity of despair due to fear. Only in faith do humans comprehend that in all their despair they were constantly missing [*gefehlt*] *God* and that only in this lack [*Fehlen*] of God they *had to* miss [*verfehlen*] themselves. Hence faith — and only faith — uncovers the factual necessities of evil in psychoanalysis and existential analysis as a false, even culpable existence. It reveals the whole desolation of the compulsive causality of evil arising from one's own culpability as a self-incarceration of human existence in the ghetto of fear without God. (ibid., 501–2)

Despite Drewermann's appreciation of Kierkegaard, he radically breaks with this great Protestant philosopher of religion on one central issue which is of significance in light of Drewermann's later reinterpretation of the central symbol of Christianity: the Cross (ibid., 504–14). Drewermann charges that Kierkegaard, in his later writings, especially *Practice in Christianity* (1991) and *The Moment* (1998), and in view of the nature of the suffering of Christ in relation to the suffering of human beings, more and more loses sight of the key idea he developed in earlier writings: that faith is not only a relativization of everything that is finite in its turn to infinity, but that the movement of faith is completed only in the decisive " 'repetition' of the finite in faith" (Drewermann 1986b, 508).

Biographically, Drewermann developed this criticism of Kierkegaard only *after* he himself had struggled with psychoanalysis. From the ascetic youth and self-sacrificing seminarian up until the late 1960s, Drewermann developed into someone who questioned the sacrificial mentality of traditional Christianity. Kierkegaard, Drewermann notes, interpreted Christianity in his later writings in a manner which was more and more "hostile to life and to humans" (1986b, 504). Drewermann believes that the inability of Kierkegaard to regain "the finite in faith" was a clear result of "the old Protestant identification of human nature and 'concupiscence' with human sin," where God and humans are absolute opposites. In *The Moment*, Kierkegaard goes so far as to declare that " 'God is love' " means God is " 'your mortal enemy,' " that God wants " 'that a person shall die... that what God then does — out of love — is to torment him in all the agonies designed to take life away from him' " (Drewermann 1986b, 510, quoting Kierkegaard 1998, 178, 251). "Instead of saying that God contradicts human *anxiety* and its mechanisms of flight for the sake of humans, now Kierkegaard portrays the situation as if God would have to say and command principally the opposite of what humans want themselves. Contrary to his own aim, Kierkegaard now identifies human existence more and more with its desperate form of existence, which now means the same as natural existence" (ibid.).

In terms of Kierkegaard's biography, Drewermann the psychoanalyst believes that this inconsequence was basically due to the Oedipal' conflicts which Kierkegaard struggled with in relation to the idea of getting married to Regine Olsen.

It is as if all that remains for Kierkegaard of the development of faith in *Fear and Trembling* [1983] is only the image of a God who — because of love! — demands the killing of his child and is above all concerned to prohibit if possible any thought of a god-pleasing marriage. One does not need any great psychoanalytic insights to recognize behind such a God-image the oppressive traits of Kierkegaard's father whose own marital life left a shadow of evil. In his melancholy he "sacrificed," by smothering everything childlike in the young boy, the elementary pagan in his son which the son was never able to overcome. (ibid., 510)

It is in his critique of Kierkegaard that we hear Drewermann for the first time express explicit criticism of neurotic structures in Christianity. Drewermann considers Kierkegaard's critique of Christianity in his later writings to be

completely neurotic. He evidently dismisses here as paganism everything which he himself originally (of course, only in the half-hearted play of writings published under pseudonyms!) sensed as healing possibilities for the overcoming of anxiety and despair through faith. Here he clearly elevates Christendom to a principle which is diametrically opposed to life, which no longer has the power to liberate and to free from fear but only to destroy and to instill fear. But the problem is not that Kierkegaard rationalized his neuroticisms theologically. The problem is that Kierkegaard could accurately think himself the heir of (Protestant) theology precisely in the neurotic forms of his "Christendom" and that Christianity obviously contained in itself all the neurotic traits that permitted Kierkegaard to call "pagan" what would have allowed him to live in faith and to call Christian what had caused his sickness, his failure in regard to the task of a "synthesis" of the self.... The challenge of Kierkegaard demands nothing less than an examination of the Christian message in its core content: the doctrine of the suffering and death of Christ.

[I]t is precisely the necessity of the *suffering* of Christ to which Kierkegaard again and again refers when he contrasts Christianity to the "natural" struggle for happiness in humans.... Through the example of the Cross of Christ it becomes evident for him that the teaching of Christianity, presented to a child, will and should lead to the most enduring revaluation of her entire natural sensibility (Kierkegaard 1991, 174–78).... Since Christ had to suffer it becomes an unshakable certainty for Kierkegaard that Christianity runs contrary to the natural in humans, that neither the feeling nor thinking of humans possesses a preparatory point of connection and that, along with this, Christianity distinguishes itself from all other religions of the "world" precisely through its doctrine of the suffering of the Son of God.... Christ, according to Kierkegaard's argument, had to be killed because his message basically killed humans. From a Christian perspective, Kierkegaard thinks, it would therefore be generally better not to have been born into this world at all (Kierkegaard 1998, 250). (Drewermann 1986b, 511–12)

Instead of blaming Kierkegaard for demonizing as pagan and unchristian "all human wishes, passions, and longings," Drewermann asserts that something in Christianity itself provided the basis for Kierkegaard's misinterpretation of Christianity in which the will of God is pitted mercilessly against the will and nature of humans. Drewermann argues that the

difference between paganism and religion ... does not lie in the doctrine of the suffering of the Son of God, but in the difference between fear and self-redemption on the one hand and faith and overcoming of fear on the other. Everything depends on understanding the suffering of Christ not as a principle that generates new fears but as the way in which the basic situations of fear in human existence are worked through and opened up in view of God. (ibid., 513)

In an Excursus titled "The Hostility Toward Myth in Christianity, the Conflict Between the Denominations, and the Inner Disunity of the Human Being" (ibid., 514–33), Drewermann analyzes the intellectual-historical developments that led Christianity into its suspicion of "the natural" and its devastating consequences for the history of the West. We reserve a detailed analysis of this Excursus for the second chapter since it deals explicitly with the social implications of a particular spiritual attitude dominated by fear and Drewermann himself cites it in his analysis both of the dynamic of war (1992a) and of the destruction of nature (1991e).

An Existential Proof of God and the Reality of Psychic Images

Drewermann argues that the Yahwist's primordial history indirectly provides us with an "existential proof of God" (1986b, XLVIII). Drewermann's analysis confirms the Yahwist's view that all structures of human existence become psychologically "crippled" and philosophically "missed" and "evil" outside of a unity with God, "that, speaking with Kierkegaard, a human being *must* despair who in fear loses faith in God, and that humans without God must, pressured by excessive amounts of suffering and wasted efforts, attempt to set themselves up as absolute beings. If it is so inhuman not to believe in God, should one then not come to the conclusion that faith in God is something basically necessary and natural for humans, something that is beyond doubt as much as the existence of air is in the face of the torture of suffocation?" (ibid.).

We saw above that the Yahwist employed mythic imagery to portray the fear and despair of humans who feel separated from God. In the psychoanalytic interpretation Drewermann appreciates both Freud's idea of the phylogenetic foundation of psychic imagery and Jung's psychology of archetypes. In discussing Jung's notion of archetypes, which attempted to overcome Freud's pessimism by asserting that the psyche naturally aims toward wholeness, Drewermann argues existential-philosophically and theologically that the assumption of such a natural tendency cannot be maintained and that the imagery, if it should not eventually lead toward destruction, needs to be grounded in an absolute reality. The radically destructive effects of the "archetype of the God-human" in the Third Reich refute Jung's intrapsychic optimism. Whether archetypal images lead in the life of the individual and the collective to wholeness or destruction, Drewermann holds, depends on whether the ego — philosophically, the human spirit — is characterized existentially by a basic attitude of fear or of trust. Humans need to assure themselves *philosophically* of "the *absolute* meaningfulness of their factual natural constitution," hence also of the images of the human psyche. Otherwise "the radical accidental nature and the devastating subjectivity of these images would never be taken from them." "Everything, literally everything depends [on the belief] that the images point to something real which is the [philosophical] ground for their existence.... The symbols of hope and longing become [existentially] meaningful only if they are understood as images which God has put into the human psyche in order to reveal herself in it" (Drewermann 1985a, XXVII). That religious beliefs are not *only* images of the human psyche" but point to a reality beyond the scope of psychology is vital if they should have existential significance as the language within which humans discover the absolute meaning their spirit longs for (ibid., XXVI).

This implies, on the other hand, that the reality of God must be philosophically and theologically clearly distinguished from God-images, although humans can perceive God only with the images of their natural constitution. Whether God-images connect with the life-giving reality of God or distort it into the demonic depends on whether the human spirit is under the spell of fear or not. The ambivalence of the God-image is not native to the human psyche but is itself the result of the fall. Archetypal images are in themselves neutral, neither positive nor negative. It is lack of integration of the archetypes of the collective unconscious with the personal, historical ego (philosophically: the human spirit) which leads to destructive effects of archetypal imagery. The personal integration, Drewermann reasons, is possible only if an absolute person who transcends the collective unconscious as well as the individual ego and its absolute fears comes toward us from the infinite and gives foundation to and enables us to trust the absolute value of our existence.

Moreover, God has to be absolutely distinguished from the experience of our parents, of authority figures, and of the social group. In the psychoanalytic interpretation, Drewermann employed the theory of ontogenetic development and of neurosis as a model for what happens between humans and God as humans fall prey to the fear of separation from the creative ground of their existence. God was identified in the psychoanalytic analysis with a child's experience of the parents in order to understand the emotional significance of the process of the fall. Under the spell of fear the God-image becomes mentally violent, confused with parental introjects or self-images, and has to be defended against. Psychoanalysis is indispensable for an understanding of a violent God-image, but it would be rash to identify God with a God-image distorted by fear. Drewermann argues that instead of holding psychoanalysis "to the old theory of S. Freud of the illusionary character of religion, one can show by means of the Yahwist's symbolic narratives about the desolation of human existence without God that the entire structure of human existence without God takes on neurotic and insane traits" (1986a, LXXXVIII). By means of existential-philosophical analysis, Drewermann reads the drives and defenses against drives in psychoanalysis as expressions of a basic human projection of life. The theological analysis in turn relates the existential projection of life to questions of ultimate concern. If humans become neurotic or quasi-neurotic when their spirit is held hostage by existential despair then it is essentially the spiritual neurosis before God which does not allow them to grow up psychologically. In a pointed statement in volume 2 of *Strukturen des Bösen*, Drewermann puts it this way:

> If the psychoanalytic part of the present work has any value it is to prepare the philosophical thesis that humans can only find themselves if they become *theologically* "children" and if God stands face to face with them as a free, absolute person, as "father"; that they are capable of overcoming the fear which prevents them from becoming a self only if they know themselves to be accepted in all parts and areas of their created existence; and that they find the trust [necessary] to decide in favor of independence and freedom only if they are able to give their freedom hold and direction in God. Only when humans become theologically 'children' can they cease psychologically to remain children and to transfer their longing for father and mother onto human authorities or to make themselves into God. (1985a, 241)

Drewermann indicates what kind of therapy is needed to free humans from a violent God-image. Chapter 3 will explicate his interpretation of the Christian imagery of Cross, resurrection, and Eucharist as symbols by which the hate provoked by a violent God-image toward God and self can be worked through. In *Strukturen des Bösen*, Drewermann likens the process of healing from sin as despair to the process of therapy. "What a neurotic learns with his therapist, humankind had to learn through faith in the God of the people of Israel (cf. Drewermann 1985a, 585), with one essential difference: while the healing of neurosis consists in also leaving the therapist behind, the healing from mythology [i.e., here: mythic imagery experienced under the spell of fear] consists in coming ever closer to God. The 'Shema Israel, the Lord our God is Lord alone' (Dtn. 6:4) is the embodiment of redemption from everything which hinders the human being from being a human being" (Drewermann 1986b, XXXVI). The difference is this: the therapist is there to help a person find some way to replace the security of being held by the mother (figure), help the person to become emotionally more and more free from stifling attachments to early caregivers, because these caregivers can be replaced. But God as the one to help us find absolute hold cannot be replaced. The existential security, the security of the human spirit with its longing for the infinite, can only be found in an absolute person, God. While the security of being held in the lap of one's mother can somehow be replaced through the experience of security with another human person, the existential security people need to exist as ultimately meaningful can only be found in an absolute person and can thus "not be replaced." All attempts, therefore, which try to replace God by anything less than God, including a rigid superego image of God, will only cement the self-alienation and serve to repress the actual loss of God (ibid., XXX).

Drewermann stresses that if God should really be what the Yahwist portrays him to be: the only one who can ground our lives in a true sense of absolute existential meaning, then God can theologically not be seen to oppose but must be seen to essentially confirm our true longings and wishes. In other words, humans "choose" God, to use psychoanalytic terms again symbolically, as an object on a "narcissistic basis." "The 'narcissism' in 'object choice' . . . represents merely the psychoanalytic correlate of the theological statement . . . namely, that humans cannot live without God, that . . . if they love God they love their own life, themselves; any love of 'God' is psychoanalytically in this sense 'narcissistic'" (Drewermann 1985a, 161). Only a God who allows humans to love their own life and wants to bring that life to full expression is worthy of being called a God for humans, a God who "becomes human," incarnate.

Conclusion

This chapter provided a first glimpse into the historical context of Eugen Drewermann's work, establishing that his concern with structures of evil is shaped by the underlying question how a nation steeped in Christianity could be swept away by the destructive ideology of Nazism. The nature of human evil analyzed in *Strukturen des Bösen* attempts to understand how the worst crimes against humanity are done in the name of some of the most cherished ideals of humankind (such as duty, allegiance, obedience). Humans become evil by wanting to be better than they need to be (the woman in Genesis 3 at first repeats God's instruction and taboos the tree) for fear of losing the ground of their existence. This is the lesson of Adam and Eve. Humans become killers by wanting to be better than others after they have lost through fear a sense of absolute justification of their existence. They sacrifice themselves and die unto themselves in the name of religion or of absolute ideals substituted for God. Their sacrificial mentality sooner or later turns into deadly rage against the Other who is perceived as the rival in the search for absolute recognition. This is the lesson of Cain and Abel. This, too, is the lesson of Eichmann and of the millions of dutiful citizens of Nazi Germany who, by simply doing their duty, by following the *Führer* and the leaders of the collectivity, and by repressing the objections of their own conscience, helped create the death camps of the Third Reich.

In *Strukturen des Bösen,* Drewermann shows why moral appeals fell short of being effective in stopping the inhuman horror of the Third Reich. Morality had been put in the service of evil in Nazi Germany. Drewermann proposes to understand moral evil as a secondary symptom of a preceding existential projection (sin) of life in relation to the absolute (God) under the spell of fear. Drewermann's theology of sin does not want to judge but to understand. By understanding the absolute forms of evil of humankind as expressions of compensations for the loss of an absolute person who wills humans absolutely, Drewermann seeks to get at the spiritual root of the problem of human evil. Above all, he sees evil as the result of the reaction-formation of a violent God-image which unconsciously or consciously, in pious or atheistic garb, drives humans to create through their own effort an absolute ground to stand on — by absolutizing the violent God-image of their own projection, by absolutizing themselves, the Other, work, or society — a feat which inevitably alienates them from themselves and from others. In *Strukturen des Bösen,* he alludes to the fact that Christianity itself has fostered, against its best intentions, an ambivalent and violent God-image that supports a sacrificial mentality which, secularized, could easily become harnessed by dictatorial and absolutistic rulers.

Drewermann's focus on the development of a violent God-image serves as a blueprint for all of Drewermann's later interpretations of religious and spiritual texts. *Strukturen des Bösen* shows that an ambivalent, psychically, and ideologically violent God-image is itself the result of the existential fear of humans who lose sight of God against their best intentions. A violent God-image is itself the result of sin, an expression of the loss of trust in the absolute person who wants us and justifies our existence. The exegetical analysis of Genesis 2–11 showed that humans do not intentionally turn their back on God but do so actually in the very attempt to defend God against the distortions of God's image by the serpent. The question of the serpent first evokes the fear of an untrustworthy God. Humans try to deal with that fear on their own and thus end up doing what they actually did not want to do. Their fear becomes all-consuming as they lose sight of the nonambivalent and nonviolent God of Genesis 2. Attempting to recover the lost God, they sacrifice the best of themselves in a deadly competitive strife for God's absolute recognition.

Psychoanalytically, Drewermann employed the development of ambivalent parent images as a *symbol* for the development of a violent God-image. A violent God-image is analogous to the defensive process against fears of separation stirred up by forbidden oral-sadistic and Oedipal impulses, at the end of which the image of God (the parents) has become internalized as deeply ambivalent and has fostered a desire in humans to become psychologically God, that is, completely self-sufficient in oneself (orally) or completely self-sacrificing to divinized successors of parental figures (Oedipally).

Existential-philosophically the violent God-image is seen as the result of a certain way of becoming conscious of oneself. Self-awareness includes recognition of one's nothingness which in turn creates existential fears of ultimate worthlessness, insignificance, and lack of justification. An adversarial and violent God-image emerges when humans battle those fears on their own, that is, when humans through their own desperate efforts try to compensate for and "stop up" the existential "lack" of being, thus absolutizing consciously or unconsciously finite, relative aspects of life such as their work (Cain, Genesis 4:1–16), their aggression (Lamech, Genesis 4:23–4), their sexuality (Gen. 6:1–4), their leaders (Gen. 10) or society (Gen. 11). God then appears as the ultimate competitor who opposes anything humans do or want. A violent God-image that essentially contradicts all human desires and wishes and requires humans to sacrifice themselves or the best of themselves is an expression of the sense that one cannot fill the "lack" of one's existence and that one will be annihilated by the "look" of the wholly Other.

In the theological analysis Drewermann tries to show that the fall from God and the subsequent emergence of the distorted — because violent and ambivalent — God-image, is not necessary, although the immanent perspectives of psychology and philosophy must suggest so. These perspectives are indispensable for an understanding of the concrete existential and psychological effects of the fall. There is, Drewermann argues, however, a different way of responding to the fear which nothingness stirs in us: allowing absolute fear to be calmed by an absolute person.

Chapter 2

War, Christianity, and the Destruction of Inner and Outer Nature: Effects of a Violent God-Image

Fear, Trust, and the Importance of Psychic Images

Several ideas of *Strukturen des Bösen* explicated in the previous chapter weave like a thread through Drewermann's later works and are highlighted below as preparation for his treatment of the problem of war as an outgrowth of fear.

First to note is the importance to Drewermann of the radical alternative between fear and trust. The analysis of the Yahwist's primordial history established theologically that fear of separation from God in the face of nothingness leads to sin, that is, loss of sight of God. Sin results not from the temptation of the passions of human nature but from the fear of the human spirit. This important correction of traditional Christian interpretations of sin has far-reaching implications which Drewermann outlines in his critique of Christianity's traditional repressive stance toward matters involving sexuality and its ecologically devastating devaluation of nature (Drewermann 1991e). Sin as the result of the human spirit's fear is at the root of all human evil. Sin as freedom's liquidation of itself leads even-

---

1. Drewermann placed this statement as an epigraph above the introduction of *Die Spirale der Angst* (The spiral of anxiety) (1992a, 15). A paraphrased version appears in his autobiographical essay *Was ich denke* (What I think) (1994a, 32), reading "No Christianity has existed in the West, otherwise it would not constantly have been the source of wars."

tually to the liquidation of the Other. Sin is the fearful attempt to create through one's own finite and best efforts an infinite foundation for oneself, that is, the attempt to be like God. Under the spell of fear the best intentions and the most moral efforts to create good become subject to the counter-finality of aim and result. The alternative to getting caught up in the spell of fear is an experience of trust that, despite the experience of one's nothingness, one's existence has an infinite foundation. Faith is confidence in oneself based on trust in an absolute person who calms the absolute fear of the human spirit by letting it feel that its existence is absolutely willed and justified.

Drewermann distinguishes between three levels of fear: biological, psychosocial, and spiritual (existential) (Drewermann 1986b, XVIII–XX; Drewermann 1993a, 309–84). Humans share biologically grounded fears (Bilz's "primordial fears") with other animals. These fears are responses to situational dangers such as starving to death, being ostracized (guilty) and punished, being trapped, or being segregated (abandoned). The reflective capacity of human consciousness is able to isolate these fears from their immediate situational context and transform them into psychosocial fears present even when there are no real external danger situations. Psychosocially, fear emerges not only in response to an external danger situation (Freud's "realistic anxiety") but in response to internally perceived dangers (from the drives or the superego) based on past experiences of danger (Freud's "neurotic" and "moral anxiety") (see Freud 1933, 78). The evolutionary fears of being segregated and punished, for instance, are psychologically transformed into the psychosocial fear of "the loss of object," that is, initially of the mother (see Freud 1926, 136–39); they evoke in the course of the four classic psychoanalytic phases of drive development (schizoid, oral, anal, Oedipal) various "fear-based" character adaptations (character structures) aimed at avoiding the internally perceived danger (Drewermann 1993a, 321). Human existence is, however, characterized not only by biological and psychosocial needs and dangers but — and here religion proper enters the picture — by spiritual needs and dangers. The situational fear an animal experiences and the psychosocial fear humans experience in relation to other humans expand spiritually into more fundamental fears characterizing human existence as such. The self-reflective nature of the human spirit turns the primordial fear of starving to death and the psychosocial fear of not having one's oral needs met by another human being into an infinite "hunger for life which can basically never be stopped up — especially in the face of the certainty of death" (Drewermann 1986b, XIX; cf. 258) — and which corresponds to Kierkegaard's "despair of infinity." The fear of being trapped by an enemy and the corresponding psychosocial fear of losing the battle of wills during the anal stage, especially in regard to the "first possession," is transformed into absolute fear due to the awareness that ultimately our will is impotent in the face of death, a fear which evokes "an infinitely heightened desire for possessions...and self-control" and corresponds to Kierkegaard's "despair of necessity." The fear of loneliness (segregation) and the corresponding psychosocial fear of Oedipal loss of love in the form of castration anxiety is transformed into a fear that one's existence is not absolutely recognized, evoking the "principally unfulfillable" Oedipal striving "to find somewhere an absolutely necessary degree of security, hold, justification, and recognition from another [human] person" (Drewermann 1986b, XIX; cf. 310–24). This corresponds to Kierkegaard's "despair of possibility." The spiritual dimension of fear is an expression of the fact that the "human being is the only living being which has and must have questions that cannot be answered by biological means" (ibid., XIX). While situational fears of hunger, loneliness, illness or premature death can be — and have been to a certain degree — solved through technological and civilized improvements of the biological and social environment, humans have at the same time become more and more aware that "one day they have to die; as much as they may fight against the poverty of existence and against the fear of being alone, one day they will be utterly poor and all alone" (ibid., XVIII). By reducing situational fears the self-reflective human spirit becomes increasingly aware "that all individual situations of fear are only representations of basic threats which belong to created existence itself and which can by no means be gotten rid off" (ibid.). The human spirit infinitizes all biological and psychosocial fears into existential fears of *Dasein* whose absolute nature require nothing less than an absolute answer. The spiritual dimension of fear is responsible for the fact that the "advances of human civilization in no way represent a solution to the central problem of anxiety. They are unable to remove the danger of transforming the best and most noble cultural achievements of humanity in a heartbeat of fear into instruments of barbarous destruction" (Drewermann 1986b, XVIII). To use biological, that is, material, technological means to answer the absolute fear of the human spirit is simply inadequate. A person, "far from mastering anxiety in that way, to the contrary will increase her own instinctual needs beyond all limits, will drive [*peitscht*] by means of the boundlessness of her spirit, of the fear generated in consciousness, her instinctual wishes into immeasurable proportions — thus ruining herself and the Other through overexertion" (ibid., XX).

In addition to the basic alternative between fear and trust and the three-dimensional perspective of human existence and fear, Drewermann stresses the importance of psychic images that give concrete expression to human longings as the necessary language of religious/spiritual beliefs. Psychic images, too, correspond to the three dimensions of human existence (Drewermann 1993a, 269–308). They are understood by Drewermann first as expressions of archetypal scenes developed in our evolutionary past in response to the experience of primordial fears and needs. Psychosocially, they become affective symbols for the psychodynamic interaction among humans. In terms of the absolute longings of the human spirit, psychic images become symbols for the infinite. Because biological and psychosocial fears are infinitely magnified by the human spirit's absolute fear in the face of its own nothingness, humans need images that, rooted in the affective evolutionary heritage and the psychosocial matrix of significance, can open up existence experientially toward the infinite. On the spiritual level, psychic images become symbols that connect finitude with infinity. Without the integration of psychic images, religion becomes empty and rationalistically one-sided — a theory Drewermann elaborates in his analysis of Christianity's inadvertent contribution to war. Mythic imagery provides the language necessary to heal the whole human person, from deep down in her evolutionary, affective roots to high up in the heights of the spiritual fears of her reason. But — and here we return to the alternative between fear and trust — whether the human spirit experiences psychic imagery as calming fears or as further increasing fears depends on whether the images of the collective unconscious can be integrated with the historical individual's ego. Whether the historical ego of a person is drowned or controlled by the collective images or is strengthened and built up by these images depends on whether or not they are experienced vis-à-vis an absolute person in whose presence they become symbols for one's absolute worth. Drewermann finds this spiritual dynamic symbolically expressed *par excellence* in the gospel story of Peter (the historical ego) who is able to walk on water (the unconscious) as long as he looks at the person (Jesus, God) coming from the other shore (the infinite) but who begins to drown as soon as he loses sight of the person he can absolutely trust (Matt. 14:22–32) (1985b, 29–31).

Fear, War, and God

In a certain sense we Germans owe history reparation: "We were the ones," we should say, "from whose territory the worst war originated which humankind has ever waged. We have systematically and intentionally committed atrocities.... We Germans therefore consider it today, at a time when history is beginning to take the debt of fascism from our shoulders, as our honor and task to voluntarily give up all military power and to devote all our power, one third of our gross national product, to fight hunger and misery." It would be the first time in history that a generation of youth would grow up which could escape from the stone-age logic of violence and counter-violence, of armament and war. It would mean morally in the world a huge step forward.   —Drewermann, *Die Spirale der Angst*[2]

In the 1982 publication of *Der Krieg und das Christentum* (War and Christianity), reissued in paperback as *Die Spirale der Angst* (The Spiral of Anxiety), Drewermann (1992a) analyzed the role of fear as motivator for war and the question why the most extreme means of human aggression, such as the atom bomb or the Nazi extermination camps, originated in the Christian West. Drawing on historical, ethological, paleoanthropological, sociological, and psychological findings, Drewermann traces the development of war from its earliest roots to its modern face. He reviews moral and religious

---

2. Cf. Drewermann 1995a, 226: "As a reunified Germany we have today a great opportunity to implement what was pledged in 1945: after the most atrocious war of this century we commit ourselves to pay *reparations* to damaged humanity [by fighting hunger and social injustice]. It is *here* where we would have an obligation of 50 billion German marks annually [i.e., the amount Germany actually spends on the military]. They are just as important as the rebuilding of the former East Germany. They would be an important contribution to the debt service which we should accept *morally* in the sense of an expanded responsibility as a nation today."

solutions to the problem of war and advances the argument that Christianity inadvertently promoted war through a moralistic misunderstanding of the Sermon on the Mount. A basic similarity joins his analysis of Genesis 3 and of the problem of war in Christianity for in one as in the other the problems relate psychologically to oral-sadistic and Oedipal dynamics and existentially to longings for the infinite.

At the center of the study stands a comprehensive analysis of the element of fear in the development of war. Drewermann wrote *Die Spirale der Angst* expressly for theological reasons. He holds that without an analysis of human fear all talk of original sin, faith, being good, grace, etc., remains far removed from the true needs of humans and, through moralization, may actually contribute to human misery. Writing in 1982, Drewermann finds it "incomprehensible how theologians generally, with the exception of P. Tillich, cannot or do not want to understand that the entire interpretation of faith removed from the backdrop of fear can be nothing more than moralizing overexertion or boring talk. Only the notion of fear allows us hermeneutically to set against sin not the ethics of virtue but the necessity of faith" (1992a, 205).

In the remainder of this chapter I will explicate Drewermann's analysis of the paleoanthropological, psychological, and spiritual reasons for war; follow him as he considers ethical attempts to solve the problem of war, including a discussion of the Christian just-war doctrine; present his analysis of elements in the Christian religion that tend toward war; portray his discussion of the role of the suppression of women and the role of Oedipal dynamics in the Christian stance toward war, exemplified by a reading of Henrik Ibsen's *Peer Gynt*; and recapture Drewermann's interpretation of elements in Christianity that, if understood deeply enough, could promote a truly peaceful mentality. Where useful, we will supplement the ideas presented in *Die Spirale der Angst* with arguments developed first in his Excursus in the third volume of *Strukturen des Bösen* (1986b, 514–33), which addresses connections between Christianity's hostility to myths, its denominational battles, and the inner disunity of the human type it fostered in Christianity, and with the analysis, developed in depth in *Der tödliche Fortschritt* (Deadly Progress) (1991e), of the Christian underpinnings of the Western exploitation of external nature.

Roots of War—from Struggle for Survival to Fears of the Spirit

> As the likely failure of our training strategy became more apparent in the months ahead, we tilted gradually — almost imperceptibly—toward approving the direct application of U.S. military force. We did so because of our increasing fear — and hindsight makes it clear it was an exaggerated fear — of what would happen if we did not.
>
> —Robert McNamara, *In Retrospect: The Tragedy and Lessons of Vietnam*

Drewermann begins his study of war with a descriptive account of paleoanthropological and psychological research into the origins of war, followed by a discussion of how the unique type of fear that accompanies the emergence of human self-awareness plays an intrinsic part in the belligerent tendency of the human spirit.

Paleoanthropological literature indicates that human evolution went hand in hand with a steady increase of aggressiveness. In an effort to *escape biological death and enhance chances for survival, homo habilis* began about two million years ago to form social groups for the purpose of communal hunting (Drewermann 1992a, 48). While hunting enhanced social interaction and promoted the ascent of humankind, it also increased intraspecies aggression which found expression in cannibalism and in the hunting of humans (war). "The hunting and eating of animals went hand in hand with the hunting of humans and cannibalism" (ibid., 50). Cannibalism was practiced as early as 300,000 years ago by *Pithecantropus pekinensis,* the Peking human (ibid., 51). As cannibalism became ritualized, it functioned to channel aggressive impulses within the in-group into "socially binding" rituals (ibid., 53). While raw aggressive drives were thus deprived of their socially destructive power within the in-group, they were redirected in form of war against the out-group, thus gaining through their social organization an effectiveness and strength which they never possessed in their " 'wild' state: war—cannibalism as ritualized aggression—is far worse and dangerous than the aggression of a beast of prey" (ibid., 53). A common idea associated with cannibalism, especially of enemies highly esteemed and honored for their strength, was that by eating their flesh and drinking their blood one could become like them. Drewermann believes that this is perhaps the only "ritual idea" which, in its symbolic form, has the "religious power" that could "overcome the problem of war at its root" (ibid., 54, see 290–300).

Why cannibalism disappeared is not clearly known. It seems that "it was pushed aside as killing during war got out of hand: an enemy may not be venerated nor devoured if one wants to slaughter him *en masse*. The honor which cannibalism gave to the killed person becomes superfluous through the praise the conqueror and fighter gains by bringing *as many* enemies to death as *possible*. . . . *In that sense* one may even say that cannibalism presumably was and is less atrocious and aggressive than the wars which humans wage against each other without satisfying a (ritual) interest in food" (ibid., 55–56).

Drewermann supplements paleoanthropological findings of the connection between hunting, heightened aggressiveness, cannibalism, and war, with *psychological* reasons for the waging of wars based on studies of ethology and group dynamics. Among them is the primordial "principle of territoriality" (ibid., 57–60) which humans share to some degree with animals. This principle can be defined as the aim of animals or humans to defend a certain territory needed for hunting (food) and for the protection of females and offspring within secured and inviolable borders (sex), thus securing the perpetuation of one's progeny. This is "psychologically" perhaps "the most profound and most original motif for war" (ibid., 57). As humans proliferated in search of ever new territories to secure food and progeny, races[3] began to develop in accordance with the climatic requirements for survival in relatively isolated areas of the globe. What was biologically a useful process of adaptation became psychologically a source of war as soon as different races of the same species would meet again after thousands of years of isolation. "What is foreign, incomprehensible, or at least different, is then experienced as contradicting, dangerous, and hostile, and thus awakes first the inclination for eradication and destruction, or at least the suppression of what is unfamiliar. A human now appears to another human as if something from a foreign species which he can hunt like animals" (ibid., 60).

In addition to the principle of territoriality, three basic laws of group dynamics are listed by Drewermann among the psychological reasons for war, heightened by a fourth law according to which these three laws intensify the more a group feels threatened from within

---

3. Drewermann follows the paleoanthropological definition of race biologically as a (once) isolated "community of procreation [*Fortpflanzungsgemeinschaft*]" (Drewermann 1992a, 58 n. 19).

or from outside (ibid., 60–64; citing especially Hofstätter 1957 and G. C. Homans 1950) — that is, "the greater the *factor of fear* is" (Drewermann 1992a, 63). The first of the three laws of group dynamics says that groups tend to require the convergence of opinions and of behavior and to suppress dissenting views and practices. The second law holds that groups form by binding intraspecies aggression through the establishment of a clear hierarchy and pecking order, with those in the alpha position deciding who is assigned the omega position. The third law consists in the fact that any group defines itself through a common enemy to be fought together. The common enemy may be experienced as external to the group as well as within the group, either as those who may threaten the status quo or as those who are assigned "the role of the collective scapegoat" in relation to whom the group acts out all those aggressions which it is yet unable to turn against the external enemy. "The suppression of the omegas — particularly horrible, for instance, of Jews during the Third Reich — functions then as a sort of internal substitute war for the destruction actually intended for the enemy, for instance, Soviet Russia. The absurd association in Nazi propaganda of international Judaism with bolshevism, for instance, had to do with this association of the omega position with the enemy image" (ibid., 63). Punishment of dissidents, hierarchical structure, and aggression against commonly defined enemies increase the more a group feels threatened from within or from outside. The result is frequently the emergence of a dictatorship in which the group rallies around a "strong leader [*Führer*]." Drewermann emphasizes that dictatorship should not be seen as the result of war but rather as a result of the dynamic of fear. "When a people produces or accepts a dictator, it does so usually because it already is in a state of fear. Dictators come to power and stay in power due to fear. We would confuse cause with effect if we considered the political form of dictatorship — because of the fear it spreads — *a priori* as belligerent. Dictatorship *comes into existence* rather through an exacerbation of the laws of group dynamics by the factor of fear. Fear mobilizes aggressive forces for a defense of a possible danger — dictatorship is merely its tool" (ibid., 64). Based on the fact that the life of early human groups was characterized by a radical struggle for survival, Drewermann suggests that we cannot overestimate the factor of fear as a cause for war and for the attempt at the eradication of the Other (ibid.).

While roots of war can be found in the struggle for survival of early humans, shaped by fears of biological death as well as by psychosocial fears related to the protection of offspring and to laws of group dynamics, Drewermann proposes that the distinguishing *human* characteristic of the phenomenon of war cannot be understood fully either by biological or psychosocial models or by related economic models. A key element that distinguishes humans from animals is that the human being "is the only being which, based on its intelligence, could learn that a conflict can be solved *permanently* if one kills the enemy" (ibid., 74). Drewermann sees this human capacity to seek final solutions, that is, to seek the death of humans that pose or seem to pose a threat to one's existence, as an expression of the unique ability of human consciousness to reflect situational dangers in terms of future recurrences of the same dangers (ibid.). This solution of conflict is the result of the unique *fear of the human spirit*. Referring to R. Bilz's five primordial fears, Drewermann notes that human consciousness has the ability to "perceive the situational fears to which animal life is exposed as fundamental and, in the last instance, unavoidable threats. Fears of hunger, of loneliness, of being exiled from the group, of sickness, of persecution and of death [a footnote refers to Bilz 1971, 427–64], to which animals respond from moment to moment by means of certain emergency reactions [a footnote refers to Cannon 1932], are reflected by human consciousness in such a manner that they press toward a final solution of what, in the end, cannot be avoided. The human being wants to avoid once and forever the dangers which threaten her, although she knows that in the face of death, the epitome of all dangers, there is no escape. In that sense, consciousness does help to overcome certain anxiety situations through action based on foresight, but at the same time it increases the factor of fear, and with it the will for excessive defensive reactions, to infinite proportions" (Drewermann 1992a, 74–75). Killing other humans in battles is thus a function of the illusive aim of reflective consciousness to *prevent* the emergence of all future danger situations. The human spirit has therefore been preoccupied since its dawn with the manufacture of ever better weapons, of instruments for killing aimed at "calming a fear which came into existence with such poignancy only through consciousness. While it is sufficient to an animal to chase away a competing member of the species, a human being has to kill his enemy in order to get rid of him *forever*" (ibid., 75; a footnote refers to Tinbergen 1969). Human intelligence, with its unique capacity for reflection, is thus a two-sided sword. While it has allowed humans to master situational fears through preventive measures, thus giving them a tremendous selective advantage in the course of evolution, it also has been the source of the *absolute* character which human aggression has taken in the course of history. It is the fear of self-reflective human consciousness which spurs humans to disconnect from present feelings of empathy in the name of morality (i.e., of avoiding future suffering) and promotes wars in the name of reason. Reason run mad is the worst threat to humankind.[4] In the following passage, Drewermann succinctly sums up his analysis of such reason under the spell of infinite fears.

On the whole, we are confronted with a quasi-pathological reality. Over the course of millennia the feeling of fear has brought forth and employed human reason as an organ for the avoidance of situations of fear; conversely, human reason has been able to reflect the individual situations of fear into infinite proportions and, at the same time, has taken defensive measures which themselves spread fear to infinite levels. . . . It is a kind of reason which stands under the dictates of fears it has been increasing for millennia under the pretense of eradicating them; such reason can without hesitation be described as ill, as a *pathological* phenomenon: a kind of reason which literally creates ever new suffering and which forces humans to suffer ever more under themselves and the consequences of their actions.

Psychologically and, specifically in its highly technological and ingenious form, war is thus a symptom of the pathology of human reason, and its immanent rationality proves to be thoroughly the thinking of a madman, the logic of pure fear or of a behavior which objectively creates the very threats which it tried to escape due to fear subjectively. . . . Nothing exposes the human being as a sick animal more than the hypertrophy of fear and violence which has gotten out of hand.

We can formulate the diagnosis of the madness of the human psyche also in terms of the physiology of the brain: the cerebrum reflects and operationalizes the programs of the archaic

---

4. In the postmodernism debate, Vattimo (1992, 78, 81) has pointed to the phenomenon of reason turning against itself as a "counter-finality of reason": "the rationalization of the world turns against reason and its ends of perfection and emancipation, and does so not by error, accident, or a chance distortion, but precisely to the extent that it is more and more perfectly accomplished."

brainstem — unchanged since the stone age — in such a way that those programs become utterly crazy.... The age-old programs of evolution are indeed, if not disturbed by fear, actually still infinitely wiser than the conscious thinking and behavior of humans based on the small scope of insight into nature and self. The task is thus not to simply abolish the "old human," but rather to decrease the fear that comes into existence through her reason, distorts the original programs into madness and transforms her in the end into an ill animal. The actual question that needs to be answered if one wants to get rid of the symptoms of human insanity in the form of war is *this:* How could the human being use his reason in such a way that it does not merely become the fear-increasing henchman of archaic fears but that it would be transformed into a true organ for calming fear. (Drewermann 1992a, 103–5).

As evident in the examples from wars presented in Chapter 1, the fear of the human spirit leading reason to go mad does not need to be experienced consciously as the affect of fear. Rather it characterizes a person's or group's *Entwurf* or — to use W. Reich's term as an analog — spiritual "character armor" (Reich 1972; see Drewermann 1990a, 94). Only in light of the peculiar fear of the human spirit which tends to seek absolute answers in the face of the absolute fact of one's future death do several other common features of human conflict and war become intelligible. That positive stereotypes for the in-group and negative stereotypes for the out-group gain absolute character and combine with the belief that the in-group (whether a people, a race, or a religion) is at the center of the world must be attributed to a process of infinitization due to the fear of the human spirit (Drewermann 1992a, 65–74). Drewermann finds the most extreme illustration of this dynamic in the Nazi propaganda slogan "The world shall be cured through German nature [*Am deutschen Wesen soll die Welt genesen*]" (ibid., 66). Drewermann believes that the universal tendency to see the in-group as the center of the world turns historically into "genuine self-centered insanity, an absolute self-arrogance and -overestimation" only if this tendency is combined with a feeling of fear and threat about the group's existence (ibid.). Then a people may, as did "the German people between 1918 and 1945," regress like a neurotic in thinking, feeling, and action to an archaic state that was "thought to have been overcome culturally and psychologically long ago" (ibid.). This very "human" dynamic, Drewermann believes, was at work in extreme form in "the moral monstrosity and inhumanity, for instance, of the Nazi regime": "all fear is ego-centric, and any people in fear circle around themselves like a neurotic" (ibid.).

Wars that spring from religious fanaticism seek to convert or eradicate all pagans or infidels, based partly on the familiar laws of group dynamics, but such wars also receive their absolute character from the absolute fear of the human spirit. We will elaborate Drewermann's analysis of religious and quasi-religious wars further below. Race wars which aim at the subjugation or eradication of other races presuppose a mentality in which the in-group considers anything ethnically or culturally "different...as not 'human'" (ibid., 71–72). Drewermann points out that race wars were preceded in evolution by wars aimed at the "eradication of anything foreign" (ibid., 72), including wars between different hominid species: "30,000 years ago, the species of Cro-Magnon human in particular, whence all modern human races originate, seems to have hunted down the older species of Neanderthal human outright.... The brain of Cro-Magnon human is none other than that of modern humans. It contains the whole range of possibilities, from cave drawings to hydrogen bomb. In it lie, however, also the behavioral schemes which have again and again led to wars and all sorts of monstrous acts" (ibid., 73–74).

Historically, wars have been fought by men, who in turn gained recognition from women for their bravery and their protective acts. Questioning the notion that the rule of women would be more peaceful than the rule of men, Drewermann notes that paleo-anthropologically "the peacefulness of female behavior does not represent a contrast to male aggression but is rather the condition for the latter" (ibid., 78). Females could raise the young in peace only if they felt protected by physically stronger males. As in the biblical song of Lamech (Gen. 4:23–24), men's strength and bravery in battle have from primordial times provided the conditions upon which women based their love. This implies, Drewermann points out (against W. Reich 1970), that two popular notions cannot be maintained: first, the notion that the problem of human aggression could be solved through an increase of "sexual and mating activities"; and secondly, the notion that the reason for an increase of aggression would lie in the culturally conditioned suppression of sexual drives.

In response to the first, Drewermann refers to ethological and historical research showing that in male-female relationships, including those among humans, "sexuality does not overcome or make superfluous aggressiveness, but to the contrary: it outright promotes and rewards aggressive behavior" in that the victorious male traditionally gains (sexual) recognition from females. In response to the second notion, Drewermann argues that sexuality does not necessarily exclude aggressiveness but that, to the contrary, the two can go together, as can be observed in competitive courtship behavior (Drewermann 1992a, 76–82). The all-or-nothing quality that characterizes the human desire for recognition and becomes a key source of wars is, too, fueled by the particular fears of the human spirit longing for absolute recognition.

Drewermann notes a number of other reasons for war related in one way or another to the human spirit's longing for absolute recognition and its corresponding absolute fears. There are wars which seem necessary to preserve one's dignity and self-respect (ibid., 82–86). Drewermann lists a wide range of battles and wars which evidently were fought not necessarily with the intent of victory but more with the goal of preserving or repairing a group's dignity, among them the famous battle at Little Big Horn in 1876, the resistance at Masada, the uprisings in the Warsaw Ghetto and the concentration camp of Treblinka, the Yom-Kippur War, and, as "the most awful example..., undoubtedly World War II. This last war was expressly waged against France and Great Britain in order to undo the shame of Versailles and to make sure that November 1918 would never again be repeated" (ibid., 86). Other wars are waged, especially when a certain cultural era comes to an end and a culture seems hollow and hypocritical (ibid., 87–88). They are provoked not by an external attack on one's dignity but from within by a sense of the meaninglessness of traditional values, of inferiority, and of self-loathing. Drewermann sees the enthusiasm with which World War I was greeted by so many (including his own father) as a case in point.

Another psychological reason for war lies in the fear-based inability to communicate directly and nonsymbolically with the perceived enemy — instead humans tend to communicate symbolically through deterrence and gestures of threats (ibid., 89–91). The specific nature of human self-awareness gives human gestures of threat their unique character: "Belligerent gestures of threat among humans do not then, as they do among animals, serve symbolically to avoid war" (ibid., 91). Rather, the self-reflective ability of human consciousness allows humans to predict that they would be "fair game" if they could not defend themselves. Gestures of threat among humans thus are not simply deterrents but express the notion that "one is determined to go to war and that one will certainly not give in" (ibid., 90). Hence Drewermann agrees with Clausewitz (1989) that "armament is as such preparation for war" (Drewermann 1992a, 90). Since "the arms race has in its rationalized form no longer any symbolic value, the only remaining means for the avoidance of war is to replace armament...with real verbal symbols, that is, to negotiate. That, however, presupposes that one has relinquished one's belligerent intentions, which explains why genuine disarmament and peace negotiations are extremely rare" (ibid., 91). The human spirit's longing to avoid all future threats led to the development of ever more sophisticated weapons culminating in the "total weapon" (ibid., 92–98). Drewermann thus considers the development of the atom bomb, intended as a deterrent to end war *per se,* as particularly tragic evidence for the failure of an ethical solution to the problem of war.

The Confusion of Religion with Ethics

> One would like to think that God is on our side against the terrorists, because the terrorists are wrong and we are in the right, and any deity worth his salt would be able to discern that objective truth. But this is simply good-hearted arrogance cloaked in morality — the same kind of thinking that makes people decide that God created humans in his own image. (See the old *New Yorker* cartoon that shows a giraffe in a field, thinking "And God made giraffe in his own image.")
> — Roger Rosenblatt, *Time* magazine, 17 December 2001

In a review of religious and ethical efforts to solve the problem of war, Drewermann notes that ethical efforts more and more replaced religious attempts because the latter remained largely ineffective. As he explores the reason for the impotence of religions, illustrated by Christianity, Drewermann argues, however, that ethical approaches to the problem of war must eventually fail and that religion holds the key to healing human belligerence *if* only religion would avoid its one-sidedly moralistic and rationalistic stance and if it would withstand the temptation to *sanctify* either war or moralistic pacifism by prescribing what people have to *do* — that is, if religion would aim instead at helping people how to *be* in harmony with themselves, and as a result in harmony with others. To put it differently: if religion would calm the human spirit's absolute fears, then religion would strengthen humans to make truly free decisions based not on reason driven mad by fear, which infinitizes archaic evolutionary programs, but on realistic (not fear-driven) assessments of situations.

Drewermann recounts impressive religious attempts in the Buddhist, Hindu, Christian, and Taoist traditions to prevent outbreaks of war and to establish peace (1992a, 108–32). That review shows, however, that in general as soon as religion tries to secure peace by directly applying its religious truth to the realm of the political and ethical, religion inevitably appears impotent and may be taken advantage of by ruthless political or military leaders (ibid., 123–32). Thus Saint Francis of Assisi was unable to convert the Egyptian Sultan Al Kamil in a failed attempt to make the crusade in 1219 superfluous; Pope Leo I — often regarded as the savior of the Occident for negotiating a crucial retreat with Attila, King of the Huns, in 452 C.E. — did, however, not succeed in averting the looting of Rome in 455 by the Vandals; in recent history the peaceful Buddhist people of Tibet became victims of a well-planned and bloody Chinese invasion.

The apparent "impotence of religion" (ibid., 123) when war is imminent tends to lead religions — though not always — to justify war *ethically* under certain circumstances. Even Mo Ti, founder of the Chinese Mohists whose doctrine is explicitly pacifist, conceded in the fourth century B.C.E. that in a peaceless world war can, under certain circumstances, be *ethically* justifiable (ibid., 134). Drewermann contrasts the actual task of religion with the temptation to displace religion by an ethical perspective. "Instead of overcoming war from within through a reconciliation of the human being with himself and his origin, peace — which is an inner state — now [when religion is displaced by ethics] becomes a duty of moral behavior or a courageous arrangement with nonpeace. The healing of the sickness of the human heart, at which religion aims, is thus transformed into a course of action that suppresses the symptoms, the external expressions of the sickness, especially of war, by external means" (ibid., 134–35). We take note of Drewermann's metaphor, borrowed from the psychoanalytic theory of neurosis, of war as the symptom of an inner conflict whose roots lie in the spiritual character of the individuals of a certain group. Again and again, Drewermann emphasizes that the spiritually relevant "feelings of hurt pride, of a wounded self-image, of boundless longing for dominance, and of male addiction to affirmation are more important and influential than the seemingly 'rational' reasons of the business economy or of political logic" as roots of war (ibid., 157 n. 57). Though Drewermann shows understanding for the fact that leaders of religion again and again have given in to the temptation "to translate the absolute solution of religion into the form of ethical postulates for practical behavior, thus relativizing" religion, he considers the task of religion proper to lie not in the realm of ethics, but in a therapeutic calming of the sickness of the human spirit prior to all expression of that sickness in the form of violence or war (ibid., 132).

> Religion does not answer the question what is to be done or how to behave. It alone wants and can refer to the truth within one's heart. If that reference were followed, the political consequences would certainly be enormous. The whole nature of the state — with its laws and paragraphs, with its internalized violence, with its institutions and guarantees for domination, with its distribution of aggression by means of a sanctified pecking order, with its borders and egotism — would instantly totter. The religious answer would consist in a complete overthrow of the entire behavioral foundation that has thus far determined the historical reasoning of political and government action. Only thus would true peace be possible. But precisely for that reason religious teachings cannot enter the way the state acts. Political reason is not concerned with the truth of being but with immediate results, not with inner harmony with the Tao but with external impact on the mass, not with freedom from the forces of fear but with domination by the means of fear.... it has never been possible in history to change the course of political behavior from within. That fact places the religious teaching of the return to the lost unity with [one's] origin as a goal and task of human existence into the realm of a utopia... and no politician can believe [in a political crisis] that she could responsibly appropriate the utopian solution of the religious path. (ibid., 123–24)

As soon as religion begins to justify war *ethically*, it takes part in the "dilemma of the ethical," namely, that the best ethical intentions will, in the case of war, lead to the opposite of what was intended. The difficulties which "such a displacement of what is religious into what is ethical" create are extraordinary and become more complicated the higher the means and forms of war develop (ibid., 135).

By justifying war, religion inadvertently sanctifies, that is, endows with absolute approving quality, what it otherwise declares as taboo (e.g., "thou shalt not kill"). The tendency to justify war is related, in Christianity, for instance, to the notion of an externally (rationally) understood omnipotent God seen as the author of a certain "natural law" in accord with which humans are expected to live. Within that perspective wars can be justified if humans violate the "divine order." The adolescent Drewermann himself had been thrown into an intense inner struggle during the German rearmament debate in the 1950s in response to his own Roman Catholic Church's official prohibition of conscientious objection in a just-war scenario. This was the first serious conflict Drewermann experienced with the hierarchy of the Catholic Church and deeply shaped his suspicion of moral interpretations of the Christian faith.

Drewermann discusses Christianity's just-war theory as a classic example for justifying *ethically* the religiously unjustifiable (ibid., 135–58). In this theory a war is considered as just and thus justifiable if (1) it is declared by a legal state, (2) fought for a just cause (3) in response to an unjust attack, (4) by means which in themselves do not create injustice and (5) if the war has a certain prospect for success. Drawing on dozens of examples from recent and ancient history, Drewermann refutes the theory of just war by its own method of argumentation, that is, rational argumentation, on all five counts, concluding that it cannot be practically implemented. In short, his objections are: (1) Is there any state that has come into existence by legal means and not by illegal and unjust war — measured in terms of the just-war theory? Why should the war of those oppressed by a legal state be less legitimate or just than wars by sovereign states who historically only represent the result of an identification of might with right? (2) Who decides what is a just cause and what not? Any nation or guerilla group intending to wage war will consider its cause just. No unbiased agency (not even the U.N.) exists which could determine what is just and what not. (3) Preventive war may in some cases be much more effective than defensive war in reducing the number of casualties and the damage inflicted (e.g., the Six Day War of Israel). (4) The just-war theory wanted to justify means which would directly target the aggressor, not the private citizens of the enemy. In modern warfare, however, a major target are the industrial centers of the enemy; thus in effect not only civilians who work in the industrial-military facilities but also women, children, and the elderly who live in the cities are targets. By the same token, the total weapon with its indiscriminate killing of everyone and everything cannot be considered a just means. Escalation tends to totalize wars leading to efforts to inflict any possible damage on the enemy — notwithstanding the means. (5) A successful war today uses weapons which refute the possibility of ethically controlling or humanizing war.

Having refuted the just-war theory, Drewermann turns to the other extreme of moralistically misunderstood religion in which "pacifism, the moral condemnation of war" is absolutized. Based on Max Weber's distinction between an ethics of conviction (*Gesinnungsethik*) and an ethics of responsibility (*Verantwortungsethik*), Drewermann spells out the inevitable dilemma of an ethical approach to the problem of war. While the total weapon means that an ethics of conviction would have to require as moral duty the banning of any war, an ethics of responsibility shows that pacifist inactivity could be morally more questionable than active opposition to an attack.

> Many pacifists who object to military service in countries that permit it may hold the belief that their decision could preserve a status of innocence in the time of war. But they, too, cannot escape from the ethical dilemma of war. It cannot be ethical to simply serve the appeasement of one's conscience in a narcissistic manner. Ethics encompasses, in addition to the honesty of one's motives, also that one has to be responsible for the consequences of one's actions. From a perspective of an ethics of responsibility, giving up one's right to resist militarily would be unacceptable if it opened the door to the cynicism of violence and to expansionist efforts. One cannot responsibly have a good conscience if one's will for peace would from the beginning be accounted for in the plans of an aggressive enemy as "useful idiocy." One simply cannot responsibly hold pacifism, the moral condemnation of war, if that would enable an Adolf Hitler to conquer Europe or the militarism of the Japanese in 1940 to conquer all of East Asia. As long as the demilitarized status of a country continues to be understood as a power vacuum or as invitation for conquest by the neighboring country, no one who has political responsibility can agree with unconditional pacifism...hence ethics is, in the face of a war that it cannot prevent, led into a complete contradiction of itself between conviction and responsibility. (Drewermann 1992a, 160–61)

[T]he more young people ... object to military service the more they force the military today to compensate for the lack of human power and of willingness to enlist by means of an "improvement" of weapon systems. Their [the young people's] rejection of certain weapons usually contributes only to a further mechanization and rationalization of the deadly machinery of war. No single ethical decision exists which would not dialectically contradict itself in the treadmill of war, in the logic of fear, in the escalating interplay of violence and counterviolence. One cannot emphasize enough: war is itself the contradiction of ethics. It is the symptom of a problem whose solution makes ethics necessarily come too late.

It is thus a deceptive path to address the disaster of war by means of emergency measures [e.g., the theory of just war]. Ethics, born from the failure of religion, can through its own failure again and again only point to the necessity of a religious transformation of humans. That in the past such a transformation never did really or completely succeed may in the long run not need to be a reason not to believe in the possibility for such a transformation. At any rate, the current crisis [i.e., the nuclear threat] has never been so great, war has never been so annihilating, and the question of the survival of humankind has never been so total [as today]. (ibid., 171–72)

Human reason, partly motivated by a sense of ethical responsibility to keep casualties of one's own military forces as low as possible, partly motivated to deter the enemy from future attack, has developed ever more efficient and destructive weapons, culminating in nuclear weapons. The development and eventual use of the first total weapon, the atom bomb, represents for Drewermann a haunting illustration of the ethical dilemma in which a merely rational solution of the problem of war gets caught up (ibid., 152–58). Albert Einstein, "a convinced pacifist" (ibid., 152), gave essential moral support for the construction of the atom bomb by the Manhattan Project in an effort to prevent Hitler's regime from developing it first. Ethical responsibility required that the total weapon would get into the hands of the " 'right' side" (ibid., 153). On the other hand, the bomb was created in hope that its existence would once and for all deter people from waging war and that the bomb would never need to be used. The scientists who worked on the project hoped that people would think logically and that the horror the weapon instilled would lead to the abolishing of war in itself. "The most gruesome weapon imaginable thus saw the light of day as a weapon of peace" (ibid.). As soon as the bomb existed, the ethical dilemma intensified: expected to end war *per se,* it was instead immediately launched to end a particular war: World War II (ibid., 154). The reason for the use of the total weapon was in the last instance an ethical one: the United States predicted that conventional weapons could not force Japan into capitulation without an invasion that would kill more than half a million American troops (ibid., 155). Drewermann concludes that within the logic of war "morality and humanism, if they cannot prevent war from the start, are instantly transformed in their function into henchmen of war and contribute step by step to the escalation of the means of war" (ibid., 157). Wars "are not overcome logically but only when humans change in the deep layers of the psyche so far that they do not need war any more" (ibid., 154).

Drewermann attributes the dilemma that ethics "comes too late" to solve the problem of war to the fact that as a product of reflective reason (i.e., of the human spirit) ethics itself is subject to the fears of the human spirit. For Drewermann the root of the problem of war therefore does not lie in what ethically responsible and rationally justifiable *action* is to be taken but in how human beings can stop *being* belligerent. Since the analysis of the paleoanthropological and psychological roots of war showed that war is rooted both in the deepest layers and programs of the archaic evolutionary heritage and in absolute fears of the human spirit, Drewermann's thesis is that the problem of war, that is, of organized violence, requires an answer which is "as archaic as war and as spiritual as peace" (ibid., 283). Behind this statement is the belief that human peace can only be achieved if the fear of the human spirit is calmed and the archaic roots of war can lose their power. Drewermann finds such an answer in the symbols of religion which alone are capable of responding both to the archaic and the spiritual motives of war. Before we follow him into the proposed religious solution of war, we will turn to his psychological and intellectual-historical analysis of the role that Christianity, both in its explicitly religious garb and in the reactive secular movements it spawned, inadvertently played in fueling war.

War and Christianity, Or: Belligerent Consequences
of a Violent God-Image

"Truth and Theology"

To the Editor:

Thomas L. Friedman concludes a July 24 column about the Bush White House missile defense strategy with a statement that the matters under consideration "require honest arguments, not theology."

The Bush administration, we are told, is "theologically obsessed" while Mr. Friedman himself is "not theologically against missile defense, but it has to be judged by what it really is."

The clear presumption that theology is the opposite of honest arguments and more akin to unaccountable obsessions rather than judgment continues The Times's misuse of the term "theology" as it is practiced today. I still have in my files an editorial from Feb. 9, 1982, that described President Ronald Reagan's budget as "a lopsided strategy, rooted in theology alone."

If "fanaticism" is what is intended, then graduate schools of theology are fighting it every day.

—Christopher Morse, *New York Times* 31 July 2001

Drewermann's attitude toward Christianity is ambivalent: on the one hand, Christianity has the potential within its own symbols to foster genuine peace by therapeutically promoting a peaceful human attitude toward life. On the other, in its actual form, Christianity lends itself against its professed will to foster a belligerent rather than a peaceful mentality. This section will explicate Drewermann's critique of the belligerent effects of Christianity as it actually exists.

The dilemma of Christianity's attitude toward war is summed up in Drewermann's assessment that "the cruelty and frequency of wars in the Christian West [are] not a chance event but have to be considered *symptomatic* of the inner sickness of Christianity.... [The] inner inclination toward war in Christianity ... [is] the more surprising and alarming, since in its words Christianity has shown and seems to want to show extraordinary support for peace" (ibid., 181). It is important to keep in mind that Drewermann's charge is not confined to the direct influence of Christianity. Instead he is concerned with the "typical attitude," that is, the dominant human type which Christianity cultivated within its area of influence. This human type subjectively wants peace but objectively makes war. That attitude is not bound to Christian institutions and churches but, Drewermann argues, continues to dominate the once christianized world in secularized form. This attitude is compared with the mentality of a neurotic patient. "If one says that, in the first place, a neurotic, precisely with his subjective good will for peace, provokes again and again the resistances and spitefulness which he tries to avoid at all cost, then one may be justified in reproaching Christianity for embodying and living its truth as yet only to a certain degree in the form of a neurotic distortion" (ibid., 182). Focusing particularly on Western Christianity, he adds: "In fairness one can and should not dispute Western Christianity's subjective *will for peace*. But its *peacefulness* is not credible in the face of its effects in history, beginning with the battle of Constantine at the Milvic Bridge all the way to the prohibition of conscientious objection to war in the declarations of Pope Pius XII in the 1950s" (ibid., 182). In the contradiction between a subjective will for peace and an objective sanctification of war, Drewermann detects a "neurotic reversal of aim and result in Christian peace efforts" (ibid.). This counterfinality between aim and result, which we encountered in Chapter 1 as a result of the fall from God due to the fear of the human spirit, is Drewermann's primary focus as he analyzes Christianity's belligerent effects.

The Main Culprits: Anthropocentrism and Rationalism

What makes Drewermann's thesis particularly controversial is that as a theologian he dares to locate the inadvertent deadly effects of Christianity's attitude in elements of the biblical heritage itself. Drewermann justifies this move by arguing that it would be theologically absurd and "pure docetism" if one denies the human limitations of the Bible. "The Bible, looked at precisely as the Word of God, is not only in each of its parts but also and essentially as a whole a historically conditioned word of humans. Insofar it would be theologically absurd — dogmatically formulated: pure docetism — if one did not from the start count on the fact that the Bible is shaped precisely by those limitations *and one-sided emphases* which characterize the area of its formation" (ibid., 184). The key contributing factors for Christianity's inadvertent belligerence are summed up in two sections of Drewermann's book: "The Anthropocentrism of the Biblical World View and Its Estrangement from External Nature" (ibid., 185–94); "The One-Sided Rationality of the Biblical View of Humans and Its Estrangement from Inner Nature" (ibid., 195–282). The reasons for Christianity's belligerent effects are closely related to the reasons held responsible by Drewermann for the exploitation of external nature in the name of human progress as explicated in *Der tödliche Fortschritt* (Drewermann 1991e). Drewermann first developed his critique of Christianity's anthropocentric, rationalistic, moralistic, and historicist reductions in an important Excursus in the third volume of *Strukturen des Bösen* titled "The Hostility Against Myths in Christianity, the Contentious Battle among Denominations, and the Inner Disunity of Humans" (1986b, 514–33). The ensuing presentation will weave together Drewermann's intellectual-historical analysis in *Die Spirale der Angst* (1992a), *Der tödliche Fortschritt* (1991e), and the Excursus from *Strukturen des Bösen* (1986b).

Drewermann traces the radical anthropocentrism of the Christian worldview back to both Greco-Roman and Hebrew influences, while the one-sided rational attitude is attributed mainly to Greco-Roman rationalism. While Christianity was shaped by these intellectual-historical influences, its unique contributions further radicalized anthropocentrism.

Beginning with Ionian philosophy, Greek philosophers "put in the place of myth logos and in the place of feeling reason" (Drewermann 1991e, 67; cf. Drewermann 1992a, 185, 277–80), which implied an estrangement from *inner* human nature, that is, the myth-creating layers of the human mind. "[S]oon the rationality of thinking destroyed the entire spiritual basis of the old faith in the gods" (Drewermann 1991e, 68). Hand in hand went the Greek partition of human history from mere *external* natural history, thus alienating humans from nature. Human reason became the measure of all things. This one-sidedly rational, anthropocentric viewpoint of the Greeks was adopted by the Romans who combined it with "a tremendous will to rule," thus creating a mentality where "nature as a whole is declared practically to be a mere resource for human goals" (ibid., 69). The one-sided emphasis on rationality estranged humans from both *internal* and *external* nature. Christianity, politically and culturally the heir of the Romans, intensified the Roman anthropocentrism partly because of its roots in the anthropocentric God-image of the Hebrew religion and partly because of its key article of faith: namely, that "God had become human in Christ" (ibid., 71, 75).

Hebrew Scriptures, on the other hand, set "the relationship between God and humans purely anthropocentrically into the center of its theological reflection" (Drewermann 1992a, 185). "Grown originally from belief in the 'God of the fathers,'" the religion of ancient

Israel centered around the special significance of its own people based on the revelation of its tribal father. "In the center of this religion stood solely the human being and the history of a single people" (Drewermann 1991e, 71). The notion of nature and world in the form of the idea of creation was integrated only hundreds of years after the founding of the religion. "[T]he idea of creation, however, did not actually stem from a deeper experience of the 'world,' but from a claim to faith and power against the gods of Canaan" (ibid., 72). While "the Greeks dissolved the mystery of nature into an abstraction of rationality,... the Hebrews considered the world as a mere manifestation of the power of God" who rules absolutely over it (ibid., 72). But even the manifestation of God in the world was of importance not as such but only in terms of human history. History was the locus of God's revelation. Humans are explicitly created like God in order to "rule" over the earth as God rules over it (Gen. 1: 26–28). Drewermann stresses, however, that the Yahwist's creation account presents a marked exception within the Hebrew Scriptures by describing an original harmony between humans and nature which is destroyed only as a result of human sin (Gen. 2–3). The Yahwist has God place humans into the Garden of Eden not as rulers but as servants of the land (Gen. 2:15) (ibid., 73, 103–10). Drewermann charges Christianity with reading into "the Yahwist texts of the so-called paradise of humankind a fantastical, supernatural past" instead of acknowledging in them the realistic possibility of living "embedded into the cycles of nature" — a view the story of paradise shares with the religion of native American Indians and with other non-Western peoples (ibid., 130). Still, even in Genesis 2 "the relationship of power and will to creation is both from God's perspective and from human perspective principally *external*" (ibid., 73).

The ancient Hebrews, in summation, saw "nature as a kind of enemy which has to subject itself to human (and divine) will" and the ancient Greeks emphasized "nature as an ensemble of rational laws.... [B]oth ideas form the background of the 'Christian' attitude toward nature and, centuries later, their combination will found modern natural science and technology" (ibid., 74).

It is important to note that the " 'Christocentrism' of the New Testament" radicalized rather than decreased Christianity's inherited anthropocentrism (Drewermann 1992a, 185 n. 7). First, the notion that "God had become human in Christ" set humans theologically even more firmly in the center of the world than had been the case either in ancient Judaism or Hellenism. Secondly, the God of Christianity was not only or primarily concerned with the fate of a people, but with "the fate of each individual, just as Christ had been an individual" (Drewermann 1991e, 75). "The conviction of the absolute significance and value of the individual — one of the greatest and most important teachings which Christianity brought with it — was turned nature-philosophically into the idea of God's *providence* [for each individual] even in the natural order, instead of remaining a metaphysical conviction" (ibid., cf. 195). "Christian anthropocentrism eventually went as far as turning the natural order on its head and making the entire fate of nature dependent on humans: because of Adam's sin all creatures supposedly had been punished . . . and would need to be redeemed by humans — entire generations of theologians have toiled to explicate this view as a higher form of justice and wisdom of God. In reality such theorems only demonstrated that one did not know nature and did not want to pay attention to it" (ibid., 75). "Christology in its current form contributes to the fundamental confusion of an objective view of nature with existential statements from which it draws nature-philosophical conclusions" (Drewermann 1992a, 185 n. 7).

The historically and radically anthropocentric worldview of Christianity had devastating effects both in the treatment of nonhuman nature and of fellow humans, effects which Drewermann sees intricately related psychologically. The anthropocentrism of the biblical heritage fostered an attitude of fear, violence, and exploitation toward external nature, so, for example, the customary inhumane treatment of animals in the Western world. Mindful of the origins of war in the hunting of animals, he sees a link between the technologically adept mass slaughterings [*Schlachten*] of higher mammals in the West and the cold-blooded, highly technological methods developed for the battling [*Schlachten*] of fellow humans in war.[5] "For metaphysical or ethical reasons one may consider the difference between humans and animals as marked as one wants — killing a higher animal such as a dog or a monkey is for a sensitive human being *emotionally* not far removed from the killing of a human being. The experience of resistance and pain, the revolt and the twitching of the warm body, the view of blood and torn-up flesh, the bursting

---

5. See Charles Patterson, *Eternal Treblinka* (2002), who relates the technologically removed attitude with which Nazis slaughtered millions of Jews and other minorities to the mentality at work in the inhumane treatment of animals in the mass slaughter houses of modern civilization.

of the inner organs, the imploring cries of pain and of the struggle with death — all that is, just as physical death itself, the same in humans and animals" (Drewermann 1992a, 187–88). There exists an "archaic...identity, not a difference, between humans and animals. And the suffering and pain one feels entitled to inflict upon animals will soon be inflicted upon humans as well" (ibid., 188). He concludes, the "way a religion thinks about the treatment of animals by humans is the best criterion to assess its humanity [Menschlichkeit]" (ibid., 191).

While Drewermann notes that Christianity's attitude toward external nature has been particularly violent due to its radicalized anthropocentrism, he sees a generally estranged and violent attitude toward external nature at play in the other two biblical religions, Judaism and Islam, as well (ibid., 189–90). In biblical religions everything — including God — centers ultimately around humans. It is the alienation from nature in Christianity which is "one of the main reasons for the inner inability for peace; the violence against nature is in a sense only the external side of the violence against oneself" (ibid., 185). Directly linked to the hostility against inner and outer nature on the one hand and hostility against humans on the other is, for instance, the fact that "the eradication of nature by means of our Western Christian civilization especially in our [twentieth] century means that peoples who live in harmony with nature [Naturvölker] are without exception irreversibly wiped out as well" (ibid., 191).

Hostility Toward Myths, the War on Nature, Atheism, and the Secularizing Effects of Christianity

The consequences for the God-image of Christianity's anthropocentric and rationalistic bias were far-reaching: God and religion were seen as radical contrasts to human nature, that is, to the human drives and to the imagery of the human psyche. Already Greek rationality and Hebrew belief in God as absolute over nature went hand in hand with extreme efforts "to overcome the world of myths" (Drewermann 1991e, 72). In an epilogue to the third edition of Der tödliche Fortschritt, Drewermann points to the paradox that Christianity, on the one hand, adopted from the heritage of Mediterranean religions and cults a number of mythical, archetypal ideas such as the notion of the God-human or of the pre-existing Son of Man; on the other, it sought to distance itself from pagan mythology precisely because of this resemblance (ibid., 200–1). Drewermann here refers back to the

Excursus from volume three of *Strukturen des Bösen* (1986b, 514–33), where he relates the inadvertent violent effects of Christianity to developments in the Early Church's struggle for survival during which it pitted the reality of its own religious truth against other religions by historicizing and externalizing its own symbolism. He traces the connection of Christianity's violent effects with a certain *view of reality*. This analysis is a central element of the debate that eventually led to his silencing by the Roman Catholic Church: the debate around the nature of the historical reality of Christian symbolism.

In the Excursus, Drewermann traces Christianity's demonizing of the drives of the human psyche to its hostility toward myth. Early Christian apologists such as Origen, Minucius Felix, Justin, Firmicus Maternus, and Cyprian, were faced with two main objections from Greco-Roman critics of the Christian religion: first, Christianity itself is a mythology along the lines of divine sons who are conceived by virgins, who effect miracles and preach, and who die a humiliating death but who survive; secondly, Christianity is superstitious by believing that humans compared with plants and animals have a special place in nature because of a father in heaven who designed natural laws in favor of humans. "Then, in short, Christianity would be either ancient mythology or absurd theology" (ibid., 515). In response to the critics' attacks, Christian apologists tried to prove that the "mythology" of Christianity was something utterly new and unique and that its "theology" was not absurd but contained ideas that had already been divined by pagan philosophers.

Against pagan myths, the apologists argued *theoretically* — in agreement with enlightened Greek philosophy — that myths are simply unscientific ways of describing nature and *ethically* that myths contained projections of drive-based human longings, especially of hunger and love, which only idolized natural, material needs and led to practical hedonism (ibid., 516–17). What made Christianity new and unique, the apologists countered, was "precisely that it did not reduce humans to the metabolic exchange with nature, but that it declared the relationship to God as the essential element in humans. From there it provided the basis for the personhood and the freedom of humans over and against nature by taking away the terror of death and suffering in external nature through the promise of eternal life in Christ and by making possible the superiority of humans over the omnipotence of drives, the rule over their inner nature through its high moral demands" (ibid., 517).

But still, the early Christian apologists could not overlook the fact that their teachings about Christ strikingly resembled stories in pagan myths (e.g., Hermes as word of God, Perseus' birth from a virgin, Asclepius resurrecting the dead and healing the sick). A kernel of truth had to exist in pagan myth, since they contained the same motifs contentwise as did Christianity (death and resurrection, virgin birth, miraculous healer, etc.). However, it was "essential that myths could not now, as the philosophical ideas of the pagans had been, be understood [by the Early Church] as 'seeds of truth,' but that they were condemned as distorted images of the truth," as the work of demons who wanted to mislead humans (ibid., 518–19). The Early Church Fathers solved the dilemma of the resemblance of the key motifs of its religion to those of the surrounding religions not by throwing out the mythical motifs it shared with them but by declaring the other religions to be based simply on *fantasy* while its own version of the common motifs was defended as *historically* real, as something that had in Christ actually happened. "Historicity [*Geschichtlichkeit*]" became the criterion of religious truth (ibid., 522–23).

While early Christianity did not deny that the abstractly defined God of Plato and the God of Justin were identical, it *consciously* broke completely with concrete pagan, mythical ideas by emphasizing the "historical singularity and uniqueness of Christ," an idea that forbade them to see "in him *only an image* of the truth which could be applied in similar manner to the dying and resurrected Osiris, Adonis, or Attis" (ibid., 518–19). "The extraordinary spiritual [*geistige*] energy which was set free through this break with pagan mythology soon revealed itself in the *discovery of personhood* [*Personalität*]. The entire first five centuries appear intellectual-historically as a single conceptual struggle to distinguish nature and person in humans and in God" (ibid., 519). It is in terms of this discovery of human personhood that Drewermann — who otherwise has been a fierce critic of the Christian hostility against the drives, the body, sexuality, and the world — acknowledges the central achievement of Christianity:

One may reproach Christianity for whatever reason one may want to in terms of hostility toward the drives and the body, suppression of sexuality and contempt for the world; it is certain that the development of human personhood, the differentiation [*Herauslösung*] of individual consciousness from the collective psyche of the unconscious, the id, was possible only due to considerable restrictions and renunciations of drives. The spiritual prerequisite for that consisted, however, precisely in the circumstance that the contents of myths, the wish dreams of the collective human psyche were once and for all connected with the historical fate of an individual person, with Jesus of Nazareth. Because that was the scandal: in cult and rite *not* to dive back into the zones of the mass psyche, but to identify oneself as an individual with the individual fate of Christ and to find therein one's own personhood. This experience of finding oneself both in a psychological and in an existential sense through belief in Christ was so powerful that it could not be shaken by the threats of the persecutions. (ibid., 519–20)

The discovery of individual personhood "which contained *in nuce* all the cultural values that were later created and formed in the Occident" was, however, bought at a high price, because it contained "two extraordinary destructive elements" (ibid., 520). The first element we already mentioned: by attributing *metaphysically* a unique position to humans in the world, the early Christian Fathers asserted more or less that humans are the center of creation, even in the sense of *natural science* (ibid.).

Drewermann argues that this early Christian identification of metaphysical and natural uniqueness of humans inadvertently became one of the central reasons for the emergence of modern atheism (ibid., 521; cf. Drewermann 1991e, 100, 127–28): while Christianity had no difficulty agreeing with Greco-Roman notions of God and of immortality, it had to reject the Greco-Roman theories that indicated that humans did not have any special position as natural beings. With the rise of modern natural science, the identification of metaphysical and natural uniqueness led Christianity, without success, to try to deny the progressive insights of the natural sciences or to interpret them within its old worldview (Drewermann 1986b, 521; cf. Drewermann 1991e, 76–78). "The anthropocentric worldview of Christianity which actually was supposed to serve only the purpose of securing the freedom and dignity of the human person in relation to nature ended up as a theorem that eventually had to turn against the reason and dignity of the natural scientist" (Drewermann 1986b, 521). Because modern science soon showed that nature does not take any special account of humans, the notion of a God who had created the world "merely according to the needs and purposes of *human* reason" became increasingly questionable. The anthropocentric worldview of Christianity thus became a key argument for modern atheism, especially in the debates around theodicy (ibid.).

The other element which was part of the process of the discovery of personhood through Christianity was the contradictory rejection of pagan myths (ibid.). This, Drewermann argues, had far-reaching consequences for the way Christianity related to the "irrational" parts of the human psyche, to the unconscious. By demonizing the mythical ideas of the pagan world precisely because of their evident similarity to the doctrine of Christ, the apologists — without actually intending to do so — introduced a deep skepticism against the emotional dispositions of the human soul. "The world of dreams, of longings, of feelings and sensations should henceforth not serve the search for and acceptance of divine truths — rather they had to be suppressed as something hostile to Christianity, because they were competing with it in the form of myth; only philosophically trained *reason* and morally practiced *will* seemed to have prepared for belief in Christ in the pagan world" (ibid., 521).

"In a certain sense one can risk the thesis that the destruction of nature through Western technology was only the externalization of the inner devastation of the Western, Christian human. Because the successful decomposition of pagan myth through Christianity had both effects and called up both in dialectical exchange: it isolated humans from external nature and at the same time cut them off from their inner nature" (Drewermann 1991e, 139). The neurotic self-torture of the overtaxed and narrowly ideological confined Western human was acted out in form of the bizarre treatment of external nature (ibid., 140).

While the Christian discovery of personhood accomplished in terms of the history of religion the all-important step of "removing all arbitrary, demonic traits from the pagan ideas of God," this "spiritualization of the God-image" went unfortunately hand in hand with a *"denial of the unconscious in humans"* (ibid., 135). Lifting the God-image out of the ambivalent imagery of the unconscious led Christianity to the rash conclusion that "in humans, too, consciousness was what is really human" (ibid.). Christianity thus alienated humans from the unconscious layers of the human psyche which are the source of the powerful affective imagery it shares with other religions and which are in that sense truly universal. The consequence of this alienation for the God-image was disastrous: "The human psyche thus had to be *ipso facto* devalued as a hoard of untruth while the inevitable logic of this position had to make the contents of faith appear as something merely imposed from the outside; thus the truth of God became something external, something alien to humans for which no *model* [Vor*bild*] or *preparation* [Vor*bereitung*] existed in the human psyche. What was believed to be true for reason — that it contained certain innate ideas enabling it to think God — was not held to be true for human feeling" (Drewermann 1986b, 523–24).

The presence of vitally affective images in its own doctrines was seen by Christianity not as an opportunity to ground the Christian faith in the human psyche. Rather, Christianity for centuries tried to do the impossible: to explain by means of *reason* the irrational imagery (that God becomes human through a virgin birth, performs miracles, dies, is resurrected and ascends to heaven) and to make people accept as a divine mystery through an act of *will* whatever cannot be understood by reason (ibid., 522–23; Drewermann 1991e, 134–35). The Enlightenment and modern science dealt serious blows to Christianity by showing on the one hand that the irrational imagery of Christianity did indeed not derive from reason but that they were *only* "truths of the emotion" (ibid., 135, a note refers to Feuerbach 1967); on the other, that accepting as true by a mere voluntaristic act whatever could not be explained by reason would not only be against the principle of natural science but also unacceptable to an autonomous, free human person. Thus the one-sided emphasis on reason and will in Christianity sooner or later was turned against Christianity itself. Now Christianity was denounced — as it once did with pagan myth — as a mere projection of emotions, not fostering but threatening the very human personhood it officially propagated. The externally and rationally conceived divine will of Christianity could now easily be substituted by other external and rationally conceived categories such as, for instance, the category of "human society" in Marxism (ibid.).

The rediscovery and re-appreciation of the unconscious, image-creating layers of the human psyche was characteristically accomplished in opposition to Christianity and also used as an argument for atheism (in the Darwinian School, Freud's psychoanalysis) (Drewermann 1986b, 521; Drewermann 1991e, 134–35). Christianity objected particularly to the notion that not only the human body but also the *human soul* shared a common evolutionary past with other animals. Here the fact that Christianity spread false ideas about *external* nature and that it denied the unconscious *internal* nature of humans converge: "because recognizing the unconscious in humans would be the logical consequence of recognizing the evolutionary unity of humans with surrounding creation" (ibid., 136).

In his analysis of Christian notions that promoted the destruction of nature, Drewermann does not stop at Christianity's direct influence by shaping the worldview of its believers. We saw that Drewermann shows how Christian anthropocentrism and its one-sided emphasis on rationality provided the tool for modern atheism to refute the very notions of God which these ideas originally supported. Drewermann considers the *secularized* remnants of Christian anthropocentrism and rationalism in today's Western culture, particularly "the dominant notion of science, which originates in Christianity," the most serious liability of the Christian heritage as they perpetuate a war against nature (ibid., 136).

In terms of the psychological view of humans, for instance, Christian one-sided rationalism, with its denial of the unconscious and its declaration of the human psyche as the result of a direct creative act of God,

> reappears on the podiums of the academic chairs of psychology in guise of the absurd *tabula rasa* theory according to which nothing exists in humans than what they adopt from the outside. The great insights of psychoanalysis into the drive-based motivation of human behavior, the wide perspective of the archetypal theory of C. G. Jung, the multitude of analogies and homologies of behavior which ethology more and more brings to our attention — all this is shoved from the table with a stroke of the pen simply because it does not fit into the picture of the rationality of the human psyche. Instead one is concerned to bring proof that the human psyche — if not the creation of God would be at least the product of societal circumstances. Psychoanalysis is thus, if at all, integrated only within the frame of a psychology of learning during early childhood and hence becomes an auxiliary tool to justify the Marxist doctrine that the essence of a human is nothing but the mirror image of the social conditions. (ibid., 137–38)

Inadvertently the Christian doctrine of the creation of the individual human psyche and of its immortality — meant to be the

metaphysical basis for the personhood and freedom of humans —
combined with the anthropocentric emphasis on human history as
the center of reality led to an increasing dependency and unfreedom
of humans and focused the responsibility for behavior away from the
subject to larger societal groups (ibid., 138, 124–28).

Christian anthropocentrism in its secularized form is particularly
pervasive in the Western belligerent attitude toward animals and in
the technological subjugation and exploitation of natural resources.
Two developments came together in the emergence of modern science.
On the one hand, natural science showed with relentless *objectivity*
that humans are made from the same material as all nature and that
in the vast expanses of nature and of space humans are tiny and insignificant. On the other, the anthropocentric attitude of Christianity
remained active and found expression in the *subjective* claim of humans to an absolute claim to power over nature for the sake of the
well-being of humans.

> The discovery of the objective powerlessness and irrelevance of
> humans in nature and the conviction of the subjective special
> role of humans relate to each other as means to ends: while
> dethroning humans objectively, natural science is at the same
> time transformed, through a secularized Christianity's assertion
> to rule, into an instrument of power by means of which one
> can restore the lost priority in nature, or actually claim it really
> for the first time. After the religious foundations of Christian
> anthropocentrism have been destroyed due to [its] absurd nat-
> ural philosophy, all that is left is a mentality of entitlement
> which lets Christian hope for the future descend to desirabilities
> of technological feasibilities and thus lets human expectations
> expand to the level of the completely absurd. Painlessness, en-
> during health, and the almost endless prolongation of life now
> become goals for which no price is too high to pay. And since
> even the best technology cannot completely abolish but only
> displace the suffering with which religion once tried to reconcile
> us, the human portion of the burden of life henceforth has to
> be pushed as much as possible upon nature and especially upon
> animals. Nature as a whole must now be transformed into a
> mega-prosthesis, into a sanatorium for a humanity free as much
> as possible from suffering. (ibid., 79–80; cf. 197–99)

Modern humanism secularized the Christian anthropocentric morality and redirected "love of God" to "love of humans" (1991e, 197). The anthropocentrism of the Christian heritage in Western culture turned the most basic processes of nature such as death and pain into declared enemies of humans. Instead of helping people learn to live with death and suffering, the quest of medical science to overcome or avoid both is done at the expense of virtually any other 'part' of nature. With the exception of Schopenhauer (expressively in opposition to the Judeo-Christian heritage) and Schweitzer, compassion [*Mitleid*] was essentially confined to humans in the Judeo-Christian tradition (ibid., 99–102).

The already mentioned reduction of religion to morality in Christianity is effective in secularized form in the modern tendency to elevate morality to the status of a religion. The "morality of the common good" or a rationally deduced moral law substituted for "God" (ibid., 143). Continuing the anthropocentric focus, humanistic morality centers around humans and perpetuates and even worsens the war against nature because in a world without God the immanent needs of humans become infinitized. Drewermann sums up his analysis of the connection between Christianity's unintended contribution to the war on nature and modern suspicion of the God-image:

> In order to comprehend the actual responsibility [*Schuld;* lit., guilt] of Christianity for today's destruction of nature, we cannot stress clearly enough this secular transformation from love of God to love of humans, from belief in providence to the practical atheism of an active humanism. The present book does not assert . . . that Christianity would have actively and willingly called for the destruction of nature and for the exploitative greed of today's consumption-oriented society. . . . Christianity's responsibility for the ecological crisis lies, on the contrary, in the fact that it sublimated and radicalized the anthropocentrism of the Old Testament so much that its ethics of compassion and humanity in the end poisoned the sources of piety and left humans behind in a godless and homeless world without meaning and hold. When it was unable to accept the most simple facts of nature such as sickness, aging, and death as natural facts, Christianity created a mentality which, after the "death" of God due to the despair of a disillusioned compassion, retained the anthropocentric morality of the old religion but rejected its own belief

in God as illusion; [it] then tried to implement its [i.e., Christianity's] promises of salvation by violent means on earth. After Christianity had missed the opportunity to live a fulfilled life with nature in a natural way so that one could accept without objection one's lot of aging, illness, and death, it truly did not come as a surprise that, because of Christian anthropocentrism and Christian compassion [with humans], one began to keep the quantity of suffering which nature had given as its share to the human species away from humans and, if possible, displace it on nonhuman creatures. Today we have not the slightest scruple about the most cruel and mass tortures of animals if the goal is to "save" a single human life. In every single practical case, the human being is the measure of all things. And we comprehend only when it is too late that our own un-nature has turned us into parasites on this planet, although it [i.e., our own un-nature] will, in its final consequence, have to turn against humans themselves after the destruction of all that is nonhuman. . . .

The only escape from this nightmare of the future would be to do away with the excesses of medical care as fast as possible and to learn under the guidance of a kind and wise religion again to live in such a way that the natural realities of aging and dying would lose their terror. Christianity's main responsibility for the current misery lies, among other things, precisely in the fact that it has been unwilling and unable to be just that [wise religion]. (ibid., 197–98)

War Against Humans, Religious Fanaticism, the God-Image as Superego, and the Terrorism of "Ethical Optimism"

Psychologically, the harmful effects of Christianity's one-sided rationalism and its estrangement from the nonrational parts of the human psyche have expressed themselves most poignantly in its repressive, moralistic attitude against the human drives. In terms of the problem of war, Drewermann argues depth-psychologically that by repressing and moralizing the instincts, especially the aggressive instinct, Christianity, despite all its good intentions, actually

increased the field of fear and of guilt feelings by means of which the large portion of aggressive drive components are fed. Peace must turn under such circumstances into a *fata morgana*: it gets farther out of reach the more one believes that one is in reach of it by means of desertlike moralistic asceticism and by purely rational attempts at a solution.

This can be shown in both great areas of drives, those dealing with human aggression and with human sexuality. The gap between the raw aggressiveness of the Old Testament and the demands of the Sermon on the Mount is particularly notable and, in terms of the history of religions, makes the split in Christianity between instinctual suppression and fanatic sadism understandable. (Drewermann 1992a, 197–98)

Drewermann argues that while the Hebrew Scriptures, drawing on common traits of ancient Semitic[6] tribes (i.e., Babylonians, Assyrians, Hebrews, etc.), contain many openly belligerent passages sanctioning holy war against other peoples,[7] Christianity by attempting to avoid external violence through the inner violence of moralism has made war on the inner nature of humans: it has demonized the unconscious layers of the psyche, the drives and the psychic imagery related to them, and has idealized reason and will. Christianity thus inadvertently created a human type whose pent-up aggression would erupt with explosive power, take reason gone mad with spiritual fear into its services, and thus spread more harm than raw unrepressed aggression could ever have done. It thus created in effect a religion dominated by a rigid superego and a spell of fierce moral perfectionism with all its concomitant hypocrisies and defensive reaction-formations.

---

6. The term "Semitic" is here used in its wider historical meaning encompassing any group of ancient people that spoke a Semitic language (Drewermann 1992a, 27, 198). For an attack against Drewermann by Klaus Berger, a German New Testament scholar skeptical of depth psychology and of Drewermann's critique of aspects of the Judeo-Christian tradition, see Berger 1996 which reads antisemitism into Drewermann's work with the obvious intent to discredit "the most popular and widely dearly loved German theologian" (Berger 1996); for Drewermann's forceful reply refuting the charge of antisemitism, see Drewermann 1996c. See also Chapter 3 on Drewermann's discussion of the roots of Christian antisemitism due to an external-historical rather than a typological (internal, depth-psychological) reading of the role the gospels assign to certain ancient Jewish groups in Jesus' death.

7. Among the cruel, belligerent passages from the Bible which Drewermann cites in the text are Psalm 144:1; 137:9; 58:9.11; 110:1, 6. In footnotes, he points to biblical passages that call explicitly for genocide in the name of God, among them Deuteronomy 20:13–18; Joshua 8:22ff, 10:28, 31; 1 Samuel 15:3 (Drewermann 1992a, 198–201). Even passages which are traditionally cited in support of a pacifist tradition in the Hebrew Scriptures (e.g., Isaiah 2:4 or Psalm 46) do not speak of peace *per se* but of a peace in which the God of *one* people is *victorious over* "all pagan gods and their people" (ibid., 199).

The responsibility for the belligerent effects of Christianity lies, according to Drewermann, in a unique *combination* of the theologically based, anthropocentric, aggressive attitude toward (external) nature inherited from the Hebrew Scriptures, the one-sided emphasis on rationality inherited from Greek and Roman philosophy, and the radicalization of theological anthropocentrism in the Christocentrism of the New Testament. All three elements culminate in an idealistic and moralistic interpretation of the Sermon on the Mount in the service of a radical suppression of aggressive and sexual instincts and "a kind of despite-implementation by means of violence of what had been inhibited" (ibid., 198).

L. Tolstoy's pacifism serves Drewermann as a tragic example of a life where the subjective will to follow the Sermon on the Mount resulted in the opposite of peace (ibid., 219–22). For Drewermann, Tolstoy's pacifism was based on a melancholic fear of death and a rigid repression of sexuality and aggression in later life. While Tolstoy consciously loved peace, he in effect cultivated in himself an "aggressive attitude" by repressing his aggressions, thus heightening the aggression of his superego which found expression in his aggressive moral perfectionism (ibid., 220–21). Though Tolstoy represents an extreme form of the moralistic attitude of Christianity, Drewermann believes that this superego-based moralistic attitude pervades in more moderate form official Christian theology (ibid., 221). In the Roman Catholic Church he finds this attitude classically expressed in "the great Saint" Ignatius' "inner disunity," characterized by an ascetic "fight against the self," in which "asceticism, the suppression of the self, dominates the ego" and reactively creates "absolutely" fanatic character traits in response to the violent repression rather than integration of the aggressive psychic forces (ibid., 221).

We are already familiar with Drewermann's agreement with both M. Klein and K. Abraham that the earliest roots of guilt feelings providing the basis for superego formation reach back into the first year of life and stem from oral-sadistic conflicts of the infant in relation to the mother (ibid., 306–8). Drewermann points once more to Genesis 3 as a model story representing the oral-sadistic, depressive conflict. He maintains, however, that the oral guilt feeling in relation to the mother can receive a religious meaning of existential depth only because "the individual mother in the biography of the individual is only the first carrier of the *archetype* of the mother by directing the instinctual needs of hold and security, of unconditional acceptance and affirmation upon herself. These needs determine in an absolute sense the foundation of human existence and represent in the life of adults the core of religious longing and promise" (ibid., 307). Drewermann considers it "a psychological necessity of *all* religion that in it the longings of humans for protection, acceptance, and hold, which are experienced psychogenetically first in relation to the mother, are later related in their absoluteness to 'God' " (ibid., 256 n. 64). "The emotional ambivalence the child" experiences in the oral-sadistic stage "anticipates the question which will later accompany life constantly: whether one is able to accept one's existence from ground up despite the torturing shadow of the guilt feeling, whether one can presuppose that one is justified to exist, or whether, to the contrary, one feels deeply rejected and superfluous due to fear" (ibid., 307–8).

In a religious attitude dominated by a superego mentality, the guilt feelings stemming from these ontogenetic oral-sadistic conflicts are not calmed by the experience of unconditional acceptance from an absolute person but are instead absolutized, thus metaphysicizing the repressed aggression that feeds the superego. The result is an identification of the God-image with the superego: moral reason becomes infinitized while it is fueled by repressed aggressive impulses from the id. While such a superego-based God-image rages neurotically against the ego in moralistically forbidding fashion, it becomes the motor force of religious fanaticism when turned outside. Identified with the superego, God blesses wars against infidels or other enemies in the name of each party's notion of the good. In this context, Drewermann's speeches against the Gulf War in 1991 note that both the American President George Bush and the Iraqi President Saddam Hussein prayed at the beginning of the war to God for victory and for the protection of their soldiers (Drewermann 1991c, 84, 118–21). The identification of God with the superego finds its extreme expression in religious fanaticism. In a superego-based religious attitude it becomes inevitable

> to find goals and enemies of the ego toward which the suppressed aggression can be set free for the purpose of accomplishing holy orders. This is the hour of birth of fanaticism. It appears like an act of liberation, as an inner need. In it the neuroticizing

moralism of religion creates its own vent, and the members of such religions now are not even able to notice that they henceforth speak of God only in order to rationalize their repressed aggressions. The legitimation or rationalization of religious fanaticism is rather simple: after the unconscious forces of the human psyche have been repressed and humans are seen merely as beings of reason and will, henceforward the relationship to God and the profession of faith is seen as an act of reason, commanded by the will, and in the service of this faith the repressed, nonintegrated aggressiveness must then be discharged.

The rational appearance of the religious attitude — clearly enough documented in the biblical religions of Judaism, Christianity, and Islam, above all, in the lack or even theological mistrust of any genuine mysticism — does not, however, make religion more rational. To the contrary: the teachings of religion remain as deeply paradoxical and unprovable as ever. Henceforth they must, according to the self-understanding of that religion, be declared to be rational statements. One must supplement whatever persuasive power they lack for the judgment of reason by external pressure: anyone who does not submit to such a religion has either not yet been instructed, that is, indoctrinated, sufficiently, or she has an *evil* will and must thus be *forced* [to believe]. Religious wars [*Glaubenskriege*] without and inquisitions within are the inevitable consequences of the moralizing one-sidedness of religion. (ibid., 224–25)

We alluded earlier to Drewermann's observation that in the Christian West, the rationalistic one-sidedness of religion turned eventually against Christianity itself in the Age of Enlightenment, entailing Christianity's loss of external, political power. Since the days of the Enlightenment, Christianity was stripped of the external pillars of "propaganda and power" and has had to fear for its own existence. The lack of "possibilities to exert external power for the purpose of deflecting its aggressive impulses must once again lead to a damming up [of those impulses] accompanied by corresponding neurotic symptom formations: fear, guilt feelings, inferiority feelings, masochistic reaction formations, and so on. Not the pacification but the neuroticization (or the sadistic perversion) of human aggression is the result of such a religiosity" (ibid., 226).

How the heritage of religious "moral pacifism" can in secularized form assume a mentality akin to a "medieval inquisition" and to "militant terrorism" is evident to Drewermann in the attitude of the "ethical optimism" of respected German politicians with high moral authority such as the Berlin mayor Heinrich Albertz or the politician Helmut Gollwitzer during the terrorism crisis involving the terror group *Rote Armee Fraktion* (RAF, i.e., Red Army Group) in the 1970s (ibid., 227–30). The leftist RAF had been formed originally in protest to the Vietnam War and presents an example of how "pacifist aims turned into radical terror," based on the splitting of the world into absolute good and absolute evil. Though Drewermann does not agree with accusations which assert that Gollwitzer and Albertz sympathized with the actions of the RAF, but instead acknowledges that both were consciously against use of violence in the service of peace, he finds their thinking to be based on the same division of people into the morally good and the morally bad. Albertz, for instance, proclaimed the possibility of *"peace now"* and "translated the message of the Sermon on the Mount with a moral directness and simplicity into a political action prescription" which seemed to suggest that "the means for peace are actually known and freely available and that with some good will peace could be 'made' without any problem. If there is still an increase in armament and if preparations for war are still being made, then — this view suggests — the reason lies in a lack of good will of a few people in powerful positions" (ibid., 228). The "simplistic moralistic externalization" of the religious message of peace in the Sermon on the Mount must necessarily increase the tension within those who try to follow this view but find that there are always people without good will. "Once it is clear who and what has to be considered as the absolute evil, then the pacifism of moral repression turns instantly into terrorism [e.g., in the case of the RAF] toward the outside, just as it had been psychologically from the beginning" (ibid., 229). No appeal to good will is then capable "to prevent the explosion of violence. And it is precisely those of good will and of good faith among the students of a theology of the kind of Albertz or Gollwitzer who are in danger of no longer comprehending why peace is so difficult to achieve after it has been portrayed as so simply attainable. Ethical optimism or, put dogmatically, the factual Pelagianism of Christian affected behavior is in itself terrorist" (ibid., 229–30).

That "factual Pelagianism" is where Drewermann's critique of the failure of the Christian religion to promote peace and of its effectively belligerent heritage has its core: its own misunderstanding of the doctrine of original sin (ibid., 206–9). We saw (Chapter 1) how Drewermann emphasized that an understanding of the story of the fall in Genesis 3 or of the story of Cain and Abel in Genesis 4 as the result of pride or ill will, that is, as a result of a lack of good will, misses the meaning of the Yahwist's account. Drewermann's analysis showed instead that the human spirit's fear of losing God in the face of nothingness is at the root of the fall from God, at the root of what Christian theology calls sin. To confuse sin with a lack of good will means to moralize sin and to miss its actual deeper, religious meaning as an attitude based on a sense of fear due to absolute ontological insecurity.[8] If sin and its consequences such as the alienation from fellow human beings and from fellow creatures is the result not of hubris or evil will but of an absolute fear of losing the ground of one's being, then the consequences of sin cannot be cured by simply appealing to ethical efforts of a good will. What is required is a religious solution in which the deep fear of the spirit is calmed. Only then, Drewermann believes, will the very fears and the unresolved guilt feelings which are at the root of war have a chance to subside, thus reducing the spiritual and emotional fuel that prevents people from solving conflicts through talk and negotiations. "The 'commandments' of the Sermon on the Mount are for him [Christ] really not instructions for a super-morality of human legal behavior, they simply describe what kind of power God can gain in people who entrust themselves to him and who have therefore once and for all overcome fear with its longings for security based on money and power, righteousness and heartless [*mitleidloser*] self-assertion. Without the grace of God it is not possible for humans to be good" (ibid., 205).

Drewermann proposes that theology can best learn from depth psychology how to interpret its own doctrine of original sin in a nonmoralistic fashion (ibid., 209–15). Theology will not understand the religious doctrine of original sin unless it "learns from depth psychology how totally human existence needs to become sick of itself

---

8. For Drewermann's use of Laing's term "ontological insecurity" (Laing 1965), see Drewermann 1990a.

if it is most deeply shaped by the feeling of a lack of grace [*Gnaden-losigkeit*]" (ibid., 205). "Only the notion of fear allows us to set hermeneutically against sin not the ethics of virtue but the necessity of faith...; only in the field of anxiety, in the border zone between existence and nonexistence does it become evident whether a human being is 'radically' held in God or radically separated from God" (ibid., 205 n. 26). Only as a result of the absolute fear of the spirit caught up in itself, "which has to be interpreted theologically as a fall from God, does the 'pecking order' of any human group become murderous" (ibid., 207). Thus the story of the murder of Abel by Cain in the desperate attempt to regain a sense of absolute recognition of one's existence which was lost under the spell of fear is the matrix of war. In the background of all wars thus lies an ambivalent, psychically violent God-image, often not explicitly present but rather repressed and disguised by absolute claims to power and recognition, which are the result of a projection of life under the spell of spiritual fear. Only if fundamental anxiety and the experience of "lack" bind a group together does aggression become dangerous in a group (ibid., 210).

Drewermann hence sees wars as the arena in which deeply spiritual fears are violently acted out. He argues that war "as a battle for existence, the instrumentalization of death against the constantly possible threat of death can lose its justification and its necessity if life shows itself to be confirmed, recognized, and *everlasting*.... The source of the evil [of war]...[is] the eternal fear of humans in view of mortality" (ibid., 329). A main reason "why wars break out again and again consists, as we have seen, in the feeling of humiliation, of contempt, and of national shame — the valuelessness of the militarily weak or defeated ones in the face of the stronger one.... The superiority of violence is spiritually again only a *symbol* for the desire for *inner* recognition and respect: were it given, most wars would no longer occur" (ibid., 326). From a religious point of view one should hence ask what is at stake *spiritually* when people wage wars, in terms of recognition, dignity, status, and so on; what spiritual *fears* are at play in the midst of all the economic, sociological, cultural, and psychological fears (ibid., 325). The question of war, then, requires a spiritual, that is, in Drewermann's language, "religious" solution that begins prior to any concrete action, prior to any ethical solution. Because there is nothing that ethics can *do* to truly calm the fear of death of a human *being*.

The Suppression of Women, Christianity's Oedipal Conflicts and Patriarchal
God-Image, and Ibsen's *Peer Gynt*

> Drewermann's thinking is in many respects very close to femi-
> nist theology. At any rate, it is not sexist but humanity-wide and
> holistic. Sexuality and soul are integrated in such a way into
> anthropology that a confusion of human with man can hardly
> occur. His understanding for the role of individual women in
> the New Testament is highly developed. . . . His pastoral advo-
> cacy, too, for those who have been psychosexually damaged
> by ecclesial notions of morality is feminist insofar as it names
> the victims of patriarchal-clerical violence: those strapped to
> sadists, the divorced, the remarried, people who use contracep-
> tives, and all who are afraid to be free. Who falls more under
> these forms of internalized violence than women who were and
> who are most of the victims of the authoritarian religion of com-
> pulsion?! His theology is also feminist in the liberation of feeling,
> in his attempt at wholeness, above all in the application of the
> psychoanalytic method.
> —Dorothee Sölle, "Heilung und Befreiung"

Drewermann understands the relationship between the evolutionary
heritage of archetypes of the human psyche and the freedom of the
human spirit dialectically. Clarification of this relationship is important to avoid misunderstandings, especially with respect to his use of
phrases such as "the feminine aspect of the human psyche, the unconscious" (ibid., 254, cf. 248), "masculine aggressiveness and one-sided
rationality," and the notions of a mother and a father archetype. The
evolutionary heritage of the human species is considered to be shared
universally by all races, while cultural manifestations vary due to
sociological differences and to the human spirit's capacity to reflect
on the programs of the evolutionary past. While certain experiences
which the human species has accumulated in relation to mothers or
fathers over hundreds of thousands of years are affectively connected
to an archetypal experience of mother or father, the human spirit's
"indeterminateness" — to borrow a term from Clifford Geertz (1973,
45) — allows humans to refrain from reifying psychic images into social roles and to vary social roles so that both men and women may
take on social functions which evolutionary patterns associated with
the opposite sex. When Drewermann speaks in the following then of
the suppression of feminine attunement to feeling and to the art of
being and of the masculine mentality of doing, he does so in terms

of factually dominant roles that females had in giving birth to life (being) and males had in hunting for food and in protection (doing) in the course of human evolution (roles, for instance, evidenced in the different physique of the sexes). But he does so not in terms of the absurd notion that human biology is also social destiny. To think that biology is social destiny is to deny the human spirit, is to liquidate human freedom, which Drewermann considers itself as a version of the Kierkegaardian despair of finitude. In fact, as we have seen, Drewermann sees the very problem of Christianity in its rational one-sidedness and calls for a psychological and spiritual integration in both men and women of the archetypes of mother and father of the collective unconscious. But he does assume that the suppression of the feminine aspect of the psyche found cultural expression in Christianity through the patriarchal suppression of women and of female sexuality. A move toward psychic integration in Christianity would thus require that men would relinquish such suppression and learn from women the attunement to feeling they have feared and dismissed as feminine.

Religion is characterized by a use of evolutionary-based archetypes to create symbols for eternal meaning in the life of the individual. This is the other side of the dialectic: the human spirit's fear cannot be calmed by abstract philosophical concepts, that is, by reason, but only by symbols which reach deep down to the affective roots of the human psyche as well as high up to the spiritual dimension of *personhood*. The archetypes are the indispensable language of the human spirit, but whether the images which derive from them culturally are experienced under the destructive spell of fear or the constructive calm of trust depends on whether the human spirit experiences these images in relation to an absolutely accepting person, God. Geertz's "significant symbols" of religion are thus rooted in evolutionary-acquired patterns of the human psyche but vary in their cultural arrangement due to the human spirit's capacity for freedom (Geertz 1973, 45). The "information gap" (ibid., 50) thus does not consist in terms of the *content* of religious symbols but only in terms of the specific *arrangements* and *manifestations* of that content in each culture — and each individual!

With this important clarification in mind we will turn to the final question of Drewermann's book on war: whether Christianity's inadvertently belligerent effects are related to its sexually repressive attitude and to its historical suppression of women (1992a, 232–82). A link of the belligerent effects to a sexually repressive societal attitude seems plausible in light of Christianity's severe suppression of sexuality which led, for instance, to "reactively strong aggressive sadomasochistic impulses" during the witch-hunt between 1400 and 1700 (ibid., 238–39). But a cultural comparison makes this link questionable. If a direct correlation existed in the sense that the more a society suppresses sexuality the more aggressive that society would be, then one might assume that men in Islam would be less aggressive than in Christianity and men in Buddhism just as aggressive as in Christianity. While Islam gives men rather liberal sexual rights, including the institution of polygamy, such sexual freedom does not prevent the passion with which the idea of the Jihad, the Holy War, is embraced. And Buddhism is considered to be, despite its sexual asceticism, the most peaceful of the great world religions (ibid., 242). In addition, "the sexual permissiveness propagated since the late 1960s has not automatically made the Western European population more peace-loving" (ibid.). Drewermann concludes from this cross-religious comparison that "it is not the suppression of sexuality but the suppression of women in a society ruled only by men which could indeed encourage wars" (ibid.). Not the suppression of sexuality as such but the suppression of female sexuality is seen as a contributing factor to belligerence.

The sociological suppression of women, the fearful suppression of female sexuality and of the "feminine in the human psyche" are for Drewermann the other side of the coin of the anthropocentric, rationalistic *and* patriarchal reduction of religion in Christianity (ibid., 232–54). In assessing the archaic roots of the patriarchal attitude of Christianity, Drewermann reminds us of the prehistorical sociological role patterns of the hunter-gatherer period. In prehistory it was the "duty of men to kill life [i.e., during hunting] and the task of women to give birth to life" (ibid., 242–43), men's attitude was associated with doing and women's attitude associated more patiently with being. A patriarchal society favors characteristics associated with hunting. Psychologically this is of serious significance for how a patriarchal society answers the basic religious human question of whether and why one feels justified to exist. "The overvaluation of the father-image means psychologically that human recognition and acceptance is primarily bound to achievement and diligence rather then bestowed unconditionally because of one's mere existence" (ibid., 246).

But this does not mean that women would contribute less in a patriarchal society to a psychology of war. "[W]ar is indeed closer to a patriarchal society than a matriarchal community, but — to stress this once more — not because women are psychologically more peaceful than men, but because the *execution* of wars, which resulted from the complementary psychology of man *and* woman, has to date been primarily or even exclusively a male business: men, to say it pointedly, conduct wars with women in mind — for their protection and their admiration" (ibid., 248). The warrior seems to receive the kind of admiration and recognition his spirit is longing for from women. Such recognition often appears in sexualized form: a man's power makes him sexually desirable for women.

Drewermann argues that the patriarchal suppression of women in the Christian religion went always hand in hand with a repression "of the female aspect in the human psyche," that is, "with a certain aversion to and shying away from the emotional possibilities and values in personal and public life" (ibid., 248–49). The rationalism of the patriarchal attitude leads to a devaluing of psychic phenomena which are not simply rational. "[T]he *piety* of a patriarchal form of religion *correspondingly* tends toward a kind of religion of reason from which rites, images, the sacramental, the mystical, and the mythical are gradually banned and must be substituted through clear laws and instructions" (ibid., 250). In doing so, Christianity cut itself off from the very foundations from which its own doctrines spring. Christianity "cut off the world of religious experience from psychical foundations and transformed it into a system of psychical alienation, of institutionalized suppression. Especially through the Christian way of talking about peace a human type had to emerge which is technologically more civilized and psychically more barbaric than can be imagined" (ibid., 254).

In the history of biblical religions, Drewermann observes a progressive increase of hostility against the emotional, feminine aspect of the human psyche, which found expression particularly in the tendency to suppress or rationalize the mythic imagery of religion. Agreeing with the South Sea chief's (Tuiavii of Tiavea) astute analysis of the latent aggressiveness of Western rational one-sidedness (Tuiavii and Scheurmann 1997), Drewermann writes that such intellectualism, rational superstition, and rational one-sidedness leads to inner disunity in humans. Such intellect does not just become belligerent when it invents tools of war or thinks of war but is in itself, as Tuiavii correctly observed, thoroughly "loaded with ammunition." ...

[A]fter the Old Testament had laid the ground through its battle against Canaanite mythology, its iconoclasm, and its increasingly legal type of piety in the time after the Babylonian exile, Christianity at first attempted a synthesis of Judaism, Mediterranean — largely mythical — thought, and Hellenistic rationality. But the tensions within this religious brace were too strong to allow Christianity in the West to retain its unity: especially Protestantism tried, with certain justification, to purify Catholic syncretism again from its pagan additions and to leave behind only the pure, imageless word of God.* Islam, on the other hand, as the last of the great biblical religions, already began in the seventh century where Protestantism started in the sixteenth century: in the demythologization of Christianity. It became the only truly myth-free, completely rational religion[9] which knew how to appropriate, especially during the Middle Ages, the ideas of Greek philosophy without problems. The patriarchal God-image reduced itself to omnipotence, intellect, and a law-giving will — a God superior to the world whose adoration with feminine feelings almost had to be embarrassing, or at least undignified. This dangerous distortion of religion in the direction of the ethical-rational seems to be very strongly connected with the basic patriarchal tendency of biblical religions.

*Protestantism is in the history of religions a reaction against the increasingly maternal [*maternistischen*] character of the Catholic Church of the Renaissance period and derives, especially in Calvinism, from an extreme identification with the father, including everything that belongs psychologically to it: the danger of fanaticism, the sexual repression, the degradation of woman, the burden of constant feelings of guilt and of fears of hell etc.... Regarding the psychology of iconoclasm and its origin from the Oedipus complex see E. Drewermann 1985a, 451–60....

(Drewermann 1992a, 250–51)

---

9. Drewermann notes in a footnote that Sufism is the exception through which "the idea of *Islamic mysticism*" did gain an important place in Islamic piety (Drewermann 1992a, 251 n. 59).

Drewermann relates the suppression of women in Christian society and the corresponding repression of the feminine in the psyche of this Christian human type *depth-psychologically* again — as in his interpretation of Genesis 3 — to conflicts on the oral and the phallic level. While we saw that he considers the oral conflict dynamic of Genesis 3 as universal and hence capable of becoming a universal *symbol* for a theological notion of sin, Drewermann interpreted the phallic dimensions of the story in terms of a regression to the oral level in the service of a defense against emerging sexuality during the phallic stage. While no universal biological Oedipus complex can be assumed to exist, Drewermann suggests that the emergence of sexual-genital impulses in a child creates certain patterns of relating to the parent of the opposite sex (and implied, of the same sex) which influence adult relationships with the two sexes. In Christianity, Drewermann holds, a human type was culturally created which promoted Oedipal conflicts (1992a, 269).

Based on a conviction that modern art increasingly filled the "place of feeling" as Christianity suppressed it, Drewermann's analyses rely much on the interpretation of dramatic plays, fairy tales, poetry, prose, and the visual arts to portray plastically what has been suppressed by Christianity and which "therapy proposals for the sickness of the Western type of human" exist (ibid., 261). In Henrik Ibsen's play *Peer Gynt* (Ibsen 1962), Drewermann finds a clear embodiment of Western Christianity's "problem of the fear of woman and of the exaggerated will to maleness" (Drewermann 1992a, 261). Two key aspects of the Christian type of human are observed by Drewermann in the main character Peer and in his relationships to women: "the splitting of dream and reality" (ibid., 268–71) and "the obsessive compulsive splitting of the feminine into the roles of madonna and whore" (ibid., 271–73).

"Peer Gynt's central problem is the ambivalent attitude toward woman" (ibid., 262). Peer is to his mother, after the death of her husband, everything, "her hope, her love — and her disappointment." She provides everything to him. In return he is actually only expected to take care of the farm. But Peer thinks he should be like an "emperor" to his mother and feels overtaxed by her. "His great-man dreams spring from and serve a deep self contempt; they force him to flee his own reality more and more and to work himself into a lie, into megalomania." His mother adores him like an idol but she also curses him because he does nothing. She raised him by making him conjure up fairy tales and day dreams, but also hates his "useless-dreamy substitute life" (ibid.). Peer's attempts to relate to other women are characterized by initial lack of interest on the part of the women he tries to court, then by his violent abduction and rape of Ingrid whom he ends up chasing away because she ended up "*not* refusing intimacy with him (ibid., 263). She appears to him like a whore and in response he longs for the "pure" Solveig. When he sees her "the grace of God descends" on him (Ibsen 1962, 22 [act II, sc. I]). "But his splitting of lust and love delivers him" to the curse Ingrid put upon him when he rejected her: "the daughters of trolls" appear to him, piglike animal-humans, "lovers of a desperate lust" whose maxim is not a human one ("Human, to thyself be true") but instead "Troll, to thyself be enough" (Ibsen 1962, 26 [act II, sc. vi]; Drewermann 1992a, 263). Peer fathers a child with one of the troll daughters but narrowly escapes from their realm just before they are able to mutilate him and make him their leader.

Lost, he stumbles for the first time upon the "Great Curved One [The Great Boyg]" who is the only one able to answer the question "Who are you?" with "myself"; (Ibsen 1962, 26 [act II, sc. vii], Drewermann 1992a, 263). "The one who is 'I am myself,' it is said, is victorious throughout time without violence, forces Peer into a *change of path*": he begs the "innocent Solveig" to leave everything and join him (ibid., 263–64). She does, but "her self-sacrifice does not reach" Peer. The troll daughter appears with the child he fathered and threatens never to leave him alone. Peer now has to engage in a long journey of "work" where even Solveig cannot help him, but can only "wait" till he comes back — if he comes back at all. "Peer's 'work,' his step from dream to reality, begins meanwhile with the death of his mother" (ibid., 264). He comforts the dying mother with stories she told him when he was a child to calm his fears. After her death he steps, still unchanged internally, into the "reality of the world of adults." He "still dreams the power-possessed, narcissistic dream of his imperial status, now, however, using money as the medium" (ibid.). He learns that everything in the world can be bought: "honor, religion, power." Such a world is internally desertlike and Peer tries to compensate for it by once more reviving his megalomanic fantasies, this time by becoming a prophet, a "religious messenger" (ibid.). He fails, however, and then tries to become a scholar and to make a name for himself.

When meeting the Egyptian sphinx, Peer is able to hear in her, half woman, half lion, again the "Curved One." Once more the life-and-death question arises "who he himself is and for what he could be loved" (ibid., 265). But all he can hear in the decisive moment is merely "the echo of his own questions and chattering" (ibid.). "His *alter ego,* with the name 'Field of Concepts [*Begriffenfeldt*]' declares him instantly to be an emperor of exegetes." But the power-possessed, one-sidedly rational dream to be the emperor of exegetes reveals itself to be what it really is: "pure madness." Hence Peer finds himself in the next instant in a mental institution (Ibsen 1962, 48–51 [act IV, sc. xiii]). His unfulfilled desire for unconditional love led him into a madness of doing, first by trying to make himself into a man by violently taking the women he wants, followed by a search for refuge in the relentless world of monetary combat, and eventually by desperately trying to create a reality of his own through being an exegete and scholar. Barely escaping the mental institution, he finds himself on a ship in search for gold and fur which, however, shipwrecks. Peer then has his first close encounter with death, and he is more and more worried by the question what his life is all about (Drewermann 1992a, 265). He discovers that his problem has been that he was never able to attach himself to anything or anyone, symbolized by the "button without a buttonhole." He barely escapes the "casting-ladle" of the button-moulder which would melt his individual existence completely back into the indistinct mass of all other lost existences. He feels that his "worst 'sin' is: to be a *nobody,*" not himself (ibid., 266). In the end the question of who Peer Gynt has been is answered only by "the eternally waiting Solveig"[10] who rescues him with unconditional acceptance once he finds his way home to her. His powerful, male actions could not save him but "only the words of a love which does not grow tired waiting for him until his eventual exhaustion, until his death. Peer Gynt who was fleeing from his mother all his life returns at the end of his life's dramatic odyssey back home. His burdens are replaced

---

10. Solveig's "waiting" for Peer as a *religious* symbol for an attitude of "being" versus the masculine attitude of "doing" is strictly understood in view of the existential search for *absolute* meaning, hold, and justification of one's life which cannot be "made." The *religious* association of "feminine" and "patiently waiting" is based on the archetypal association of "feminine" with "giving birth" to being and must not be confused with a *social* role of passivity and 'waiting' forced upon women in a patriarchal society. Thus Peer sees in her in the end "My Mother! My wife! You holy woman! Oh, hide me, hide me within your love!" (Ibsen 1962, 66 [act V, sc. x]).

by the mercy of the motherly Solveig, and after escaping from the demanding-suffocating mother he comes to tranquility through the absolute kindness [*Güte*, connotes goodness] and patience of the unconditional grace of a truly motherly woman. The image of this *eternal* mother stands at the end of the wrong track of male megalomania as the last place of a religious experience of inner peace. *That* then is what it could mean to rediscover the role of woman *religiously* and similarly it should serve Christianity as a lesson" (Drewermann 1992a, 267): that is, Christianity should end its desperate attempt to create or cultivate existential meaning and sense of self through doing moral deeds and instead reintegrate the archetypal feminine aspect of the psyche of love and of patiently being. This reintegration, Drewermann believes, could be facilitated and catalyzed through the integration of women into the priesthood of the Roman Catholic Church (ibid., 332 n. 62).

Drewermann sees the split between dream and reality and the split of the image of woman into whore and madonna in Peer as conditioning each other within a "basic Oedipal syndrome" (ibid., 269). The split between dream and reality presupposes "psychologically a fearful relationship to oneself" (ibid.). The love Peer experiences is never unconditional, but always dependent on what he does. It is partly suffocating, partly rejecting. And it approached him in form "of (super-)claims and internalized (super-)demands." Peer is loved by his mother always "like a small, dependent child," but she has demands too great for him to fulfill. Such love creates "abysmally deep anxiety, a never ending feeling of inferiority and, in reaction, immeasurable demands toward oneself" (ibid., 269). This is the key aspect of the "Oedipal syndrome" for Drewermann: to ask from a child too much, that is, morally too much, in terms of deeds too much. Underlying is the conflict of the earlier oral stage: the desire to be unconditionally accepted.

Acknowledging that Ibsen did not intend to portray a specifically Christian type of human (ibid., 267), Drewermann nonetheless observes in this Oedipal syndrome with its underlying oral issues a central parallel between Peer Gynt's mother and the Christian "mother Church":

The spiritual location where humans should feel unconditionally accepted would be the realm of religion. In contrast, Christianity, the "mother Church," in its long history, cannot be acquitted from spreading and preaching — as Peer's mother did — more fear than a sense of security, more moralized demands than faith, more conditional than unconditional acceptance. The question of what to do was always much more important to Christianity than the question what kind of human being someone is, which feelings shape him and from which truth he lives. External conformity with the demands of the public seemed much more important than the religiously more decisive and important question of the conformity of the individual person with herself.... Instead of reconciling the individual with herself thus creating the indispensable presupposition for the reconciliation with others as well, such a religiosity with its moralizing and rationally oriented one-sidedness even blocks the central location for the finding of the self [i.e., the location of religion proper]. It sabotages thus what it actually wants according to its word and its claim: it does not mediate the "grace of God," but commits the human being in the name of a never experienced "grace" to a form of life which — due to fears never worked through — mentally can only have neuroticizing and in every respect damaging effects. The actual task of religion would consist in embodying *in the midst of life* the figure of that "mother" which Solveig appeared as to Peer Gynt at the end of his life: as the decisive agency of an unconditional acceptance....

Measured by this primordial image of religion, the Christian "mother Church" with its rule of men appears rather as an embodiment of Peer Gynt's aspirations to become like God while actually missing restlessly all possibilities to hear anything but his own voice, the logic of his own reason. The state of today's "theology," above all of exegesis, in its absurdly domineering [*herrisch-absurden*; lit., lordly-absurd] devotion to concepts and in its historicizing externalization has probably found nowhere in modern literature as apt a portrait as the scene where Peer Gynt lets the Egyptian Sphinx speak his own echo. (ibid., 269–71)

In view of the question of war and peace, this analysis means that Christianity as a religion would have to stop demanding from people to "do" something and instead address the deeper question of how to be — how to feel loved merely because one exists, how to *feel* justified to exist. "Not what can be 'done [*machen*]' for peace, but how the humans are whom Christianity has over two millennia constantly 'made [*gemacht*]' through its 'doing [*Machen*]' — that should be the first problem a Christian theology of peace should present itself. It would then become very humble, because the answer to this question looks rather bleak" (ibid., 271).

The ambivalence toward women due to the Oedipal feeling of never being enough takes in Peer Gynt's psyche the form of an "obsessive-compulsive splitting of the feminine into the roles of madonna and whore" (ibid., 272). Drewermann sees the same dynamic at work in Christianity's "hostility toward sexuality." "It is not difficult to recognize in this *obsessional alternative* of the image of woman into mother and whore the same sexual dilemma which has essentially shaped the Christian churches.[11] Especially the leadership of the *Catholic* Church seems to be deeply shaped by Oedipal ambivalences toward women and in turn has been decisively influencing for centuries the ideas of sexual ethics in the Church — in a manner that 'permits' libido only in marriage" (Drewermann 1992a, 272–73). Drewermann consequently believes that "the attitude toward human sexuality will find a solution on the part of Christianity only if Christianity could give up its historical battle of despair against the inner nature of humans, against the unconscious as a whole and against the feminine of the human psyche in particular" (ibid., 273).

Situating his critique of Christianity's one-sidedly rational attitude, its suppression of the impulses that gave rise to the concrete mythic imagery of its own symbols, and the reactively violent compensations, within the historical context, Drewermann writes: "One only needs to recall, for instance, the experiences during the Third Reich: how powerless the voice of 'reason' was in the midst of the collective mass madness, in order to understand right away that only religious symbols can be effectively humanizing against the vortex of mass psychology, against the psychotic symbolism of the collective fear with its regressive ideas and mythologies"[12] (ibid., 283).

---

11. In a note, Drewermann refers to Freud's thoughts on the splitting between madonna and whore in relation to an Oedipal mother fixation (Freud 1909) and his observation of the ambivalence of love and hate within obsessional character neurosis (Freud 1910, 237–45).

12. Cf. Drewermann's analysis of Hitler's "Nimrod complex" (named after Nimrod, "the first on earth to become a mighty warrior," a "mighty hunter before Yahweh" Genesis 10:8–9), with its characteristic oscillation between a sense of inferiority and a megalomanic will to power in Drewermann 1985a, 495–503.

Drewermann sums up his analysis of the inadvertent belligerent effects of all three biblical religions and of Christianity in particular — radicalized through the individualization of anthropocentrism and through Christocentrism — as follows:

> [T]he circle comes to a close and one sees that all of the one-sided attitudes of biblical religion(s) mentioned so far are in the last instance connected with each other and condition each other: the alienation from external nature corresponds with the alienation from internal nature; the latter is identical with the repression of the unconscious and encompasses the suppression of female sexuality which, in turn, is the condition, at least indirectly, for an increase of male aggressiveness and one-sided rationality; that, in turn, brings forth a social role distribution which prefers the man in such a way that from it spring once more the defense against the deep layers of the human psyche and the progressive destruction, too, of external nature. The entire arrangement in the relationship of the human being to nature, to himself, and to his fellow humans is based on a form of latent structural violence: the theological doctrine of the rule of a male God over the world corresponds psychologically to the domination of intellect [*Verstand*] over the drives, reason [*Vernunft*] over feelings, and this manifests itself sociologically in the domination of man over woman. The work of the man shows itself in technology and war — in working on nature and on humans — and both, technology and war, escalate within this worldview: *ecologically* up to the brink of the final destruction of the environment through humans and *politically* up to the destruction of humans through humans. [This is] a form of being-in-the-image-of-God based on the exertion of pure power, which counteracts the actual image of a Creator God. Honestly, it is mere self-reverence [*Selbstanbetung*], an idolization of money and power. (Drewermann 1992a, 251–52)

The one-sidedly rational image of God is itself a reflection of the human spirit binding itself desperately to one pole of existence under the spell of fear, which — as we saw in Chapter 1 — Drewermann considers with Kierkegaard as one of the forms of despair in which sin manifests itself.

A Religious Solution for the Problem of War

Recognizing the Element of the Tragic: Avoiding Both Religious Justification
and Condemnation of War

> Inability to understand resignation and the relations prevailing
> between ethics and resignation, is the fatal weakness of modern
> European thought.
>
> —Albert Schweitzer, *The Philosophy of Civilization*[13]

What, then, is the task of religion in general and Christianity in particular in the face of the problem of war? How could Christianity
interpret the Sermon on the Mount in a manner that does not do
violence to psyche and spirit (ibid., 209)? Drewermann argues that
this is possible only if the instructions of the Sermon on the Mount
are understood *internally,* that is, as inner guidelines rather than as
moral laws of *external* action. The Sermon on the Mount's call for
"absolute nonviolence and readiness for reconciliation" is "a clear
rejection of any ethical or political pragmatism in favor of a purely
religious resolution of fundamental human fear and of its redemption through a deeper faith in the foundations of human existence"
(ibid.). Thus the task of Christianity should be "to make humans
aware of the reasons for their fear and to overcome it through an
experience of faith" (ibid.). In order to do justice to the "empirical"
expression of the human spirit's absolute fear in the form, for instance, of the infinitization of aggression, Drewermann believes that
it is essential for Christianity today to learn from "the insights of
depth psychology into the structures and mechanisms of the unconscious as it experiences and acts on fear and aggression. As long as
theology does not really acknowledge the unconscious in humans, its
only choice is either to suppress or demonize the drives of humans"
(ibid., 209–10). Christianity could expand its notion of original sin in
accordance with the theory of neurosis to show "that human aggression as a drive with all its instinctive mechanisms of threat, defense
of territory, and group hierarchy only becomes really dangerous and
evil if human groups are kept together by fundamental fear and the
sense of radical lack and of internal and external threat" (ibid., 210).
Drewermann argues that all approaches to the problem of war which
bypass human fear "increase rather than calm human aggressiveness"
(ibid., 211).

---

13. (1949a, 295), cited in Drewermann 1992a, 183 n. 6.

Theology, however, can learn from depth psychology not only to see "failed attempts at working through fear as a kind of phenomenology of human existence without God" (ibid., 214; see Chapter 1), but also that the "grace of God" is not some magic fix, for it, too, needs to be seen in light of the complexity of the problem of human fear. "It would be rash to declare the correctly observed connection between grace and peace (and of lack of grace and war respectively) simply as a ready-made program for the solution of the problem of war and peace, without the mediation of depth psychology, that is, without taking into account actual experience permeated by lack of grace and by fear. If theology continues to disavow the psychoanalysis of fear in the unconscious of the human psyche, it would condemn itself to a total abstractness which would prevent an understanding of the issue of war" (ibid., 211).

An acknowledgment of the complexity of human fear would above all require the recognition of the *"tragic* structure of redemption" (ibid., 213). This is probably the most important and contentious aspect of Drewermann's critique of the moralistic misunderstanding of the Sermon on the Mount and has implications for Christian moral theology in general, because it holds that a nonethical, purely religious solution of the problem of war would be required to abstain from *judging* and instead confine itself to *understanding* — "even in the face of war" (ibid., 212). The following passage succinctly describes the implications of such a spiritual-therapeutic attitude in healing the roots of war, including the recognition of the "tragic inevitability" of war under certain circumstances.

When dealing practically with fear many things appear contradictory, paradoxical, and at any rate more difficult than can be accepted within the frame of the elaborate abstractions of a theology that decrees eternal peace. Psychotherapy provides the opportunity to observe again and again that there is no straight path from fear to peace. An increase of trust and "grace" and a slight decrease of fear succeed initially in psychotherapeutic treatment often at first not to bring about greater peacefulness in a patient but rather lead, as her ego strength grows, to a setting free of aggressive impulses. Increasing self-confidence stirs the desire to no longer have to continue the pattern of avoiding existing conflicts and issues by giving in or by retreating. Many conflicts that had been repressed due to fear must now be made conscious and worked through: that is, it is precisely in the name of "grace" that many repressed aggressions now surface for the first time. Instead of moving directly on to peace, the "grace" of unprejudiced acceptance provokes — often for the first time — the fears and aggressions which had until then slumbered under the cover of repression. And only through the becoming conscious *and acting out* [i.e., within the context of the therapeutic relationship] of the jammed [*eingeklemmten*] affects do the hitherto repressed aggressions become accessible to conscious steering and free decision.

What we can observe already within the narrow confines of an individual psychotherapy takes place in far more complicated ways among various peoples [nations] on their way to peace. One does, at any rate, understand, only based on such experiences, that even Christ did not immediately create peace and reconciliation through his message of grace but that he, against his will, could not but provoke and bring upon himself certain forms of hate, enmity, and murderous rage. "I have not come," he did indeed say, "to bring peace, but a sword" (Matt. 10:34). The peace of Christianity always lies beyond the neuroticisms of fear, of the repressions of aggression and their working through. It is, if at all, a peace of truth. And it always comes only after the — in a certain sense, necessary and forgiven by God in advance — destructive work of the Cross on the way to insight into self and inner honesty. Otherwise one may never understand the statement of Saint Paul that sin had to become ever greater so that grace could show itself even more abundantly (Rom. 5:20). If one is not willing, especially with regard to the issue of war, to recognize the deeply *tragic* structure of redemption, one cuts short the message of Christianity just as much as the problems of human existence in fear and coping with fear are cut short.

From here the paradox emerges that theology, instead of categorically or *a priori* condemning war, would have to recognize its tragic inevitability under certain circumstances, which are not external, political-practical, or responsibility-ethical reasons but rather inner reasons of a deeper understanding of human fear and its "no exit" situations.

This is particularly true for wars that are waged, as described ... [ibid., 82], for a sort of mental self-healing and which actually do not serve the classic goals of war such as protection of women and children or the preservation of territorial integrity, but only the demonstration of one's dignity and the preservation of a remnant of a feeling of self-worth. Especially a religious evaluation of war should be capable of freeing itself from a mere condemnation of war. It should recognize and emphasize that the human being does not have to be aggressive if his sense of self-worth is secured through faith in God, but it should also admit that the path to this [experience and attitude] can be very long. . . . [Taking a middle path] between the alternative of blessing or condemning war, religion should be able to make war transparent in its concrete reasons and to overcome it from within through a *deeper understanding* of human tragedy. (ibid., 212–24)

Calming the Fear of the Spirit with the Symbols of Religion

But how can religion overcome the reasons that propel humans toward war? We have seen that Drewermann suggested that the key root of war and its tendency toward totalization has to be sought in the human spirit's conscious or unconscious fear of death. This is not so much a fear of physical death as a fear that one's existence is ultimately insignificant and lacks an absolute justification, a fear — theologically — of a loss of relationship with the absolute person who can give foundation to one's existence. That this is the particular nature of human fear and that it provides the fuel for what is theologically called sin was shown by Drewermann in *Strukturen des Bösen* (see Chapter 1). In war it is fear of having the significance of one's existence put explicitly into question — expressed in such sentiments as feeling one's national dignity violated, or one's status questioned, or feeling threatened by other ideologies, or claiming one's rights — which leads to a desire to see the rival dead. Fear of insignificance — a notion we use here as a shorthand for all the connotations just mentioned — leads to a Sartrean world in which the Other is a painful reminder of one's finitude and hence to the desire to kill off the Other forever.

On an individual level, Christianity has dealt with such fear-based wishes to kill the Other by suppressing the aggressive instincts rooted in the evolutionary heritage of the human species through a moral censorship of such impulses in the name of a God-image distorted by fear. The moralistic understanding of the Sermon on the Mount was not only unable to contain the spiritually infinitized aggressive impulses but through it Christianity inadvertently contributed against its will to the spiral of violence by feeding guilt feelings that weaken the individual ego and make it able to be swept away as soon as a collectively sanctioned form of aggression could be found. Drewermann notes that strangely enough collectively expressed *"aggression* — unlike sexuality — has never really become conscious as an issue for Christianity after the Constantinian turn. The origins of Christianity are evidently too belligerent for human aggression to be experienced as a central issue" (1992a, 198). Individually pent-up aggression sooner or later becomes redirected outwardly on the enemy or the infidel and paradoxically is then often justified in the name of preserving a divine order that, too, has been reduced to moral or rational-legal categories.

We saw that Drewermann argued that the issue of war cannot be solved by ethical means. The human problem of war as such presents thus "a last cry of help for a deepened form of religion" (ibid., 281). It provides an opportunity for Christianity to recover its own emphasis on a theology of sin and grace in contrast to the moral reductionism of religion. "The question of war and peace is the most vivid example for demonstrating the necessary *failure* of ethics in its fight against the evil in humans and for proving in a paradoxical way the indispensability of religion. In addition, the religious position of Christianity emphasizes — along with many other religions — that ethical optimism represents an illusion and heresy and that humans cannot be good without divine help" (ibid.). Drewermann highlights why the "nondoing" of religion is absolutely necessary to solve the problem of war in contrast to the "doing" of ethics.

[T]he issue of war is able like little else to point to the absolute necessity of religion. War is that concentration of evil in the face of which literally nothing can be "done." But it is really the failure of the ethical position that creates the possibility, even the necessity to consider the apparent impotence of religion as the only remaining hope. Religion, especially when it refuses to answer the all too practical questions of ethics, is indeed the only remaining agency which could as such get at the roots of war. It is the only perspective in which the question "who is the human being?" or "who am I?" is more important than the question "what do I have to do?" Only for religion does the inner truth of the human being, her importance as an individual have priority over the correctness of deeds. Only religion is not concerned with the external correction but with the inner reconciliation of the human being, not with his improvement, but with showing him mercy. Only religion is able to face the human being so unbiased, so understanding, so kind [*gütig*, connotes "good"] that it would be able to calm the fear in the depths of the human heart which again and again provides the reasons for war. . . . Only the nondoing of religion could make peace possible. (ibid., 230–31)

Religion calms the fear of the human spirit by pointing to a preexistent grace, to the unconditional acceptance by an absolute good will that is at the same time absolutely compassionate. But such grace to calm the deepest, preverbal and emotional layers of human existence depends on the very images of the human psyche that humans share universally and to a degree even with higher animals, images which are capable of making us *feel* grace, love, free, secure, justified, and peaceful. Drewermann's self-understanding as a Catholic theologian emphasizes the importance of images, especially against Protestant theologians who may agree with the importance of the grace of God or the justification by faith through grace but may reject any idea of a point of connection for grace and justification in human nature (see ibid., 250–51). He holds that the problem of Christianity is not that it has not talked about grace, love, peace, justification, security. "Christianity, in its current form, speaks much of love, but it fears love as a feeling. It speaks of freedom, but this passion of the subjective, this most feminine of all attitudes, is fought like a cancerous evil" (ibid., 259). It is the combination of the primacy of grace and of the key importance of psychic images which are at the heart of Drewermann's creative, therapeutic theology.

Healing Symbols of Religion: The Eating of the Godhead in the Holy Meal

Religion with its archaically rooted images has essentially the task of helping people experience their unique and absolute value, prior to anything they do (ibid., 326–27). Instead of confusing itself with superego morality, religion should strengthen what psychoanalysis calls the ego. "One does not need war anymore if by means of religion the feeling for one's own value has grown strong enough. Such an *ego strength* as a function of faith is psychologically the exact opposite to the depressive internalization of war under the compulsion of the ethical" (ibid., 327). "Religiously founded self-respect and self-recognition . . . [i]nner freedom and firmness are psychologically the most effective instruments for avoiding wars. Religion, however, if it does not lose itself to ethics, consists precisely in enabling and affirming the absolute self-respect of each individual from the perspective of God, and its effectiveness can be seen in terms of how much it is able to mediate credibly in its rites such a feeling of self-respect and recognition" (ibid.). In order to overcome war one needs to find value and recognition internally (ibid., 326).

This leads Drewermann to look for religious images which are capable of calming the fear at the core of the human spirit and to provide a sense of being absolutely wanted. Drewermann proposes that the symbolic ritual of the eating of the Godhead in a holy meal — for instance, the Holy Eucharist of Christianity — has the symbolic depth and the spiritual profundity necessary to calm the fear that propels the human spirit to fight wars. This symbolic ritual addresses the fears, guilt feelings, and oral needs for hold and security. As one coming from and trying to reinterpret the Christian tradition, Drewermann is mainly concerned with the question how Christianity can contribute to peace rather than war. He believes that in the symbol of the Holy Eucharist, Christianity has the opportunity to understand itself as a truly universal religion in the sense that it shares the archetypal image of the eating of the Godhead with holy meals of other religions. But it is important for Drewermann to stress that the symbol of the Eucharist is not meant, as it is often celebrated, to reinforce guilt feelings due to a moral misunderstanding of the death of Christ. The symbol of the Eucharist instead is meant to work through the guilt feelings and to experience an acceptance of the very aggression that could be deadly. In Chapter 3 we will explicate Drewermann's thesis that only a symbolic understanding of the Eucharist can avoid a sadomasochistic understanding of the historical killing of Jesus and a sadomasochistic instrumentalization of his death for purposes of legitimizing the mental or spiritual suffering of Christians by a religious power elite. Drewermann instead thinks that the death of Jesus could become a symbol only because people believed in him as one believes in a lover who died to maintain his integrity and that people were able to connect their psychic imagery of the Christ with Jesus, thus with a historical person. It is this connection of the archetypal imagery of the eating of the Godhead with a historical person which

Drewermann considers to be the truly unique contribution of Christianity as the cornerstone for an integration of the collective human unconscious with the historical ego of each person. But more on that in the next chapter.

Earlier in this chapter we saw that Drewermann considers war as a "symptom for the pathology of human reason" in its failed efforts to eliminate fear. He pointed to the misrelation of human reason to the archaic evolutionary programs of the brainstem. Any viable solution of the problem of war would have to be able to calm the fears that drive reason to go mad through moralistic self-destruction. For Drewermann, the sacraments of religion offer the last opportunity to serve as "the key to the understanding of the possibilities of a religious pacification of humans: because only the symbolism of the sacraments is as archaic as war and as spiritual as peace" (ibid., 283). *"The sacrament of the Eucharist* is the central sacrament of Christianity. It is the act in which Christianity expresses itself most deeply and by means of which it has attempted to provide a genuine answer to the problem of human hostility and evil" (ibid.). Understood deeply enough, Drewermann believes that the Eucharist accomplishes three key tasks in view of human aggression and human fear. It (1) *ritualizes* human aggressions effectively, (2) *prevents* [*kupieren,* also: to cut, arrest development of] fundamental feelings of guilt and fear in relation to aggressiveness, and (3) *sublimates* the instinctual aim of aggression (ibid., 284).

We will follow Drewermann's argument for each of these three elements in some detail as they amount to a broad-scale reinterpretation of central Christian imagery — comparable to the related reinterpretation of Cross and resurrection in his biblical commentary *Das Markusevangelium* (1990d, 1990e), which forms the basis of the next chapter.

Ritualizing Human Aggression Effectively. Combining research from the field of ethology and the work of Sigmund Freud, Drewermann assumes that, in addition to the external stimulation of the drives of sex and aggression along the lines of "innate release mechanisms," drives are also an "endogenous, periodically appearing need" which must be *"playfully* acted out" in "created, *artificial* scenes" if one wants to avoid "the danger of 'wild,' culturally destructive discharges of drives" (1992a, 284–85). This is where religion enters the picture. According to Drewermann's notion, religion "accepts, integrates, and interprets as part of a meaningful order" the aggressive human impulses instead of "prohibiting them in the form of a radical moral cure" (ibid., 300). Religion "sanctifies and includes the aggressive potential of the human psyche by means of certain sacred acts. The illusion of a life without destruction is not the real religious promise of such rites, but that the necessary part of human destructive work in itself does not need to be destructive [intrapsychically or interpersonally] if it is sanctified and permitted as part of life" (ibid., 301). "The religion of Christianity, together with the age-old rites of peoples, possesses a deep wisdom in *repeating,* as they did, the death of the Lord again and again in the sacrifice of the Mass in the Catholic Church" (ibid., 302). By providing it with a "ritually permitted realm,"[14] human aggression can "lose its explosive danger" (Drewermann 1992a, 302). Drewermann stresses that though Christianity in its "factual appearance" has failed to provide a solution to the problem of war it has available "in its dogmatics" (ibid., 303) what would be necessary for the "religious pacification [*Befriedung*]" (ibid., 283) of humans. Christian dogmatics "circumvents the danger of unforeseen, 'wild' outbursts of drives by *permitting* their ritualized — hence in itself *limited* — acting out.... It thus assumes that the human drives are not *as such* evil" and that they serve life as long as they are not "fearfully suppressed and repressed" (ibid., 303–4). "Only when the religious sanctification of human existence fails does the dilemma of the ethical and the powerlessness of the religious, of which we spoke, begin" (ibid., 304).

Preventing the Development of Guilt Feelings and of Fear as Responses to Impulses of Aggressiveness. Playing out aggression in ritual form *as such,* however, does not yet solve the problem of war. Drewermann points to the fact that in sports, too, society has developed a playful mode of expressing aggression. But unlike religion, sports does not aim at an *inner, symbolic* "interpretation of the meaning of life" or at a connection of the individual with "the order and wisdom of nature" (ibid., 288). In sports, "aggressions are superficially discharged externally,

---

14. Drewermann points to Erikson's work in this context: "The value of ritual for the socialization of humans has been pointed out by E. H. Erikson, *Gandhi's Truth* [1970], 433, where he reminds us of the pacification gestures in the animal realm and considers the expansion of human identity an essential means for peace: one can only wage war if one — unlike animals — denies the biological unity of the human species. The movements of peace are seen by him as a 'fight for the anticipatory developments of more inclusive identities' (ibid., 347 n. 72)." Cf. Erikson 1966, 1977.

but are not really worked through. To the contrary! The external-ization of the ritual contributes as such even to the disintegration of the drives. Especially modern mass events do precisely not promote the consciousness of the individual, as would be imperative for an education toward peace, but they let it sink into the delirium of the collective. In addition to the disintegration of the drives through ex-ternalization, the destruction of the personality through ecstatic mass experiences" tends to increase rather than calm aggression because of the pressure of the raw, collective pull by the mass (ibid., 289–90). Religion, in contrast, has the potential through its ritual of the holy meal to "help do away with the problem of human aggressiveness from the ground up" (ibid., 290).

The key reason for the difference of sports and religion in view of the problem of aggression is that religion addresses the deeply personal and ambivalent issue of oral guilt in its sacrament of the Eucharist while sports merely encourages the expression of aggres-sion through a mass experience without addressing the ambivalence of such expression. In psychoanalytic terms we could say that while sports gets around the defense, religion takes the defense serious and works through the ambivalence of oral aggression. How does Drewermann see religion work through the deep ambivalence of oral aggression?

The experience of human guilt has to do with the experience that one has to kill life in order to live. Paleoanthropologically, myths especially have connected the act of killing with the experience of guilt. In myths the killing is not merely confined to the killing of humans (as in the practice of cannibalism) or of animals (as, for instance, in the Siberian bear cult), but even the killing of plants (as in the myths of Osiris, the God of grain, or Dionysus, the God of wine) is connected with the experience of guilt. Though Drewermann considers the psychological (archetypal) and historical roots of the sacrament of the holy meal to go as far back as the ritual meals of the early hunters, thus making this sacrament a truly "primordial sacrament [*Ursakrament*]," he notes that "the Christian Eucharist has received [the basis for] its particular form not from the hunters of the ice age, but from the ideas and rites of the early agricultural cultures" (ibid., 293). "[T]he ritual of 'the eating of the Godhead' was obviously — through a transformation of the older rites of the ice-age cultures of hunters — widely disseminated as an archetypal thought among the ancient agricultural cultures of the Mediterranean for thousands of years. It simply needed to be taken up and realized by the Early Church for the interpretation of its own experiences of faith. In the religions of the early agriculturalists the fruit of the fields was seen as the child of father sky and mother earth, and the harvesting of grain and the crushing of grape vines was seen as the killing of the divine child which — like the divine animals of the ice age — sacrificed itself as food for humans" (ibid., 296). This idea is effectively behind the Christian Eucharist: "that the son of God sacrifices his flesh in the form of bread and his blood in form of wine in order to be present with his believers and to have them participate in his death and his resurrection" (ibid.), thus connecting to the deepest oral-sadistic and cannibalistic impulses.

Drewermann stresses that this idea also "connects to the very contents of fertility religions which were *denied* in the Jewish Passover meal" (ibid., 298 n. 19). At the same time, the sacrament of the holy meal is closely related — in many religions — to the "sacrament of *baptism,* that is, with the symbol for death and resurrection" (ibid., 299). Besides the obvious parallels between the Christian Eucharist and the mystery cults of Eleusis, Drewermann points, for instance, to the Indonesian myth of the death and resurrection of the God Hainuwele who is killed and eaten during the great Maro-dance. "In the same way a Christian today is baptized into the death of his Lord which he or she commits to in the Eucharist," thus participating in resurrection and immortality (ibid., 300).

Drewermann highlights that the actual problem of religion is, however, not that one has to kill in order to live. If this were the actual problem, "one would ethically have to accuse and declare as guilty existence itself and the natural laws," which would — as has happened frequently in modernity — lead to ethical efforts "to be *better* than one has been created" and "to substitute the order of the world generally with a supposedly higher order" (ibid., 305). The issue of religion is not that one has to kill life in order to live, but how one can overcome guilt feelings that derive from the experience that one wants to kill what one loves and admires most. Reconnecting once more with the story of Genesis 3, Drewermann writes: "*Psychoanalytically* the first experience of guilt at the beginning of each human life consists in having destroyed through a prohibited eating the paradisal unity" (ibid., 307). Especially "the process of weaning appears to the infant — as many studies of depressive guilt feelings show — as a deserved punishment for her or his oral excessiveness and greed" (ibid., 307).

Oral guilt feeling, however, receives a religious meaning, as we saw above, only if the needs for hold and security experienced in relation to the individual mother figure are seen as expressions of fundamental needs that characterize human existence and are represented psychically in the archetype of the mother. As fundamental needs they are needs of the human spirit. What gives a religious quality to the experience of oral guilt, that is, of depression, is the sense that one is guilty merely for existing at all. We noted in Chapter 1 and earlier in this chapter that Drewermann considers the spiritually broadened notion of depression as at the root of war, even when from a purely psychoanalytic point of view elements from other clinical impressions may predominate. We need to keep in mind that Drewermann uses the clinical categories as a phenomenology of the human spirit under the spell of fear. "The depressed person experiences the very fact that he exists on this earth as a guilt which can never be paid back." The key feeling of the depressive is: "life as a constant working off the guilt of the mere fact that one exists on the earth" (ibid., 308). Christianity has consciously connected the doctrine of original sin with the oral story of the fall from paradise. It thus gave a central dogmatic place to "this experience of human existence profoundly put into question through the feeling of fundamental guilt." In response it has "tried to find an answer to the oral experience of guilt precisely in the symbol of the holy meal, an answer which is as universal as the fundamental doubt of existence itself is" (ibid.).

According to Drewermann, the achievement of the sacrament of the Holy Eucharist is that it connects with the deepest phylogenetic and ontogenetic feelings of guilt and declares humans to be "free of guilt" for merely existing and for needing to kill for food in order to live. The following passage sums up Drewermann's argument how the ritual of the holy meal, of the eating of the Godhead, responds both to deep-seated psychological and existential guilt feelings which question one's very existence as such.

Particularly on the background of oral guilt feelings the celebration of the Eucharist in its oral symbolic language wants to *acquit* human existence *from the ground up,* coming from the experience of taking in food, and redeem it from the fear that again and again entangles it against its own will into the

dilemma of the aggressive movements of the drives. If oral cannibalism represents the deepest experience of guilt, well — this
sacrament seems to say — *we allow* the cannibalism from God's
perspective. If the human being is most deeply confused and
shaken by the fact that she has to kill what she loves most —
well, *we allow* her from the perspective of God to kill from what
she lives. It is as if the sacrament of the Eucharist attempts —
very much along the lines of Saint Paul's logic — to dam up,
radicalize, and unite the whole experience of human guilt to
its maximum in order to redeem it and take it away as a whole.
The guilt feeling of the depressive results from the sense of being
able only to steal what he needs to live. The sacrament of the Eucharist wants to assure him from the perspective of God, against
his fear, that his existence is a *gift* from the ground up and that
he is *given* freely what he thinks he is appropriating violently.

The Eucharist is thus — far deeper and more radical than
the sacrament of "confession," which deals only with individual
failures of the human will — an absolution [*Lossprechung;* lit.,
"a speaking free"] of all of existence, deep down into the roots of
the unconscious. It is a comprehensive attempt, in the manner of
a psychodrama, to *heal* by means of *acting out* what is actually
destructive. It is like an attempt *to make* and *to do* consciously
what is eternally guilty, eternally prohibited, in order to accept
it *in the doing* as not guilty. The Eucharist is like a desperate
and extreme effort of religion to tell humans what no mother is
able to say in a psychologically convincing way to her child in
depression: that the child's feelings are baseless, that, contrary to
the child's guilt feelings, he is no murderer and that he can stop
feeling like a cannibal and living like a cannibal merely because
he has to live and *eat.* The God who one thinks one kills in
the sacrament will live — he gives himself — it is the God's own
sacrifice, not murder, which happens there. . . .

Religion could not be in sharper contrast to ethics than by
blessing sacramentally what ethics condemns most and by trying to eradicate what ethics particularly demands: namely, that
humans should feel *ashamed* and *guilty* for their greed and their
rawness. Religion — not only Christianity, mind you, but religion *as such,* if one considers its dogmatic teachings — seems
to be sustained by the knowledge that one cannot achieve anything in humans if one tries to suppress by means of reason

and will, feelings of shame and of guilt, the "beast" in humans. It [religion] — infinitely more courageous and wiser than any ethics — is trusting enough to believe that humans have nothing evil in themselves *if* their drives and reactional readinesses are not magnified to excessive proportions through the distorting mirror of fear. (ibid., 309–11)

Religion is able to acquit humans from their conscious or unconscious sense of existential guilt because of its belief in an absolute grace, an absolute and unconditional acceptance of human existence. "Religion wants to risk life, it believes...that humans can only be good by means of a preceding and absolute grace...to the point that a human being, instead of experiencing her entire existence as guilt, becomes grateful for the fact that she lives: the eating of the Godhead then becomes literally '*Eucharist,*' a *giving thanks* for the gift of existence" (ibid., 313).

Sublimating the Instinctual Aim of Aggression. At this point we might have serious concerns about Drewermann's notion that the Eucharist would present an acquittal for oral-sadistic, yes, cannibalistic impulses by acting them out within a limited ritual. Such concerns are warranted and lead us to "the last contribution of religion to the solution of the issue of war" which "is actually the most important one and today probably the most difficult one": in addition to "*integrating* and *taming* human aggression" religion "tries to *transform* and *sublimate* it" (ibid., 314).

The ritualized expression of aggression in the form of war, in the form of headhunting or in the form of cannibalism did obviously not solve the problem of collective violence. It may have served to "calm anxiety and strengthen the sense of togetherness in one's group, but...the factor of collective violence is as such not yet solved...[and] instead is merely made possible in the first place in larger organized associations" (ibid., 315). The ritualization of aggression in these *external* forms of acting out within a dynamic of pseudo-speciation[15] are actually the basis for holy wars (Drewermann 1992a, 315).

---

15. For the potential of "human ritualization" to overcome "pseudo-speciation," see Erikson 1993, 423–36. For Erikson the division of humans into "pseudo-species" is characterized by a "cumulative aggravation of *bad conscience, negative identity,* and *hypocritical moralism*" (ibid., 434).

Only by adding to the ideas of the integration and of the forgiveness of aggressive impulses *"the idea of sublimation or transformation"* — "found precisely in the symbol of the eating of the Godhead" — does religion make "a third important, and in the last instance, decisive contribution to the solution of human aggression" (ibid., 315). Particularly the idea that the external signs of the holy meal are spiritualized makes this sacrament capable of transforming raw human aggression into forces which support the unity of self and the world:

> Instead of changing humans in their deeds and behavior, religious efforts aim therefore at an inner *transformation* of humans in their being, and its [i.e., religion's] central symbol is since antiquity — in form of the ritual of the eating of the Godhead — the *transubstantiation* of the offering, the *spiritualization* of the external signs of bread and wine into an inner, divine reality. The immediate drive movement of eating with all its oral-sadistic, cannibalistic implications shall be transformed into an act of spiritual union, into a *unio mystica* of God and human, consciousness and unconscious, female and male, mental and bodily, into a birth of the true human. (ibid., 316)

That a cannibalistic symbol is open to such spiritual sublimation presupposes an "openness of each archetypal symbol which signifies from the start the crudest and the most noble, the most external and the most internal, the lowest and the highest, and which encompasses in its breadth the entire tension and developmental possibility of the human psyche" (ibid.).[16] In the religious use of the archetypal symbol of the eating of the Godhead the "tendency of an inner spiritualization" dominated *"from the beginning"* (Drewermann 1992a, 317). Such a tendency can already be found, for instance, in the monstrous practice of the Aztec human sacrifice where the heart is cut out as a symbol for the opening of the heart toward the light of the Godhead (ibid., 319). One has the impression, Drewermann suggests,

---

16. Cf. Erikson (1993) who noted with reference to K. Lorenz in a similar vein that the nonviolent *"revolutionary* kind of human ritualization . . . may derive some of its obvious strength from an *evolutionary* potential, namely, the one so dramatically illustrated by the pacific rituals of animals" (ibid., 435). But, Erikson stressed, "only faith gives back to man the dignity of nature" (ibid.). Thus he suggested that Gandhi was able to create "a ritualization through which men, equipped with both realism and spiritual strength, can face each other with a mutual confidence analogous to the instinctive safety built into the animals' pacific rituals" only because he had faith (ibid., 433).

that the more "the external expression is removed from the actually intended spiritual content the more the latter remains itself unconscious and the more one has an intuitive knowledge of oneself only in the most externalized projections of oneself" (ibid., 320). There is thus a tendency to ever further spiritualization of sacrifice: from human sacrifices to animal sacrifices to unbloody sacrifices of vegetables to, finally, the simple unbloody sign of the Eucharist (ibid., 321–32). The goal of religion, be it that of the Buddha or that of the mysteries of Elysium or that of Christianity, is eventually that "the sensual human being [*sinnlicher Mensch*] be transformed into a human being living more from within [*innerlicher Mensch*]. Instead of perceiving the external happening as the essential, the external should rather be understood as the symbol of the essential spiritual content" (ibid., 322).

The spiritual answer to the acting out of aggressive impulses in war is the belief in immortality grounded in archetypal images of the psyche. "The sublimation of human aggression" means that "war could really be overcome by *spiritual* means. It [i.e., war] would appear as something unspiritual or, better, as a mere preliminary step of the spirit, as something outdated. For the first time we could awake from the spiritual madness of the nightmare of war and could find spiritual health in the 'therapeutic means of immortality'" (ibid., 323). Moreover, "[t]he spiritualization of humans, which is intended and expressed in the symbol of transformation, is not only the single means for the overcoming of war but is the overcoming itself" (ibid., 324). The path is the goal.

Religion, by providing an *inner* foundation for one's existence, makes it unnecessary for the human spirit to seek existential, that is, absolute recognition and respect in the external world. "Religion does presuppose in its archaic images that this recognition and respect is spiritually pre-existent in an absolute way. Its sacraments, especially the rites of the eating of the Godhead, precisely want to say that each human being has reason from God's perspective to feel his existence to be unconditionally wanted and affirmed" (ibid., 326–27). By grounding one's sense of self-value spiritually in this pre-existent, divine affirmation, religion achieves by implication several things at once which are required for the pacification of humans.

First and foremost, it provides the basis to resolve conflicts, not through external but through spiritual means. Spiritual here means both self-reflective and religious. "From a spiritual perspective it is absurd to seek one's right or what one considers one's right in the superiority of external power and violence. Spiritually there is only one way to find and sustain one's right: argumentation, that is, persuading the 'enemy' by means of a reciprocal exchange of claims to rights and with a readiness to accept mutual limitations and an ability to compromise. From a spiritual perspective right is a function of truth not of violence" (ibid., 324). Drewermann adds:

> Only such a spiritual transformation of the external into a symbol of what is internally meant, only an awakening ability to see and express verbally the external deed as an expression of the internal creates the condition necessary for overcoming war from within as something *only* external, unspiritual, raw. . . . One has to show clearly for what humans *spiritually* fight when they scrap for lands and power interests. One must see what they want, mean and stand for *spiritually* when they wage war against each other, only then will the battle of ideologies, religions, cultures, and different spirits of people no longer be acted out on the battle field. (ibid., 325)

Secondly, by validating the underlying claim for recognition and respect of one's existence religion avoids the fallacy of an ethical solution which requires the suppression instead of the working through of the aggressive impulses. It is precisely because the spiritual perspective, the sublimation of the aggressive tendencies, requires "a considerable amount of self-confidence and ego strength" that an ethical solution falls short of its goal:

> The displacement of aggression from the external unto the internal must, if it is purely *morally* enforced, merely lead to a war on the inside, to an increase especially of the depressive and obsessive compulsive conflicts. Religion, on the other hand, with its motif of the *transformation* is capable of doing quite something else: by spiritualizing the raw external side of human aggression it makes war itself a symbolic happening whose meaning consists in a *spiritual* aim: in the claim to right or truth. Usually a claim to right that is external is psychologically only an expression of a claim to inner estimation of worth and recognition: a main reason why wars break out again and again consists, as we have seen, in the feeling of humiliation, of contempt, and of national shame — the valuelessness of the militarily weak or

defeated in the face of the stronger. In view of this archaic sense, spiritually what kind of self-respect could one base on the ability to humiliate or kill another *physically?* The superiority of violence is spiritually again only a *symbol* for the desire for *inner* recognition and respect: were it given — most wars would no longer occur. (ibid., 326)

Thirdly, by its meaning and promise that one's entire existence is absolutely justified, accepted, and valuable, the symbolic ritual of the eating of the Godhead makes physical death lose its terror and is capable of stopping the vicious cycle of revenge. "The ritual of the dying God, if deeply enough empathized, presents the deepest assurance conceivable that what externally has to be feared most; physical death, can lose its terror *spiritually.* Life itself does not need to be horrible merely because it will end inevitably in physical death. By promising and guaranteeing eternal life beyond death, the celebration of the eating of the Godhead [means that] there is finally nothing of which one needs to be deadly afraid. Hence there exists nothing against which one has to fight *absolutely* and essentially" (ibid., 328–29).

The cycle of the mentality of revenge is broken psychologically by means of an identification with the divine person who has made the ultimate sacrifice for oneself. That religion binds the reassurance of life and the forgiveness of one's guilt to a "person" is crucial to Drewermann's argument.

In addition, this affirmation of life against the fear of death by means of the image of the dying God is not expressed abstractly, as an idea or ideal, but is bound to the person who receives the highest religious interest. The sacrament of the eating of the Godhead even requires and enables that one *identifies* most deeply with the fear, the suffering, and the death of the divine person. Through this one's own fear, the feeling of abandonment, of nothingness, of powerlessness disappears too within the connectedness of a deeper love: he, whom one loved the most, because he is life, has also died.

Only through the overcoming of fear by means of such an identification with him who overcomes death does the inner freedom for peace come into existence from the ground up. The ego strength and self-respect and the trust in the value of one's life that cannot be lost in the face of death enable one within to be

outwardly generous and to let oneself and others live. War as
a battle for existence, the instrumentalization of death with the
constant threat of death, loses its justification and its necessity
if life shows itself to be confirmed, recognized, and *everlasting*.
The sacrament of the eating of the Godhead is, seen in this perspective, really a sacrament of reconciliation: reconciliation with
the worst enemy feared — death. (ibid., 329)

Fourthly, the spiritual ritual of the eating of the Godhead is effective because it provides an answer to the infinite fears of the spirit.
The solution of religion "must consist in an inner spiritualization, because the deepest reasons for the fear stem precisely from the forces of
the spirit, from anticipatory reason and from the infinite play of possibilities in consciousness. The human species seems on the whole to
possess only one choice: either to forcefully work off the fear of death
in ever new wars to the point of actual death and self-annihilation
or to respond spiritually by means of religion to the fear which falls
upon humans from the spirit" (ibid., 330).

Fifthly, the psychological effectiveness of the ritual of the Eucharist
lies in the fact that its symbolism integrates the feminine in the human
psyche.

War is and has been, as we have seen, a matter of men and
it stems partly from an overvaluation of male "virtues" in a
society.... For that reason it is all the more important that the
masculine parts of the psyche fuse with feminine strivings. The
meaning of the sacramental symbolism of the eating of the Godhead consists... precisely in such a synthesis of the masculine
and the feminine, of the conscious and the unconscious. Already the oral act of eating on the *object level* means a merging
with the mother,[17] inclusive of all the qualities of feelings which
are connected with it: the permission to feel unconditionally accepted like a child, the sensation of security, protection, hold
and warmth, etc. The divine appears in the sacrament of the
meal itself as something feminine with which the human being
merges. And vice-versa, in the sacrament of the meal the experience of the feminine becomes credibly present archetypally

---

17. In a note Drewermann cites here the same passage from Szondi which he had quoted
in *Strukturen des Bösen* (1985a) to support the notion of an innate "drive to cling" which is
originally directed toward the mother and which he considers to be the emotional basis for the
religious need for unconditional acceptance. See Chapter 1.

as a final metaphysical givenness [*Gegebenheit*] of existence. Only thus do we understand the meaning of the meal as a sign of reconciliation, pacification, and provision for the journey — as a means for immortality. On a deeper, *subject level* the act of eating means at the same time a fusion with the feminine archetype of one's own psyche. The gifts of bread and wine themselves symbolize the feminine and masculine parts of the human psyche. They stand for matter and spirit and their association corresponds depth-psychologically to the mystery of the Holy Wedding, the unification of the soul . . . the unity with the lost anima. (Drewermann 1992a, 331–34)

This aspect of the Eucharist provides to Drewermann "the theological foundation of the possibility, even the necessity of the priesthood of women" — which is one of the controversial issues for which Drewermann was branded by the official Catholic Church as violating its teachings.

Finally, the ritual of the Eucharist supplies a symbol which, according to Drewermann, has the potential for a real humanity-wide peace, for a universal siblingship in which hunger and death are no longer the reasons to fight one another under the spell of fear but become reasons to come together and share.

The sacrament of the Eucharist picks up precisely the motif of hunger, of eating, in order to transform what divides as something that binds together. Historically, religion here undoubtedly leans on the model of the early hunters for whom hunting, together with the *communal* sharing and devouring of the captured prey, contributed essentially to the creation of a sense of community within one's hunting group. But out of the thousands of years of history of the stone age an archetype emerged whose psychological significance reaches far beyond its historical origin and which exists innately in all humans as a psychical readiness for experience [*Erlebnisbereitschaft*]. By appropriating the *archetype of the meal* sacramentally, religion wins *ipso facto* an energy which is directed toward a universal siblingship of *all* humans. (ibid., 335–36)

Drewermann thus envisions the sacrament of the Eucharist, of the holy meal as a means for a "humanity-wide psychotherapy" (ibid.,

337), and religion as a "dream of trust" against the "nightmare of fear" (ibid., 339).

It would perhaps be easy to consider the images of religion which Drewermann draws upon as utopian. We need to keep in mind that for Drewermann the most important consequences of distinguishing religion from ethics are its stance of unconditional understanding and acceptance and its notion of grace. This has far-reaching implications: in terms of the issue of war and peace, every human being has to be accepted at their actual level of peacefulness. Separating himself explicitly from Gandhi's practice of nonviolence, Drewermann clarifies, that

> religion should beware of making "pacifism" a doctrine. According to its basic attitude it should take its departure from the truth of the individual and her situation and not from an ideal or idol — not even that of nonviolence.... Violence could under circumstances be closer to the cause of Christ than the external correctness of pacifism [NB: which is not to say that it would be religiously justified!]....

> More important and basic than the question of violence or nonviolence, war or nonwar is the question of the true motives of one's action and, together with that, the question of the truth of one's person.... Mahatma Gandhi, the only truly peaceful political leader of the twentieth century, called his "program" of nonviolence *satyagraha,* "the power which is born from truth," and emphasized ... that it is not possible to be peaceful and nonviolent as long as the state of fear continues ... [a long quotation from Gandhi, *Freiheit ohne Gewalt* (Freedom without Violence) 1968, 26, follows which ends with] "Violence is necessary for the protection of external things, nonviolence is necessary for the protection of *atman,* for the protection of one's honor." One should perhaps better translate: for the protection of one's actual self, one's true dignity. But it is nonetheless clear what Gandhi means: by means of the power of religion through trust in God one must have been freed from fear in order to be peaceful and act peacefully....

> But even such statements are still in danger of being too ideal and too abstract. Who can really be that: a truly religious human? Another great *homo religiosus* of modern India, Ramakrishna, thus very truly bound the absolute insight into

religion to the relativity of the path. "At a holy place of bath there are numerous stairs (Ghâts) which lead down to the water," he said. "Thus there are many Ghâts to the water of the eternal."...What is valid for religion as such has to be all the more valid in the particular issue of war and peace: each person has to act and be accepted depending on the level of spiritual and mental development at which she experiences herself. Someone who is internally filled with fear and therefore a man of war may not be coerced into peace in the name of religion. And reversely: nothing can be more rejected in the name of religion than the *egalité*-principle of the French Revolution, according to which every "citizen" is condemned to "general" military duty....Religion, of whatever kind, should foremost demand from the state that in the question of war and peace everyone has the right and the duty to act in accord with his inner character at the time of decision. On the score of *satyagraha,* the acting from the truth of one's being, Christianity has once more reason to learn from the religiosity of Indians. (ibid., 375–78)

Situating his search for a religious answer to the problem of war once more within the historical context of World War II, Drewermann responds to the possible objection to his proposed religious solution that such an answer would hardly be able to "heal someone like Alexander the Great, Frederick the Great or Adolf Hitler of their hate toward the father, their hate toward themselves, their feeling of inferiority, their need for power and revenge, in short, their belligerent rage and danger" (ibid., 373). Following Fromm's interpretation of Hitler's psychology (Fromm 1973, 369–433) and Fest's biography of Hitler (Fest 1974), Drewermann notes that Hitler's father seems actually not to have been the kind of sadistic or tyrannical personality which Hitler perceived him to be, but that the father "became the Oedipal opponent of his son above all through the exaggerated and spoiling tenderness with which Klara Hitler raised her son" (Drewermann 1992a, 373 n. 97; see Drewermann 1985a, 495–503). The fascination which the neurotic personality of Hitler exerted on the "mass psychology of the Third Reich rested without doubt on what J. Fest...called 'the great fear' which in its despair saw in the collective promises of heroic greatness and explosive violence yet some comfort" (ibid., 373 n. 98). Drewermann agrees with the assessment that neither a "religious" nor a "secular" form of psychotherapy could prevent someone like Hitler at the height of his megalomanic dreams from acting belligerent; however, "such eccentric characters must no longer pose a danger to neurotically infect a people if its members are sufficiently strengthened [*gefestigt*] within the archetypal images of an intact religion against the vortex of collective fear. No other starting point exists than to begin through a religious 'therapy' with oneself and with every individual. Religion presents the only collective proposal of therapy for the pacification of the human being, but this proposal, too, has only prospect for success and endurance if the individual is led by means of religion to her own identity and inner firmness [*Festigkeit*]" (ibid., 373–34). Thus religion is viewed by Drewermann as less capable of solving existing wars and more as a prophylaxis preventing the emergence of the dynamics that lead to war in the first place.

Chapter 3

Recovering the Nonviolent God-Image of Jesus: Working Through a Sadomasochistic Interpretation of the Cross

The moment we begin to fear the opinions of others and hesitate to tell the truth that is in us, and from motives of policy are silent when we should speak, the divine floods of light and life flow no longer into our souls. Every truth we see is ours to give the world, not to keep for ourselves alone, for in so doing we cheat humanity out of their rights and check our own development.
— Elizabeth Cady Stanton, *Womanliness* (1890 Address to the National American Woman Suffrage Association Convention)

Eugen Drewermann's reinterpretation of the Christian doctrine of original sin emphasizes that sin does not result from a lack of good will but is instead a deformation of human existence as a whole due to the fear of the human spirit. The attitude religion takes toward the fear of the human spirit decides whether religion heals or harms, redeems or violates, liberates or oppresses. Drewermann understands Jesus' death psychologically in light of Jesus' opposition to a certain universal type of religiosity: because Jesus opposed a type of religiosity based on an ambivalent, violent God-image, and dared to live by a nonambivalent God-image, he drew the repressed rage associated with the violent God-image upon himself and was killed. In this chapter, we will travel into the heart of Drewermann's therapeutic reinterpretation of Christianity where the beliefs in Cross and resurrection are seen as essential elements of a drama of the "cleansing" of the God-image from its fear-based projections of ambivalence (Drewermann 1990d, 77).

Drewermann's two-volume commentary on the Gospel of Mark, *Das Markusevangelium* (1990d), supplemented by a dense article on the symbolism of tree and Cross in view of a history of religions (Drewermann 1979), is the main source for this chapter. In a substantial introduction to the commentary on Mark (Drewermann 1990d, 11–123), he employs depth psychology as a model for a comprehensive reinterpretation of Cross and resurrection. With the experience of the fall leading to an ambivalent God-image as portrayed in the book of Genesis in the background, Drewermann presents the dramatic psychospiritual dynamic of redemption from an ambivalent God-image as found in the narrative of Mark. We will first follow Drewermann as he argues that a religion based on sacrifice and moral effort is itself the fruit of a God-image distorted by fear and that it must inevitably demonize both God and humans. Then I will present two complementary aspects of Drewermann's interpretation of the symbolism of the Cross. The first aspect deals primarily with the questions why the historical Jesus was killed, how to avoid an interpretation that perpetuates a sadomasochistic understanding of suffering and death, and how a typological rather than historical interpretation can avoid blaming past (and present) people or groups for his death and, instead, can focus on the factually universal mentality that leads to the killing of the one who questions a violent God-image. The primary model Drewermann employs to elucidate this first aspect is the transference situation of Freudian psychoanalysis. The psychological perspective is on an "objective level" or object-related in the sense described in Appendix 2 and in Chapter 1. The core conflict finding expression in Jesus' cruel death is "historical" in the sense that it involves the radical alternative between fear and trust of the "historical" ego, that is, of the human spirit in its concrete existence. Though Drewermann alludes in his interpretation of the symbol of the Cross from this first perspective to the oral-sadistic conflicts of aggression which we described at length in our presentation of his analysis of the symbolism of the tree and the forbidden fruit as symbols for both mother and father in the story of the fall, the full significance of the symbolism of the Cross beyond the ontogenetic meaning can be grasped, according to Drewermann, only if one pays attention to the subjective level, the inner meaning of Cross and resurrection. This brings us to the second aspect of his interpretation of the Cross, namely, from a "subjective-level," Jungian perspective which he deepens by findings from ethology and existential philosophy and which he relates to and differentiates from a theological interpretation. The Cross is here seen as an intrapsychic symbol for the painful process of psychic integration and of the spiritual reunion with God that involves recognizing the ambivalent and violent elements of the God-image as representations of psychic opposites and taking back the metaphysical projections of this ambivalence into God. The two aspects of Drewermann's interpretation describe two sides of the same process of psychospiritual healing on various levels: the working-through of external and internal disunity and the process of emerging unity; the experiences of the historical ego between fear and trust and the transhistorical archetypal imagery which provides the building blocks for a healing of the whole human being; the human needs and struggles as reflected in the presence of a violent God-image and the longing for absolute hold, that is, for a nonviolent God; and the clarification of the God-image and the experience of a nonambivalent divine person. Objective- and subjective-level perspectives converge particularly in the archetypal imagery that has both ontogenetic and phylogenetic significance.

In the final chapter, I will present Drewermann's analysis of sadomasochistic psychospiritual structures and their domination of the current clergy-ideal in Catholicism, which can also be found in varying degrees in other Christian denominations, as well as his attempt to reinterpret the clergy-ideal in a mentally and spiritually nonviolent manner. Drewermann suggests that the current clergy-ideal in the Roman Catholic Church requires the ideal type of the clergy to live an externally defined faith that presupposes their complete identification with the office and the eradication of their subjectivity — with all the concomitant desperate ways in which the repressed parts must reassert themselves. Drewermann's analysis focuses on the notion that the identity of the clergy centers around the idea of sacrifice. The current clergy-ideal feeds off unresolved psychological conflicts in early childhood which are repressed and then projected by means of spiritual fears into the metaphysical realm in the form of an ambivalent God-image. He emphasizes that the power structures of the institution of the Church are based on and require the sacrificial mentality of its clergy. Any change to a more internally based faith grounded in the subjectivity of the human spirit, he maintains, poses a powerful threat to the collective rule of the Church over the individual. Nonetheless, Drewermann presents a therapeutic reinterpretation of the clergy-ideal from an inner, spiritual perspective which, he believes, could foster a mentally nonviolent form of faith and of religious community.

Violent God-Image and Sacrificial Religion

Drewermann has observed that in Genesis (2–11) God appears to humans as an enemy, a competitor, a moralist, and an authoritarian ruler only after humans were gripped in the jaws of an existential anxiety that transformed their entire existence into a convulsion of fear. This insight is crucial for a reinterpretation of the death of Jesus and of the symbolism that became attached to it through which Jesus became the Christ. Only an understanding of sin in light of the dynamic of fear can avoid the reification of a God-image that does violence to the human spirit and the human psyche.

> Only with such an understanding of "sin" can we avoid defining the relationship of the human being to God as problematic due to a lack of good will, due to pride or disobedience, thereby badly distorting the God-image as moralistic, authoritarian, and heteronomous.... Only thus does one, on the other hand, succeed in defining the concept of "sin" existentially as a deformation of existence [*Dasein*] entirely, instead of defining it morally as a fault of the will or as a failure of behavior. Only thus can one above all avoid deforming religion itself into an institution of heteronomy, of internalized violence and of limitless fear. (Drewermann 1990d, 16)

To "obey" God by doing one's moral duty is only necessary beyond Eden. In the story of Cain and Abel, Drewermann finds the prototypical example of how a desperate exertion of the human will to be acceptable to God by sacrificing the best of one's existence does not present a " 'progress' in culture or religious awareness" but, to the contrary, only leads humans further away from God and becomes the occasion for deadly conflict (ibid., 18). This is the background upon which Drewermann develops his critique of traditional interpretations of the notion of Christian sacrifice, which are based on a moralistic understanding of Jesus' sacrifice on the Cross. What

> takes place in a human being who believes she can regain the favor of her God only by yielding and destroying the best she has produced...is the [attempted] (obsessive compulsive) escape from all forms of inferiority and loneliness by "earning" the lack of "recognition" and esteem — because they are not "freely given" — through one's own freegiving [*Wegschenken*]. This sadistic characteristic of self-abasement and humiliation in

the fight for a lost love lives in every sacrificial religion. Not the progress of religion, but the escalating perversion of religion can be observed in this.... Precisely in the midst of a world in which recognition is based on relentless sacrifice and performance do I have to discover the Other as my enemy, as my deadly competitor whose danger threatens me more the closer he is to me. (ibid., 18–9)

The internally violent moral effort demanded by sacrificial religion, this (often unconscious) attempt to gain recognition from God by doing the right thing and sacrificing the best, inevitably ends in existential failure. To understand Drewermann's perspective accurately we need to clarify that he is not throwing out the notion of sacrifice *per se* in religion, but that he is talking about all sacrifice that is understood in the external sense: that is, sacrifice as something imposed from outside upon the self (e.g., based on internalized injunctions from authority figures in the form of the superego); sacrifice as the surrender of one's will or reason or any part of oneself to the will of another human person without regard to the well-being of the self. As will appear in our review of the second, subjective-level aspect of Drewermann's interpretation of the Cross, if sacrifice is understood instead as the surrender of a one-sided intrapsychic or spiritual attitude and as something in the service of the true self, that is, as an inner process, then it can accurately describe processes on the way to psychic and spiritual integration.

Most terrifying for humans, according to Drewermann, is when human fear reaches the level where humans perceive in God, too, someone who speaks only the language of moral instructions. "It is *impossible* for the human being within a field of distance from God, within the basic feeling of the 'banished children of Eve' of not being justified in this world, to fulfill even the most simple moral rule, namely, that one human being lets the Other live next to him. The most terrifying experience for an anxiety-ridden human being is finally to be addressed even by God solely in the language of the 'Thou shalt' " (ibid., 20). Such a God-image has truly demonic traits. Accordingly "only *pure* spirits — to borrow from the language of Christian dogmatics — are capable" of the "most dangerous" form of the demonic (ibid., 41). Referring to the story of the Great Flood in the Yahwist's primordial history (Gen. 6–8), Drewermann notes that "the Bible does not shy away from imagining what it would be like if God, too, were taken by such a spiritual attitude" (ibid., 41–42). After the fall and in the face of all the evil humans have committed, it is said (Gen. 6:5–6) that God wants to "clean the face of the earth through a Great Flood from the defilement by humans" (ibid., 42). The source of life appears under the spell of fear as the source of death who regrets the creation of human life. But after the flood, the Yahwist portrays the same God as regretful, as pledging never again to curse the earth because of humans; for God accepts that after the fall — that is, for Drewermann: under the spell of fear — the human being is capable only of evil (Gen. 8:21). And only "because God does *not* insist on a 'clean' world and a 'purified' human being do we really exist.... That God does *not* ultimately reject us but continues to count on us, this extremely antiprophetic, antiapocalyptic characteristic of the divine lets us exist.... And yet the monstrous thought existed and exists — a thought actually worthy of a God but which God evidently has to reject repeatedly and emphatically: the temptation of a kind of perfection of creation that would devastate all of life. God, the biblical primordial history tells us, has rejected this temptation once and for all" (ibid.).

If the thought of a God who seeks "absolutely just and universal judgment" is seen in itself, apart from the God who shows unconditional acceptance, one would "probably have the most perfect image of the figure of a 'Satan': of a pure and most high angel who becomes devil by striving to serve God better than God could be served" (ibid.). The image of the devil in the Gospel of Mark essentially comes down for Drewermann to this: "if humans are befallen by a spiritual attitude which forces them, with reference to God, to appear more just and pure than the Eternal One, then the highest ideals, the instructions of piety as well as the rules of morality become cruelly fanatical, terroristic, and fixedly rigid" (ibid., 43).

Against the tendency to understand religion externally as a set of instructions for being perfect, for being-like-God, in the moral sphere, Drewermann emphasizes with the Yahwist and Mark that "nothing in God is devilish and nothing in the human being must be devilish. What kind of poor devils, however, do humans need to degenerate to if through sheer fear they... hallucinate a God who stands ready at all times to impose a new Great Flood and who with constant threats wants to force all humans to be 'better' than they can be — angels instead of humans and devils instead of angels!" (ibid., 44). Drewermann believes that humans can escape from fear and its resulting evil only when they "are allowed to put their trust in being loved and necessary — precisely in their lowness. We can only stop having to exist as children of darkness if we can gain trust that, though poor like dust from birth, we belong to an invisible kingdom in which we are guests and royalty before God at the throne of eternity. With *this* image of the human being Jesus wanted to liberate us from the power of evil. The sons of humans[1] should find trust in the vision God has of the human being" (ibid.).

Drewermann notes that the Gospel of Mark shares the Yahwist's perspective that human existence without God is a "picture of extreme hopelessness and need for redemption" (ibid., 27). Such a world is completely "in the hands of the power of evil which has erected within the hearts of humans a closed system of domination. The only difference is that Mark no longer speaks of the origin of evil by means of a symbolic image such as the 'serpent' " but instead of Satan and his demons, ideas adopted from ancient Jewish apocalypticism (ibid., 27–28). These "spiritual forces" are understood by Mark as *persons* who hold this world and the human being captive and possess them in opposition to God" (ibid., 28). Drewermann interprets the notion of Satan and his demons — as he interpreted sin and evil in *Strukturen des Bösen* — on historical, psychological, daseinsanalytic (existential), and theological levels. In the psychoanalytic interpretation they may represent on an objective level internalized "personal" images of the parents (ibid., 37) and on a subjective level one's own shadow or one's persona (ibid., 37–8). On an existential level they appear spiritually (*geistig*) as the temptations and dangers which the repressed polarities of existence pose: of finitude in the depressive, of infinity in the schizoid, of necessity in the hysterical, and of possibility in the obsessive compulsive character structure (ibid., 39). Drewermann argues that as a first step a radically anthropological reading of "devil" and "demons" is required if one wants to avoid the temptation to demonize humans theologically. Anticipating the objection that an anthropological reading focused around the notion that "the fear which springs from the human spirit can take on demonic traits" would not coincide with the notion in Mark that

---

1. *Der Menschen Sohn* is a play on words on the title *Menschensohn*, which is traditionally translated as "Son of Man." Drewermann here wants to establish that Jesus was called "Son of Man" because he showed us a God who allows us to live as humans and does not require us to live as if we were God ourselves. We are reconciled with our being human, and thus can be truly human, that is, "children of humans." We no longer have to attempt to "be like God" in order to feel justified to exist.

"certain spirits exist which place the human being in demonic fashion into fear," Drewermann clarifies:

> The Gospel of Mark can indeed not be understood if one simply repeats its language. Without doubt, the first step must be a psychological demythologization in the sense of psychoanalysis and daseinsanalysis: in order to understand how *humans* are characterized in the Gospel of Mark in their drivenness and their unfreedom, it is crucial to interpret their miseries and sufferings, their errors and confusions as results of basic mental and spiritual anxieties which determine them down to their very personality organization. But if we humanize the talk of "evil spirits" in this manner, so that we once and for all no longer have to demonize anything in the human being, then the problem of anxiety is transferred completely to the *relationship* between God and the human being. And then it is — against some explications by C. G. Jung* that tend in the direction of gnosticism — at least equally important to de-demonize the image of God so that it can again appear to the human being as trustworthy. It is precisely this meaning which the talk of "devil" in the Bible can and must essentially have: it serves the purpose of removing all demonic traits from God. (ibid., 40–41)

*So especially in C. G. Jung, *Answer to Job* (1952a) and *A Reply to Martin Buber* (1952b). One has to remember constantly in the work of Jung that he speaks *empirically* of God as the center of the highest psychic energy. But it is only conditionally a psychological question which contents of human life *deserve* to concentrate all energy upon themselves, and by all means no longer a psychological but a philosophical-theological question whether a reality beyond the psychic reality corresponds to the psychic *images* of God.

Only when one focuses first anthropologically on the tragic reality of human despair can it become clear what in *humans* "need(ed)" the death of Jesus and can one avoid projecting the anthropological need into God. God does not need the Cross; humans do. Responding to a passage from Joseph Cardinal Ratzinger's book *Introduction to Christianity* (Ratzinger 1970, 214–15 [German ed.: Ratzinger 1968, 231–32]), Drewermann emphasizes that only when the projections of anthropological ambivalences into God are taken back, may one understand the significance of the Cross. Ratzinger (writing before he became Prefect of the CDF) quotes 2 Corinthians 5:19 ("God was in Christ reconciling the world to himself") to stress that God reconciles the world with himself through Christ, and that humans contribute nothing toward redemption. Drewermann questions the notion that God would need the death of a human being in order to "reconcile" the world to himself.

> That is correctly quoted but incorrectly reflected upon. Because the problem consists in the notion that God should have to kill a human being in order to reconcile himself with himself. Such a thought makes God untrustworthy and appear bloodthirsty, barbaric, and crude, and it does not help to project the entire issue of redemption into God and away from humans, while cutting out the psychological questions. The point is not that God has to be reconciled with himself, but that the human being becomes reconciled with herself by entering again beyond all feelings of ambivalence into a clear relationship with God. On that journey, it is true, there are a multitude of *resistances in the human being* which have to be worked through — battles indeed of life and death in every single case. (Drewermann 1990d, 72 n. 46)

In a discussion of writings by two Roman Catholic critics of his work, Hermann-Josef Lauter (1988b) and Rudolf Pesch (Lohfink and Pesch 1988), Drewermann further elaborates the importance of a depth-psychological awareness that is necessary if one wants to avoid the metaphysicizing of projective dynamics of the human psyche and spirit in the form of a sadistic God-image. Addressing Lauter's (1981, 77) view that psychological readings of biblical stories are in danger of "psychologizing away ... all guilt" and of trivializing guilt as "a depth-psychological curiosity" and Pesch's traditional interpretation that God atones in the death of Jesus Israel's "rejection of his son [Jesus as Messiah]" (1984b, 362),[2] Drewermann replies that Lauter's statements display

> a prejudice-happy ignorance and ideologically repressive attitude with such expressions. Anyone who has the slightest idea of the reality of analytic psychotherapy will know that here no guilt is "psychologized away," but that humans are brought to

---

2. See also Pesch's and Lohfink's critique in the same vein that it would be inconceivable for Drewermann to consider Jesus' impending death as a situation that "threatened the expulsion of the Messiah from the people of God and hence the threatening end of the history of redemption begun in Abraham" (Lohfink and Pesch 1988, 35). We will learn in this chapter why Drewermann refuses to read theology and history *essentially* in terms of categories of the historical fate of certain peoples or historical groups.

the point where they can turn their guilt feelings from the substitute themes which seem morally so important to the actual contents of their life: the forms of missing one's own existence are more original and more important than the transgression of certain norms and commandments by means of which the compulsion for the deformations of existence is usually established and legitimized. But instead of instrumentalizing depth psychology theologically precisely for the understanding of the human experience of guilt, it still seems to be broadly advantageous to arrogantly repress the unconscious. Why then did Jesus have to die? If God is willing to forgive unconditionally, as Jesus taught, there is no need for the additional atoning death of his "son." (Drewermann 1990d, 64 n. 35)

Countering Pesch's notion that the historical people of Israel has to be reconciled, which implies that Israel is theologically responsible for the death of Jesus, Drewermann continues:

... All that pleonastic effort by means of theological concepts does not in the least clarify what must and should be clarified here: why should the atrocious torture of Cross and execution be needed in order to atone any guilt before God! What kind of Moloch of a God really needs such "sacrifices of atonement"? And above all: why do *humans* get to the point where they need to punish the message of forgiveness with death? The paradox remains: anyone who declares the psychological dialectic of the unconscious in the field of fear and of reactive self-assertion simply to be a side issue, cannot avoid having to establish the "logic" of the connection between death and forgiveness in the New Testament *theologically*. Meanwhile the human action ([in Pesch's view:] Israel) remains then historically accidental [instead of representing a universally *typical* action of humans of all ages under the spell of fear], an opaque fact, while the action of God becomes just as incomprehensible as relentless. Which person with any sensibility would *want* to be "redeemed" in that fashion at all! One has to comprehend precisely *theologically* that the God of forgiveness does not need a Golgotha for his justice. But psychologically it can be shown what we humans first need to do in order to come to reason. (ibid., 65 n. 35)

The Gospel of Mark hence asks why humans killed the very person whose message celebrated humans as royalty in God's kingdom, whose life was characterized by an unshakable trust in God and faith in the inalienable worth of each human being, and who believed that religion was based on trust, not fear? "The central paradox of Christianity" is that it assumes that humans, instead of passionately longing for and accepting any kind of rescue from the field of fear and misery, "kill what would let them live, and seem to fear nothing more then their final liberation" (ibid., 46). This, too, is a key problem for Mark: why was the promised Messiah not accepted in faith but killed? Drewermann emphasizes that Mark does not answer this question by portraying humans as "bad," but instead that the Evangelist portrays the demonic dynamic: how humans kill with the very best intentions that which could let them find their own truth, that is, in the name of "the word and law of God." Drewermann's interpretation therefore looks at the kind of God-image *in humans* which may lead to killing in the name of God. Why Jesus was killed despite his role of healer or rather because he healed people is a question which, Drewermann believes, requires us to turn to depth psychology for an understanding.

This shift from theological projection to anthropological analysis is also necessary when one raises questions of theodicy after the Holocaust. "It has been said that it has become impossible to still believe in a God after Auschwitz and Dachau. The problem of Mark, however, is posed in light of the fate of Jesus precisely from the other: how can one still believe in the human being if he is downright capable of willfully [that is, with a will under the spell of fear] destroying the foundations of his own life with lofty citations from Scripture and the law book of the state held high?" (ibid., 47). Drewermann's frequent critique of the Christian churches' professions of support for Hitler in the name of God, citing Scripture and theologically legitimating state authority as part of the divine order, is a poignant application of this anthropological analysis.

The Death and Resurrection of Jesus Christ and the Redemption from a Violent God-Image

Why then did Jesus die and why could his death become a symbol for redemption? How could his death be understood other than by perpetuating a sadomasochistic identification with suffering? We find that Drewermann answers these questions from two different angles which often intertwine: from the perspective of the person of Jesus and from the perspective of those who find redemption through identifying with his death in the Eucharist (the Holy Meal) and by associating with his personal fate the archetypal imagery of "Christ," of the God-human who dies for them and because of them but who also survives death and rises again into eternal life.

Jesus Facing the Cross: The End of Fear

We will first turn to the aspect of Drewermann's interpretation in which Jesus' own perspective as portrayed in the gospels[3] is in the foreground. This angle of interpretation dispels traditional interpretations that glorify the suffering and sacrifice of Jesus as an example for believers to follow. Drewermann's understanding of Jesus' own perspective is laid out succinctly in his reading of the story of the crucifixion in Mark 15:20b-41. Due to its significance in Drewermann's overall work, I will translate here rather than paraphrase this segment, found in the second volume of *Das Markusevangelium* and entitled "The Cross of Salvation, or: Against the Masochism of Religion" (Drewermann 1990e, 648–59). Drewermann's lengthy discussion of references in the footnotes, which make up about one half of the segment, have either been omitted or merely hinted at in this abridged version.

> Why is the Cross a sign of salvation?[4] In the liturgy of Good Friday the [Roman Catholic] Church calls upon believers to step toward the Cross and kiss it. But is there even one among us who

3. Drewermann's analysis of Jesus' perspective is informed by the results of historical-critical exegesis but supplemented, as in his analysis of Genesis 3–11, by an empathic reading of the emotional meanings between the lines of the text.

4. In a note, Drewermann refers the reader to his essay *Die Symbolik von Baum und Kreuz in religionsgeschichtlicher und tiefenpsychologischer Betrachtung* (1979) (for a discussion, see further below) and takes note of Rank's interpretation of the crucifixion as an Oedipal merger of the son with the maternal tree expressing both wish and the punishment of the wish to transgress the incest tabu established by the father. Drewermann adds — in light of views we presented in Chapter 2 — that "if one wants to appreciate the religious meaning of O. Rank's symbolic interpretations, one must read his [psychological] style itself symbolically: The death of Jesus aims at the overcoming of the primordial anxiety [because of the mere fact that one] exists in the world. Jesus dies because against any (masculine!) reason [*Vernunft*] he believes in the power of love and of trust and becomes indeed the 'son' of (a basically maternally conceived of) God. Only in this perspective does the death of Jesus receive a function that redeems from the fear of the 'primordial trauma.' One simply needs to understand the 'primordial trauma' itself and the figure of the 'mother' as symbols of *Dasein* instead of reading them purely on an objective level" (Drewermann 1990e, 648–49, n. 1).

loves to suffer? Jesus did not want to. He was terribly afraid of
being tormented and tortured. He loved *life*, not suffering. In
the spirit of Jesus, no slogan could be more unchristian than
this one: that one has to love suffering in the name of Christ.
It is Christian to fight as much as possible suffering, sickness,
and insanity. It is Christian to commit oneself to life and the
possibility of living of each individual, not to preach suffering
or to sanctify masochism. Otherwise Jesus would indeed have
died in vain, death and the negation of life would as always have
the last word. . . .

   This must be said because no day of the ecclesiastical year
has and is supposed to have as abiding an effect on our hearts
as Good Friday — often enough in the sense: that God has loved
us infinitely, but that we are sinners and murderers; that God's
son died for us on the Cross, but that we shy away from suffering
and try to avoid sacrifice; that Christ has given himself for us
and took the path of service, but that we are egoists who want
to be in control and want to realize ourselves. If these opposites
were accurate, then the Cross would indeed be nothing more
than a signal of holy suicide and an embodiment of fatal self-
reproaches and self-accusations. It would not redeem us but kill
us by perpetuating, simply by other means, what Jesus fought
against most passionately: a kind of religion which consists only
of fear and guilt feelings and which amounts to a sadistic form
of obsessional neurosis which demands again and again that one
has to kill[5]: animals have to be slaughtered as sacrifices, drives
have to be suppressed as impure, feelings must be controlled as
dangerous, and thoughts must be avoided as too selfish. The
instruments ready and appropriate for the killing would already
be at hand: commandments, laws, regulations, and institutions,
together with a huge heap of taboos, thought inhibitions and
punishments.

   Every religion not only binds but also generates fear. And one
cannot see that Christianity is *a priori* immune against being just
as hostile to humans as any other religion which has become ossified in loyalism and moralism. The fact that the Early Church,
with reference to the teaching and practice of Jesus, summoned
the courage to untie itself from the bonds of laws in favor of

---

5. Drewermann refers in a footnote to S. Freud (1913).

a deeper humanity does not yet prove that Christianity itself
has really become better, [that is,] more humane after two thousand years. We do not even have to recall here the pyres of the
inquisition erected due to fear of the freedom of thought of humans. We do not need to recall the witch trials led due to fear of
women and disgust with one's own sexuality — always justified,
we note, with the sign of the Cross and with the necessity of the
'discipleship of suffering' of Christ.[6] It is enough to observe in
the present how, in the name of Christianity, especially the best
and the most pious feel urged to [engage in] constant self-distrust
and self-suppression. The Cross means for them that they constantly have to flee from themselves, that they, if possible, do not
need to perceive themselves in their deeper feelings but instead
they take care of others — always with the well-worn mask of a
Christian smile and a jumble of religious phrases on their lips —
indeed industriously and with a tremendous degree of good will,
and yet in truth inhumanly and cruelly. We Christians first have
to take a good look at the monstrous fact that a genius such
as Sigmund Freud could, in view of his patients, reach no other
conclusion than that religion on the whole represents a singu-
lar crucifixion of the human being, a grand neurotic show, a
suppression of everything which wants to live humanly.[7]

One may object that these ideas do not belong to the topic of
Good Friday and to the texts of the crucifixion of Jesus. What
else, however, would the topic of Good Friday be then if not
the barbarism and the inhumanity especially associated with
religion? Hence one must ask: where in the Church can one
actually speak of the true miseries of humans without immediately coming up against a whole apparatus of rules which have
already been decided in advance and which formulate and declare without any hesitation what has to count as Christian or
Catholic and what not? Or, to ask even more specifically: Where
among the clergy, among the scribes and highpriests of *today*
does one meet people who would *not* be brimful of all sorts
of unfreedom, of cruel fears from childhood, and of a whole

---

6. Drewermann refers in a footnote to Lea (1887, 468) who takes note of the practice of
the "penalty of *bearing crosses*" (Drewermann 1990e, 654 n. 12) as early as the thirteenth
century.

7. In a note, Drewermann refers to Freud's paper "Obsessional Acts and Religious
Practices" (Freud 1907).

ensemble of fearfully internalized prejudices which were later declared as sacrosanct? One thing seems clear: if one wants the mass, large numbers, one needs institutions and ordinances, one needs obedient colonies of humans. But if one wants the human being, one must value the individual infinitely higher than the mass, one must — as Jesus — be absolutely more concerned with the hundredth sheep than with the other ninety-nine. But the decisive issue now is: If one only brings into this world of regulated fears even a single spark of confidence and freedom [i.e., in the individual] — the hunt is on immediately, immediately one fears chaos, immediately one resists them [i.e., confidence and freedom] as if they were the devil incarnate.

One has to understand *this* paradox in order to understand why Jesus had to die. But one has to stop the habit of humiliating people in the name of God with reference to the Cross of Christ and of destroying them through guilt feelings. One has to stop nailing people to the Cross in the name of the Cross and calling this travesty of religion discipleship of Christ. If we understood the message of Jesus in an interpretation so hostile to humanity, then we would be not a bit different from Annas, Caiaphas, Herod, and Pilate [as portrayed in the gospels]. If Jesus had wanted *that,* then one would without doubt have to depict blasphemously . . . a God who feeds on the suffering of humans and who, as the Sun God of the Aztecs, only lives by devouring daily hecatombs of slaughtered children and young men.

Against the pietistic perversion of the Cross into an ideology of the mysticism of suffering one cannot forcefully enough repeat: Jesus did not want to die on the Cross and he never thought to declare inhumanity and torture to be signs of a true trust into God.[8] To the contrary: he lived so that humans would receive back their dignity as creatures of God, so that they would regain their innocence and uninhibitedness in relation to God, and so that the unceasing suffering which afflicts humans because of God [as portrayed] in the religions of human history would find an end.

All the signs and miracles of Jesus transmitted to us speak for this attitude. In closeness to Jesus it happened again and again

---

8. In a note, Drewermann cites a passage from Kahlil Gibran's *Secrets of the Heart* (1968) and comments: "The only form of *suffering,* in other words, which Jesus wanted is *compassion,* but not the abstract masochism of a hypocritical ideology of theologians."

that people who were crippled for their whole life were able to stand up through their trust in God, that through his words they would receive back their senses, and that they would again be able to see the world as it is. In response to his word they learned again to trust their own ears, their own judgment, and their own thinking. It did not pose a contradiction for Jesus but was one and the same thing: to find God and to find oneself. Both happened for him through the power of one and the same trust, and the one was for him only the sign for the other. Precisely for that reason people who understood him called him *the life:* because what he spoke allowed them to live and brought them to life. Exactly for that reason they called him *the way:* because thus they found direction and perspective in their life. Exactly for that reason they called him *the truth:* because through him their life and all things around them found again their true *gestalt.* Because they could live in him as they were actually meant to and created to they called him *Son of God* (John 14:6).

And killed him? Crucified him? Simply because he allowed them to live humanly?

Yes, only for that and no other reason. Only those who had nothing at all to lose could follow him without fear. All others began at some point to resist his plain truths and to defend their inhumanities. This whole world and every human being in it consists in reality only of fear. Everyone tries in her own manner to defend against her nothingness. And those who succeed most are in the end worst off. Nothing is as difficult as to remain human, true, and kind in the face of fear and not to escape into power, lies, and destruction. But this is what Jesus wanted to say and what his whole life was about: that from the perspective of God we could defeat fear and would be able to live as free humans. Really only for that reason did he *have to* die, and precisely for that reason can the Cross, this cursed stigma, this monstrous embodiment of all human torture, become despite everything a sign of salvation.

If one brings into this world a little kindness and compassion in the spirit of Jesus; if one goes so far as to slightly transcend with it the narrow sphere of nurse- and Red-Cross-morality; if one engages beyond the charitable care of symptoms the structural background and origins of our dilemma, then one soon will experience how little such an effort fits into this world and soon will begin [to encounter] the intentional distortions, the setting up of traps, the know-all attitude, and above all, the recourse to how things have always been — and are certainly written down somewhere. *Due to fear* everyone has an interest to lie to himself and to 'hide' himself, so that he has to kill the one who tells him the truth. Humans kill Jesus not because they would as such be against God, not because they would naturally be egoists, not because they would principally not want to suffer, but because due to fear not a single one has the courage to simply be a human being.

Therefore it is decisive for Jesus to show himself and us that what he believes is true: that it is possible to overcome fear through trust in God and to stay loyal to the truth of one's own existence. At this moment when everything is at stake, words and miracles are no longer useful — at the end of the story of suffering in Mark Jesus no longer makes a single comment. Instead, all that counts at this hour is to do the decisive "deed," which the Gospel of John mentions so often and which is the only possible and valid way that can attest to all that has been said and done: by risking one's own life, through death (John 17:4).

Therefore the all-decisive question to us is: To what extent do we accept the death of Jesus as this attestation? If we do [accept it] then salvation indeed comes from the Cross. In itself the Cross is the sign of the most abominable and the most base which we humans can do to each other. But if even the Cross loses its power to instill fear, then we could finally and truly begin to live as humans, then nothing would exist from which we would have to escape.

Often it is said that a human being needs another human being to believe. True, but all [human] fear consists precisely of the inability to believe any human being anymore. Beyond the fear of all humans we have only this single example of Jesus. If we believe him as to his death then the world changes entirely. Then those who mocked him, the highpriests, the soldiers, and the men hanged with him (Mark 15:31) are once and for all made wrong by the brutal logic of their impotent power and by the very limited truth of their coercive anxiety-ridden obedience. Against the possibility for humanity then, no objection exists any longer which in principle could not be weathered and borne in view of the Cross of Jesus. Then all of his words of the dignity of even the least human being, of the power of trust, and of the opportunity for kindness are irrefutably true. But if we cannot even put our faith in the death of Jesus then indeed the earth is now shaken to its core and the sun is darkened (Mark 15:33, Matt. 27:45, 51), and we remain unredeemably what we have always been: inhumans [*Unmenschen*] of pure fear, living-dead without resurrection. No God can do more in order to take the fear away from us than to die for us in this cruel way as a human being. (Drewermann 1990e, 648–59)

The redemptive significance of the Cross thus does not lie in the suffering of Jesus, but in Jesus' overcoming of the fear of death through trust in God and in his loyalty to the truth of his own existence in the face of a world and a type of religiosity ruled by fear and collective alienation. His refusal to compromise with a system of fear and death, with the way we are used to living, his refusal to compromise the truth of his personal existence, and his belief that not even physical death on the Cross could destroy this nonviolent truth could transform the atrocious symbol of inhumanity into a symbol of fearless resistance to all inhumanity. Jesus had to die on the Cross not because God wanted him to suffer but because we humans are under the spell of fear, terrified of the truth of our existence, and paradoxically we kill what would let us live. Not God's will but the dynamics of fear in humans led to Jesus' death. The paradox that his tragic death could become a symbol for the working through of an ambivalent God-image and thus for our redemption can be understood only if we understand the anthropological needs under a spell of fear that were played out in the crucifixion and are played out symbolically in the ritual of the Eucharist, which Christianity connected early on with the death and resurrection of Christ.

The Historical Jesus and a Typological Reading of History

Before we proceed to this second angle of Drewermann's interpretation of the Cross, we must first attend to an issue addressed by his depth-psychological interpretation that has occupied modern exegesis since its inception: how can we know the historical Jesus today and how can the historical Jesus take on transhistorical meaning? This issue is central to the controversy surrounding Drewermann's work because it involves the broader question of reality on which the Christian faith is based and because Drewermann's answer to the

problem critiques what he considers to be the traditional externalistic interpretation of the historical dimension. Drewermann's solution
appreciates the historical uniqueness of Jesus while at the same time
correcting a kind of historical understanding of the fate of Jesus that
became the driving force for Christian antisemitism, which singled
out a particular historical group of Jews or all Jews as murderers of
Jesus. Two premises guide Drewermann's interpretation of the historical Jesus and of the response he evoked that led to his death: on
the one hand, a typological reading of history; on the other, the assumption that history has *meaning* religiously not because of certain
facts verifiable by hard science, that is, not by physical, biological,
hence *external* facts, but because of the *quality* of the spiritual and
emotional, that is, the personal, hence *internal* experience of external reality that the historical actor had and evoked in his time — in
other words: whether this experience was shaped by and led to *fear*
or *trust*.

Overcoming the Antisemitic Tendency of Historical Readings of the Gospels by Means of a Typological Reading of History

In Drewermann's depth-psychological interpretation of the death of
Jesus presented above, Drewermann stated the thesis — which I will
elaborate further below — that Jesus' death on the Cross was the
result of a human projection of life under the spell of fear which
principally all humans share. It is Jesus' attitude of trust that is unbearable to a life ruled by fear and the letter of the law. Because Jesus
reveals how much our human existence is shaped by the powers of
fear and death — despite all possible substitutes, overcompensations,
and rationalizations we have created to escape from fear and death —
because he arouses in us those parts of our life which we have fearfully
repressed, "we will hate him precisely for his straightforwardness"
(Drewermann 1990d, 54).

Addressing the historical effects of the fear of the human spirit,
Drewermann stresses that the " 'neurotic' structure of life around
fear does not merely possess subjective value: it is, to the contrary,
the result and the basis of institutionalized, societally fortified forms
of the petrified fear of all" (ibid.). The Gospel of Mark sees particularly "the leading religious power-circles of the *scribes*, the priests,
the Sadducees, and the Pharisees" as social representations of the
"petrified fear of all" which kills in the name of God what comes

from God. Drewermann notes, however, that historical-critical studies have clearly shown that the negative role which Mark has the
Pharisees especially play is not accurate in terms of external facts but
is rather a projection back into Jesus' time of the tensions between
the Early Church and Judaism after the destruction of the Jerusalem
Temple in 70 C.E. (ibid., 55–59). Historical criticism is indispensable
to Drewermann as a tool for dismantling inaccurate external historical notions in religious texts. It is precisely this (external) historical
inaccuracy in Mark — and in the other gospels — which has contributed tremendously to an "anti-Jewish ideology" in the midst of
Christianity (ibid., 57 n. 17). But this was possible only, Drewermann
argues, because Christianity has tended to identify history with external facts. This tendency also characterizes historical criticism. If
Christian theology retains *this* historical perspective it may shift the
blame from Pharisees to Sadducees or to the Romans, but it will still,
at least latently, remain trapped in the attitude of blaming some historical group in the past for the fate of Jesus. Against this external
understanding of history, Drewermann sets a depth-psychologically
informed *typological* reading of the gospels which, he argues, is alone
able to avoid vilifying whole groups of people as historical enemies of
Christ. In a *typological* reading of the groups which Mark portrays
as the religious enemies of Jesus, they are understood not as external
historical groups but as symbols for a type of religious attitude which
is a danger "in all nations and all religions (Christianity itself is no
exception!), where external direction [*Außenlenkung*] by power and
external obedience are valued higher than the power of personal experience and inner conviction" (ibid., 57). It is of utmost importance
to see "that from a theological perspective the Gospel of Mark is not
concerned with certain groups of [ancient] Later Judaism, not at all
with the history of a certain people at a certain time" and to see the
reaction he portrays of the Jews and the Romans to Jesus "rather as
an expression of our own being" (ibid., 56–57). While clarifying his
case for a typological reading of the gospels, Drewermann points out
the devastating effects which a historicizing, externalistic [*äußerliche*]
interpretation of religious texts had in theological education during
the Third Reich and must have as long as theology refuses to adopt
a typological, symbolic, inner way of interpretation.

If one wants to avoid a relapse into anti-Jewish ideology [in
Christianity] which undoubtedly exists and has existed, it is

indeed decisive to understand and interpret the *seemingly* historical stories of the gospels in their *typological* content valid for
all times. Not historical groups but existential attitudes make
up what is pharisaic and always deadly that opposes the message of Jesus. . . . It is true: If one reads the New Testament
historically instead of typologically, externally instead of internally, sociologically instead of psychologically, one cannot
avoid doing theology as ideology. Any external understanding
of religion is violent and provokes violence. Recall, when the
word "Jews" was spoken in the lecture hall of the Theological
Academy in *Paderborn* forty-five years ago [i.e., in the 1940s]
during an exegetical lecture on the Gospel of John, the can-
didates for priesthood hissed and pawed [*scharrten*] dutifully
[*pflichtgemäß*], in order to give expression to their theological abhorrence of the people of Jesus-murderers. To a certain
degree it is of course useful to show by means of historical
criticism how the image of Judaism becomes systematically falsified, particularly in the Gospel of John. But it is much more
important to comprehend that the battle between the realm
of light and the realm of darkness, as John portrays it, runs
thematically throughout all of human existence and cannot be
relativized historically (politically, sociologically, racially, etc.).
(ibid., 57 n. 17)

Drewermann elaborates the overcoming of Christian anti-Judaism
through a detailed typological reading in the introduction to his
commentary on the Gospel of Matthew, *Das Matthäusevangelium*
(1992d, 102–39). Noting how the combination of the general historical emphasis of biblical theology and Matthew's tendentious
attribution of the death of Jesus to the historical Jewish groups
of Pharisees, scribes, and highpriests has led and must continue to
lead to an anti-Jewish trend in Christian theology unless an (external) historical understanding is replaced by a typological, existential
understanding, Drewermann writes:

We have to stress here at any rate that the Romans executed
Jesus as a self-declared "King." Whatever "complicity" Jewish
circles had in the execution of Jesus, to fabricate out of it a
main or sole responsibility has been historically completely dis-
credited. . . . The worst effects of Matthew's historical theology
of retribution are when he interprets the fall of Jerusalem in the

year 70 after Christ as punishment and consequence for the execution of Jesus (Matt. 21:41, 22:7, 23:37–39, 27:25)....From a
humane point of view it is, of course, absolutely necessary that
nowadays Christian exegetes genuinely regret the anti-Jewish
theology of Matthew, that they try to relativize it through its
historical context and simply declare the entire history of its effects as a terrible error. But that does not yet change any of the
presuppositions and damaging consequences of a fundamentally
false thinking about the relation between history and revelation
even around this important issue....

One could — as is often the case today — now be inclined to
consider the problem solved simply by declaring the Pharisees
historically innocent with regard to the death of Jesus and to attribute all blame to the Romans....[But] the historical question
of who is responsible for the death of Jesus — the Jews or the Romans? — only distracts from the only question that is religiously
decisive: who or what bears the *essential* [*wesentliche*] responsibility not for the historically accidental but for the necessary
dying of the Son of God. The question of the supposed guilt or
lack of guilt of the Pharisees, of the scribes, or of the Romans
back then only obscures the far more important question of the
"Phariseeism," of the "Scribalism," and of the "Romanism" in
one's own existence, within the Church and within society today. Even within the framework of historical-critical exegesis it
has now been recognized that Matthew did want to castigate
through his wrathful words about the "scribes and Pharisees"
in Matthew 23:1–36 not only the "Jews" but, among others,
also certain conditions within his own Church. But in the last
instance the question is not whether Matthew also included the
Church in his critique of Pharisees and scribes when he blamed
these circles for the murder of the Son of God. The issue is rather
that, from a religious point of view, it is on the whole a grave error and an insoluble paradox if one follows the theology of the
Gospel of Matthew and tries to pin down the responsibility for
the death of Jesus historically....Unless one wants to throw out
the whole theological dramaturgy of the "redemptive death" of
Jesus in Matthew at the same time as one throws out his anti-
Jewish attacks, one must untie from its historical bracing what
the Evangelist says about the Pharisees and scribes as the true
henchmen of the death of Jesus and try to understand it as an

essential statement about the human being, about ourselves. To say it differently: If the Gospel of Matthew is to offer us today at the heart of its theology more than anti-Jewish propaganda, a lie about the responsibility of the Jews for the death of Jesus, then we must once and for all stop seeking the Pharisees and scribes two thousand years ago, then we must henceforth seek them where they have all this time really been hiding: within ourselves. The word "Pharisees," however, has to be set in quotation marks from now on, if not eliminated all-together as too misleading. From here on, this word describes in the language of the Evangelist not a group of historical Judaism but a type of piety within the Church and within ourselves.

In other words: We need to transform at this important juncture the historical exposition of Matthew about "the Jews" into a psychological and existential, Church- and society-critical question and may not let it stand historically-externally. Once again: The "anti-Judaism" of the Gospel of Matthew cannot be done away with without the loss of the whole doctrine of redemption of the Evangelist unless we realize that the talk of "Jews," "Pharisees," "scribes" and "highpriests" means essentially something that lies in ourselves. Only when we take back into our own psyche the anti-Jewish projection of the theology of the Gospel of Matthew by means of the typological understanding of depth psychology will we be capable of paying off the terrible burden of guilt of the Christian hate of Jews and at the same time let that which Matthew really has to tell us come close to us in a liberating and redemptive way and share it with others. Reik was correct in his psychoanalytic conviction that the Christian dogma itself must necessarily lead to a disavowal and repression of the doubts in our own inner life, only to transport them all the more intensively toward the outside and to then persecute them out there fanatically. A "christology" of dogmatic teaching traditions must indeed split the "faithful" into a verbal obedience of faith and an emotional state of opposition or of latent rebellion, and it is not only the content, but especially the form of the Christian doctrine which requires in its rational externality again and again a projective self-exoneration: "not Christians themselves — but 'the Jews' are the ones who disavow Jesus as the Christ; it was (or is) 'Judas,' the 'eternal Jew,' not the individual Christian who has betrayed his Lord; not the Christians, but the 'Jews' are the ones actually guilty." All doubts and split-off parts within the psyche of believers in Christ which have accumulated due to the historicizing externalization of the christological mythologem have to be transported outside into anti-Jewish (antiheretic and antipagan) projections. A depth-psychological interpretation of the Gospel of Matthew is under those circumstances therefore indispensable simply because only a symbolic or typological understanding of the "Pharisees," "scribes" and "highpriests" in this gospel can overcome the alternative between anti-Jewish historicism or historically enlightened insignificance in matters of christology and the doctrine of redemption. (ibid., 115–18)

The *type* of attitude which Mark (and Matthew) portrays as leading to the death of Jesus is "an issue of *all* humans in the ensnarements of morally good will" (Drewermann 1990d, 58). It is then theologically not important which external historical group was responsible for Jesus' death but rather which attitude is portrayed by the gospels as leading to the death of Jesus: namely, an attitude of doing violence in the name of God or in the name of divinized laws or states. This is, according to Mark, the internal, that is, existential reason why Jesus had to die. Mark does not provide an accurate picture of the external historical facts of the people involved in Jesus' physical death sentence but an account of the historical implications of an inner attitude shaped by fear which leads to death on the inside and the outside. This attitude exists in every stage of history and can manifest itself particularly in religious righteousness and in a legal understanding of religion. And wherever this attitude is found, the death of Jesus is committed. To Drewermann, the story of Cain and Abel is the prototype for this attitude. That story portrays the devastating effects of a mentality in which

> God comes face to face with ... humans *essentially* as a moral admonisher and lawgiver: the drives [*Antriebe*], which were dammed up under the censorship of the "good will," eventually assert themselves against all resistances with eruptive violence and enforce access to their own implementation. It is impossible to calm the anxiety of humans by means of morality. Nevertheless it is precisely the increase of the anxiety in humans which will demand ever more procedures of legislation and external direction. And these procedures in turn contribute in themselves

to an increase of the degree of one's own lack of independence and to dependency. In the end one has people who exist merely as protectors of the law, as officials, as functionaries of the objective spirit. In the lack of aliveness of their existence the wounding cruelty of the established system of social fear fuses with the cruel sickness of their own individual compulsion. By binding their entire self-respect and valuation to the agreement with and the execution of certain roles and norms such people save themselves the emotional shake-ups which are the cost for being human. They do not exist as people, as individuals, but exist only as executive organs of the collective.... [A]ny argument of visible suffering of people appears to them as below the level of their concepts, even as a suspicious case of subversion and insubordination.... This group of teachers of the law, of scribes, of "Pharisees" *as types,* supplemented yet through the political ambitions and plotting of the "Sadducees," make up the eternal opposition to any freedom of opinion, any deeper feeling, any humane impulse of compassion, phantasy, and creativity. (Drewermann 1990d, 58–59)

The Historical Uniqueness of Jesus Lies in His Person

> Psychoanalysis has long since ceased being merely a therapy and has been generally recognized as a basic theory to the study of the human personality. How can it be that the historian, who must be as much or more concerned with human beings and their motivation than with impersonal forces and causation, has failed to make use of these findings?... Since psychoanalysis is concerned primarily with the emotional life of the individual, its most immediate application is in the field of biography.
> —William L. Langer, "The Next Assignment"

Drewermann's second premise in the interpretation of the historical Jesus and of the response he evoked that led to his death is that the significance of the "historical" in the historical Jesus refers not to the particular time and space in which Jesus lived but to the particular spiritual and emotional attitude which characterized him as a *person* — namely, an attitude of absolute trust in God and in the dignity of every human being. In terms of religion, it is ultimately not historically significant to which race, gender, social group, or time period Jesus belonged, but which attitude he personified. His particular attitude had such power that it evoked the deepest archetypal imagery of the human psyche and merged it with his historical person, an integration symbolized in the name of Jesus the Christ which refers both to the historical person characterized by an attitude of trust (Jesus) and to the universal archetype of the savior (Christ as the concrete cultural manifestation of that archetype).

One of the most notorious accusations against Drewermann by Church officials and theologians defending the traditional view of Christianity that the suffering of Christ is a sign of his unique sacrifice for others and of his selflessness is that Drewermann neglects the uniqueness of Jesus and of Christianity among religions (cf. Lohfink and Pesch 1988, 26–36; Blank 1985, 26; Venetz, 1986, 35; Lauter 1988b, 16–23). Drewermann supposedly relativizes the absolute uniqueness of the Christian message by comparing the motifs of death and resurrection, of virgin birth and of Son of God with material in other religions and drifts into gnosticism. His talk of universal archetypes, the critics continue, opens the field to random subjectivity and neglects the unique and final revelation of God in the historical person of Jesus.

Careful study of Drewermann's major works shows that he clearly rebuts these charges throughout his writings,[9] yet his critics either seem not to understand his argument or simply choose to ignore it. The key issue here is what is meant by "historical." We are by now familiar with Drewermann's important distinction between external and internal reality. Drewermann applies this distinction particularly to the notion of "historical." With "external" Drewermann refers to the observable facts of history which can be established with approximate, scientific certainty — physical, cultural, sociological, historical-critical. With "internal" he refers to the meaning which is attributed to external facts, a meaning which is based on the inner perception of external facts and does not need to present these external facts accurately in a scientific, objective way.

What about the historical Jesus made him unique? Drewermann answers that we should not look for Jesus' uniqueness in terms of externally historical facts because historical criticism has shown over the last 150 years that most of the events central to Christianity cannot be verified as external historical facts: neither virgin birth, nor transfiguration, nor miracles, nor Last Supper, nor resurrection. What

9. See especially Drewermann 1985b, 762–72; 1986b, 514–33; 1986c, 59–66; 1988, 78–118.

can be verified, however, is the internal meaning of the historical person of Jesus — but verified only "with the eyes of the spirit" of one's own existence (Drewermann 1990d, 100).

> It is true and correct...that for the foundation [*Begründung*] of faith the person of Jesus of Nazareth has to be thought of as a historical figure. But that does not at all mean that one has to "know Christ according to the flesh" (2 Cor. 5:16) in order to reach the kind of trust which has taken shape in the person of Jesus in relation to God. The Gospel of Mark by all means speaks of the "historical Jesus," but it does so by means of types of narratives that render the history [*Geschichte*] of Jesus in the religiously relevant form which alone can claim a meaning for humans of all times and places: in the form of symbolic condensation [*Verdichtung*[10]]. (ibid., 92–93)

These two characteristics *together,* Drewermann argues, make the historical Jesus unique: through his person, Jesus conveyed primordial trust in relation to God, and he did so while evoking in others the rich symbolism of the human psyche that can have therapeutic power for mind, body, and spirit only in relation to an absolute person who is capable of calming the fear of the spirit. It is through the "effect" of the "inner truth" in history of the historical Jesus, of the particular kind of person he was, that we know him (ibid., 93). And only because the stories of the gospels employ the symbolism of the human psyche as a means for expressing the struggles humans face in their journey from fear to trust can we today become "contemporaneous" with Jesus.

> Not what one could see in Jesus of Nazareth externally [*äußerlich*] is the "object" of such descriptions [in the stories of Jesus]. The question and the content of the gospel tradition is instead what reality [*Wirklichkeit*[11]] becomes visible if one opens oneself to Jesus. Not the externally observable side of historical facts that is irrelevant for faith, but the effect [*Wirkung*] of the inner truth of the figure of Jesus upon the self-experience and the self-interpretation of humans in the middle of the tightrope walk

---

10. *Verdichtung* shares the same root as *Dichtung,* which means "poetry." This is intended and reflects that Drewermann thinks of the symbolic condensation as a poetic process.

11. The German word connotes the meaning "effective reality."

between fear and faith constitutes the level of *reality* [*Wirk-lichkeit*] — **which by all means should be called historical** — of this eminently religious and therefore *symbolic,* hence "un-historical" manner of biblical presentation. (ibid., italics in the original; bold added)

The historical reality of many of the religious stories which his-torical criticism simply cannot verify externally can, Drewermann proposes, be easily confirmed if one takes depth psychology as a model. In psychoanalysis, a client often recalls memories from the past. Drewermann reminds us that Freud reached a point in his work when he realized that it was often simply impossible to distin-guish between historically true events (external facts) and emotionally charged fiction. This led Freud (1900) to acknowledge the existence of the reality of "psychical truth" and allowed him an understand-ing of dream symbols which he presented in his *The Interpretation of Dreams* (Drewermann 1990d, 94 n. 28). Freud coined the term "screen memories" to recognize that even memories which "recall" events that never happened in that way in external history were con-veying immensely important insight into the emotional history of a patient (Freud 1899). "They contained truly experienced history, but instead of reflecting history as external facts they narrated the his-tory of emotional and existential meanings" of the past (Drewermann 1990d, 95). Screen memories thus worked similar to dream images which in their "timelessness ... let something that is long past ap-pear *symbolically* as present" and thus help us understand a meaning which "characteristically escapes conscious perception" (ibid.).

Drewermann believes that this depth-psychological model can be particularly useful for an understanding of those religious stories which historical criticism would otherwise have to devalue as unhis-torical or which were declared in opposition to historical criticism by the Roman Catholic Church "as historical for dogmatic rea-sons." This latter commanded faith which requires that people believe against all reason in facts which have no external-historical verifiabil-ity "is definitively no longer possible. It is once and for all impossible to swipe from the table the results of historical criticism by means of the demand of faith, although the Catholic Church has tried to do precisely this with rigorous strictness for more than an entire cen-tury. It is hopeless because violent, inhuman, and 'nihilistic' — in Fichte's sense of the word — to demand a dogmatism of faith which turns polemically against thought and against reason" (Drewermann 1990d, 98).

Instead of doing such "violence" to human reason and thinking, Drewermann proposes that depth psychology provides a way out of the dilemma of either the one-sided rationalism of historical criticism — which Drewermann associates particularly with Protestant theology and its iconoclastic tendency — or the coercive identification of religious symbolism with external historical facts against all reason by a dogmatism that tends to foster superstition — which Drewermann associates particularly with Roman Catholic theology (see 1984a, 31–37). A depth-psychological solution requires, however, that "one recognizes and admits that 'contrived fables'[12] exist and can exist which very well include in a symbolic sense a historical [geschichtliche] truth and even more: an eternally valid meaning, although they have never happened historically in the external sense" (ibid., 98).

Drewermann holds that depth-psychological appreciation for the inner historical value of screen memories and of dreams is particularly useful in understanding the meaning of stories evoked in response to the historical person of Jesus. These stories, Drewermann argues, are not only grounded, as the Bultmannians thought, in the "faith and the proclamation of the first Christian community [Urgemeinde]. On what then does the faith of the early Christian community base itself?" (ibid., 97). Drewermann instead understands these stories as the result of experiences in the life of Jesus which resonated in those who encountered him and which therefore became worth telling. Drewermann exemplifies this by means of the story of the transfiguration of Jesus (Mark 9:1–13). Prefacing his interpretation he writes:

It is hermeneutically decisive to interpret stories of this kind [i.e., of the baptism and the transfiguration of Jesus] not as literary constructs of the faith of the Early Church but to see in them condensed [verdichtete], symbolically expressed experiences which really took place in the inner life of Jesus, even if they, externally looked at, never occurred in this way. By means of depth psychology it is often possible to trace and make plausible a psychical truth in the background of texts which under

---

12. A reference to 2 Peter 1:16–17 (Drewermann 1990d, 97).

direct historical-critical scrutiny repeatedly vanish into thin air.
Instead of reading the respective texts with a focus upon the
disciples in the past, it is decisive to interpret them as the inner
experience of Jesus himself. Only thus do they also become
evidential and receive their binding significance for one's own
existence. (ibid., 93 n. 27)

By focusing on the inner historical meaning of religious stories,
theology could learn from depth psychology the importance especially of the "personal" dimension of historical reality. Since religion,
for Drewermann, never speaks of reality only objectively and can
never be understood only by objective methods of interpretation, the
method of depth psychology with its objective appreciation of the
historical significance of subjective experience takes on importance
for a theological interpretation of religious texts. "In reality, talking
by means of religious symbols serves essentially the purpose of reversing the subject-object dichotomy which is the basis for the modern
concept of science" (ibid., 98). Instead of holding on to "an inap-
propriate concept of science," exegesis and theology should interpret
religious texts so that these texts can do what they aim to do:

to grip the reader in such a way that she dives with her existence
into the encompassing mystery which can never become "object" because it is that "subject" to whom we owe the fact that
we can be "subject" at all: God. Stories in which God speaks
cannot be understood "objectively," but only when one is affected by them in one's very "subjectivity." All the same, such
an exegetical attitude which includes the subject in the process
of understanding is not "unscientific." It merely follows other
rules of interpretation than are dictated by the objectivity ideal
of modernity which principally excludes all forms of religiosity. If exegesis wants to be a *theological* method, it therefore
needs depth psychology today because it [i.e., depth psychol-
ogy] offers a model of scientific insight. For the purpose of
personal understanding, this model thus demands, describes,
and enables the risking of one's own person with one's own
feelings, expectations, interests, miseries, and transferences. One
cannot understand a religious text other than as one tries to
understand a friend: by being interested essentially in the psychical significance of his communications instead of on the
level of fact and of thought. In a certain sense one literally

has to dream the dreams of the other with him in order to understand him deeply enough.... What appears to historical criticism as mere "fantasy," consequently presents itself psychologically often enough as the only possible further development and self-communication of what [otherwise would remain] historically only in the past [*Vergangenen*] but mentally is really everlasting [*Unvergänglichen*]. What is historically "invented [*Erdichtete*]" is in psychological perspective often to be understood exactly as condensation [*Verdichtung*] of the true essence of the life of the other. Certainly, even then one still can and has to differentiate: not all dreams are similarly "enlightening" and revealing. But the criterion for this can no longer lie in history itself but has to orient itself in terms of how much the dream in question discloses itself as a progressive effect [*Fortwirken*] of the figure of the other, of her essential intentions and suggestions. In the *case of Jesus* the decisive criterion determining which kind of truth-value can be attributed to certain stories in which the Early Church "continued to dream" the figure of Jesus will consist above all in the connection between the *redemption from fear* and the *counterreaction of deadly resistance and suffering*. Measured by that criterion one can, for instance, call the story of the transfiguration of Jesus on the mountain... by all means true. To be sure, this is a truth of the historical Jesus which one can perceive only with the eyes of the spirit and not with the external senses. And it is precisely this *symbolic* manner of expression which reaches deep into the zones in which the *truth of images* resides. (ibid., 98–100)

Grounded in historical-critical exegesis but going beyond it when religious reality would vanish into thin air because of historical criticism's rational one-sidedness, Drewermann interprets the story of the transfiguration in light of this criterion of the connection of Jesus' experience and communication of the message of redemption from fear with the experience of deadly resistance which his message was to evoke. This interpretation also provides an example of how the notion of "being at the center of the world" — which under the spell of fear can lead, as we saw in the case of Nazi Germany (see Chap. 2 above), to devastating destruction if projected onto the *collective*, — can be understood constructively when it is experienced as part of the process of an *individual's* psychospiritual integration and absolute feeling of being held by the divine.

Read *symbolically,* the *story of the transfiguration of Jesus* has to be examined step by step. What real-life experiences are meant when it is said of a human being that he "went up" onto a "mountain" where there was a valid epiphany of God? Such "holy mountains" constitute in the mythology of peoples the middle point of the world. This already raises the question how one arrives at the "place" where the "world" has its center. The Christian legend empathizes correctly when it transfers Jesus' vision onto "Tabor," because *tabbur* means in Hebrew "the navel" (of the world). It is the "place" where human existence returns to its center. It is the point of the world where heaven touches earth and where the human heart is very close to God. But what happens if a human being leaves the "lowlands" of life and moves up against the law of gravity in order to gain a "position" where the whole world seems to lie at her feet? It is a moment of perfect *happiness* in which a human being feels far removed from and relieved of the world; thus one understands why in such decisive moments Jesus repeatedly takes *three* of his disciples (Peter, James, and John) with him. Depth psychologically, the *number three* means unity of the male personality — evidently one can be capable of a happy encounter with God only in the unity of one's whole person.

But what does "happiness" mean *contentwise* in relation to God?

The story of the transfiguration of Jesus says that in order to be happy one essentially needs a gradual revelation of the calling of one's own life: "Moses" and "Elijah," the two figures of the Old Testament who were able to lead the people of God into freedom from human oppression and from fear of demons speak with Jesus on the "mountain," and a heavenly voice confirms him as the "beloved son" of God. Such a scene certainly contains a "post-Easter" profession of faith. But should one think that Jesus would ever have been able to embark on his journey into suffering without such a clarification of his being [*Wesens*] and without such a high feeling of happiness? One is able to accept and bear within oneself only as much suffering as one has experienced happiness. And even if in the external-historical sense a "Tabor experience" of Jesus had never taken place, still the Gospel of Mark is perfectly correct when it declares that Jesus, the historical Jesus, must have been borne by a feeling of unconditional acceptance by God and by the vision of a deep happiness in order to be able to walk from the "mount" of transfiguration to the mount of suffering, to Golgotha. (ibid., 100–101)

Drewermann believes that, based on Jesus' experience of the overcoming of the spell of fear of the human spirit, the answer which Christianity provides to the question of anxiety makes it unique. Christianity combines a metaphysical belief in the absolute personhood of God with a belief in the absolute personhood of each individual human being — neither belief should, however, be confused with any nature-philosophical claims (see Chap. 2). Christianity holds that only the experience of being loved by the absolute person of God can calm the human fear of death. That love creates an atmosphere of trust in which the images of the collective unconscious become images of salvation that initiate a journey in which the concrete historical existence of the individual is gradually freed from the fear of the human spirit.

The Christian emphasis on the *historical Jesus* thus has significant therapeutic reasons. In the two-volume methodological work *Tiefenpsychologie und Exegese* (Drewermann 1984a, 1985b), Drewermann draws an analogy between the relationships portrayed between Jesus and those he healed in the gospels and the nature of a psychotherapeutic relationship which can only work if a concrete historical person, the therapist, aims to provide an atmosphere of unconditional acceptance and trust and thus allows the patient to learn to trust her psychic images. Theological exegesis can learn from depth psychology that the healing "symbols and symbolic narratives of the [Jesus] tradition" could never have emerged without a field of trust as it can and could only develop around "the center of a historical person" (Drewermann 1985b, 770). Thus, even though Jesus — as historical-critical research has shown — did not directly, consciously, teach many of the symbols of healing which later emerged in the Christian tradition, Jesus awoke those symbols in the psyches of others through the experience of a profound trust that he conveyed

and that sprang from his own relationship to God. It is this profound *trust* that uniquely characterized the *historical* Jesus and that
became the foundation for the Christian faith.[13] Thus — and this
is crucial — Drewermann locates the significance of the historical
Jesus not merely in external, objective facts, nor in the abstract Bultmannian[14] "that" of the life of Jesus, but in the concrete *inner attitude*
that the *historical* Jesus embodied in his person (1985b, 771). It
is this inner attitude that is *historically* relevant. And it is in the
historical *person* of Jesus as the one who evoked the symbols of
healing in an atmosphere of trust that the Christian faith is historically grounded and through which it has been established (ibid., 770
n. 6). The continuity between the historical Jesus and the dogmatic
Christ thus lies in the trusting attitude of Jesus which evoked the
archetypal symbols of healing necessary for the process of redemption
(ibid., 763–69).

Again the process of psychoanalytic psychotherapy provides the
hermeneutic model for an understanding of the relationship between the historical Jesus and the healing images he evoked in his
followers — here especially the role of dreams in the therapeutic
process.

> That a therapeutic process effects healing can be recognized
> when images emerge from the deep layers of the psyche which
> signal with great regularity certain maturational steps and mark
> stages of inner transformation in the life of a human being. The
> more a human being loses her fear and the more she is carried
> even in the deep layers of the psyche by trust, the more her
> dreams will change. Images of neurotic self-representation are

---

13. Drewermann frequently refers to O. Pfister (1948), who emphasized that Jesus embodied an attitude of trust which overcomes both fear and ascetic moralism in religion (see
Drewermann 1990d, 17, 68, 77).

14. Drewermann notes that *"Bultmann* tried to make the fact of the mythological speech
of the Bible and of Christian dogmatics *historically* intelligible. His tragedy was (and is within
the frame of historical-critical exegesis) that in doing so that which is historically understood
became and has to become devalued itself as part of history. It is, however, also possible and
in the sense of Christian dogmatics indispensable to evidence the *truth* of the mythological
images and to thereby deepen the existential hermeneutics of Bultmann by means of depth
psychology in such a way that it becomes adequate to the concrete contents of the mythic
images" (Drewermann 1990d, 91 n. 22). Drewermann holds that one can retain the poetic
language of mythic imagery without declaring it "in a fundamentalist sense [a vehicle] for
historical reports" only if one asks "the decisive question of what kind of *reality* is it that can
be conveyed *only* in the symbolic language of *myth*. Only through depth psychology can the
objective validity of the *symbols* of faith be regained beyond the Bultmannian critique" (ibid,
86 n. 14).

replaced by image-sequences with a guiding quality, and these very images not only *indicate* the beginning of healing but the healing is effected through them and would never come about without them. In addition, we deal here with images which are not to be "grasped" in a rational sense but are to be made part of consciousness in a meditative sense and to be obeyed with the direction of one's entire existence. They are not pregiven from outside, and in that sense one may call them "unhistorical." Nonetheless one has to keep in mind that these images of healing can become effective in the psyche of the individual only if he enters a space of trust which is mediated through the presence of another person. (ibid., 767–68)

This experience of the historical Jesus allowed Christianity to connect the *archetype* of the divine savior with the individual *historical person* of Jesus (ibid., 776–79; cf. Drewermann 1986b, 533). It is Jesus' experience of the fear of dying and his overcoming of this fear through an experience of feeling absolutely held by God, together with the fact that his message of trust and love provoked the deepest spiritual conflicts of fear and aggression that would tragically lead to his physical death, which became the foundation on which Christianity could connect the archetype of the "God-human" with a historical person (hence Jesus the Christ). "And precisely in this *connection of personal trust and archetypal dreaming* seems to lie the most important point of connection for a foundation-theological establishment of what is specifically Christian" (Drewermann 1985b, 777). It is such faith, that is, such trust by means of which archetypal imagery becomes integrated constructively with the personal historical ego, which bans the type of *fear* that leads humans either to regress — flooded by collective unconscious forces and by extension to enslavement by collective social forces — or to construct a rigidly rational point of view (Drewermann 1986b, 533). The archetypes of the collective unconscious can lose their ambivalence only if experienced in relation to another human person who incarnates the absolute love that God has for each human being. The finding of self and the finding of God are *empirically* the same, even though they must be strictly differentiated *theologically*, in the sense that the finding of God is the condition for the possibility of self-integration (Drewermann 1985b, 245).

The Symbol of the Cross and the Redemption from a
Violent God-Image

Wieviel Trost ist im Bilde; ja alle unsere Tröstungen kommen
von Bildern her.[15]   —Reinhold Schneider, *Iberisches Erbe*

We have so far focused on the attitude of trust of the historical person of Jesus and his perspective on death as he faced his sentence of death. We have alluded occasionally to the archetypal imagery which Jesus evoked in those who encountered him, imagery that is capable of healing the fear of the human spirit and the fragmentation of the ego. I will now present Drewermann's interpretation of Cross (and resurrection) from the other angle: from the perspective of the psychospiritual dynamics that led, according to Drewermann, to the killing of Jesus and that, read symbolically, is the basis for the atrocious event of the Cross becoming a symbol of ultimate redemption. We learned in the previous section that Drewermann is not interested in the external-historical reasons why people ultimately rejected and killed Jesus. Instead he is interested in the *type* of attitude portrayed in the gospels that is responsible for the killing of Jesus: an attitude of fear that cannot bear the unconditional acceptance that he lived and offered. This type of attitude stems from a deep ambivalence to what is absolutely good, God. Following both the Evangelist Mark and the Yahwist, Drewermann holds (see Chap. 1) that this spiritual attitude characterizes all human beings outside of Eden and that it finds psychological expression especially in oral-sadistic conflicts. The connection between the killing of Jesus and the oral-sadistic dynamics is, according to Drewermann, particularly evident because Christianity very soon connected the ritual of the Eucharist, of the eating of the Godhead, with the doctrines of the Cross and resurrection. Drewermann's main tool for an understanding of the dynamics that led to the killing of Jesus is the psychoanalytic situation. The situation of psychoanalytic transference provides the model for an understanding of the *type* of attitude in all humans — and not just in those historically "responsible" for the death of Jesus — that leads to a rejection of and aggressive reaction to the one who offers healing. As a model for the spiritual issues of life and death which were involved in the message of Jesus, psychoanalysis can help understand what rage was

---

15. How much comfort lies in the image; indeed, all our solace comes from images.

unleashed when Jesus preached a nonambivalent, nonviolent God that shattered the established ambivalence of the God-image.

The Transference Model of Psychoanalysis and the Vicarious Killing of the Son of God

Drewermann finds the classical psychoanalytic formulation of the patient-therapist relationship, with its emphasis on the importance of the basic rule, of resistance, of transference, and of the Oedipal conflict particularly useful for an understanding of the conflicts involved in a redemption from an ambivalent God-image within a patriarchal religion. The psychoanalytic situation serves Drewermann as the place where human despair is revealed in its unmistakable clarity and as the central model for understanding how the deadly end of Jesus on the Cross could come to be interpreted as a redemptive symbol for humanity. Drewermann emphasizes particularly the importance of the experience of transference. He describes the model of the "ideal" psychoanalytic situation as follows:

> Ideally an analytic therapy consists in keeping a contract agreed to at the beginning by analyst and analysand: the patient commits himself to say anything which comes to his mind, "the most embarrassing things first." The therapist, on the other hand, promises to accept everything which is said unconditionally as psychical truth, that is, without rejecting, correcting, directing, or manipulating it. Only on the background of such a general permission to be [zum Sein], only based on such a request for unrestricted truth will it be possible to express all those feelings which the patient — under threat of severe punishments, including the deadly loss of the love of the parents — was prohibited since childhood to even experience consciously. And precisely at this point a curious form of relationship — which varies in intensity — regularly emerges between the therapist and the client. The inner ambivalence and — possibly — positive development of this relationship offers an exact model for understanding the Christian drama of redemption, too. In experiencing for the first time in his life a kind of care, esteem, and attention which he needed previously as a child but received in his childhood only in part, the patient places upon the therapist a quite childish extent of trust and of longing for hold. Inevitably he regresses thus at first into childhood and step by step once again lives through

and suffers through its feeling states and experiences — now, of course, in conscious form. "If you do not become like children, you cannot enter into the realm of God" (Mark 10:15, Matt. 18:3) reads the established maxim of what is probably the most important part of any analytic psychotherapy: the building up of a relatively stable *transference*. The word "transference" means that the client puts upon the therapist feelings and expectations which do not belong to her [i.e., the therapist] as a private person, but which basically derive from the early childhood pattern of the relationship to the parents and which become visible only now through the therapist as a suitable plane of projection. (Drewermann 1990d, 73–74)

The transference gives the patient permission "to re-experience and live out" those layers of the psyche "which, like the famous 13th room in the spellbound castles of fairy tales, was until then off-limits"[16] (1990d, 74). Drewermann compares the analyst's attitude with the words of Jesus in the Sermon on the Mount: "If someone asks you to go with her one mile, go with her two" (Matt. 5:41).

No analyst does anything else principally than translating this attitude of Jesus into practice. Still...as the patient comes increasingly close to the home of her childhood, not only the old feelings of longing for hold and security become loud again but also simultaneously feelings that had been repressed in the past: of disappointment, of revenge, of anger, of jealousy, of rage, of powerlessness, of loneliness, of guilt, and of reparation....Although, or rather: precisely because the therapist wants nothing more than that his patient, with all good will and all readiness for acceptance, find his way from the fears and dependencies of childhood to an independent life, he really must appear to his patient as a reincarnation of the old parental figures of father and mother. If a really new beginning is to be possible for the client, then the therapist must adopt *their* role for a long period of time; by trying to be understanding, as the parents of the patient in her childhood actually would have had to be, he sets free for the first time all the aggressions, cravings for revenge, and power struggles around the fact that her father and mother were

---

16. For Drewermann's interpretation of the forbidden thirteenth door in the fairy tale *Our Lady's Child* as a symbol for the suppression of a girl's curiosity about her own sexuality and about love through a moralistic misunderstanding of religion, see Drewermann 1992e.

back then not exactly as she would have needed them in order for her own life to unfold without falsifications. (ibid., 75)

The therapist thus takes on a vicarious role, a notion which allows Drewermann to elucidate the vicarious character which the person of Jesus has as Son of God in the gospel stories.

For quite some time the therapist embodies *vicariously* the figure of a positive counter image to the ambivalent memory images (the *"imagoes"*) of the parents. Thus she can in a certain sense only wish with all her heart that the repressed anger of child-hood [of the patient] finally erupts at least in relation to her person. Only if all the words of protest, of rebellion, of accusation, of reproach in the form of the therapeutic substitute figure of father and mother, which one, as a child, was not permitted to express — because one had to assimilate to the will of the parents in order to survive — can be worked through, only then can that experience be catalyzed which in the language of the Bible may indeed be called "reconciliation [*Versöhnung*]": Reconciliation is a sense of being from the ground up, prior to all censorship and conditioning to certain ways of behavior, justified to exist in the world and hence to be allowed to *firmly* set [*fest*setzen] one's own boundaries, carry *through* [*durch*setzen] one's own wishes and *employ* [*ein*setzen] one's own skills and abilities in life. (ibid., 75)

Unconditional Acceptance and the Cleansing of the God-Image from Ambivalence: Where Depth Psychology and Theology Meet and Need Each Other

The *experience* of unconditional acceptance is where the aims of Jesus and the aims of psychoanalysis converge and where psycho-analysis can *experientially* be more than a model for redemption. But this experiential convergence requires that psychoanalysis draw the theoretical consequence and acknowledge that its notion of un-conditional acceptance and trust can only stand on a theological basis. Drewermann's integration of theology and depth psychology attempts to overcome both the *"soullessness of today's theology"* and the "theoretical *atheism of today's psychology*" (Drewermann 1985b, 762–73; cf. Drewermann 1989a, 128–29). He clarifies the *experiential* connection between psychoanalysis and the process of redemption and the *theoretical* difference between the reconcilia-tion in psychoanalysis and in Christian theology. The experiential

connection lies in the attitude of unconditional acceptance which
characterizes both psychoanalysis and the Christian doctrine of redemption and implies in both a necessary "suspension of the ethical"
in Kierkegaard's sense (Drewermann 1991h). The emotional and spiritual correlation between the dynamics of human aggression and the
finding of self hinted at by Drewermann in the passages we just cited
are deepened in the following in view of the connection between developmentally early psychological needs and fundamental existential
needs of humans. Leaning on M. Klein's work, Drewermann writes:

> The details of the relation between aggression and the finding of
> self at the earliest stages of mental development present them-
> selves as follows. In any child who does not feel accepted in his
> entire existence by his parents, especially by his mother, a deadly
> fear emerges. In his fantasy, all the way to sadistic wishes of
> death, he will try to kill the "evil [böse]," withholding mother
> in order to regain the "good" mother. But at the same time he
> feels guilty for his (oral) aggressions, that is, he fears the punish-
> ing persecution by the "evil" mother. This fear of punishment,
> however, only increases the rage of the child against the mother.
> Hence a vicious circle is created which can only be solved if the
> child represses his rage and exerts himself all the more to com-
> ply with the supposed expectations of his mother.[17] But even if
> he succeeds with this the feeling remains henceforth that first of
> all one has to *earn* the love of the parents. The recognition thus
> acquired is given in the best scenarios only for externally correct
> behavior but not for one's own person, and the morality which
> develops under these circumstances really consists in an elab-
> orate system of punishments and rewards, which are given as
> premiums for the repression and suppression of one's own feel-
> ings. According to psychoanalysis such processes already play a
> role in the mental development of any human being during the
> oral-depressive phase of her childhood. This is precisely why it
> is not possible to return to the truth of one's own person unless
> a trust has been built that — beneath the threshold of socially
> enforced conformity and of fears of loss of love — one can be
> allowed to be absolutely justified and wanted in this world de-
> spite all and with all the malice [Bosheit] and destructive rage
> of an unloved child. (Drewermann 1990d, 76)

---

17. Drewermann here refers to M. Klein's "On the Theory of Anxiety and Guilt" (1975b).

The feeling that one is only acceptable to mother when one re-presses one's aggressive, "evil" impulses, the feeling that one needs to live a super-morality to be assured of some right to exist, is also transferred to the father-image as the triangular, Oedipal, relationship emerges developmentally. If the God-image, in a patriarchal religion, is confused with the moralistic super-demands of the Oedipal fa-ther figure, God in the form of a superego becomes the ultimate sadist requiring the impossible: complete denial of self. When the repressed aggressive impulses and unresolved conflicts in relation to the parental figures resurface in the course of a psychoanalysis of an adult, the task is, however, not only a psychological working through of conflicts from the psychological past (oral, anal, Oedipal) but also a working through of the (corresponding yet) more encompassing and more fundamental existential, spiritual conflicts around one's ex-istence as such (feeling guilty for existing at all; sacrificial mentality aiming at attaining justification of one's existence; feeling that one's existence is never good enough). It is here where dynamics of psy-chological beginnings, of *in principio,* take on — as in Drewermann's analysis of the Yahwist texts of the primordial history in Genesis 2–11 — symbolic meaning expressing the character of one's *Dasein,* of how one experiences or longs to experience existence principally, *a principio.* Hence Drewermann proposes that at the point where in "analytic psychotherapy" a trust emerges that lies "beneath the threshold of socially enforced conformity and of fears of loss of love," psychoanalysis

> becomes not only a *model* for the Christian doctrine of redemp-tion but leads in itself [*in sich selber*] to experiences of religious quality which centrally shape Christianity. A *child* has to ask whether *her parents* can love her. An *adult* who lives once more through the hell of her childhood in psychoanalysis, also asks, to be sure, about the significance of her parents in respect to the first years of her life. In doing so, she is fundamentally no longer concerned only about regaining the past but far more about forming a primal trust [*Urvertrauen*] in *the background of her existence* as a whole. (ibid., 76–77)

Although psychoanalytic practice, if successful, may lead to experi-ences of religious quality, Drewermann stresses that within its theory psychoanalysis cannot establish a basis for the absolute trust neces-sary for this experience. This, he believes, requires a theological basis, that is, the belief in the unambivalent and absolute affirmation of our existence. Theologically speaking, psychoanalysis presupposes a non-ambivalent, nonviolent God-image and is itself a tool for the working through of the ambivalence associated (in a patriarchal society) with the image of a Father God.

> No psychoanalytic treatment can be the foundation of this trust. All it can do is clear away the psychological reasons which get in the way of such a fundamental attitude of trust. But in doing so, the analytic practice of treatment itself presupposes a spiritual [*geistige*] conviction such as the one which the religion of Jesus essentially wants to catalyze: the conviction that *the origin* of our existence beyond all the ambivalence necessarily contained in the image of the *human* parents does *not* need to be imagined in itself as frightening, rejecting, hostile, revengeful, and jealous. It would indeed equal the slander and falsification of God if one wanted to transfer the fears and ambiguities which are common among humans into the relationship to God. Psychoanalysis as well as religion in that sense aim together, although with different approaches, at the *cleansing and clarification of the father-image,* at the end of Oedipal sadism. And both know that it is futile if one wants to build a temple of humanity on the shaky ground of all sorts of repressed anxieties, aggressions, and guilt feelings. Both therefore try through the person of a *vicar* [*Stellvertreters*] of the frightening father authority by way of a substitutive assumption of age-old suffering to set free again those powers of one's own life that were buried alive early on in order to enable a new beginning which is truer, more honest, more understanding, less frightening, ego-stronger [*ichstärker*], and more trusting than the previous path of inhuman sacrifices and dutiful cruelties. (ibid., 77–78)

Without the emotional and existential background of the feeling of being ultimately unjustified and superfluous in the world, Drewermann considers it impossible to understand the Cross and resurrection other than as a sadomasochistic tool for moral asceticism. Only a life under the spell of existential fear — with its desperate attempts to gain some justification either by denying ourselves as much as we can in order to appear good in the eyes of the Other or by striving mercilessly toward a perfection in which no human weakness has a place — inevitably leads to our killing of the one who upsets this life of fear (Drewermann 1990e, 625–42). And only when one is cognizant of the deepest human experiences of fear, guilt, and aggression, can one make the cruel event of the crucifixion intelligible and understand why it could take on symbolic meaning as a *therapeutic* cipher of redemption for the whole human person.

One understands the paradoxical human meaning of many words and references in the Gospel of Mark, in relation to the necessity of suffering, to the inevitability of the Cross (Mark 8:34–35) and to the resurrection from the realm of the dead (Mark 9:30–32, 10:32–34), only in the sense of such a therapeutic working through of the most difficult feelings of anxiety and guilt which a human being can live through: the primordial fear of and the primordial protest against being unjustified and unloved on earth. Anyone who, in contrast, does not constantly keep in mind the dialectic of all human intentions in the face of the counter-finality of the unconscious, repressed material in the deep layers of the human psyche, inadvertently plainly misunderstands, in the sense of an ascetic moralism, the entire concept of the Gospel of Mark and its fully consistent sequence leading up to the story of the Passion. He thus will condemn himself inevitably to distort the religion of freedom and redemption into an ideology of obsessive compulsive nightmares within which the God of Jesus Christ has to appear even more horrible than the bloodthirsty gods of war, of the sun, and of fertility of the meso-american Aztecs, as Huitzilopochtli, Tonatiuh, and Xipe totec ("our Lord the oppressor").[18] In a *redemptive* sense, as a *therapeutic cipher,* the death of Jesus on the Cross means precisely that it is not worth being afraid of humans because it is no longer necessary to be afraid of God. It was and is precisely this belief of Jesus which found expression in all his words to and encounters with humans and which was confirmed in his death: we humans may do what we want and we can have done what we want — the first and the most important word of God on all human fear and guilt will be a word of understanding and a word of forgiveness. Exactly because this contradicts at first everything which we have become accustomed to learn and to follow in our everyday life, this conviction of Jesus generates at

---

18. All three gods required human sacrifices, which were thought to nourish them or clothe them so that they could maintain the cosmos.

first a tremendous resistance. However, in the course of this resistance all of the suppressed feelings, too, are washed from the
depths to the surface until the water cleanses itself and becomes
transparent to its bottom. (ibid., 78–79)

The Symbolism of the Cross and the Holy Meal: A Ritual for Working Through Emotional and Spiritual Experiences of Ambivalence

It is in response to the experience of unconditional acceptance that
the repressed material emerges in varying degrees: in psychoanalysis,
it is associated with the oral, anal, and Oedipal stages and, correspondingly, in *daseinsanalytic* perspective, with feeling guilty simply
for existing at all, believing that through one's own sacrifices and efforts one could create a justification for one's existence, and feeling
that one *is* never enough no matter how hard one tries. That Christianity itself thinks particularly of the oral background of the guilt
feelings which have to be worked through and which are conceived
of as the core and foundation of all later psychosocial and psychospiritual conflicts finds expression for Drewermann in the fact that
the death of Jesus very early on became connected with the words of
the Last Supper.

> Precisely because the Early Church connected the death of Jesus
> with the words of the *Last Supper,* from the perspective of the
> *oral* background of the childish feelings of guilt one has to say
> that the death of Jesus does not so much mean atonement and
> justice in the juridical sense but represents the consequence of
> a simple as well as life-saving experience. If the first confusions
> of fear and guilt, as psychoanalysis has shown, are created from
> the ambivalences of *oral* sadism — long before they are later
> transferred from the experiences of the child with her mother
> to the father in order to falsify *his* person, too, within a field
> of fear, competitive envy, and self-mutilation — then there is no
> other way than to evoke and relive vicariously in relation to a
> *new* mother- and father-figure this whole drama of fear in form
> of an oral ritual until it becomes clear and trustworthy enough:
> that God is more fatherly than any father and more motherly
> than any mother. Unambiguously, God wants us to live. Even
> if we are as bad as we have been taught to fear we are since
> our childhood, God nevertheless wants us to live, beyond death,
> beyond guilt, and beyond fear. Because only in this trust of God

[*Vertrauen Gottes*], when all the distorting masks of duty, of possessions, and of cruelty have been lived out and laid down will we notice how rich and how valuable we truly are. Exactly for that reason the crucified Christ becomes bread for the world, because he embodies in his life as well as in the manner of his death an abiding certainty: what no mother is able to tell her child, God, with no ambiguity whatever, wants to say to the human being: we are allowed to live without having to wrap the simple fact of our existence in shrouds of old feelings of fear and of guilt. God is like bread and wine, like flesh and blood, primordially maternal from the very beginning. (Drewermann 1990d, 79–80)

When these conflicts, however, are not worked through within religion, they lead to a form of religion in which all the unresolved psychosocial and spiritual fears, guilt feelings, and projections are perpetuated in a doctrinal system where God is reified as ambivalent and is identified with the ambivalent parental imagoes to which the superego is structurally the heir. And those who live most conscientiously according to the precepts of such a superego religion inadvertently represent most clearly the *type* of mentality that has to kill in the name of God the one who lives unconditional acceptance and trust. This type of mentality represents "the incarnation of fear against the incarnation of the divine in humans" and is confronted in the person of Jesus with "an absolutely decisive struggle for the clarification and purification of the God-image from all ambivalences and admixtures of distorting fear" (Drewermann 1990d, 59). Psychologically, this is a challenge "which must, in a concentrated way, bring to the fore all resistances of the superego as well as the demonized, repressed material of the deep layers of the human psyche" (ibid., 60).

It is, Drewermann believes, precisely the kindness, the tenderness, the humanity of Jesus which forces the conflict with any inhuman law-and-order faith. "It is his quiet, tender tolerance which provokes the screaming fanaticism, his humanly open heart the inhuman faith in laws, his universal love the narrow hate. And again one needs depth psychology to understand in this crucial point the inner logic of the Gospel of Mark according to which an extreme degree of aggression has to catalyze itself precisely around an extraordinary degree of patience before the inner disunity, the internalized violence of all possible compulsions and guilt feelings can give way to a credible peacefulness in dealing with oneself and with others" (ibid., 60–61).

In contrast to Freud, Drewermann proposes that the Christian symbolism of Cross and Resurrection, with a God imagined as Father and a human being represented by the Son, actually contains the material by means of which the specifically Oedipal dynamics involving an ambivalent (patriarchal) God-image are worked through rather than perpetuated. For this, Drewermann turns, however, to the admittedly "fantastically sounding theory" of the killing of the primal father presented by Freud (1913) in *Totem and Taboo*. Drewermann acknowledges that from an external historical perspective, Freud was far off the mark in his "scientific myth." But, he suggests, Freud's argument contained a very true intuition which can provide the key to an understanding of the symbol of the Cross and of the kind of God-image which needs to be overcome if humans should be able to live as humans. In *Totem and Taboo*

> Freud wanted especially to solve the energetic problem of how it could be possible to subjugate the strength of the drives of the id to the dictates of cultural demands. The problem seemed to him solvable under the presumption that the moral-religious conscience itself would be nothing but the internalized violence of the strivings of the id of an absolute (father) authority. Its replica would actually be what the religions of humanity call by the name of "God."
>
> ... What is essential in our context, against all the objections [to Freud's theory], is the absolutely correct description which Freud has provided in exemplary clarity of the *ambivalence of the God-image in a patriarchal religion* as well as his portrayal of the extremely paradoxical processes of inner liberation from all the aggressions which have been dammed up since childhood days, which first are directed toward one's own father and then, however, also toward the figure of the "Father in heaven"; it is chiefly this analytical process of the working through of ancient Oedipal aggressions, of the *mental* "prehistory" in the human being, which also allows us to understand the archetype of the killed God as a symbol of redemption. And it is at this point that every existing religion has to learn from one of the great atheists and humanists of our century how "God" may *not* be if humans want to live humanly. (Drewermann 1990d, 62–63)

As we saw (Chap. 2), Drewermann's interpretation of the Eucharist as the ritual in which the symbol of the killing and eating of the God-head, if deeply enough experienced, ritualizes aggression, prevents feelings of guilt and fear in relation to aggression, and sublimates the instinctual aim of aggression from humans onto God. Drewermann now elaborates that the redemptive significance in the symbol of the Cross is that it gives humans absolute permission to put all their repressed murderous oral, anal, Oedipal aggression on God who is capable of bearing it. The universal presence of sacred meals of the Godhead in religions, suggests the archetypal nature of this ritual. That both Freud and Jung have thought in terms of archetypes, of phylogenetic dispositions of symbolizing, is important for Drewermann. He believes that the difference between Freud and Jung "is not one in terms of content but purely dogmatic" (ibid., 63 n. 32).

As we proceed to Drewermann's constructive interpretation of the symbol of the "killing of the Son of God," we encounter his passionate deconstruction of traditional interpretations of the Cross which set the suffering of Jesus as an example for self-denial and for suffering in the name of the Cross or of Christ. A constructive interpretation of the Cross requires the working through of Christianity's tendency to project into the God-image unresolved psychospiritual conflicts rather than to face the anthropological reality of these conflicts. We again note that Drewermann sees the symbolism of Cross and Resurrection as responding to primary human psychological and spiritual needs at the different stages of human development. Drewermann cautions against a reading of the death and resurrection of Jesus Christ that fails to begin with a psychoanalytic demythologization and instead tries to establish the meaning of the texts directly from the perspective of God.

> If one considers the *symbol* of the crucified Christ independently from depth psychology and possibly even independently from the many parallels of the archetype of the killed Godhead in the history of religions,[19] then the danger is inevitable that one simply recognizes the event of Golgotha as an external-historical fact whose truth is not evident from within but at most impresses as a moral model. If Christ died for us on the Cross then, according to this psychology-distant approach, every Christian

---

19. Drewermann here refers to A. E. Jensen (1966) and J. Kott (1973).

has henceforth the "duty" of "discipleship of the Cross" —
many passages of the Gospel of Mark seem to fit in with such
a demand. Then a Christianity of suffering and sacrifice categorically opposes the immediate pursuit of a fulfilled and happy
life. Under such circumstances it even has to be held to be downright sinful and egotistical if someone wants to *find himself* or
to "realize" himself. If humanity could only be redeemed by
reconciling an infinitely offended and angry God through the
vicarious sacrifice of his son on the tree of the Cross, then the
individual could share in such a liberation from the "punishment of sins" only by realizing the suffering of Christ in her
life (Mark 10:28–31). A psychotherapeutic theory and practice, such as psychoanalysis, which intends to enable the human
being to become capable of happiness and enjoyment quite in the
earthly sense, to reduce her guilt feelings and to expand her ego-
strength, assertiveness, and identity — such a "philosophy" can
under these circumstances only be understood as anti-Christian
hedonism, as value-subversive egoism, even as methodical and
practical atheism. In light of the Christian self-presentation, it
was, conversely, more than understandable that psychoanalysis
declared war completely on such a father religion of suffering.
Freud even expressed in the end the hope that humanity might
one day be permanently healed from such ideas of infantile fear
of and dependency on the father as the embodiment of a collective obsessional neurosis — hence a redemption not *through*
religion but definitively a redemption *from* religion. Indeed, if
the theology of Christianity, particularly exegesis and dogmatics, continues with its externalistic understanding of suffering
and redemption which avoids any psychological mediation, it
inevitably will draw upon itself from psychoanalysis the reproach that it is nothing but a ceremonialized and religiously
painted-over derivative of the Oedipus complex. The arguments
which psychoanalysis advances here can all be confirmed by experience. The "infinite offense" given to the father(-god), this
sin crying to heaven of the human children, consists in psychoanalytic perspective in the very natural wish of every (male) child
to be and remain the only lover of his mother. With this wish,
however, the child threatens the older claims and rights of the
father who in return threatens the son with castration as punishment. And it is eventually only this castrative submission under

the sadism of the authority of the father which is able to mollify the rage of the jealous patriarch. A religion which declares ideas of this kind as central dogmas of its teaching, according to Freud, does no less than elevate in barbaric fashion the archaic sexual suppression as its ideal — the mutilation of the human ability to love through the dictates of severe masochistic guilt feelings as well as a constant ambivalent attitude of self-humiliation and self-renunciation. The Oedipus complex, the obsessive compulsive neurosis, constitutes in this way the experiential background and also interpretative model for the historical fact of the execution of Jesus. (Drewermann 1990d, 64–68)

Drewermann then goes on to charge that the superficial, external self-understanding of Christianity indeed tends to reify just such an Oedipal structure and is therefore the cause of unimaginable mental and social suffering.

This is how things are as long as Christianity understands the doctrine of the redemptive death of Christ *externally:* it serves not redemption but alienation, not liberation but oppression, not humanization but repression. Does this have to be this way? Does this need to continue this way? It is an outrageous and scandalous state of affairs that the religion of Jesus, born from the struggle against the authoritarian suppression of humans in the name of a despotic God has been subject for the last 150 years to the well-supported suspicion and exposed to the often corroborated reproach that it is basically nothing more than the ideology of this kind of morally garnished sadism, a form of institutional external direction and fear, a grotesque new edition of just that scribal mentality which Jesus with the power of his whole person wanted to overcome.[20] (ibid., 68)

Addressing the historical reasons why Christianity became sidetracked into a superficial, external reading as opposed to an internal, existential reading of the Passion story, Drewermann finds that certain reasons lie in the very dialectic of the Bible itself. In order to make intelligible particularly to its Jewish listeners why Jesus was the expected Messiah although he was killed, the Early Church tried to

---

20. Drewermann points, for instance, to O. Pfister's *Christianity and Fear* (1948) and Th. Reik's *Dogma and Compulsion* (1951) in this context.

portray the suffering and killing of Jesus as fulfillment of Old Testament prophecies. As much as this argumentation made sense at the time, "it yet contained two weak spots which had to become extremely dangerous psychologically as soon as they were separated from the immediate experience of the humanity of Jesus: *the positivism of theological reasoning* and *the psychological return to the ambivalence of the God-image*" (ibid., 69). Sooner or later the argument of the promise-fulfillment paradigm of the killing of Jesus raised ever more urgently

> the question not only *whether* but above all *why* God at all could have wanted his own son to die on the Cross. The Gospel of Mark or the tradition of the Passion from which it drew was content to declare *that* God wanted it this way. But the question remains what kind of God this is who can will this way.... [P]*sychologically* the "proof of Scripture"...led inevitably to a monstrous God-image in that one tried to ground the process of redemption from the perspective of God (rather than from the conditions of human experience). A God who does not spare his own son but "gives" him up on the Cross, a God who demands from his son "obedience" under cold sweat and tears and who declares himself for the manifold tortured [son] — whom, as the pious legend on top of it all assures us, he could have easily saved — only after everything had already been "finished," such a God does not at all appear only as a God of redeeming love, he appears rather as incomprehensibly paradoxical, as unimaginably cruel, even as archaic, barbaric, and crude. It is a God-image which is even more terrible than the notion of a punishing just God in the Old Testament which Jesus himself wanted to supplement, correct, and overcome by means of his message and the visible proof of a forgiving love. (Drewermann 1990d, 69–71)

Drewermann stresses that one can only understand "the God of Good Friday as a cipher of redemption" if one thinks and argues *"psychologically,* from the perspective of humans" rather than theologically from the perspective of God. Here he is deeply indebted to the "experiences and descriptions of Freud of the archaic crudeness of the human psyche," although he fiercely rejects Freud's reduction of religion to a neurotic offshoot of the Oedipus complex. It is this very "archaic crudeness" in the human psyche which needs to be addressed in an effective ritual of redemption. If one wants to prevent this "archaic crudeness" from being acted out externally in the form of war against Others or against self and instead wants to provide a forum in which such spiritually infinitized impulses can be worked through and sublimated, then one needs rituals within a safe space in which the repressed impulses can be playfully acted out and directed toward the innocent person of God (instead of directing it toward innocent humans) by means of symbolic gestures. Drewermann's model is here the patient's "acting out" of repressed impulses in the transference toward the psychoanalyst. Only when the significance of the crucifixion is seen not in the external, physical event of the past but in symbolism which the human psyche stirs up, can the crucifixion as a *symbol* become a cipher of redemption from fear throughout the ages. Then it can be a symbol for God being almighty in the sense that God can bear all our worst human impulses and it permits us to direct them toward God. For a constructive interpretation

everything depends on understanding the drama of the crucifixion not as a symbolic etiology of the Oedipus complex but, to the contrary, as *a psychodrama of healing,* as a symbolic-vicarious working through of the repressed feelings of hate, destruction, and revenge, hence as a depiction of everything which humans first have to experience and do before they can truly and unambiguously believe in the ghetto of their anxiety in something like forgiveness beyond *all* guilt. Theology has — especially through the experiences of analytic psychotherapy — an interpretive model available which primarily enables us to elucidate the very human character of such paradoxical intricacies. The most puzzling paradox of the Gospel of Mark as well as of Christianity becomes truly understandable only based on psychoanalytic experience: that it requires the killing of *an innocent person* [i.e., God] in order to be liberated from one's own lack of life. What was expressed in the Old Testament ritual expression *through the image of the sacrificial lamb or the scapegoat* has its basis and confirmation in the process of *"playfully acting out."*[21] Paradoxically, it is also just the attitude of

21. Drewermann here refers to Anna Freud's observations that children in analysis may need to act out their material in the form of actions (A. Freud 1965, 29–31, 39–41), which he thinks may also be the case in certain "adult" neurotics. Drewermann here also supports H. Kohut's

acceptance that is free from violence as much as possible and of letting-be that is free from prejudice as much as possible which may provoke the most intense outbreaks of aggression. (Drewermann 1990d, 71–73)

To understand Drewermann's argument that the symbol of the Cross in which Christians are participating through the ritual of the Eucharist is meant to work through rather than perpetuate Oedipal sadism, we have to remember his definition of the Oedipus complex existential-philosophically, that is, spiritually (see Chap. 1) as the infinite longing of a human being under the spell of the fear of nothingness "to become one's own creator, the foundation of oneself, and the origin of one's own being so that finally one gains a feeling of justification in *Dasein* and of a sense of security in the very 'homelessness' of this world" (Drewermann 1986b, 405). The Oedipus complex is thus the wish to be like God (psychologically, to be one's own parent) which Drewermann understands spiritually as a reaction-formation to the distortion of the God-image due to the spiral of existential fear (see Chap. 1). By acting out in the ritual of the eating of the Godhead the infinitized and repressed aggressions (psychologically, both oral and Oedipal aggressions) which are the very fuel for the competitive strife of replacing God and of becoming like God (of replacing the same-sex parent), the Oedipus complex can be worked through by means of religion rather than perpetuated by it. The Oedipus complex, this fear-based complex focusing around guilty submission to or enraged rebellion against God (the ambivalent father or mother), is overcome when one experiences through that ritual, in which God does not punish us for our deadly aggressions but willingly takes them upon himself and unconditionally accepts and justifies us, that God is not someone to be feared and hence cannot be used by humans to intimidate other humans (Drewermann 1990d, 78–79). Just as the one-sidedly rational ego dies, which itself is a result of repression of the unconscious under the spell of fear, so the one-sidedly rationalistic God-image dies intrapsychically. A nonambivalent God-image emerges that is existentially both more motherly and more fatherly than any mother or father could ever be. It is then, Drewermann believes, that humans can cease to have to become like God or turn other humans into gods and that the God-image can cease to become

---

term *"action-thought"* for actions which take on the value and function of "associations" (H. Kohut 1977, 34–37) (Drewermann 1990d, 72–73 n. 47).

like an ambivalent human being. Drewermann believes that we then can stop the futile attempt of creating for our own existence an absolute foundation, can lose the fear to discover freely the true richness of ourselves, and can feel anchored in a truly preexisting, absolute foundation.

Cross, Baptism, and Rebirth: Psychic Unity and the Longing for Reunion with One's Origin

We have so far explicated the objective-level aspect of Drewermann's interpretation of the Cross which focused essentially around the existential alternative between fear and trust and employed the model of the psychotherapeutic process hermeneutically. This view of the Cross allows an understanding of the oral-sadistic conflicts and the symbolic existential significance they take on spiritually which have to be resolved. But it does not yet spell out why the symbol of the Cross should have healing significance for the whole person. Above all, how can the symbol of the Cross, not merely a return of the repressed aggression in ritual form, lead to intrapsychic change through which the one-sidedness which characterizes the human psyche and the human spirit under the spell of fear can give way to a true integration of consciousness and the unconscious, reason and the drives, individual ego and collective psyche, words and affects. Drewermann (1979) answers this question in two steps: first, he highlights the subjective-level aspect of an interpretation of the Cross which complements the objective-level aspect. Second, he shows how the subjective-level, intrapsychic interpretation of the Cross can serve as a *symbol* for the relationship of humans and God.

In preparation for the subjective-level interpretation, Drewermann cites findings from the comparative study of religion, from ethology, and from research on early psychological childhood development. He shows that the symbolism of the Cross is not the unique heritage of Christianity but is found in mythology all over the world by analyzing in detail images in the Aztec religion which developed apart from Christianity and which bear striking resemblance to its very contents (ibid., 5–12). As with the Cross, the rituals described below are repulsive and cruel as long as they are externally understood. Only when one sees them as symbols which are not to be acted out physically but experienced as internal imagery — in the language of psychoanalysis, only when they are present in sublimated form — can they be intrapsychic symbols of human healing. The Codex-Fejérváry-Mayer, for instance, shows on the first page a cosmic map in the shape of a cross with cross-shaped trees representing among other things the four directions of the world and the world as a whole, different gods, and the eternal cycle of death and renewal in vegetation. In the center of the cosmic cross lies the fifth area of the world in which the fire god Xiuhtecutli is nurtured by bloody sacrifices. This image of the cosmos was the basis for the cultic place in which the Aztecs presented sacrifices to the gods — which is similar to the cruciform shape of Christian churches with the altar in the center (ibid., 8). Ideas very similar to the crucifixion can also be found in images from the Mixtecs, who are related to the Aztecs, namely, in the Codex Nutall. It records that during the Spring feast, in which a human sacrifice was given to the fertility god Xipe totec, two other rituals took place: a "sacrifice of battle" during which a prisoner, tied to a pierced stone disc evidently symbolizing the heavens, is killed in a mock fight which was associated by the Aztecs with scratching the earth; and the so-called sacrifice of arrows in which a chief is bound in a ritual to a ladder and shot to death by arrows, which was associated with the fertilizing of the earth. "Both ceremonies of slaying served the resurrection of the earth: the mock fight evidently symbolized the dangers of the corn and the piercing during the sacrifice of arrows pointed to the breaking through of the tips of the corn plants through the soil" (ibid., 9). The "sacrifice of battle" was replaced by some tribes with the "game of flying" in which four figures disguised as birds slowly descended from a high mast symbolizing the heavenly descent of the food plant.

Drewermann observes the following similarities in the *symbolic* content between the Aztec and Mixtec rituals and Christian teachings. "The death of Christ, too, deals sacramentally with the foundation of the heavenly food; his death on the Cross serves, as the death of Attis, Osiris, and as the Aztec sacrifices, the growth of grain for the life of humans. His body, too, must be opened at the Cross, just as the seeds have to break through the hard shell of the earth in spring. His blood is, as described in Tertullian's *Apologeticum,* the seed and the rain of fertility. His life itself falls as seed into the earth for greater life (John 12:24)" (ibid.). The cosmic dimension of the Aztec ritual thus finds a parallel in the notion "that the sacrifice on the Cross makes possible the continuation of the vegetation and of life in the entire cosmos. The fruit of heavenly food is based, as fertility itself, on a prior dying of the God or a vicar of the God who eventually gives himself in the form of grain or corn as food. All eating is hence basically sacramental. Life would not exist without the killing and eating of the gods" (ibid., 9–10). Similar ideas are also found in nonagricultural societies of hunters.

But what does this similarity of tree symbolism mean in which both life and death come from a tree? Further analysis of Aztec mythology shows that the tree is associated in various stories with maternal functions. For instance, in Tamohuanchan, the land of the split tree, the children who died early were believed to suck on a tree which was their source of fruits and milk. Tamohuanchan is also the location where the tribes originated, hence the place of the origin of humankind: "the symbol of the birth of primordial femininity" (ibid., 11). These and other stories in myths and fairy tales around the world establish a "remarkable, and to all appearances archetypal symbolic equation of tree and woman (mother), with a noticeable emphasis on themes of birth and cannibalism" (ibid., 12–13). Thus the question for the psychology of religion is: "Do . . . certain innate regularities exist in the human psyche which can provide the basis for the symbolic combination of tree and woman (who gives birth and is eaten)?" (ibid., 13).

We already saw (Chap. 1) that Drewermann answers this question affirmatively. Drewermann briefly recaptures findings by Szondi,[22] which established the instinctive connection between oral movements of sucking and movements of clinging, primate studies, and paleo-anthropological studies (by Bilz), which show that all primates once transferred onto trees the experiences of security first made in relation to the body of the mother animal (with the exception of humans and rock-inhabiting baboons primates still do so) (Drewermann 1979, 13). Even in humans one can observe clear relics of the tendency to vertical flight upward characteristic of tree life: "in moments of sudden fright, an involuntary shortening synergism of the extremities leads during a start to a movement sequence which, if completed in eventual action, would represent a clinging and climbing movement" (ibid., 13–14). "The tree represents for the grown primate and human being a continuation of that security which was first experienced in relation to the maternal organism. Hence the

---

22. Note that the reference in n. 36 of Drewermann's article (1979) should correctly read "L. Szondi, *Lehrbuch der Experimentellen Triebdiagnostik,* 1. Bd." instead of "L. Szondi, *Triebpathologie,* 1. Bd."

symbolic identity of woman (mother) and tree seems to be determined drive-psychologically" (ibid., 14).

Why the tree, beyond its maternal symbolism, could also represent the divine is a question Drewermann answers with reference to the evolution of the human species in the open steppe in which the prior security experienced in relation to trees was missing, which in turn led to "an extraordinary lack of protection and accordingly to a strong feeling of anxiety. Basically an attempt to manage the fundamental anxiety of human *Dasein,* religion in all its forms consists essentially of the promise of metaphysical security [*Geborgenheit*] as it is biologically preformed in the security [*Sicherheit*] of tree life. Evidently, the religious language of security in God cannot but connect with those primordial experiences of security which were first made phylogenetically at the stage of tree life" (ibid., 14). This connection sheds light on many ritual acts such as, for instance, the position of prayer or of devotion in the Roman Catholic liturgy: kneeling, the priest raises his arms wide open: "the shortening synergism of the lower extremities, which belongs to the movement of climbing, is coordinated with the clinging of arms and hands. The gaze is directed 'upward' because 'up' is in the memory of the species still associated with the security of treetops. Prayer as a clinging to God utilizes precisely those expressive movements which derive from the clinging to the (mother-)tree. The symbolic-ritual unity of Godhead and tree could not be clearer" (ibid., 14–15).

But the symbol of the tree does not only draw positive associations. As Drewermann tried to show at length in his analysis of Genesis 3:1–7, many primordial myths report a forbidden eating from the tree of paradise, of heaven, or of the underworld. In the essay on the symbolism of tree and of cross, Drewermann alludes to his psychological interpretation of such stories, following K. Abraham and M. Klein, as reflecting the ontogenetic experience of oral-sadistic impulses and the corresponding ambivalence in relation to the maternal (tree). What he stresses, however, is the fact "that the oral ambivalence which forms the content of the guilt feeling of a primordial forbidden eating regularly finds in the religion of peoples an oral dissolution too: the same act of cannibalistic appropriation of the killed (mother-)Godhead serves not only to recall a primordial guilt but at the same time as a sacrament of atonement and forgiveness in the sense that the Godhead of grain, corn, banana, etc. offers itself to humans in death as food so that in its death and in its being eaten eventually its own will is carried out" (ibid., 16–17). On a deeper level the death of the Godhead is even seen as the indispensable condition for the resurrection of the vegetation or for the transition to a higher form of life, as the Gospel of Luke, for instance, has the resurrected Christ tell his disciples in Luke 24:26. The sacrament of the eating of the fruit that represents the Godhead (of bread and wine in Christianity) thus transforms the forbidden into the opposite. "What as act of an unlawful, forbidden appropriation would have to pronounce the human being guilty for existing at all is transformed into a merciful permission-to-be [*Sein-dürfen*] because the (maternal) Godhead assents to her killing for the preservation of human life. The tree and cross symbolism thus encompasses the tension arc of the abysmal experience of guilt and of the experience of a deep permission to be" (ibid., 17).

But Drewermann goes one step further than the (objective-level) interpretation of symbolism of tree and cross on an oral level: prior to the experience of guilt in the form of oral ambivalence lies the guilt of incest "which, as far as we can see, all peoples prohibit and punish most severely" (ibid.). Connecting with Rank (with the qualifications noted above), Drewermann sees the roots of the incest wish and the incest prohibition in terms of the prenatal sense of security and peace through which "ontogenetic memories from the time of primordial unity with the mother" and "regressive longings" of humans are fueled. While noting Freud's interpretation of the incest theme in terms of Oedipal dynamics, Drewermann opts for a Jungian interpretation in order to do justice to the religious significance of the incest theme (ibid., 17). The "incest wish for (sexual) union with the mother is only the expression of a deeper and more original tendency of a return of one's entire existence into the womb of the mother" (ibid.). The reason why incest is banned everywhere, even outside of patriarchal societies which are not shaped by the Oedipus complex, is "that in it the psychic energies would be purely regressively wasted and hence could not be used for the managing of life's difficulties in the present. The incest prohibition thus fulfills psychologically the important function of directing the psychic powers forward and cutting off retreat into the longed-for regression into the maternal womb" (ibid., 17–1–8).

But the tendency to regress is not in all cases neurotic or pathological. It is dangerous if it aims at avoiding "*external* difficulties in

neurotic fashion," but it represents "an absolutely necessary movement of the psychic drive direction if life has thus far been adapted
in a certain sense too diligently toward external reality and thereby
the needs of the 'inner human being' are neglected" (ibid., 18). For a
character who is one-sidedly oriented toward external reality, the "regressive incest tendency" of the psyche, "the 'union with the mother'
means to let himself be carried by the maternal in his own psyche, to
begin life from the ground up and to let it be more merciful from the
start, more contemplative [*innerlicher*], freer, and more spontaneous.
In terms of contents, one deals here with a working through and integration of wishes, hopes, and possibilities which have thus far not
been lived, have been repressed and neglected as useless, in favor of
a more encompassing and richer personality" (ibid.).

Since the symbolism of tree and cross has been shown to relate to
an archetypal image of the mother, Drewermann points out that it is
not surprising that the themes of "incest, of regression to the maternal
womb, of dying and rebirth essentially codetermine the symbolism
of the cross" (ibid., 18–19). Drewermann holds that one approaches
the "*religious* meaning of the symbolism of the cross, of course, only
when one draws on the *subjective-level* meaning of the incest issue
for the interpretation and sees in the Oedipal constellation only an
image for the union with oneself.... with the 'maternal' in one's own
psyche" (ibid., 19). Here he agrees with Jung that the incest motif expresses subjectively "the longing for union with the archetypal
symbol of the mother in one's own psyche" (ibid.). In a subjective-
level perspective the symbolism of the "crucified redeemer" is thus
not understood in Freudian terms as the sadomasochistic Oedipal
victory of the son against the father (by the son uniting with the maternal Cross) but as "an image for the paradoxical union of the ego
with the unconscious, hence as an image for the paradoxical wholeness of the human person. By pointing to the latent unity of death
and life and to the return to the origin and to renewal of life, *this*
meaning comes closest to the religious message of the symbolism of
the Cross" (ibid.).

Drewermann stresses that this subjective-level meaning finds expression in the fact that Christianity has connected the symbolism of
Cross and resurrection with the sacrament of baptism, that is, "the
act of *rebirth* in the unity of death and resurrection" (ibid., 20). This
connection, he states, is religiously even "more fundamental" than
the connection to the oral-sadistic sphere of experience in form of

the Eucharist. It is "more fundamental" because it addresses the aspect of a fundamental intrapsychic change in the relation between the historical ego and the collective unconscious. The crucifixion is on this level understood as a dying of the one-sidedly rational and external orientation of life in the service of an integration of the vital forces of the unconscious. Only when interpreted as an intrapsychic process can the crucifixion in its concrete symbolism be understood not sadomasochistically. Drewermann sums up the relation between Cross and resurrection as follows:

> The union with the mother figure of the tree of the Cross appears as an expression of a deeper longing to return to the truth of one's own origin after having lost one's way in a life of fearful externality [*Äußerlichkeit*], coerced diligence, and empty compliance with others . . . one may call this "regressive" movement of renewal of self in the first phase a "dying," a "crucifixion." Even though the image of union with the origin emphasizes basically that one opens up to oneself in a more trusting way and that one lets oneself be led more by the unconscious reason of one's own psyche, this step of disavowal of ego and surrender of the ego position produces the greatest fear. Then one indeed deals with a dying, namely, with the death of the entire attitude toward life to this point. And nothing is tougher in the long run for a human being who, sheerly out of fear, constantly escaped into a world of notorious overcompensations and self-validation than to enter the road of nondoing, of being-carried, of trust. The step in that direction is usually only accepted if it seems inevitable due to the pressure of external symptoms and if one's own existence is experienced literally as tortured and crucified. Nonetheless it is part of redemption that the surrender of the ego is performed from a certain point in time *consciously* from within. The truth of inner healing consists precisely of giving up the will to be healed *from* the torturous symptoms; inner recovery presupposes that one is healed eventually *through* the symptoms, by assenting to the *meaning of the symptoms,* and that what was forced upon the ego through the symptoms against its will is in the end recognized as part of the ego and voluntarily accepted. *Only voluntary surrender into the death of the ego makes regeneration and the new beginning of an expanded, greater life possible. Only accepted death*

creates the presupposition of resurrection, of a reborn, renewed life. (ibid., 20)

Based on this subjective-level interpretation, Drewermann also re-interprets notions such as Christian obedience or the symbolism of the virgin birth.

No image is better suited than the symbol of the Cross to express the inner contrast between the experience of sickness and wholeness [*Heil*]. No image, moreover, is better suited to express the decisive element in the renewal of life: that it happens not through the strength of will or the assertion of the ego but through trust in and obedience to the order of one's own inner life [*Innern*]. The miracle of the resurrection, the emergence from the grave of the womb of the mother is the beginning of a life which no longer depends on one's own "will or exertion" (Rom. 9:16) but is determined entirely by that which is given as a present, which is not-made, which is graceful. According to the religious-psychological symbolism it is therefore one and the same thing to believe in the miracle of virgin birth at the beginning of a redeemed existence or in the emergence from a sealed rock tomb, in the resurrection from the death of the Cross. Because womb of the mother or tree of the Cross or underworld and tomb all describe the orgination point of a redeemed existence who has given up even the fear of ego-preservation and has found one's true self. (ibid., 21)

It is this obedience to one's true self which theology means when it says "that God demands *obedience* from humans" (ibid., 22). Drewermann assumes that spiritually each human person has an inner "law," a unique destiny which only she or he can know, discover, and follow. By following that "law of herself," a human being does in the last instance leave herself to her Creator who placed this law into the human being.

Theology, on the other hand, understands the laws of the human psyche as created by God. It names the metaphysical ground on which one can get involved with the forces of one's own unconscious. It considers obedience to the instructions of the unconscious implicitly as obedience to God. It thus understands the process of self-realization as the empirical manifestation and consequence of an underlying trust in the ground of human

*Dasein. ... The psychology of self-realization is hence theolog-
ically a phenomenology of faith.* And the symbol of the Cross
is a cipher whose psychic constitution points to a trust which is
directed *psychologically* to the ground and beginning of *biological* existence (the mother) but *theologically* refers to the ground
and beginning of *Dasein* as such. (ibid., 23)

This is the point where Drewermann emphasizes on theological
grounds in critical differentiation from Jung the absolute importance of the *personal* and *relational* dimension as a condition for
the process of self-realization and intrapsychic unity.

Only the psychology of *fear* shows how blocked a human being
must remain if he does not see himself in his existence completely carried by an absolute freedom. The inner process of
self-realization does not come about merely because the psychic
image of the self, of the "God" of the psyche, pushes toward
unfolding. Rather the forces of self-discovery and self-unfolding
are only awoken if there exists a person who faces us and
through whose love one's own person for her own sake can feel
completely meant [*gemeint*], carried [*getragen*], and embraced.
Roses bloom only through the medium of light and warmth into
their shape, and only within a space of love are humans capable
of developing into the shape of their being.

    This *absolute dimension of the personal* cannot be reduced
to intrapsychic processes because the experience of the absolute
significance and importance of one's own person can only come
about in relation to another person who through her devotion
takes one's own person as absolutely important and significant.
(Drewermann 1985b, 458)

If the archetypes of the collective unconscious should have healing instead of destructive effects, Drewermann argues, a human
person needs to feel firmly grounded by an absolute person. Discussing the need for both Jung and Freud to understand this dynamic,
Drewermann writes:

One can correctly say that the God-*image* cannot "exist apart
from humans [C. G. Jung 1952b]. But Jung declares: "God
cannot [exist apart from humans]," and that is undoubtedly a transcendent gnostic assertion, in the sense that God

is understood as nothing but the "God-image." It is, however, even psychotherapeutically very important to avoid a metaphysicizing of the psychical and a psychologizing of the metaphysical. Because the manner in which the archetypes approach the ego of the human person depends very much on the manner in which the ego feels firmly grounded [*gefestigt*] or not vis-à-vis another person. At that point, Freud's "objective-level" perspective will always be right: humans fail because of people before they fail because of themselves. And beyond all the images it is important to believe in a person who lives in all the images and yet, in order to integrate these images, must be more than all the images. In order to embark on the path of becoming a person [*Personwerdung*], the human being must be allowed in her *consciousness* to believe in God as an absolute person who takes away the fear that prevents her from facing the onslaught of her own images. (ibid., 457 n. 37)

While the process of self-realization and of finding God are empirically identical, they are theologically distinct. This is what Drewermann means when he calls the psychology of self-realization theologically a "phenomenology of faith." The experience of intrapsychic wholeness, of the paradoxical unity in the human psyche of consciousness and the unconscious is theologically a symbol for and empirical expression of "the unity with God" (Drewermann 1979, 22). While the Cross is in psychological perspective "an image for the surrender of the ego to the unconscious, theological interpretation understands it as a symbol of the giving of the entire existence, including consciousness and the unconscious, to God" (ibid.). Addressing a moralistic, externalistic misunderstanding of the Cross, Drewermann emphasizes that it actually skips the difficulty of the " 'crucifixion of the ego,' and actually prevents it in the form of an ascetic, self-tormenting disguise. As long as one does not understand the symbol of the Cross — as depth psychology shows — as the expression of a law of life of inner maturation and self-realization, but as a *moral demand* of self-renunciation, one inevitably turns an integrating symbol of inner healing and of becoming whole into an image of self-destruction which is not only senseless but plainly absurd" (ibid., 24). The ethical implications of such religious healing are profound. "Only a human person who has in this sense found himself and has overcome the fear of himself through an increase of trust in the capacity to be carried by the ground of his own *Dasein,* can then, too, meet the Other with the kind of freedom which does not focus on itself, which can look away from the petty interests of his own ego and is truly 'selfless' — because it presupposes a true self" (ibid., 24). A moralistic misunderstanding of the Cross instead refuses to be carried by the deeper powers of one's own unconscious and demands from the ego the absurd: namely, to fight against itself by means of its own capacities, "reason and will" (ibid.). "Instead of truly surrendering one's ego position one thus arrives precisely at an absolutism of ego-orientedness by making the ego through its *willful* suppression of its egotisms only more ego-centric, fear-possessed, and tense" (ibid.).

An important result of tracing religious "images of suffering and Cross" as anchored in the human psyche itself is that it is then absurd if one wants to use these symbols moralistically as arguments against "human nature," as is commonly done in Christian churches. These images "owe their effective power precisely to the natural constitution of the human psyche. *The meaning of the symbolism of the Cross can therefore not lie in the suppression of the forces of the human drives but only in their integrating inclusion against the resistances of fearful ego-preservation*" (ibid., 25). And it is here where Drewermann credits Christianity with first seeing the images as symbols for the inner human being instead of projecting them out into nature. "Christianity has the merit to recognize the images of suffering and death — which are projected in the myths of people into external nature and correspondingly acted out externally in barbaric rites — completely as laws of life of the 'inner human being' " (ibid.). But, Drewermann is quick to add, if "theology refuses to put depth psychology into service as an epistemological organ in its study of the 'inner human being,' then even the most correct dogmatic teaching of the redemptive suffering and dying of the God-human — of his resurrection and ascension, of the forgiveness of guilt in the sacrament of rebirth (baptism) and of the nurturing unity with the divine (Eucharist) — can, on the whole, not prevent the tragic psychical renewal of the horrible externality of pagan rituals in the shadow of the Cross, in the midst of Christianity" (ibid., 25–26).

Chapter 4

Analyzing the Clergy-Ideal
of the Roman Catholic Church

That is the other side of selflessness: its tyranny.
— Margaret Atwood, *The Blind Assassin*

In 1989 Drewermann published *Kleriker: Psychogramm eines Ideals* (Clerics: Psychogram of an Ideal), analyzing how a violent God-image, through the moralization of religion, internally mutilates the psyche and spirit of the clergy and externally stabilizes authoritarian power structures within the Church. The debate around his reinterpretation of Christian theology by means of depth psychology was in full swing. For several years, officials of the Roman Catholic Church had voiced concerns about certain of his statements on moral theology, on the need for the historical-critical and depth-psychological (symbolic) study of biblical texts and Christian doctrines, and on the relativity of the Church's hierarchy.

Five basic, interrelated ideas which we encounter in all of Drewermann's work also are woven throughout *Kleriker*, providing structure to the many details of the study. The first is the assumption of an existential anxiety of *Dasein* as such which precedes all specific psychological fears and conflicts. Second the tendency to short-circuit being with consciousness in Christianity and the repression of the unconscious (Drewermann 1990a, 34). The third is the necessary differentiation between the individual and the collective for the sake of the mental health of both individual and community (ibid.). The fourth is the confusion of questions of being with questions of doing, of religion with ethics, of the absolute with the relative, of the metaphysical with the practical. The fifth, finally, is the analysis of the temptation to psychologize the metaphysical and to metaphysicize the psychological (ibid., 75, 53–55).

273

In a radio interview, Drewermann (1992i, 291) commented that writing *Kleriker* was a way of processing his own development as a priest in light of his encounter with psychoanalysis. While working with people in his first years as a priest it became clear to him "that people suffered but were not guilty and that, if I wanted to understand them, I had to get to know areas of *Dasein* which I had not become familiar with during all my theological studies: areas of the unconscious. Thus I came to psychoanalysis, though still with the crazy notion that I studied it basically for other people. For a long time I did not realize that it questioned my entire journey into the priesthood, which is what I later processed in *Kleriker*" (ibid.). *Kleriker* thus provides a picture of the ideal by which the young Drewermann was guided and can in some sense be compared to the autobiographical character of Freud's *The Interpretation of Dreams*. Just as Freud arrived at his far-reaching conclusions about the unconscious dynamics of dream life and of psychoneurotic symptoms in patients (objects) only by discovering these dynamics first in himself (subject), so Drewermann could reach his conclusions about the unconscious dynamic interaction between the human spirit and the psyche in relation to parents and to God as manifested in the psychospiritual conflicts of clergy (objects) only by discovering this dynamic interaction first within himself (subject).

If we follow Drewermann's emphasis that the essence of religion is by definition subjective in that it deals with ultimate concerns stemming from our human subjectivity (freedom, spirit), we may say that his analysis of the psychospiritual effects of the conventional clergy-ideal is an analysis of the vicissitudes of subjectivity under the spell of fear of a metaphysicized superego. Drewermann wrote this book not *about* clergy but *as* a cleric, as someone who is himself concerned with and who attempts to process the effects of an externally interpreted clergy-ideal. Hence he can use the plural pronouns "we" and "us" when speaking of the clergy (e.g., Drewermann 1990a, 657). Drewermann writes as a "subject" about what he considers to have inevitably subjective character: religion. The use of "subjective" is not pejorative but reflects the constitutive capacity of the human spirit. Nonetheless he expects that those who will vigorously object to his call for the inclusion of subjectivity into a study of religion may try to brush off his analysis of the required clergy-mentality as " 'a mere projection of his own difficulties,' 'a nasty running-down,' 'a presentation of purely subjective significance,' 'the psychogram of the author but not of the clergy" (ibid., 32). Drewermann sees in such anticipated (and materialized!) objections the very mentality at work which he attempts to analyze. In analytic fashion he therefore uses these questions diagnostically and replies: "It is indeed the question: How can one make people whose self-confidence is essentially based on the repression of the issues detailed [in *Kleriker*] aware of certain problems of the unconscious by means of a book? How can one capitalize positively on their insecurity, even their shock, and prevent renewed secondary repression [*Nachverdrängen*] which usually follows upon the uninvited enlightenment of unconscious connections" (ibid., 32). Drewermann chooses to write the book in such a way that the "presentation gets unmistakably close" to the reader's own experience, to the degree that "he must against his will admit or actually feel liberated to see that, unless he pours sand in his eyes, he and no one else is the subject here" (ibid., 33).

Written in response to the psychospiritual suffering of both clergy and laity in the Roman Catholic Church, *Kleriker* studies the effects of the prevailing clergy-ideal of the Church on the mental life of priests, nuns, and monks from a depth-psychological, that is, both psychoanalytic and *daseinsanalytic,* perspective (ibid., 43). Though it touches basically on all the controversial issues in the Roman Catholic Church today, from celibacy to abortion, from homosexuality to women's ordination, from the Church's secret support systems for so-called illegitimate children of the clergy to child molestation by pedophile clergy, from freedom of speech to conformity with Rome, we will focus in the following not so much on specific issues but on Drewermann's analysis of certain necessary mental structures the clergy must possess if they want to follow the Church's clergy-ideal. In other words, we will not focus on the manifest symptomatic conflicts but on the underlying latent psychospiritual structure which Drewermann observes and finds ossified in the external interpretation of Christian doctrines.

Drewermann maintains that the origin of the clergy's suffering and of the Church's lack of vitality lies in "the objectively preexisting structures" within which it orders the lives of its officials (ibid., 27). He is quite aware that this focus gives the study an important "political dimension" within the Church. Drewermann's main analytic tool is psychoanalysis. By trying to shed light on the very " 'earthly' repressions and transferences from which the image of the heavenly loftiness of the clerical caste is to an extent created," Drewermann hopes to "psychoanalytically demythologize the image of the clergy" and reintegrate the clergy more with the rest of the Church, the so-called lay-people (ibid., 29–30). "Through the power of making [things] conscious psychoanalysis has the social-psychological effect of being a definite democratic agent against all institutions that are based on unexplained venerabilities" (ibid., 30). The fact that in the course of Church history every detail of the ideal and life of the clergy has been "dogmatically elaborated and defined" is the reason that "every piece of psychoanalytic working through is always also a piece of ideological critique" (ibid., 85); this will naturally be "experienced as threatening to the power of the Church" (ibid., 161, cf. 100). Drewermann describes the cultural significance of an analysis of the clergy-mentality for the health of society as follows:

> In all cultures, it is the task of religion to close the field of contingency that characterizes all human institutions and performance and to set up havens of the absolute where it is possible to be led from acting to listening, from having to being, from planning to hoping, from judging to forgiving — from the finite into the infinite. A society in which such open spaces of eternity do not exist or are only insufficiently developed dies of itself due to lack of air to breathe. Hence no culture or society can be indifferent to the manner in which the official carriers of the dominant form of religion mediate or obstruct the content of its faith. Therefore the mental hygiene of the leadership of a religion especially is of immediate interest even for the part of the population which has no religious ties. As long as an existing form of religion has not degenerated to a sect, it decisively shapes through the mentality of its key groups the morality and attitude toward life in the culture in which it lives. Conversely, it is forced to be transformed and provide new answers again and again in response to changes in its social surroundings. The question of the psychology of the clergy in a religion hence requires an open discussion, that is, a public debate. (ibid., 31–32)

As Drewermann analyzes the conflicts that tend to plague clergy, he does so not to condemn but to understand, not to blame but to accept the clergy in their struggles to live with inhuman ideals. *Kleriker* is a plea "to restore within the frame of the mega-group of the Church... unconditional freedom of speech before God" (ibid., 27).

This book wants to show that even as a priest, a nun...or a monk one is allowed to have or, so to speak, must have certain problems in order to be suitable as a cleric, and that it is absolutely rewarding to speak openly about these problems, always guided by the conviction that it is not the existence but the concealment and repression of mental difficulties that first creates real conflicts and makes it impossible to truly solve existing conflicts. This book wants to be a plea on behalf of those clergy who cannot handle their life any longer — that is, for all those who feel unworthy, feel like failures, feel condemned, who experience themselves as chronic hypocrites, as hired liars, as living character masks, who feel "degenerated" in their frustrations and decompensations into people who have no internal hold, who are addicted, who deem themselves as or really are "perverts." Beyond that it will also be a plea for all the unlived and rejected (from guilt) aspects of the human psyche in the shadow of the official life of the clergy. It thus wants to correct the impression that the seemingly private and exceptional negative aspect of the clergy's psyche has the character of personal failure and instead to anchor the problem where it evidently has its origin: in the objectively preexisting structures within which the Church "rules" the way of life of its most loyal and devoted followers. (ibid., 27)

As in this last sentence, Drewermann often uses the term "the Church" to refer to the Roman Catholic Church's hierarchy which makes decisions regarding the formulation and interpretation of her doctrines and structures. *Kleriker* analyzes the psychodynamics which support not only the "objectively preexisting structures" but their underlying philosophy and theology as well. The book is intended to contribute to a "collective psychotherapy of the whole system of the Church" (ibid., 854 n. 43). In a direct and straightforward style, *Kleriker* is written with the explicit intent of reviving the Church and Christianity (in the West) through an analysis of the psychospiritual dynamics that threaten to make them more and more irrelevant. "Anyone who cares about the Catholic Church can no longer do it the supposed favor of showing patience, forbearance, or a kind of tolerance that deems itself generous. Rather, as much as possible, he must try to bring to its awareness *for its own sake*, without evasion or excuses, the reversal and inversion of its own ideal formations. Some mistakes are simply inexcusable because they have existed for too long. Some false attitudes cannot be explained [away] by saying that they may have had a certain function under past circumstances. Anyone who wants to reduce rust on iron cannot do without aggressive reagents — we have *sprayed over* the rust long enough" (ibid., 660).

A similar sentiment has recently erupted in response to the Roman Catholic Church's handling of its pedophile priests in the United States and throughout the world. Though Drewermann is aware that pedophilia is a complex phenomenon and clearly not confined to the Church, he argues that the pattern found in pedophile clergy must be seen within the overall context of the Church's repressive attitude toward sexuality (Drewermann 2002a). He suggests that the repressive attitude imposed on its future "ideal priests" leaves them with a particular vulnerability to pedophilia. While all cases are unique, he observes certain factors which typically play a part when that vulnerability turns into a reality. In youth, the future "ideal" priest is expected by family and Church to sacrifice all heterosexual contacts with girls. Often, according to Drewermann, this leads to a compensatory form of homosexuality which the parents and the Church usually naively disavow as impossible in the first place. The young priest-to-be's mental energy in his loneliness is thus often channeled into a first friendship with a young boy. That friendship, which usually does not enter into the "taboo zones of genital sexuality," enables the priest-to-be to break away for the first time from the mother. The homosexual form of pedophilia in priests, Drewermann says, is typically the result of a fixation on that early experience of pubertal intimacy with another boy. "Even at a later date in the life of homosexual priests there is a preference in love relations with boys or youths whose age corresponds to the age in which they [the priests] had their first 'experiences' of love which were immediately forgotten because of dutiful self-suppression" (Drewermann 1990a, 598). Drewermann thinks that this inner sense of tension between obedient repression of heterosexual impulses and stunted compensatory homosexual longings even presents a "strong additional motive to enter the priesthood: since marrying a woman is excluded as a possibility anyway but the fear of a breakthrough of homosexual acts and of relationships still persists, the sexually repressive attitude of the Roman Catholic Church promises something like a redemption from the whole dilemma. Reality, of course, looks quite different. Theological seminaries are filled with scores of people who have the same experience and who attract each other according to rules which are no less mysterious than the hidden signals of heterosexual lovers. In other words, anyone who thought he would be out of the woods has to realize, to the contrary, that, in reality, he has jumped from the frying pan into the fire" (ibid.).

The immensity of the task of a "collective therapy" of the Church accounts for the length of *Kleriker*: 900 pages, and for its division into diagnosis, etiology, and treatment suggestions. Methodologically, Drewermann structures his argument by first constructing *models*[1] of the psychological structure, dynamics, and thought patterns of the clergy that are required to completely fulfill the conventional clergy-ideal (ibid., 39, 657). The clergy-ideal is specifically expressed in the vow to uphold the evangelical counsels of poverty, obedience, and chastity. Drewermann's distinction of external and internal interpretation is again essential. His analysis concludes that in its current, externally interpreted form the clergy-ideal is neither humane nor healing, but instead promotes neurotic conflicts, capitalizes on ontological insecurity, and inhibits healthy personality development (diagnosis) (ibid., 41–268). When Drewermann refers to the official, externally understood clergy-ideal, he sometimes uses qualifiers such as "conventional" or "today's" (ibid., 657) but often simply uses the short-hand "clergy-ideal" where the context makes it clear that he is talking about the external interpretation. To prevent confusion, I will, where indicated, add either "external" or "internal" to clarify which interpretation of the clergy-ideal is meant. References to the "official" or "current" clergy-ideal imply the external, moral orientation of interpretation.

After constructing the model mental structure which corresponds to the external clergy-ideal, Drewermann analyzes the psychogenetic development which is likely to create the psychological reality necessary for the implementation of that ideal in the individual cleric (etiology) (ibid., 269–654). Drewermann does not suggest that all clerics live completely by the official clergy-ideal of the Church. Rather, he suggests that the more the reality of an *individual* cleric's

---

1. We note the similarity of Drewermann's "models" with Max Weber's "ideal types" (Weber 1952; cf. Drewermann 1990a, 621). The difference lies, of course, in the fact that Drewermann constructs his models depth-psychologically while Weber constructed his "ideal types" from a social-psychological perspective.

life approximates the current clergy-ideal of the Roman Catholic Church, the more valid in that particular cleric's life will be the assumptions made in the construction of the *model* of the genetic and dynamic psychospiritual reality of being a cleric (ibid., 39). In a final step, Drewermann proposes a reinterpretation of the clergy-ideal, in which the evangelical counsels are understood not as external (i.e., in terms of doing) but as internal (i.e., in terms of being and of the projection of being in Heidegger's sense) and that would foster the development of a strong, coherent personality instead of inhibiting such development (treatment suggestions) (ibid., 655–750). Drewermann's study aims to reinstate again the *"prophetic"* and *"poetic form of existence"* (ibid., 17) of the clergy which is closer to the mentality of a "shaman" (ibid., 47–60) in the history of religions than to the mentality of a "boss" as described in J.-P. Sartre's story "The Childhood of a Leader" (Sartre 1972) (Drewermann 1990a, 61–83). Though *Kleriker* often examines the psychology underlying fundamental Roman Catholic doctrines, Drewermann explicitly states on many occasions that he is not discussing the value of Christian doctrines themselves but only the effects on the psyche of the clergy and, by extension, of the laity of a certain type of interpretation of Christian doctrines (see ibid., 272, 287, 511).

Drewermann's depth-psychological analysis of the effects of the current clergy-ideal is based on material gathered from his own clinical work with the clergy; religious writings, creeds, and other official documents of the Roman Catholic Church and of other Christian churches; studies which have critically addressed the status of the clergy (e.g., works by Ranke-Heinemann 1990, Deschner 1972, Denzler 1973–76, 1988, de Rosa 1988 etc.); passages from well-known pieces of world-literature and from philosophical writings (e.g., works by Dostoevsky, Greene, Nietzsche, Sartre, Zola) which amplify the analysis; and research from fields such as comparative religion, anthropology, ethology, and history.

Diagnosis

At the heart of Drewermann's analysis of the mentality suitable for the current clergy-ideal is the sacrificial psychology of the clergy. Manifestly, Drewermann observes two key elements that characterize the required psychology of a Roman Catholic cleric and differentiate it from the psychology of, for instance, healing shamans in other religions: first, while the calling of shamans is rooted in and verified by initiation dreams, in the Catholic clergy the psychological elements of the experience of the calling are displaced "away from the dream into the conscious 'decision' "; secondly, while the shaman can only heal because as a person he has weathered the very sickness (which often delivers him dangerously "to the edge of the psychotic") that he is later able to help heal in others, the Catholic cleric is required to "replace the personal character of communication through an objectification of the office" (ibid., 49). We will take a closer look at both elements as they build the phenomenological base of Drewermann's analysis.

Drewermann points out that strict emphasis on the conscious decision to follow a calling by God in the Catholic Church is the specific Catholic solution to an issue that has occupied theologians throughout the history of Western theology: the question of "the relationship between divine election and human free will" in the calling or election to a life as a cleric (ibid., 51–52). Drewermann argues that the way the Catholic Church has solved this problem directly reflects the self-experience of the cleric, namely, a self-experience which is required to "*split in two* human will and the will of God. On the one hand, it is insisted that in order to become a cleric of the Catholic Church one must have chosen that form of life freely; on the other, God in his grace must co-perform that decision of will by anticipating it through his grace, accompanying it, and leading it to completion" (ibid., 52). Whatever the theological implications of this view may be in view of the ecumenical discussion between Catholics and Protestants, Drewermann is more interested in the "psychological implications and consequences" (ibid.). The cleric's participation in the call or election involves an *anthropological reduction*," that is, a reduction of the participation to a "*conscious* part of the '*free decision*'" and to a "moral will," while "the entire part of the unconscious" is repressed and ignored, that is, the mental motivational history that is shaped by psychical and social influences in early childhood, the subjective ways in which these influences were digested, and the factors of personal gifts and unique characteristics (ibid., 52–53). This external, conscious, moral understanding of the calling henceforth is used as a moralistic tool: if one has once consciously and freely accepted the "grace of the office [*Amtsgnade*]," it is henceforth forever his "*duty* . . . to work together with the grace of God and if he does not do so in the manner desired [by the Church], then he is either sinful or guilty or unfree and sick" (ibid., 53). While this externalization of the calling and the repression of the unconscious allows the Church to *"standardize* and objectify" the education of the clergy, it has devastating consequences for the mental and spiritual health of both the clergy and the population at large by fostering not only *"psychic* alienation" but, even more importantly, *"religious* alienation"* through a distorted God-image (ibid., 54). Drewermann elaborates while addressing Feuerbach's (1873) critique of religion as a projection of alienation.

> [T]he repressed part of the unconscious does, of course, not simply get lost, but is rather directed away [*abgezogen*] from humans and transferred into "God," or, to put it differently: the psychic repression of the unconscious leads to a theological projection of the repressed into the divine. In terms of a psychology of religion thus the very situation occurs which provided the basis for Ludwig Feuerbach's critique of religion in which religion as a whole is the representation of the essence of the human being in projected form, which then is received by the human being in alienated and alienating form [i.e., as if it came from outside!]. Today we can and must, of course, formulate Feuerbach's thought more precisely: it is not the essence [*Wesen*] of the human being but instead an essential aspect of the human psyche in the theological theory of the election of the clergy which is projected from the unconscious into the divine. This, however, does not represent the essence of religion but merely that form of religiosity which is indeed personified today in the cleric in the Catholic Church: a permanently divided mentality through which the human being becomes monstrous to himself and through which God appears ambiguous to the highest degree. Since the problematic, frightening [*ängstigenden*] contents of the unconscious especially are cut off from one's own human ego during the defensive process of projection, all the feelings of ambivalence and contradictions which once lay unresolved in the biography of the cleric are henceforth placed upon the person of God. (ibid., 53–54)

In addition to this projection of repressed unconscious material into the God-image, Drewermann observes "that, as a result of these same psychodynamics according to which the content of the divine has to be sought in principle outside of the human dimension [*dem Menschlichen*], the communications of the revelation of God have to be demonstrated as *historical facts*, as *facts in time and space*. The fear of the subject, psychoanalytically viewed, pervades all of the theology of the Catholic Church; but it is personified most clearly in the depersonalization of the clergy themselves" (ibid., 152).

Three factors hinder a subsequent solution of the psychospiritual conflicts of the clergy. First is the fact that the projective process not only remains unconscious but is "theologically fortified through the idea of divine election" (ibid., 54). Hence any attempt to "revisit one's own motivational history" would equal serious "doubts of faith" (ibid.). Secondly, "the original alienation in regard to one's own psyche has been multiplied through the process of the projection, namely, in that the state of *psychical* alienation has been reshaped into a state of *religious* alienation. The resulting God-image, which now appears as a kind of overpowering opponent, subsequently prevents, by means of all the compulsions and guilt feelings which have found objective expression in it, one's own ego from ever again finding the courage to risk itself in a trust toward God" (ibid., 54). Thirdly, "the separation of and contradiction between the 'demands' of 'God' and the desires of humans have now become a constituting part of the psyche of the clergy — they form henceforth the unconscious premise, too, of theological understanding" (ibid., 54). Drewermann adds: "It is clear that under such conditions mental conflicts are not solved but infinitized [*verewigt*] by means of the idea of election" (ibid.). The current clergy-ideal thus requires both mental and spiritual alienation which in turn results through the projective process in an objectification of the unresolved personal conflicts as God's will. God and God's calling are experienced as external and faith is moralized through the one-sided emphasis on the conscious and external element of free will.

Corresponding to this inner alienation and this externalization of God and faith is the reduction of the person of the cleric to her or his office and role. The form which the ideal of being a cleric has taken today is described by Drewermann as "existing *ex officio*" (ibid., 83). The clergy-ideal requires an "alienated being" which completely identifies with the role (ibid., 96). The mentality of alienation involves an objectification of human life as such and a drying up of the subjective elements which, according to Drewermann, are constituting aspects of religion. The objectification of human life in the Church finds expression in an overemphasis on the importance of the office.

The Church, unlike any other system in the West, has given such importance to the office that it becomes the "truth of the self" (ibid., 73). The clergy are expected to be simply "functionaries"[2] (Drewermann 1990a, 82). This expresses a lack of differentiation between the individual and the collective. In terms of the clergy-ideal, subjective psychical motivation to follow the ideal tends to be confused by the Church with the objective social function of the ideal, that is, the social role is taken to be the person. In Jungian terms, this identification of office and person is a process whereby the *persona* takes the place of the ego (ibid., 226). In Freudian terms, the superego becomes the dominant power in the cleric's psyche (ibid., 111). The psychogenesis which leads to this development of the "official" is the focus of the largest portion of *Keriker* (ibid., 269–654). Drewermann finds that the model cleric who agrees to an identification of person with office suffers existentially from Kierkegaard's "despair of resignation [or weakness]" (unlike Sartre's "boss" who suffers rather from "despair of defiance") and finds in the office great relief from the fear involved in personal existence (ibid., 83–85). In theology "an extreme ideology of ego weakness and of ego restriction" corresponds to this, which finds particular expression in the required sacrificial mentality (ibid., 85).

The alienation required by the identification of self with the office is expressed in the whole life of the clergy: in areas of thinking, of basic everyday structures, and of human relationships. On the cognitive level, the clergy are to think in accordance with the precepts of the hierarchy of the Church and not independently (ibid., 96–169). The clergy are expected in their thinking to identify completely with the thought of the group and to give up any thoughts that might diverge from it. Drewermann pointedly calls such impersonal thinking "structurally fascistic [*faschistoid*]" (ibid., 129). As he traces the historical origin of this type of thought in the history of the Roman Catholic Church in *Dictatus Papae* of Pope Gregory VII (1073–85) and in Innocent III's theocratic identification of the power of the pope with the spreading of the "truth of Christ," Drewermann relates it explicitly to the structure of thought in Nazi Germany which required absolute obedience to the *Führer.*

No religious fanaticism exists which does not express itself objectively as will to power in order to be internalized subjectively

---

2. Cf. the title of the French translation of *Kleriker* as *Fonctionnaires de Dieu* (1995b).

as obedience of the individual. It was *Innocent III* who stated the aporia of the demands of obedience by the Church most succinctly: "Any cleric," he demanded, "must obey the pope even if he commands evil, because no one can judge the pope."* No question: in the twentieth century there is *only one* word in German which can describe this attitude: such thinking is fascistic [*faschistoid*]. The "leader [*Führer*]" as Lord over truth and right** and the demand for obedience as means for the implementation of commanded truths — what perversion of the "truth" of Christianity. And what kind of theology is this which through its teachings takes on ideologically the responsibility for the uniformity of a creed of all true believers [*Rechtgläubigen*] in such a Church! How far removed is all this especially from the sarcastic words of Jesus in Mark 10:42 on the "arbitrary rule" of the rulers of nations over their subjects and from his emphatic command: "Among you it should not be this way." (ibid., 441)

*P. de Rosa, *Vicars of Christ*, 1988 . . . [in the German ed.: de Rosa, *Gottes erste Diener*, 1989, 92].

**Cf. J. C. Fest's *Hitler* (1974, 469) for a statement from *Hitler's* speech justifying himself after the murder of *Röhm:* "In this hour I was responsible for the fate of the German people, and thereby I became the supreme judge of the German people!"

The absolute claim to truth of the Church also explains why the Church has the attitude that officially it "can never have erred" (ibid., 114). All responsibility for participating in or silently condoning evil is therefore defensively deflected. For instance, the Church may acknowledge "that *antisemitism* existed through the centuries in the West; but the Church, of course, has always considered the Jews as the elder children of Abraham and as the brothers of Jesus" (ibid., 115). The ideology of absolute truth makes it virtually impossible for the Church to take responsibility for the devastating consequences of its ideologies. When doubts creep up in the clergy about the Church's view of the truth, especially when that view commands evil or when the Church's official position lacks persuasion, the lack of that persuasive power is compensated for by the exertion of administrative pressure (ibid., 154). "Clerical thinking with its rationalistic, objectivistic thinking removed from the personal dimension is psychoanalytically not only structurally based on internalized violence but replicates itself as a form of violence, or, put differently: the structure of clerical thinking produces not only violence but itself functions as the ideological basis for power and violence" (ibid., 161–62).

Especially anyone who points out (as Drewermann does) that the very contents of the Church's faith derive from a common store of symbols of the human psyche will get into serious difficulties with the Church as an institution because "that would instantly touch on the traditional exclusive thinking of Christian theology.... If one declares that all religions draw from the same sources of the human psyche and that it is hence also possible and even necessary to listen to the interpretations of the same symbols in non-Christian religions to comprehend the Christian creed above all in its richness and its humanness, then one has the greatest difficulties with the teaching office of the Church. The claim to an unsurpassable, final, exclusive truth is part of any ideologically fixated thinking which is based on the absolutizing of its own contents rather than on living human experiences" (ibid., 117).

In addition to the alienation of thinking, the basic everyday structures of the life of the clergy (especially in religious orders) are symbolically determined by the Church at all levels (ibid., 169–225): their personal space is determined by standardized clothes; their time regulated by the Hours; their conscience shaped by public penance; their feelings manipulated by the prohibition of private friendships; their past removed by cutting them off from their families; their future given to the Church through the oath of allegiance; their deeds guided by a meticulous definition of their service. In interpersonal relationships, the clergy are supposed to have relationships mediated only through their role (ibid., 225–68). They live under a principle of constant availability, are torn between being spoiled and being under surveillance by the Church, have strong feelings of ambivalence toward their superiors, and are caught in the dead end of an authoritarian centralism. They suffer from both a fear of entering committed relationships and from loneliness. On the surface they may appear jovial and friendly. But when it comes to their office, they tend to become authoritarian and paternalistic.

Drewermann notes that the life of the clergy is thus made up of an odd combination: the comfortable, conservative life that comes with offical status is strangely wedded to the special calling which requires an "extremely antibourgeois life formed by the so-called 'evangelical counsels' " (ibid., 57). Drewermann suggests that "anyone who today becomes or is a member of the clergy must psychologically have been shaped in the direction of that contrast" (ibid.). The psychological question regarding the specific election of the clergy is thus sharpened to read: what are humans like who "want to have *at the same time* both life as a complete exception, on the one hand, and the safety and security of the ordered life of an official, on the other; and how do these opposite aims relate to each other?" (ibid.) Drewermann's analysis suggests that a cleric has been mentally forced all his life to be an exception and that the wish to be appointed as an official is due to extreme pressure of the original family situation (ibid., 58).

At the root of clerical psychology with its combination of exceptional calling and secure official position and the related *"excess of responsibility"* (ibid., 269), Drewermann perceives a certain type of "ontological insecurity" (ibid., 269–72). Philosophically speaking, ontological insecurity is a metaphysical condition of being human, since every human being is contingent and therefore existentially has a feeling of ultimately not-being-necessary. In the case of the model clergy, Drewermann finds that ontological insecurity becomes a constant issue because they have linked their feeling of not-being-necessary to accidental rejection by the earliest primary caregiver instead of directly confronting the contingency of "being itself" (*Sein an sich*) (ibid., 270–71). A metaphysical problem thus becomes a psychological one. The psychological conflicts, in turn, become metaphysicized, that is, they are projected into the God-image of the future clergy (ibid., 53–54).

Drewermann holds that the Roman Catholic Church responds to the ontological insecurity by displacing the metaphysical anxiety into the "categorical realm of the possible contents of life," that is, into the realm of morality (ibid., 74). The Church distracts from the basic anxiety of human life by focusing on particular, small anxieties of everyday and moral life. In other words, the Church attempts to dissipate existential anxiety into categories of anxiety with which it is better able to cope. The price is an objectification of human life and a phobic fear of "the subject" (ibid., 152). Since religion, as Drewermann defines it, is a response to the existential insecurity of humans, the Church, by trying to "stop up" the sources "of that anxiety which characterizes human life essentially" through the pseudo-security of the office (ibid., 76, 191), deprives itself of the very foundation upon which it rests. Drewermann concludes that this inevitably leads to a "spiritless" Church, since the human spirit cannot exist without existential anxiety. Drewermann's "central reproach" of the Catholic Church is *that it attempts to answer the fear and misery of humans who turn to it not with the means of Jesus, not with the forms of a personally mediated trust, but with a procedure of institutional safeguards* by stopping up[3] the springs of anxiety which are constitutionally given with the freedom of a person and hence, conversely, mobilizes the worst of all fears and instrumentalizes it: the fear to risk one's life in independence and personal responsibility. What seems helpful at first — and is from the promoters probably also meant that way — reveals itself in that way eventually as a *reinforcement of fear* in the form of institutionalized directives" (ibid., 191).

Drewermann holds that the actual task of the Church would not be the eradication of existential anxiety through killing off the subjectivity of the human spirit, but rather the calming of existential anxiety through the images of the human psyche within a trusting relationship to the subject which is the ground of all subjectivity, God, and mediated through the trusting relationship to another human being. Instead, the Church, in order to compensate for a lack of spirit, replaces persuasive power with administrative power. Ontological insecurity is compensated for by a "fanaticism of authoritarian thinking" (ibid., 161). Thus the Church itself becomes a major source of anxiety. Instead of responding to the ontological anxiety of its clergy by strengthening their egos, the Church increases anxiety through mass-psychology, setting up social control mechanisms based on anxiety (ibid., 213). Drewermann finds that the consequences are devastating not only for the clergy but for the Church and the culture it shapes: the externalization of religion which is expressed in overemphasis on office and in the special institution of a caste of clergy inevitably produces a type of religion which is unable to provide the healing the human spirit yearns for. Drewermann contrasts this with the experience in a shamanic religion.

> Just as the personal conflicts involved in the idea of election are withdrawn during the projective process from the person of the individual who feels called to the clergy and are objectified

---

3. We take note of Drewermann's use of the metaphor of "stopping up" in *Strukturen des Bösen* as the central characteristic of sin: humans attempt to stop up the sources of their fear through their own efforts, a process which Drewermann sees at play in the Church's requirement of the self-sacrifice and self-liquidation of the cleric's ego through an act of free will.

as God's will, so, too, do *the healing images* become removed from the psyche and are reified and depersonalized as divine revelation in the form of objective symbols of faith and of the rite in the life of the Church....

The caste of shamans in tribal cultures forms, no doubt, a separate institutional entity too — but with what a difference! A shaman gains his occupational place and his public recognition in a way that is possible in our culture today only to artists: they emerge at a certain point, when they feel mature enough, with their images and dream stories in public and present themselves with their experiences to their contemporaries or their tribal members. *In our days,* hardly anyone expects a poet, a sculptor, a musician, or a painter to convey anything beyond the description of mental misery and disunity — the search for what can heal has long left the cultural life of the present. This question [i.e., what can heal] essentially has to be answered by *religion.* Hence the damage is clear which is created by the fact that, yes, the theology of the Church does indeed store in the archives of its dogmatic declarations all possible images of salvation and healing, but only in order to contrast them to subjective experiences as ... works which work through themselves, as *opera operata;* thus to separate them from the context within which the rites and symbols could have mentally healing effect. A shaman certifies his calling before the members of the tribe by actualizing in dramatic form for the well-being of individuals the images which have freed his very self from severe illness. A priest of the Catholic Church is ordered to present in the form of the transmitted sacraments ritual signs which precisely do not spring from his own soul but rather all the more from the controlled tradition of the Catholic teaching office. These images are *signs* for the faith but they are themselves impotent to work through effectively by means of that faith the illnesses of the soul and the body. A shaman takes on his office within the life of a tribe based on the power of his own personality. A Catholic cleric enters the state of his calling at the price of a deep rift between his person and his office: the office which he has to take on does not result from his person but from the objectively preexisting structures of the Church....

It is obvious that this procedure of *objectifying the calling,* too, has its advantages [for the Church]. If one succeeds in defining the type of the "carriers of the office [*Amtsträger*]" of a religion essentially as officials [*Beamte*⁴] so that they are able to effect "something divine [*Göttliches*]" through their objective appointment by the Church and not through their own person, then one achieves a form of religion in which the *prophetic*, visionary, and ecstatic element is consistently eliminated in favor of the bureaucratic, administrative, and conservative element. (ibid., 55–56)

The required complete identification of the cleric with the office, the virtual eradication of his person, leads to tremendous suffering in the life of the clergy and to deep feelings of self-loathing and guilt over any desires for pleasure. Drewermann's psychotherapeutic work with the clergy has shown that behind their ever-present extreme feelings of ambivalence is "an extremely cruel idea of God which stands in glaring contrast to the verbal profession of a loving and forgiving God" (ibid., 87). He defends the individual cleric against the view that her difficulties are due "to the failure of the individual" and asserts that the depressive suffering of so many of the clergy "is clearly the responsibility of a relentless system of inhuman moral ideas, of unchristian images of God and of cruel mental tortures" (ibid., 185). Drewermann compares the effects of that "cruel idea of God" psychologically to "a vampire" (ibid., 187) or to the God Tonatiuh of the Aztecs who could maintain the world only if humans were sacrificed to him. Drewermann has a picture of Tonatiuh hanging on the wall of his office as a reminder (ibid., 88). "When I was ordained as a priest more than 20 years ago, I did not (yet) know how much the God-image of the clergy, if one only listens long enough, resembles the God of the Aztecs, the blood-thirsty *Tonatiuh,* far more than the 'Father' of Jesus Christ — a genuine 'return of the repressed' in the sense of the philosophy of religion as well as psychoanalysis" (ibid., 89). Drewermann stresses that this violent God-image is not the one that Jesus brought but is instead the result of projections of unresolved conflicts due to fears in the clergy themselves on which the system of the Church capitalizes. Making a not so subtle allusion to the mentality of total self-eradication fostered in Christianity and the projection of such a mentality in the total eradication of the Other in Nazi Germany, Drewermann writes:

---

4. This word is more commonly used for "civil servants" in German-speaking countries, but is analogously used in churches in Germany.

Who actually "benefits" from the self-sacrifice of the clergy, from their mystical-existential and officially appointed participation in the Passion mystery, in the redemptive sacrifice of Christ, in his "total giving," in his Holocaust to the "Father"? What kind of "Father" is one who, as theology has it, is so infinitely loving that he wants to forgive the human being infinitely but who, at the same time, is so infinitely just that the sin of the human being offends him infinitely; who therefore needs an infinitely valuable sacrifice, that is, his own son, in order to reconcile the opposition between mercy and punishment into which the sin of the human being has driven the All-knowing and the All-wise? ... The God of Jesus Christ did not know the theological problem of the infinite opposition between his love and his justice. The God of Jesus Christ might have hoped that his messengers would realize someday how much they multiply with theories of this type of "benevolence [*Güte*]" their own contradictions into infinite proportions by making God's problem something which is, at best, their own, but at any rate a purely human problem: how *we* reconcile the eternal conflict between love and justice, of grace and law, of forgiveness and retribution. (ibid., 89–90; cf. 284)

In psychoanalytic psychotherapy with the clergy, Drewermann found that the "theology of sacrifice" is the source of the greatest resistance to treatment: "how great really is the need to hold on with all one's might to the ideology and mysticism of the idea of sacrifice. If one shakes *it*, one rocks the ego of the clergy which has been stabilized with difficulty" (ibid., 91). "It is this longing for sacrifice and nonbeing which has to be considered as the primary aspect and which eventually *falsifies* even the descriptions of redemption in the New Testament by misinterpreting the message of Jesus by means of [externally understood] primordial archetypal patterns of ritual ideas of sacrifice" (ibid., 91).

How do clerics arrive psychologically at an identification with such a violent God-image? Drewermann explores the complex answer to this question in the section "etiology" (see below). Here we should simply note that though the answer to that question is unique in the biography of each cleric, Drewermann found in his work with the clergy that certain regularities in development could be observed: the developmental process is not linear but involves typical complex interactions between four main aspects of life, "family, individual, Church, and society" (ibid., 37). All four aspects of life directly and indirectly relate to one another to create the mentality of a cleric who longs to identify with the conventional clergy-ideal. While the influences of the nuclear family, the Church, and society are important, Drewermann emphasizes that it "would be a grave error to believe that it is sufficient to consider a human being as a mere passive product of education and milieu. Instead, at every step, one has to take into account simultaneously what reactions were possible to the individual in response to her surrounding influences, how the 'world' appears to her in her own 'projection [*Entwurf*]' and how she re-externalizes the internalized structures through her action and behavior in the surrounding circumstances" (ibid., 36). It is this focus on the individual's reaction, on her life's own *Entwurf* which, Drewermann believes, is necessary if one wants to elicit the clergy's potential for therapeutic change. Such focus can be done without harm only, however, in an atmosphere of trust in which the cleric is not morally judged for her choices but existentially understood in the depth of her fear to risk her own freedom.

Etiology

How does the sacrificial identification, the longing for nonexistence in the form of a special calling to an existence *ex officio,* most likely develop psychogenetically? In other words, which "conditions must exist in the constellation of one's own parental home to predispose someone to take on a clerical office in the 'family at large' of the Church" (ibid., 269)? We already mentioned one of the essential building blocks of that development: a certain type of ontological insecurity experienced in relation to the earliest caregivers. Drewermann elaborates the dynamics of this particular type of ontological insecurity as the lack of existential justification; this "produces as a compensatory result the wish to earn despite everything through a certain kind of usefulness something like a justification to exist" (ibid., 270). This accounts for the cleric's *"characteristic excess of responsibility"* and the extreme *"will to be useful,"* or, in other words, for the structure of the cleric's being as dissolved "in altruism," as a being which is permitted only as a "being-for-others" (ibid., 269–70).

As indicated, Drewermann finds behind the sense of ontological insecurity of a cleric the experience that the feeling of nonnecessity is linked in the mind of the cleric to a rejection by the mother or father (or any other primary caregiver). Though Drewermann draws most of his examples from the relationship between mother and child and believes that in the "psychogenesis of the cleric" the central contact is "usually the mother," he again and again emphasizes that this same dynamic can also be experienced between father and child (ibid., 270, 275–76). The parent's rejection is not willful but rather "involuntary," typically not due to an outright wish of the parents not to have the child at all. The psychological ambivalences that are found in the psyche of a cleric characteristically stem from an "involuntary [*unwillentliche*] rejection, for instance, due to the simple fact that one parent is mentally overwhelmed" (ibid., 271). The will, for instance, of a mother who really wants to love her child is thwarted because "due to certain emotional reasons she is unable" to love the child but she "*forces* herself through exertion of her will [*willentlich*] to build up an affirmative relationship to her child — only to realize all the more that in this effort she by far overtaxes the store of her true feelings. The entire relationship between mother and child thus lacks a genuine warmheartedness" (ibid., 271). The lack of "spontaneous benevolence [*Wohlwollen*]" creates guilt feelings in the mother and hence "is replaced by even greater efforts of the will which, in turn, must reinforce again the basic feelings of the original rejection" (ibid.). The increase in feelings of rejection, in turn, reactively creates even more guilt feelings which will once more radicalize efforts to "dutifully" perform the "correct behavior" (ibid.). This "*first vicious cycle* on the part of the mother (or of the primary caregiver) of repressed feelings and moral performance of duties based on tendencies of reparation due to feelings of guilt already preforms the later clerical attitude to a great extent: no relationship exists outside of certain morally coerced actions of the will; everything has, at least in principle, to happen rationally, orderly, and responsibly; and everything is pervaded by a chronic ambivalence of feelings together with a curious ambiguity between willing and being" (ibid.). Drewermann adds: "If ever it should be as plain as day that the widespread superstition of moral theology is nonsense which holds that the lives of humans would be in good order and on the whole infallibly successful if only they would direct all their good efforts and will in line with the instructions of the Church and the divine commandments, surely it is in the case of all the tragic relationships between mother and child where precisely the *particular* extent of good intentions becomes the cause for the never-ending failing of each toward the other" (ibid., 274).

As for the child who grows up with a mother who, with the best of will, is emotionally unable to provide the love which the child needs, that child "will not attribute the responsibility" for the lack of love "to the inability of the mother but to himself: if the mother does not love him it must be because he is not worthy of love. And he must think of every possible thing he may have done wrong to lose the favor of his mother" (ibid. 275–76). If the mother herself, for instance, has physical or mental ailments which can be so threatening to her health that the child has reason to fear for her life (e.g., if she suffers from "asthmatic heart attacks" (ibid., 274)), "the child must think how he can possibly preserve the life of the mother" and the vicious cycle between excessive feelings of responsibility and guilt feelings for failure between mother and child will become radicalized. "The fear of harming the mother simply through one's own existence is converted into the attitude of constant worry and attentive observation in relation to the mother, so that *a system of reversed responsibilities* emerges: the mother is not allowed to live her own life as a woman since she has a child who cannot live without her while, conversely, the child lacks permission for his own life because he has a mother who cannot live without him. The result of this *dual union of reversed dependencies* consists — against the moral will! — of a persistent *reversal of really good intentions* to be as little a burden or obstacle to the other as possible into objectively almost unbearable burdens and obstructions of all kinds" (ibid., 275). Here lie the ontogenetic experiences corresponding to the "counter-finality of aim and result" which Drewermann analyzed by means of the Yahwist's primordial history as an essential element of sin — of the attempt to restore a unity with God lost under the spell of existential fear by means of one's own effort and one's sacrifices. We now understand more clearly what Drewermann meant when he referred to *Strukturen des Bösen* as a "Trojan horse": he analyzed there within a religious text — and to the enthusiastic approval of theologians and Church officials — the very mentality of sacrifice which he was to analyze in *Kleriker* within the religious system of the Church.

But if the sacrificial mentality of the clergy has its roots in the sacrifice of a mother for her child and the child's attempt to save the mother and thus "the world" through the sacrifice of his person, how could the predominant role of the "father" in the sacrificial drama of the clergy be understood? Because the clergy think ideologically that they have to offer themselves as sacrifices to God the Father by taking upon them the Cross just as Christ sacrificed himself to the "father" to redeem "the world." Drewermann here, too, traces ideology back to psychology. "In order to appreciate especially the role of the *father* in the Christian theology of sacrifice, we must here, too, isolate it psychoanalytically from its projected (metaphysicized) form and translate it back into the biographical experience of early childhood — during this process every detail must, again, be taken as literally as possible" (ibid., 284). Just as the Christian theology of sacrifice portrays the Father as a benevolent and just ruler who accepts the sacrifice of the Son out of love and for the sake of the preservation of the world, so the psychological family situation does usually involve a father both loving and just who for some reason requires sacrifices so that the family world can be preserved.

The fixation on the "sacrifice of the Son" has its psychological genesis in this early childhood experience: the loving and just "Father" (the cleric's father) requires the sacrifice of the obedient "Son" (the cleric's mother) in order to save the "World" (the domestic world, which includes the cleric). That the mother plays this saving role of the "Son" is confirmed by the strong emphasis placed in the Roman Catholic Church on the Virgin Mary's participation in the mystery of salvation. Through the strong identification with the mother ("the Son"), the child assumes the sacrificial "spirit of Christ" (ibid., 288). Herein lie the psychogenetic roots for the cleric's later sense of being chosen to save the world: as a child, the future cleric often had to save the marriage of the parents, that is, the domestic world. The child often had to perform early on a *"shuttle diplomacy between father and mother"* (ibid., 297).

This sheds light, too, on the excessive preoccupation of Catholic moral theology with the "insolubility of marriage": psychologically and existentially the admission that marriages could fail would deeply shake the cleric's existence which is built ontogenetically around the attempt to preserve the marriage of the parents (ibid., 277). At the same time, however, the cleric's own hallowed choice of a celibate life and the cleric's emphasis on the insolubility of marriage betray something else: they "serve to a large extent as a defense against one's [the cleric's] own aggressiveness against the marriage of the parents, which has to count before God just as 'consecrated' and 'eternal' as eventually one's own being a cleric" (ibid., 196). As the child grows older and strives to become more detached from the mother, she or he will readily identify with the ideals of the Church and transfer unresolved emotional conflicts into the relationship with Mother Church (ibid., 334). It is this displaced identification which pushes the ideal cleric into the office of the Church (ibid., 287–88).

While the circumstances which give rise to the father's need for the sacrifice of the mother can vary significantly, they typically involve the father's conscious or unconscious demand for the mother's obedience. Failure to do so on the part of the mother could threaten peace or even the existence of the domestic world. Since the father is typically a good-natured person rather than an overtly abusive person, the mother will obey and sacrifice herself in order to save the domestic world for the sake of the child. She will try to be a good mother for the future cleric, repress her negative feelings, and not ask for fulfillment of her own psychospiritual needs. The result is that emotionally she is unable to love her child as much as she would like to. Drewermann illustrates this sacrificial dynamic within the nuclear family of a future cleric by presenting two typical situations in which the mother feels forced to sacrifice herself in order to preserve the relationship between mother and father, which in turn lead the child to identify with her sacrificial spirit: in the first, the father is absent either physically or emotionally; in the second, the father is present in a smothering way (ibid., 291–98). Among the examples where the father is absent, Drewermann mentions first two situations in which the father was away to fight in a war. In light of Drewermann's own experience of his father's brief absence at the end of World War II, the following passage seems particularly important. Addressing the feelings which the mother of a future cleric had whose father had not yet returned from the war, Drewermann writes:

The real anxiety [in Freud's sense] of the mother on the one hand and her holding on to the possibilities which nonetheless continue to exist on the other can generate in the consciousness of a child a tension as such which can be resolved only through the formation of religious, world-transcendent expectations. "I recall clearly," a nun [*Ordensschwester*] said, looking back on her childhood, "how I, about four years of age, was lying in bed with my mother and she said that soon the entire town would be destroyed by the Americans. We prayed together that father would return from the war." It is certainly of great significance that in this childhood memory the mother tried to console herself in her existential fear by means of religion. But more important than this is this girl's psychological experience of participation in the fear and the mother's inner lack of hold. The foundation of the whole "world" collapses for a child when the person to whom he clings for protection is unable to provide security [*Geborgenheit*] due to her own fear. In the case of this four-year-old girl this even resulted in the task of consoling the mother in her despair and encouraging her decision to keep on living. This girl sensed clearly that she represented through her own existence to the mother a big, even unbearable burden. On the other hand, she had also become through the fact of her existence something like the only content of life and of meaning in the *Dasein* of her mother. And both experiences together condense into the described interplay between guilt feeling and savior fantasy, between the impression it would be better not to live at all and then again to be born in the world as the "savior." In this, too, finally there is a religious component. Since, of course, a child can objectively do next to nothing for the wellbeing of his mother, he himself would in a way have to *invent* the religious consolation for himself and his mother if he did not already find them within the faith of his mother: the ontological insecurity itself, in its dramatic worsening, naturally brings forth religion in the mind of the child and utilizes all its elements as if it were building for himself and his relatives a house made of basalt right above the mouth of a volcano. (ibid., 292–93)

Drewermann emphasizes that in this example the father may subjectively through his absence have no awareness of the sacrificial drama between mother and son, but that the objective situation nonetheless often leaves no other choice emotionally for both mother and child. "This short example shows, too, how the motif of the 'sacrifice of the mother' for the sake of the 'father' has to be understood: the father does not subjectively, morally have anything to do with the whole process" (ibid., 293). What is crucial is that *"as substitute for the absent father the child* takes on in the life of his mother the central, literally 'saving' place of mediation of meaning and content of life" (ibid.). In another, similar example Drewermann emphasizes "that the constellation 'the father is at war' can exist in the form of any 'ordinary' marital war: it is sufficient that father and mother have already drifted apart after the birth of the first child so that the mother clearly sees before her the end of the marriage unless she creates through two additional births and the responsibility that comes with them additional stabilizers for the continuation of the marriage" (ibid., 305–6).

Intrapsychically, the identification of the cleric with the office corresponds to an identification of the ego with the superego (ibid., 345). In contrast to Freud, Drewermann emphasizes, as we have seen, that the formation of the superego begins long before the Oedipal conflict arises in the psyche of the child (cf. ibid., 457). The peculiar sacrificial mentality of the cleric develops out of the earliest emotional identification with the primary caregiver rather than as the result of a sense of guilt stemming from Oedipal death-wishes against the rival parent (ibid., 288). At the root of this earliest identification lies, however, not only what psychoanalysis calls the oral-sadistic feelings of guilt. Rather, as we have seen throughout Drewermann's work, he sees the oral-sadistic conflicts *daseinsanalytically,* that is, essentially as conflicts around the justification of existence *per se.*

> The redemptive sacrifice which "mother" as well as "child" have to make in order to save the world of the "father" consists first of all not in the suppression of certain sexual strivings but in the justification of existence *per se.* As true as it is that the life of a human being can only succeed if he is permitted to risk loving, so true is the observation that only someone who has become happy in his *Dasein* because of the love of another is capable of loving. The psychology of sacrifice with all its ambivalences begins only outside of the existential security which is portrayed in myth through the symbol of a primordial paradise. The decisive question, which usually determines the *excessive feeling of responsibility and self-sacrifice* for saving the "world" in the later life of the Catholic cleric is not how one can compete with the father for the love of the mother but how one can save the mother who attempts through the sacrifice of her life to save the future of the family. (ibid., 290)

During the early years of childhood the child learns that she or he can justify her or his own existence only by being there to preserve the family, that is, by living a form of "being for others" (ibid., 270). This is the familiar Cain-and-Abel problem which Drewermann explicated at length in *Strukturen des Bösen*. The childhood maxim of the ideal cleric was characterized by an extreme attempt to live out the mentality of Cain and Abel: "One will be accepted if and as long as one *sacrifices* not simply something but oneself. . . . Only those who sacrifice themselves are loved" (ibid., 302). From this follows the competitive strife of "*a narcissistic wish* or *compulsion to be good*" (Drewermann 1990a, 312). In order to be suitable to identify "later," that is, during puberty, with the theology of sacrifice of the Church, the future cleric must "from a psychoanalytic perspective have been 'sacrificed' already as a child in major areas of his personality development" (ibid., 91). The later clerical office functions as the place in which this narcissistic need to exist only for others becomes repeatedly implemented. It puts an overload of responsibility for others on the shoulders of the cleric, while at the same time giving the cleric all the material and ideological security for which she or he craves. The price is a loss of subjectivity and healing creativity.

Drewermann also throws light on the psychological motivations which make "abortion" the premier social issue of the Roman Catholic Church today. "Ever since the Catholic Church lost its power to force anyone by means of external pressure back to the teachings of Christianity, it lays great stress not so much on the questions of faith but on the questions of morality. Among the latter, no problem is as important to it as the question of abortion" (ibid., 309). While not discussing the question of the objective ethical meaning and justification of the Church's attitude, Drewermann is concerned with the "obvious *subjective* meaning which this question has for the psychic equilibrium of the clergy themselves" (ibid., 309). Drewermann recalls a discussion with a student of theology who was devastated by Drewermann's suggestion that one may need to "recognize the possibility of inevitably *tragic* situations" in the question of abortion (see Drewermann 1991i, 40–45). He gradually learned in the conversation where the extraordinary passion around the issue of abortion stemmed from in the life of this theologian. The young man had grown up with the stigma of illegitimacy. His father had abandoned his mother who, pressured by a moralizing public opinion, reluctantly "chose life." All his life this theologian had suffered under the "ambiguity of a morality . . . in which artificial birth control, premarital intercourse, and abortion all counted as grave sins." His mother had borne him "like a document of public shame." With her child she

could not see any prospects of gaining a new "guiltless partnership."
To carry her child thus felt to her like

> the hardest sacrifice of her life. How should she find access to
> his life other than along the narrow bridge of doing her duty?
> This theologian, who was horror- and panic-stricken at the mere
> thought of the "permission" of abortion, as a child had no-
> ticeably been such a living obstacle in his mother's life that he
> literally needed the absolute, exceptionless *prohibition* of any
> termination of pregnancy in order to feel safe in his own life.
> The prohibition of abortion by the Church was (or had been) in
> a certain sense for him really the only guarantee of his existence;
> thus he defended with correspondingly violent emotional in-
> volvement the teaching of the Church in this respect. The rigidly
> compulsive assurance against the "killing of the child in the
> womb" all the way to the logically incomprehensible compar-
> isons by Josef Cardinal Höffner who put abortion on the same
> level as the mass-extermination of "life unworthy for living"
> in the Nazi gas chambers — this assurance appears clearly mo-
> tivated if one presupposes psychoanalytically in the advocates
> of such views an early childhood experience which made it un-
> mistakably clear to the growing child that he owed his existence
> solely to his mother's heroic will for sacrifice. Consequently, it is
> expected *from him* to sacrifice himself in the role of "Abel," and
> as the priest of a strict God he will also demand later from all
> people, foremost from women and mothers, that they so act in
> similar situations and sacrifice themselves "voluntarily." (ibid.,
> 310–11)

Development Through Psychological Stages,
Or: Psychogenesis of the Evangelical Counsels

Identification with the clergy-ideal, which finds expression in the
evangelical counsels, is a process which spans the different stages of
the childhood of the future cleric. The formation of the three evangelical counsels takes place throughout these stages. Drewermann's
analysis concludes that in their current ideal form, the evangelical
counsels are based on unresolved childhood conflicts: conflicts of
orality underlie the ideal of poverty, conflicts of anality underlie the
virtue of obedience, conflicts of genitality underlie the conception

of chastity (ibid., 347). Drewermann points out that the historical emergence of these three counsels took place long before the birth of Christianity in the period between the eighth and fourth century B.C.E., when personalities such as Lao-tse, the Buddha, Isaiah, and Socrates arose. This period, which Karl Jaspers called the "axial age" (*Achsenzeit*), marks a point in the development of human consciousness in which humans tried for the first time to overcome their sense of finitude and their experience of suffering by "means of the spirit" (ibid., 351). Drewermann sees this period as the culmination of a development which had begun with the neolithic revolution 10,000 years ago: the discovery and growing consciousness of the individual (ibid., 350). "Humans stopped understanding themselves as part of nature" (ibid.). This development meant both greater freedom and the awareness, and fear, of one's own death. The first appearance of the counsels of poverty, obedience, and chastity falls into this culminating axial age as responses to the lack of orientation which accompanied the newly gained freedom of the spirit, and the dreadful acknowledgment of the inevitability of one's death.

The awareness of one's freedom and death was also the fertile ground from which the monastic movements of Christianity and the development of the Christian evangelical counsels arose. From the very beginning, monastic movements were a serious challenge to the established Church (ibid., 352). One of Drewermann's main critiques of Catholicism as it actually exists (ibid., 613, 623) is that the Church, as a whole, failed to face up to the real challenge of the evangelical counsels. The Church avoided this challenge by externalizing their function: the counsels were elevated to the status of objective ideals for its clergy and thus turned into a powerful tool for the control of its personnel. The Church also used them to deepen the gap between those elements which ought to be a unity: "creation and grace, church and society, clergy and 'laity,' priest and human being, sainthood and responsible living, soul and body, feeling and thinking, woman and man, drive and spirit, nature and culture" (ibid., 654). It did not apply the counsels to itself as an institution, however, but maintained instead both its wealth and its power (ibid., 353).

The functionalization of the evangelical counsels also entailed their moralization. Their original purpose, to decrease the feeling of ontological insecurity by inner spiritual means, was reversed; as objective ideals which the clergy must live up to, the counsels rather increased the clergy's anxiety. In addition, the methods through which the

Church regulated the lives of the clergy, thus enforcing the counsels, also became a source of anxiety. Meant to reduce anxiety within the subject, the counsels instead became means by which to increase the Church's fear of the individual.

Psychologically, the externalization and functionalization of the counsels corresponds to a process of rationalization causing an emotional alienation from the healing images of the psyche (ibid., 55). Such alienation accounts partly for the loss of the Church's relevance in contemporary Western societies. Dealing with each ideal counsel in depth and illustrating his conclusions with a plethora of examples, Drewermann demonstrates how they must produce in their external interpretation a predominantly neurotic feeling in the clergy (ibid., 371).

Poverty and Oral Conflicts

Drewermann describes how the Church, especially those at the top, uses the counsel of poverty not only to make the clergy materially dependent on itself (see ibid., 643) but also to impoverish the clergy's sense of self. Instead of understanding poverty as an attitude which can grow only from within a person's existence, the present form of the ideal virtually requires a "poverty in the sense of inability, dependency, and lack of personal value" (ibid., 371) imposed from outside upon the clergy. Drewermann illustrates this point, for instance, with the dynamics in the fairy tale of *Hansel and Gretel*[5] in which the theme of " *'poverty'* is essentially condensed *as an oral theme"* (ibid., 391) which contains a mental "script" for the children: "Only if you give up everything from which you can and must live, may you return home" (ibid., 390). This fairy tale illustrates how a boy may feel mentally and spiritually "incarcerated" in the presence of a mother who herself is emotionally and spiritually in deep distress — to the point that all that can safely be shown of his life to the outside is a bare bone for fear that anything else would be devoured. Drewermann sees this pointedly as a metaphor for the inner sense of those of the clergy who feel "incarcerated" in their rectories, their convents, their bishop's palaces, or simply behind the bars of an official existence (ibid., 393). But, in contrast to the happy, growthful ending of the fairy tale, the external interpretation of the Christian

---

5. For Drewermann's book-length depth-psychological interpretation of *Hansel and Gretel*, see Drewermann 1997b.

"myth of redemption" (ibid., 395) requires from the clergy "instead of rebellion [*Auflehnung*] and struggle [*Kampf*] submission and conflict avoidance, instead of open hate the eternalization of guilt feeling together with corresponding attempts at reparation, instead of self-assertion and freedom a mentality of self-sacrifice and dependency — everything which Freud described under the topic of the '*castration complex*' within the context of the Oedipal conflict is already represented here, in the fairy tale of *Hansel and Gretel*, as a developmental direction based on oral and not just 'sexual' experience" (ibid., 392). Turning to another fairy tale, *The Girl Without Hands*,[6] Drewermann illustrates a common underlying psychological dynamic in the experience of women religious who do not feel entitled to take anything into their own hands: a dynamic in which a "father suffering from misery" finds himself tricked by "the devil," and against his own will, to cut off the hands of his daughter — with her sacrificial consent. In that story the script at play to guarantee the "poverty" of the girl is: "Only if I am sad, I am not bad; only my tears wash me clean; only my oppressed feeling and depression save me the trouble that others become 'hopping mad [*fuchsteufelswild*; lit., devilishly wild like a fox]' about my wishes" (ibid., 400).

Psychodynamically, the mentality of poverty has its root in early oral conflicts and has as its psychogenetic background the self-sacrifice of the child which resulted from identification with the sacrificial mentality of the primary caregiver. The Church capitalizes on this early self-sacrifice. Instead of fostering a spirituality of poverty that helps a person come to terms with the reality of death and freedom, that is, with the poverty of being itself, the Church, by responding to spiritual problems with moralism and externalization, unconsciously and unwillingly, yet inevitably, promotes the poverty of spirituality instead. At the same time, the clergy become fully dependent on the Church materially. Such dependency perpetuates a child-mother relation between the clergy and the Church and prevents the clergy's maturation (cf. ibid., 386).

Drewermann also points out the tragic and inevitable perpetuation of material poverty if the motivational fuel for helping the materially poor comes from a moralistic duty of self-impoverishment.

---

6. Drewermann presents a detailed depth-psychological interpretation of *The Girl Without Hands* in Drewermann 1985c.

It feels so good to forget the poverty of one's own ego by feeling magically drawn to those who are supposedly even poorer!
We have to emphasize once more: We are not objecting to the
attempt to fight with all one's strength distress and misery in the
world; but such an investment of one's strength is mentally not
possible where one really needs the misery of others in order to
draw from them some permission or justification to avoid working through one's own conflicts and to continue to live with them
[i.e., the conflicts] as usual. Anyone who makes a virtue out of
misery is not particularly suited to work off someone else's misery. By the way, one should use terms correctly: where the task
is the just distribution of existing *prosperity* the problem is not
poverty but rather justice, that is, the implementation of the
Bill of Rights, not the counsel of "evangelical poverty."[7] (ibid.,
424–25)

A mentality which needs the misery of others in order to find some
reason to live tends to "confuse *suffering* with God" by actually projecting "one's own unlived and unsatisfied life into the realm of the
divine and then bringing it back down to earth as a moral mission to
seek solidarity with the unhappy others" (ibid., 714).

Obedience and Anal Conflicts

Instead of understanding the counsel of obedience internally as a way
of listening to and obeying one's own being, the Church uses this
counsel to eradicate the personal will of its subordinates (ibid., 431).
Hidden behind the idealization of obedience lies the ideologizing of
the power of the Church (ibid., 437), which replaces an authentic
personal conscience with social anxiety, in the form of a permanently
bad conscience (ibid., 447–49). I will present this part of Drewermann's analysis in greater detail because of its particular relevance to

---

7. See Drewermann 1990a, 674–708, for his critique of First World political theologians
(particularly J. B. Metz), especially in view of the danger of elevating the criterion of material
poverty itself as a sign of being chosen by God: such a view would inadvertently turn misery
into virtue and metaphysicize problems of economic injustice which require urgent political,
practical solutions. "The problems of Latin American campesinos exist in a bitter reality and
cannot be solved psychoanalytically. But psychoanalysis can dissolve the urge to constantly have
to redeem one's own (mental) unfreedom through the 'social' unfreedoms of others.... The
misery of the campesinos...requires the best possible rational and de-ideologized *political*
solutions. Those, however, better succeed the less their reality can be envisioned and created
without distortion by the neuroticisms of one's own subjectivity" (ibid., 694).

his own struggle between identification with and differentiation from the official directives of the Church.

For the clergy, obedience to the collective institution is like a drug which appeases the spiritual "fear of oneself," of one's own freedom (ibid., 450). Drewermann mentions three key elements which come together to make the attitude of *unconditional* obedience" (ibid., 456), from childhood on, first a duty and later a need (ibid., 452–80). The *"'classical' situation of origin of the obedience of a cleric* is best described as the interaction between a rather anxious mother and a father who seems rather robust" (ibid.). The first element is an authoritarian intimidation, usually by the father, which leads to the destruction of the cleric's sense of self, a process which Drewermann calls a "castration on the anal level": one must dispense with one's own will in order to save the world (ibid., 459). Here, too, Drewermann locates, in contrast to Freud, conflicts around authority and power prior to the Oedipal stage (ibid., 457).

The second element is an identification with the "example" of the parents which prepares the clergy for an identification with the model of a suffering Christ as presented by the Church (ibid., 464–72). Drewermann calls this the "St.-Francis-attitude" because he finds it classically expressed in St. Francis's biography (ibid., 464–70). Francis's father is usually portrayed as someone who tries to force, at times violently, his son against the latter's will to do what the father wants. When Francis chooses the life of a cleric, the father violently tries to change the son's mind and even locks him up. The submissive mother, though also not in favor of Francis's decision to give up a worldly life, nonetheless has pity on him, speaks tenderly with him, and eventually frees him. Francis openly vows obedience to the heavenly father in place of his earthly father Pietro Bernardone.

At that moment, Francis directly *contrasts* the image of the heavenly father with the image of his earthly father. Both are completely opposed to each other so that he must *disobey* the one in order to *obey* the other: while the earthly father is violent and crude, his son will meekly and peacefully walk through the world in obedience to God; while father Pietro Bernardone urges possessions and bourgeois recognition, his son, trusting the heavenly father, will choose poverty as his "lover [*Geliebten*]" and despise the applause of the crowd. Everything which the Father-God of Francis wants is obviously the opposite of what father Pietro wants. Psychoanalytically we note above all that Francis does not face his father in his own person — it is not he himself, not his ego, which dares to contradict the father. Rather he projects his protest into the God-image which not only legitimizes but demands it outright. A subjective conflict between father and son thus turns into a conflict between father Pietro Bernardone and the Father-God. Disobedience to the earthly father appears thus as absolute obedience to God, personal revocation [*Widerruf*] as divine vocation [*Berufung*].

But it seems that the contents which Francis believes in his God-image as objective were also objectively in existence prior to his own experience, so that the conflict between the earthly and the heavenly father only reflected in superelevated form what already existed in the contrast between father and mother. It is apparently the soft, obedient manner of the mother which expressed itself in the soul of the saint as a divine conscience and as an insatiable source of longing for love, harmony, and world-encompassing reconciliation.…

[I]t is really *the image of the mother* which is wrapped in the experience of St. Francis with the aura of the absolute, the divine. (ibid., 465–67)

The model of the parent with which the clergy classically identifies is the submissive obedience of the mother to the father. But the cleric does so not by obeying the "earthly" father; rather, he metaphysicizes identification with the mother's submissive obedience to the father by obeying the Father-God. This explains to Drewermann why St. Francis could become a saint in the Church rather than a rebel or reformer.

In Church history no one criticized and provoked through his character the power apparatus of Rome more than he, but it is precisely not the ego of the saint but rather the content which he projected and divinized in his superego as *objective* which becomes a challenge, without him uttering any personal word against Rome and in humble obedience toward God. Only that explains, too, why Francis was eventually willing to come before Pope Innocent III and to ask this giant-Bernardone to recognize his life in monastic poverty. If it had not been just that identification with the obedience of the mother which drove Francis into disobedience to his father and if the entire aggressive part of his attitude had not been completely removed from his ego [and used by his superego against his ego], then Francis — equipped with a stronger will to assert himself and a smaller willingness to submit — would have felt called to become a rebel or reformer [*Reformator*] rather than a saint and a member of a religious order. (ibid., 469)

Drewermann adds that the projection into the divine of the mother's attitude of "submissiveness," seen by the cleric as her "secret strength," develops more easily if the mother herself attributes her attitude to a transcendent source without which she could not be so obedient (ibid., 470). "The transcendent part in the life of the mother promotes the 'transcendentalizing' or idealizing of the mother-image in the growing child and plants in him something like a 'mystery [note the importance of the *mysterium* in Catholic theology!]' to which he feels absolutely committed all his life long" (ibid., 471).

The third element in the formation of unconditional obedience that is both duty and need for the cleric is the cleric's experience that his opinion, his thoughts, do not really count. Particularly if the future cleric senses that, despite all appearances, the marriage of his parents is not really happy but, for instance, built on an affinity of the contents of the superego of the parents rather than on genuine love as persons, as egos, the cleric will learn to identify with the parents' taboo against thinking that something could be wrong with the parents' marriage "because the truth would be unbearable" (ibid., 474). The future cleric will experience "fears of punishment for perceiving" (ibid., 476) the actual reality and, in order to preserve the 'world' of the family, will become irritated at his own thinking and feel a need to obey the thinking which is prescribed by the parents. This is ontogenetically the origin for the cleric's characteristic "false-bottomedness [*Doppelbödigkeit*]" in thinking (ibid., 474), which is required in an existence identified with the office: the cleric has continuously to disavow and repress all thoughts which threaten the illusion that everything is true that Mother Church says. Drewermann points out that the Church capitalizes tremendously on the attitude of those among its clergy for whom obedience to the hierarchy is not just an annoying formality that comes with the job but "*a need*" (ibid., 477). He holds that "the reciprocal relationship between the individual insecurity and submissive attitude on the one hand and

the institutional fixation on the claim to truth in the form of a hier-
archically structured apparatus of offices on the other is not at all
restricted to the area of the personal issuing of orders and following
orders, but provides the basis for the whole structure of thinking of
the Catholic Church" (ibid., 478). He stresses that it was not possible

> to erect the dogmatic edifice of the teaching of the Church in the
> course of centuries and would be just as impossible to maintain
> this edifice completely today even 200 years after the Enlight-
> enment, unless the "faithful" had not first been intimidated and
> made uncertain in matters of religion to such a degree that they
> could not trust their competence as "lay people." *Obedience in
> matters of faith* [*Glaubensgehorsam*] is literally not just some-
> thing in the Catholic Church but its center, its very heart. Any
> public talk which departs from the line of the usual Sunday
> sermon will be questioned in the subsequent discussion not ac-
> cording to what was said but according to what "the" Church
> will say about it — whether one is permitted to think what was
> said, *that* is the parameter for a good Catholic. No Western
> institution as much as the Catholic Church has been able to dic-
> tate to humans as to what outside [*fremde*] thoughts — whether
> they understand them or not — they have to repeat in order to
> be "saved" in time and eternity. Not freedom of thought but the
> static structure of coerced thinking and will is the highest goal
> of theological training in the Church even today. (ibid., 478)

Addressing the difficulties that this creates particularly for Catholic
academic theologians who are not permitted to share their scientific results with "believers" lest they be condemned as "heretics,"
Drewermann comments:

> Today we have come so far that theologians have to keep secret
> their own knowledge, for instance, regarding the historicity of
> biblical texts, vis-à-vis the mass of believers in Christ, so that
> they can avoid being denounced as heretics by those who go to
> Church and then also by the respective Commission on Faith
> of the Bishop's Conference. This layer of *obedient* bearers of
> the teaching office floats like a layer of fat above the seas of
> uninformed believers who are and remain misinformed to the
> degree of massive superstition, so that their childish faith is not
> damaged [cf. ibid., 110, 123–27]. How else could one explain

that according to a report by the FAZ [*Frankfurter Allgemeine Zeitung*] from March 1989 *more than half* of the population of the Federal Republic of Germany still holds the opinion that, for instance, the biblical story of creation has to be understood *literally?* If one evaluates such numbers correctly, one must conclude that the only people who go to church today are those who in their "obedience in matters of faith" have been spiritually arrested at the level of awareness of their fellow believers centuries ago and, with respect to their own biography, at the stage before puberty, while those less intimidated stop wanting to be "obedient" in that sense no later than at the age of 14. St. Ignatius hoped that by means of a militaristic form of obedience in religious orders the Church could be more effective in its outward mission since it would be internally more united. This hope has long turned into the fact that it is precisely that formalization of the demand for obedience which has *devoured* the spiritual powers upon which a truly religious life would depend. This much is certain: The future of the Catholic Church depends essentially on a new and credible definition of the "evangelical counsel" of obedience so that it could withstand the psychoanalytic and philosophical critique of the nineteenth and twentieth centuries. (ibid., 478–79)

The key reason, according to Drewermann, for resistance against a revision of the Church's alienating thinking and its external interpretation of the message of Christianity also lies in unresolved and metaphysicized ontogenetic conflicts of the will from the anal level, which shape power dynamics in the hierarchy.

The necessary and overdue revision in thought is made rather difficult not only by the coerced passivity of "those who are obedient," but especially by the paradoxical fixation of all subservient souls on the manipulation by their "bosses": in the final analysis, all officials are miniature editions of their superiors and have the secret wish to one day be just like the big guys. We already spoke in view of the oral level of the attitude of poverty about the inconsiderateness of the considerate... [ibid., 422]. Correspondingly we must now point to *the latent greed for power of the powerless:* In their obedience they have had to suppress so much in themselves and are so strongly identified with their official superiors and models, to whom they have to be "loyal," that from a certain point on they are indeed ready themselves to climb up the ladder of the hierarchy. The most favorable condition for that is a character that is *obsessive compulsive* enough in order to experience the internalized scripts still with a certain inner tension in relation to itself — a depressive character structure in which the ego is fully identical with the contents of the superego does not have at its disposal the necessary distance to itself and is, too, not assertive enough toward the outside in order to feel "called" to the administration of ecclesial power. The *obsessive compulsive* attitude, in contrast, provides just the type which we mainly encounter in the official representatives of the Church: human beings in whom feelings, whether their own or those of other people, do not count, who always know what is true, good, useful, and necessary, who are always "on duty [*im Dienst*]" and never notice that they stylize their own needs as metaphysical necessities, who as a rule are able to find valid only what is clear, unambiguous, proven, verified by external authorities, and, above all, familiar to them since childhood days. It is not due to ill will that they react to all questions not with their own person but with measures and administrative instructions. It rather is the lack of any will and thinking of their own which causes them to deal with other people just as they deal with themselves: "disciplined," so to speak. They have given up their own ego to "Christ" [i.e., the mother] and are structurally unable to notice that the refusal of their own life in the name of Christ must turn the message of Jesus of the freedom of the human being into the tyrannical program of a constant censorship of thought and conscience. Thus tomorrow's heads of the Church are reproduced and recruited from today's obedient ones. But what does obedience mean in the sense of the gospel? The answer will determine whether Christianity understands itself essentially as a superego-religion or whether it musters the courage to see and permit the relationship of the human to God as an ego-function. (ibid., 479–80)

The destruction of the clergy's ability to make independent judgments through the Church's domination of the their thought thus has turned the counsel of obedience in its present form into a function of superego-religion rather than a religion in which a human being is not alienated from herself, but instead finds herself and strengthens her ego in relationship to God (ibid., 480). Drewermann pointedly comments: "But one does not lose the reality of the human being, the reality of one's own ego *without also losing God*" in the process (ibid., 167). It is the "lack of personality" which also accounts for the lack of personal relevance of what the clergy have to say (ibid., 167, 170).

Chastity and Oedipal Conflicts

The current ideal of chastity conflicts with both the nature of humans and the nature which surrounds them (ibid., 498). Drewermann provides a broad historical perspective on the development of this religious ideal before Christianity during the axial age and discusses in detail the issue of celibacy, listing arguments by proponents such as Pope John Paul II and the rules of religious orders and by critics such as U. Ranke-Heinemann and K. Deschner (ibid., 480–99). The proponents' view usually is a *"functionalization of an extreme"* where remaining in the *"virgin state"* is seen as a safeguard against the chaos of the drives.

> In the background of such thinking is the constant *fear of inner chaos,* and the "evangelical counsels" are...extreme means of discipline against imminent mental disintegration. To put it in psychoanalytic terms: it is a mentality in which the ego flees from its repressed and deformed id-strivings into the superego in order to escape the danger of asocial eruption of drives. In this way the repression itself is rationalized, the repressing agency (the superego) is stabilized, and the ego is conditioned to a fearful flight into the institutionally prescribed direction of the "monastic life of the counsels." The [creative] tension between ego and superego, person and institution, individual and society disappears by means of such a pattern of argumentation, and we comprehend that the respective theological language *must* be "monophysitic"[8] or "supernaturalistic" in order to maximally legitimize and practice the process of appropriation of the individual by the collective of the Church. (ibid., 484)

---

8. The view that the human and the divine in the person of Jesus Christ constituted one nature, in contrast to the doctrine of the Council of Chalcedon which declared that the divine and the human constituted two natures which came together in one person (Schmidt 1984, 107–8).

While proponents view the ideal of chastity as a function for guarding against inordinate drives, opponents of celibacy usually argue that it is merely an outgrowth of the *"factual hostility toward sexuality in the Catholic Church,"* which is actually "unchristian." Jesus himself would not have shared such hostility but instead was relaxed about having contacts with women, even with prostitutes (ibid., 486). Radical opponents propose that the ideal of chastity should be thrown out altogether since it is neither just nor based on the New Testament, but derives from gnostic influences. After an exegetical walk through the relevant passages from the Christian Scriptures, Drewermann concludes that historical-critical exegesis cannot confirm that assessment. Rather, the New Testament portrays Jesus' own attitude toward marriage in light of his expectation of the imminent end of the world. But this eschatologically motivated attitude of distance from the things of this world was subsequently turned, as the expected end of the world did not occur, in Christianity into a moralistic demand. "What seemed natural in the attitude of Jesus under the impression of the approaching end of the world" and resulted in "the relinquishment of possessions, power, and family is transformed...into a moral demand. An originally existential attitude thus increasingly became an ethical postulate, the message of liberation through closeness to God became a kind of new legalism in order to become close to God" (ibid., 490). That the ideal of celibacy is not simply the result of hostility toward sexuality — although Drewermann agrees that it became functionalized in the Catholic Church to that end — is the case in many other religions, including Buddhism and Hinduism with their bhikkhus, sadhus, or fakirs and Muslim dervishes or Sufism (ibid., 491). He concludes that existentially the religious attitude of monastic life with its focus on the other world and its renunciation of this world stems from *"the fundamental experience of the principal insufficiency of the earthly Dasein"* (ibid., 491). The human spirit's experience of the "lack" that characterizes existence itself thus gave reason to an orientation to the spiritual, to the eternal.

It is the search for a life beyond and without death which, Drewermann suggests, also became the reason for a devaluation of sexuality. But this can be understood only, he holds, if one goes deeper into the history of religions than is usually done in studies of the religious ideal of celibacy, namely, into a time when fertility was completely attributed to women and when the man's participation in the act of procreation was not yet understood (ibid., 492). Not only has that early view of generativity been seen as the root of the "mythic image of the virgin birth" and of the veneration of the Great Mother goddess, but also as the origin of the identification in religious history of women with the ambivalent nature of sexuality. In this early view

> life and the happiness of love come from woman; but the other side cannot be disavowed: sexuality and procreation make sense only at the price of death. Only what dies needs to procreate in order to be, but every act of generation with its new life entails also new aging, suffering, and dying. The cycle of birth and death seems inevitable, and it was the mystery of woman which, in itself ambivalent enough, could call forth that contrast [Gegensatz] [between life and death]. Only this lets us comprehend that many myths of peoples see the "discovery" of sexuality within the context of primordial punishment and guilt: to perform the works of women leads to death. But men, too, are woven into this puzzling cycle: while women give birth to life as mothers, it becomes the task of men to destroy life in hunt and war. (ibid., 492–93)

How did these "archaic (and not only 'patriarchal')" (ibid., 495) views on life and death impact Christianity? Drewermann reviews the attempt in the Old Testament to deal with the never-ending cycle of life and death by means of the idea of monotheism. "Israel's Yahweh is the declared contradiction of any divinization of nature, he is in himself the radical monotheistic negation of the divinized polarity of the sexes in myths, and in his wrath, in his assertive will, in his jealousy together with his angelic hosts he has absolutely belligerent, extremely male, and, depending on the circumstances, violently fanatic traits. All this was apparently the inevitable price that had to be paid so that for the first time in human history *the experience of an absolute personality and freedom* was recognized as the decisive center of human *Dasein*" (ibid., 493–94). For the first time in human history the transcendence of the one God was seen decisively as the guarantor of human freedom in relation to nature's cycle of life and death. Besides this invaluable contribution to the development of the human spirit in this world, the religion of ancient Israel originally rejected the "idea and cult of immortal life" (ibid., 494). This meant that humans were inevitably caught far more "hopelessly in 'this world' " than in "any other religion. Was it really a consolation and a sign of hope to offer justice and well-being at the end of time under the rule of a king and savior to come from God?" (ibid., 494). However, by tying its promises to the constant coming and going of the generations "and hence to the generative power of human love," ancient Israel actually carried the idea of the fertility religions further. But this binding of the promises to the generations on one hand and the explicit rejection of the fertility cults on the other led spiritually to a "highly contradictory" attitude to human fertility. "The ecstasy, the euphoria, the pouring out of sexual longing filled the prophets and priests of Israel with horror and disgust, and by declaring the fertility religions to be sin *per se,* the shadow of sinfulness fell, too, on human fertility itself" (ibid.).

Drewermann argues that hope for a future Messiah was in the last instance insufficient to "counter the fundamental anxiety" which had shaped human history since the breakthrough of self-awareness that began in the neolithic revolution and culminated in the axial age (ibid., 495). "If the fateful forces of age, sickness, and death stand ready as godparents at the crib of each newborn child, how will it create hope and confidence to look to a far, far future in which a distant messianic king is expected to render human history and human striving more favorably and more mercifully? In the meantime, people suffer and die, and no future society, however peaceful, just, and prosperous, can change even one bit of the essential fact: 'people die and they are not happy' as long as they live on earth — in a few decades the end of the world begins for each of us" (ibid., 495–96). Drewermann thinks that in this situation Christianity revived the ancient Egyptian idea of an "other-worldly, eternal life" and tried to connect it with the religion of the Old Testament. "It thus created again a tension between this world and the other world, between 'fertility religion' and individual belief in resurrection which placed, too, the topic of sexuality into an unfavorable light in which it still stands today. Since then the question is: What is the direction of a human being's essential love — the earthly or the heavenly, the finite or the infinite, the human or the divine? Only now does love of a man or of a woman" enter into a seemingly necessary competition with love of God.[9] "Only now does the ancient *'Indian'* motif emerge again: *How*

---

9. The sentence evidently contains a misprint: "Only now do the love of a man or of a woman enter into seemingly necessary competition with each other [*Erst jetzt treten die Liebe zu einem Mann oder zu einer Frau in scheinbar notwendige Konkurrenz zueinander]*" which does not make sense within the context. It evidently should read: "...competition with love of God [*Konkurrenz zur Liebe zu Gott*]."

does one redeem the human being from the chains of his earthly imprisonment, how does one overcome suffering, sin, and death. With this question Christianity stands or falls" (ibid., 496).

Drewermann presents St. Augustine (1992) as the classical example of the Catholic Church's attempt to answer that question. With deep sensitivity this great saint of Christianity tried to find redemption by spiritualizing his natural longings for food and love in a way that had to repress and continuously fight against the "desires of the 'flesh' " (Drewermann 1990a, 497). Drewermann comments that despite Augustine's sensitive nature "it cannot be overlooked that in this conception the energy of longing exudes into infinity without ever again returning to the small, finite world. No longer does there exist any calm, fearless, happily playful manner of touching the things of life tenderly and absorbing them happily — *original sin,* Augustine taught authoritatively, has disfigured the natural tendency of humans to cling to the world of the senses in sin. Hence one has to crucify the 'natural human being' in the name and according to the model of Christ in order to attain the pure, heavenly life of the world of God. All needs of the body: the longing for food, strength, and sexual fulfillment, all desires of the 'flesh,' must be avoided as fetters and traps" (ibid., 497). As Augustine confessed, this *"battle for purity"* is fought even in dreams (ibid., 497–98).

This form of Christian theology early on in the history of the Church led humans waking and sleeping into a struggle against their inner nature, which Drewermann sees "as the exact opposite of what Nietzsche and Freud in their critique of Christianity postulated as the regaining of 'Hellenism' or as the regaining of mental health" (ibid., 498). Drewermann believes that only within this existential dynamic of life and death can the Catholic Church's fear of sexuality be properly understood. "One can understand the desperate battle of the Catholic Church against sexuality in all its contradictions, inconsistencies, and absurdities only as an instrument for the purpose of liberating the human being as 'soul,' as reflexive person in her self-determination and freedom as much as possible from nature as that which is soulless, material, lowly, and degrading. Since then and to this day sexuality appears in such thinking like a pagan relic, like a force in which 'foreign gods,' that is, *devils,* prefer to disguise themselves, namely, by effecting that someone who is sexually happy is in danger of losing sight of God simply because of his earthly happiness" (ibid., 498–99). Thus "the paradox exists that the

Catholic Church faces... everything 'natural' still filled with fear and suspicion: instead of integrating the life of the drives it declares their sacrifice, suppression, and crucifixion at least as an ideal, if not (or no longer?!) as the *duty* of a Christian" (ibid., 499).

The ideal of chastity, which sprang from the existential feeling of need for the redemption of one's earthly existence, thus developed eventually into a rule hostile to sexuality and, in effect, ambivalent toward and oppressive of women (ibid., 491). Through a review of clinical cases, of the emphasis in the Church on virginity even at the cost of life as evidenced in the choice of women beatified by twentieth-century popes, of film studies (e.g., Scorcese's *The Last Temptation of Christ*, 1988 [based on Kazantzakis 1960]), and of pertinent literature (e.g., E. Zola, L. Tolstoy, and W. Reich), Drewermann illustrates how this hostility and ambivalence is psychologically related both to the strict celibacy requirement of the clergy and to the increasing veneration of the Virgin Mother Mary which has in today's form an unmistakably Oedipal character. Comparing a certain type of "Virgin Mary piety" with the sexual self-mutilation of the priests of the ancient cult of the goddess Cybele, in which the priests castrated themselves and threw their severed genitals into the symbolic bosom of the Great Goddess,[10] Drewermann notes: in the case of the Cybele-cult no one in the Catholic Church would have objections to a depth-psychological interpretation but in the case of the Church's own "spiritual" forms of such veneration the resistance is almost insurmountable. He encounters "massive defenses against the mere attempt to propose a similar interpretation of the devotion to the Madonna, of the chastity demand, of self-castration, and mother fixation particularly for the Catholic Virgin Mary piety" (ibid., 505).

The developments of the 1960s revealed deep changes in attitude toward sexuality which the population of so-called Christian societies developed in opposition to the Church's stance on sexuality. With this, Drewermann credits the "revolt of '68" with highlighting the interconnection between patriarchal power and the repression of sexuality in the Catholic Church. Again we meet Drewermann's familiar argument that psychological conflicts are metaphysicized.

It cannot be denied that *three factors* obviously belong together in the Catholic Church's attitude of piety: the authoritarian

---

10. See Leach and Fried (1972, 352).

centralism of paternal power, the restrictive severity in the regulations of sexual morality, and the expansive veneration of a "virgin mother." Translated into the language of psychoanalysis we conspicuously find a socially expanded form of the *Oedipus-complex* which is projected into the collective: the composite of religious overvaluation of the father-authority, of the castration threat which follows from that, and of the neurotic fixation around the libidinal strivings which cling to the mother, of people whose thinking and feeling prevent them, literally for heaven's sake, from being anything but *children* who are well-behaved [*brav*], obedient, subject to directives, and uncertain of themselves; who are not allowed to become what they are supposed to be according to Christian claims: free, trusting adult personalities who are capable of love. (ibid., 514)

The present ideal of chastity requires a fixation of the cleric's sexuality during the stage of puberty which finds, for instance, expression in "purely male or female groups" in religious orders and which reinforces the cleric's immaturity (ibid., 593). Unresolved Oedipal conflicts are transferred into the relationship with the Church and influence the cleric's images of God. Drewermann argues that the patriarchal oppression of women in a Church dominated by paternal officials identified with the sacrificial attitude of their dutiful mothers has its roots in a fundamental "hatred of masculinity" among the male clergy (ibid., 588–89).

Only thus can we perhaps explain the curious attractiveness of the Catholic Church especially to *women:* They are the ones who are most oppressed by the Catholic Church, but at the same time they are the ones who alone make it possible that daily mass is celebrated to some purpose...that on Sundays a sermon can be delivered before somewhat filled pews. In the midst of the patriarchal structures of the Catholic Church one has to recognize the *latent hatred of masculinity* as the real core of the oppression of women: the men who want to rule here do not want to be men, and it is precisely their latent homosexual aura which makes them seem to many women in a certain sense better, more cultivated, more sensitive, and considerate "men." They are mothers who themselves were barely allowed to be women and who perceive in priests with their "nice" mamma's-boy and perfect-boy behavior their true dreamchildren or who discover in them something of the father whom they would have wanted. (ibid., 589)

The hatred of masculinity, the "latent feeling of shame to be a man" derives from the male cleric's Oedipal disgust at the father's sexual desire for the mother and the reaction-formation of wanting to be different from the father in relation to the mother. Drewermann finds this dynamic succinctly expressed in the "age-old myth and fairy-tale motif of the legend of St. George":

If one cannot help being a man then one has the task, as a knight astride his steed, with discipline and bravery, galloping against the fiery breath of the beast, to redeem the threatened virgin (one's own mother!) by battling and defeating any . . . physical urges in oneself and in others. All "masculine" energy thus is channeled into a battle *against* masculinity; hence the life's vocation of the cleric to come will be to complete with all ideological and ascetical means this crusade against the masculine "dragon" — the father of one's own childhood and the masculine strivings within one's own heart. The concern will then always be the immaculate purity of "the" woman, of the solely loved one, of one's own mother who must be protected and redeemed from the pestering of that "monster" (one's own father). (ibid., 553–54)

Drewermann points out how the Church, by inhibiting a mature development of the cleric's sexuality and by refusing to understand the psychological conflicts of its clergy, promotes much of what it otherwise prohibits in moral theology — a "masturbatory" and structurally narcissistic mentality (ibid., 563–80), a (latent) homosexual[11] atmosphere (ibid., 580–602), pedophilia (ibid., 597–98), as well as hidden and forbidden adulterous relationships which may or may not lead to a "clergy-marriage" (ibid., 603–29). He points to the approximately one-third of Roman Catholic priests in Germany who, often with the discreet knowledge of their bishops, live together with a

---

11. Drewermann comments that the Catholic Church's official condemnation of homosexuality, too, inflicts unspeakable suffering. "It seems that a time has come in which, once and for all, one will cease to see the meaning of sexuality, according to the Catholic example, essentially in procreation and therefore to condemn homosexuality as 'against nature,' and that one will simply ask what someone has been able to contribute with his possibilities, whether heterosexual or homosexual, for the enrichment of a human community" (ibid., 590).

woman "*without* causing 'offense,' " that is, without making it public by requesting a lifting of the requirement of celibacy (ibid., 647). Drewermann traces the difficult path of a cleric from an existence identified with the office (the superego) in an attempt to be saved from the "abyss of ontological anxiety" (ibid., 625) to an existence characterized by love of another human being and by individuation. This process requires the superego to enter a stage of "labor...in order to induce the birth of his ego" (ibid., 626), which implies that the cleric needs to be "especially *saved from his Savior complex*" (ibid., 629). Drewermann praises the potential virtues of the marriage of priests. "Married priests, especially, would give the Church the gift of a form of life in which the unholy separation between man and woman, body and soul, sensuousness and sensitivity, reality and promise, nature and grace, piety and experience could finally be overcome. And above all: married priests, by example, could show a way that leads from fear of humans to a faith that values the individual more than the collective and that even risks breaking certain sacred laws — rather than breaking the heart of a human being" (ibid., 636–37).

The Catholic Church's rigid emphasis on the ideal of celibacy is motivated by the sheer desire "to maintain power" since passionate love of another human being could free the clergy from the sado-masochistic Oedipal ties to "Mother Church" (ibid., 602, cf. 624). All talk of love in the Church will continue to lack credibility as long as the Church does not allow her own clergy to let that love become flesh (ibid., 612). Drewermann cries out: "A system which (for centuries!) has forced people again and again to choose between God and the love of a human being — what is this system but a really inhuman and ungodly system, because it is literally *loveless* and caught up in the purely external structures of power and administration! It is not disloyal priests who were courageous enough to 'lose' themselves to a woman against all the censorship of the superego who need to confess and repent before the system of the Catholic Church, but the Catholic Church itself is accused and has to confess before humans (and then also before God) its intentional inhumanity and mental cruelty" (ibid., 641). Addressing the structural hypocrisy he observes in the Catholic Church, Drewermann argues forcefully that the system of the Church is responsible for fostering and perpetuating sexually deviant behavior, including pedophilia. For the malicious presumption may have some reality to it, namely, "that probably the greatest impurity of heart can eventually be found in those who, under a cloak of purity, pretend to embody a higher morality. Jesus would have called such a condition that of 'whitewashed tombs' (Matt. 23:27); this condition is not, however, the individual's fault but the fault of the literally unrepentant system of the official Church" (ibid., 579).

Instead of the mentally and spiritually devastating opposition placed between love of God and love of humans, Drewermann asserts that the real choice is "always rather between love and the fear of those greedy for power over others" (ibid., 648). The finite world and eternity are not diametrically opposed. Rather the finite could become the "mirror of eternity." Tying together difficulties in marriages that may produce clerics with the metaphysicized psychological conflicts at work in the current ideal of chastity, Drewermann sums up:

> Surely one has experienced in pastoral or therapeutic conversations with spouses over many years how difficult it can be for people under the ideological influence of Catholic moral theology to learn first of all that modicum of "egoism" necessary for a marriage to succeed to some extent. And one cannot help noticing the gap between the clerical self-stylization even of the best among the Church's theologians when talking of marriage or celibacy and the reality of experience. And even: celibacy as anticipation of *death* — what kind of *life* could follow from that! Earthly life is no hurdle to jump on the way to heaven. It is the mirror of eternity into which one has to look as intensely as possible because all we can ever know of God on earth is reflected in it. Only one who has lived well will die with ease. (ibid., 519)

In summary, Drewermann argues that the evangelical counsels, as they are currently interpreted and enforced by the Church, sacrifice the individual to the terror of the collective and the ego to the rule of a relentless superego (ibid., 673), in an atmosphere which masks with holiness what is essentially neurosis (ibid., 549).

Therapeutic Treatment Suggestions

Drewermann's therapeutic suggestions focus on a reinterpretation of the evangelical counsels and a religious reorientation which must be reflected in a reform of clerical education. Effective treatment involves working through and taking back projections into the God-image of metaphysicized, repressed unconscious material in the clergy. Healing requires the Church to shift focus from the external to the internal, from the objective to the subjective, from doing to being, and from theological projections to anthropological dynamics.

He calls for a movement away from the functional interpretation of the counsels toward a personal, existential one (ibid., 669). They must be understood as attitudes which have inherent value rather than as attitudes both imposed and identified with from without. They are "grounded in the being [*Dasein*] of humans themselves, or they are literally groundless" (ibid., 672). In order to be considered authentic attitudes, the counsels cannot derive their meaning simply from the benefits they hold for others. Drewermann proposes that Christianity can learn something from other religions about the inner, spiritual meaning of the evangelical counsels.

For the Catholic Church, this essentially means giving up *psychologically* its defense against the "Protestant protest." Drewermann sees the heart of that protest not so much in some rationalistic, doctrinal quibbling over "the correct understanding of office, sacrament, tradition, and primacy [of the Pope]" but rather in the emphasis on "the significance of the subject with his experiences and feelings, miseries and fears, tragedies and hopes. Half a millennium after Martin Luther we in Roman Catholicism still do not know what fear is, that is, *we*, the clergy invested with the office, save ourselves from the fear it costs to be an individual by attaching ourselves to institutions and seemingly objective guarantees of divine salvation as if they would permittedly or even dutifully relieve us from the burden of our own existence" (ibid., 149). The real failure of the Catholic Church in dealing with Martin Luther was not so much the refusal to recognize his doctrinal objections but the inability "to see *the human being* Martin Luther — with his fears, his depressions, his pastoral [*seelsorgerlichen*] concern, his courage to speak the truth and his increasing rage against the formalism of the know-all attitude" (ibid., 148). The Church could not grant Luther that "the anxiety which he felt inside himself mirrored the anxiety of his whole period and of a whole continent" (ibid., 148).

It is this recognition of the experiencing subject, "so to speak, *the Protestant principle,* which Catholic priests lack psychologically in order to change the structure or, better even, the spiritual/intellectual [*geistige*] climate of the Catholic Church so that the mental, social, and theological double-bottomed nature of life and thought whose two levels lie unreconciled one above the other could be relinquished" (ibid., 103–4). Drewermann turns to Hegel's Protestant critique of Roman Catholic religion in support of his argument that what needs to be changed is the very "relationship of the notion of truth to reality," that is, whether the truth of reality is defined objectively with the exclusion of subjectivity or whether subjectivity is allowed to be recognized as the constituting element of the truth of reality. Hegel objected to the attitude that the sacred is known in the Roman Catholic Church as something "external," that humans are said to be unable to be in immediate unity with God but instead are told that they need chosen mediators. That attitude inevitably must reproduce "a state of externalized freedom or of internalized alienation" in the clergy (ibid., 104–5). "Hegel is right: no freedom exists as long as thinking remains external to itself" (ibid., 105). Without the subject, the attitude toward reality becomes *ungeistig,* meaning both "lacking spirit" and "lacking intellect." Drewermann emphasizes that "the challenges of the spirit in modernity, as represented validly and reliably in religion by Protestantism — that is, the turn to the subject, the breakthrough of the personal dimension, the anxiety of individuality, the postulate of freedom, the mediation of faith through encounter rather than doctrinaire instruction — have all been answered by us in Catholicism for centuries with a hardening of the institutional dimension, of the seemingly objective, official, and ritual dimensions" (ibid., 661, cf. in regard to concrete issues also ibid., 156, 195, 197, 288, 744–46). What is needed to heal the therapeutic effects of an inhuman ideal is hence a reinterpretation of the evangelical counsels in which the clergy are encouraged to live more the personal, "more the prophetic element of their 'vocation.' " This requires psychologically that they be allowed to learn "to build up a calm self-confidence and to seek the truth of the divine in their own person" (ibid., 142).

But Drewermann's protest does not throw out the baby with the bath water. We already have alluded to his criticism of the Protestant tendency toward radical iconoclasm: while he charges Catholicism with reifying the images of the psyche in superstitious and rationalized form, he is equally critical of the Protestant tendency to purge Christianity of its rich store of mythical images (culminating in Bultmann), thus emptying it of its experiential, and universally human content:

One may recognize in the images and symbols of religion most clearly the objective, "*Catholic* (sic!)" aspect of Christianity while the knowledge of the subjectivity of faith has gained shape most clearly in *Protestantism*. Both levels: the imagistic-objective dimension and the existential-subjective dimension belong together and condition each other as myth and history, the unconscious and consciousness, the id and the ego, and their separation, their political organization into two separate denominations reveal in a dramatic way how little we succeed today in the Western form of Christianity in developing an integrated form of being human in which the preexisting structures of the unconscious and the fears and hopes of personal consciousness combine in a synthesis rich with excitement.... The "whole" truth, from a psychological perspective, lies neither in the hands of the Catholic nor the Protestant Church, but solely in human wholeness — against which both denominations in their current shape sin gravely through their division. (ibid., 744–45)

The Spiritual Value of the Evangelical Counsels

Drewermann's reinterpretation of the evangelical counsels shifts the focus away from an external, objective perspective to an internal, subjective perspective that he also considers the precondition for any nonneurotic, community-strengthening secondary effects of the counsels.

Poverty and the Lack of Being

Poverty has many forms: social-material, psychological, and existential. Neither social nor psychological poverty necessarily belong to human beings. Hence these forms of poverty can and should be fought or alleviated by means of socioeconomic measures or psychotherapeutic treatments. Existential poverty, however, necessarily characterizes human existence, because, as self-conscious beings, humans are aware of their finitude (ibid., 670), or as Sartre termed it, their "lack of being." Drewermann points out that it is on the existential level that poverty becomes a religious issue. He explains that in the New Testament riches, not poverty, are a central problem, namely, riches which are used to secure and justify meaning in one's life (ibid., 679). The question underlying the counsel of poverty is: "How can a person be saved from clinging to material goods as though they were her or his salvation?" (ibid., 680). The counsel of poverty does not idealize material poverty as such, rather it aims at the "right amount" of possessions (ibid.). The goal of the counsel of poverty is to learn to accept one's "poverty of being" (ibid., 682). The counsel can, therefore, only grow from within one's spirit, in an atmosphere of trust in one's being, a trust that can be experienced in the accepting presence of a God who affirms one's existence. Poverty in this sense does not eradicate one's sense of self. It strengthens the ego and breaks the compulsion to use material possessions as compensation for a poverty of being. Such an understanding of poverty could also free people to give up material riches and share them with those in need (ibid., 670). Drewermann emphasizes that this is a more effective way of eradicating poverty in the world than are the moralistic appeals, which only reinforce the power of the superego and do not really result in a freely chosen sharing with the materially poor. The Christian religion can learn much from the Buddhist understanding of poverty (ibid., 354, 720).

Obedience and Listening to the Self

Drewermann contrasts the traditional understanding of the ideal of obedience, which means basically one's obedience to the superego (the collective), with an obedience which does not require disobedience to one's being. The counsel of obedience is meant to help a person to listen to and obey one's very being. Listening to one's inner nature will help one to better listen to external nature (ibid., 697). Obedience to God does not contradict obedience to oneself. And only when one has learned to listen to God in the depth of one's own being will one be able to listen to others in such a way that God speaks to them (ibid., 699). The psychotherapeutic way of listening serves as Drewermann's model for such listening (ibid., 701). He suggests that Christians could learn much from Muslim religious texts in terms of what obedience to God could mean (ibid., 707).

Chastity and the Experience of Unconditional Love

With regard to the counsel of chastity, Drewermann calls for a separation of the notion of chastity from the notion of an unmarried life (ibid., 721). Having witnessed in his psychoanalytic work the unresolved conflicts which commonly lead to the obsession with and repression of sexuality in the psyches of the clergy, he calls for an end to the fixation of this counsel around the taboo of celibacy. Currently, a time in which youth has turned from a morality of conservation

[*Bewahrung*] to a morality of proof [*Bewährung*], Drewermann calls on the Church to stop obliging its clergy to an asexual life. Instead it should allow the individual cleric to follow her or his personal development in choosing either a married or unmarried lifestyle (ibid., 716). Drewermann believes that the Roman Catholic Church does not want its priests to be married because love would make them independent from the Church. If they were in love, the heart of the clergy could not be controlled by a system that wants to control them absolutely — in the name of God. At the same time, Drewermann calls for the ordination of women priests (ibid., 738). The criterion for admitting a person to ordination should be inner maturity, not the person's sex or marital status (ibid., 715). Drewermann predicts that the Church will have to make major adjustments if it wants to avoid becoming merely one sect among many others.

Chastity can be learned from the psychotherapist-client situation: the therapist does not want anything from the client for herself or himself, but is genuinely interested in the maturation and growth of the client (ibid., 724). It is within an experience of such love that "concepts such as *duty* and *loyalty*" could also be understood in nonviolent fashion, namely, as grown from true love (ibid., 474). The clergy can also learn from poets what it means to love, since poets are among the few who realize that we are but travelers on earth, and that no one person can ever be the property of another, whether married or not (ibid., 720). Christians could learn much from Hindus about a healthier attitude toward sexuality and toward nature in general (ibid.).

Religious Reorientation and Reform of the Education of the Clergy

Drewermann closes *Kleriker* with some thoughts about a turning point in the history of religion (ibid., 730). He compares the Church to "a leukemia patient" (ibid., 731) who urgently needs a revitalization and reintegration through poetry and depth psychology. The Church has not yet sufficiently responded to the two major challenges issued by Karl Marx and Sigmund Freud. In response to Marx's assertion that religion is merely a false human attitude toward nature, the Church must demonstrate that religion can make a vital contribution in reconnecting the human species to nature. In response to Freud, who fleshed out Feuerbach's objection that belief in God is merely a projection, the Church must prove that religion does not reflect a consciousness that is being tyrannized by an overstrict superego, but that, on the contrary, religion is a function of the ego (ibid., 732). The Church must undo "the poisoning of *Eros*," of which Nietzsche rightly accused Christianity (ibid., 743). What is needed is a "synthesis which revives the concern for religious myths on a higher plane of spiritual mediation and which again integrates humans into nature, within a frame of an integral world-interpretation" (ibid., 732). The Church must still learn that the appropriate way of glorifying God lies in a "condensation of human existence" and that nature can once more become a "place of autochthonous experience of God" (ibid., 739).

The curriculum for education of the clergy should integrate sciences such as modern psychology, behavioral sciences, history of religions, and cultural anthropology. The clergy should be encouraged to develop a higher level of self-awareness. They should learn the common language of all religions which is the language of images. Theological education should be an experiential space in which clerics can interact with these images (ibid., 744). If the Church wants to survive and be true to the attitude of Jesus, then it needs to give up its one-sided objectivism and take the subject, the reality of the human person, as the point of departure for its contemplations (ibid., 715). Instead of identifying the subject with the office, the Church should be flexible in regard to the understanding of the office; that understanding should be tailored to the personal developments of the particular cleric. Drewermann calls for a religion that begins with the individual and shapes social and church structures in a way that respects the right of the individual to mature. He calls for a social order in which "the pyramid of status and power is built from below rather than from above" (ibid., 748). This, of course, threatens the current power structure in the Church. But, contends Drewermann, without such a power shift there will be no life-giving change (ibid.).

Conclusion

The German follower-mentality during the Third Reich is the historical backdrop for Drewermann's critique of a follower-mentality in matters of faith by religious institutions in general and his own Roman Catholic Church in particular. The discussion of Drewermann's therapeutic liberation theology for the West entered the limelight of public opinion in Europe during the tumultuous time of German reunification which saw in the political sphere what Drewermann came to symbolize in the religious sphere: the refusal of the individual to be suppressed in his authentic self-expression by the rule of the collective. This has stirred up a vivid public debate in Europe about the role of religion for the individual and the community. Drewermann argues that religion promotes a healthy and moral community best when the concrete, living individual is permitted by the collective to feel psychologically and spiritually healthy and true to herself.

In the center of Drewermann's work is a study of how human fear is the motor behind the individual's disappearance into the collective and how the self-reflective human spirit creates from the archetypal images of the psyche culturally conditioned violent God-images, which metaphysicize, usually in the name of the common good, claims of one group against another, of humans against nature, of men against women, of Church officials against lay people. While developing a new theological anthropology, Drewermann dialectically integrates findings from major anthropological sciences: psychology, anthropology, sociology, philosophy. The thrust of his multifaceted work can be seen in light of the postwar slogan "Never again!," that is, never again violence, oppression, and exploitation in the name of God. His mission is to counter fear-inducing violent God-images by reinterpreting biblical texts and Christian doctrines in such a way that they strengthen and defend the individual through an experience of trust against the pull and the annihilating force of the collective.

As Drewermann embarked on his work as a priest in the 1960s he began to realize that people are pervasively made to feel guilty in the name of a violent God-image and sacrificial theology simply for wanting happiness in their own life. He began to challenge age-old tendencies within Christianity that see God's will and human will as naturally opposed to each other and stresses against these inclinations that only the spell of fear makes God appear in distorted form as the ultimate opponent instead of the ultimate giver of life. Faith restores through an experience of ultimate trust the sense of self-worth which formerly was threatened with annihilation by a violent God-image. Drewermann presents a theology in which love of God and love of self are not seen as opposed to each other, but rather as two sides of the same experiential process. Similarly, he argues that love of self and love of others is not mutually exclusive as ingrained notions of Christian sacrifice, especially for the clergy, would suggest, but that constructive, noninfantilizing, and nonpaternalizing love of others requires healthy love of self. In Freudian language, Drewermann argues that religion is not an affair between God and the superego, but is rather an ego function, expresses a relation between the ego and God in the search for absolute personal psychospiritual meaning in life.

Drewermann's theological work is an attempt to understand and overcome a type of theology that imposes and reinforces a violent God-image, weakens and sacrifices the individual, and endows the collective with quasi-religious qualities. The primacy of grace and the key importance of images are at the heart of Drewermann's therapeutic theology. In his first theological work, *Strukturen des Bösen,* we have an analysis of the psychospiritual dynamics in which personal, existential anxiety snowballs into (radical) evil through a vicious cycle of loss of trust, aggression, repression, feelings of guilt and shame, failed attempts at reparation, and the eventual projection of the inner sense of worthlessness into the external world through an escalating spiral of violence against the Other in human community and the natural world. Within that spiral of anxiety all attempts to do good, even and especially in the name of God, lead through a dynamic of counter-finality into the opposite of their consciously intended result of creating peace. Drewermann came to see the spiral of violence as an attempt to somehow answer absolute longings for self-worth and recognition by finite means, or, to put it differently: as an attempt to endow what is relative, for example, a group, a country, an ideology, or a leader, with absolute meaning.

Existentialism provides Drewermann with the tools to analyze the problem of evil as the result of spiritual [*geistigen*] attitudes. It allows him to understand the process of depersonalization through which the world is turned into a slaughter house of humanity. But he finds existentialism wanting when it comes to the question how the spiral of anxiety could be turned around. Existentialism helps us see the abyss of fear clearly and confirms to Drewermann the intuition that a bridge over that abyss requires a religious solution: such a bridge can, theologically speaking, only be created by an absolute, good person, God, who provides hold to humans and calms their depersonalizing anxiety by assuring them that each of them is absolutely wanted and justified to exist. But having said this, he notes that religion and talk of an absolute person, of God, are themselves too often used to widen rather than bridge the abyss of fear.

To understand the concrete affective and symbolic manifestations of the human spirit's fear that leads to the unintended and violent uses of God-images, Drewermann argues that theology can learn from psychoanalysis. His search for a way out of the spiral of anxiety and violence led him as a theologian to discover psychoanalysis, which also made the struggle for a nonviolent God-image emotionally and spiritually poignant for him personally. He entered a psychoanalytic training program initially with the notion that he was studying psychoanalysis for others. Psychoanalysis helped him experience that the conflict between a judgmental, sacrificial attitude and an understanding, life-affirming attitude was not only something he faced in his dealings with others but something he had to solve within himself. Psychoanalysis challenged the whole notion upon which Drewermann had created his identity since childhood: the ideal of being-for-others at the expense of self and, with this, the sacrificial theology which supported that ideal. Psychoanalysis questioned a violent God-image which turned the God of Jesus effectively into the blood-thirsty image of God portrayed in the Aztec god Tonatiuh or the castrative image of the Near Eastern cult of the mother goddess Cybele. Psychoanalysis allowed him to analyze the whole ideology of sadomasochistic suffering associated with the Christian imagery of the Cross. Drewermann learned that he had to permit himself to live truly as himself before he could help others truly live rather than simply live as an official with a mission of being-for-others. He had to leave the ivory tower of an elitist, rationalistic view of priesthood shrouded in self-sacrificial being-for-otherness and discover a faith from below both in the sense of emerging from the people and in personal relationship and from the archetypal imagery of the unconscious.

But the type of psychoanalysis in which Drewermann was trained in the late 1960s questioned a part of his identity he was not willing to give up. While theology appeared to him soulless and in need of revitalization by the discoveries of the unconscious and the insights of transference experiences, psychoanalysis appeared to him godless and atheist for understandable reasons. The tension between the two became so pronounced that Drewermann left his psychoanalytic training uncompleted and began to deconstruct the theological ideology of sacrifice by means of psychoanalysis and existential philosophy. In his struggle to draw consequences from the permission psychoanalysis gave to his own happiness, to a healthy egoism as opposed to the theological prohibition of such happiness in the name of a God-commanded self-sacrifice, he engaged in working through on an intellectual/spiritual level the implications of the psychoanalytic insight that it is unconscious fear in relation to oneself and others which keeps humans from being themselves; this fear paralyzes one's whole existence through reaction-formations and defense mechanisms. This shift found expression in his call to the Church to continue and deepen the anthropological turn in theology from object to subject, which, for instance, Karl Rahner represented. Drewermann argues for a shift from theological projection of human dynamics into the metaphysical realm to an anthropological analysis of that projection so that the God-image can be cleansed of ambivalent psychospiritual dynamics under the spell of fear. Theologically, his work is an attempt to account for the anthropological element of revelation, for the human process in the encounter with the divine. The psychoanalytic concept of transference serves him as a model to understand the complex nature of human perception of the divine. Drewermann attempts to de-demonize the image of both humans and God in Christianity and in the secularized domains influenced by Christianity.

Drewermann's underlying assumption is that God as such is the creative and unambivalently good ground of human existence as portrayed in the story of paradise. Everything that follows after the unity between God and humans is destroyed presents the inadvertent human distortion of this original God-image, the attempts of humans to recover that original harmony, and the human experiences of God's attempts to help them recover that original harmony. Instead of reifying the fall as a necessary step in the process of becoming human, as modern philosophical and psychological interpretations have tended to do, Drewermann argues that a theological interpretation has to show that the fall is not necessary even if it is a universal human experience. Drewermann uses the transference model of psychoanalysis to show how the texts tell us about human transferences of intrapsychic and intraspiritual dynamics onto God. He argues that a theology which neglects these transference dynamics has been and will always be in danger of reifying violent God-images which are, however, nothing but the amalgam of psychological fears infinitized through spiritual projections onto the divine.

The very writing of *Strukturen des Bösen* — and of all of Drewermann's writings and speeches — was an exercise, in the sense of Erik Erikson, of trying "to solve for all what he could not solve for himself alone" (Erikson 1958, 67): Drewermann was working through for himself *and* for others a moralistic notion of original sin and of the corresponding violent God-image in the name of which complete self-renunciation and the sacrifice of one's "proud will" had been demanded for centuries. He attempts to reinterpret the notion of sin nonmoralistically, nonjudgmentally. He makes fear on all its levels — ethological, psychological, sociological, existential-philosophical, and theological — the central focus of his analysis. He explains how the fears psychoanalysis uncovers become infinitized by the human spirit and therefore first gain the absolute quality seen, for instance, in self-mutilation in the psyches of ideal clerics, or in the horrific mass destruction of others, for example, in the Third Reich, communism, and the use of nuclear bombs. Drewermann's exegetical analysis of the story of the fall and its psychoanalytic and existential-theological interpretation argue that the first pages of the Judeo-Christian Scriptures, if carefully read, indicate that human fear is, in a sense, at the root of all human evil, of sin, and of its interpersonal and societal, even global consequences. In a walk through modern psychology and philosophy, he elucidates the theological notion that sin, understood in light of the human spirit's absolute fears, is both universal and the result of free choice, and hence not necessary.

In works that analyze the sociopolitical consequences of a (secularized) violent God-image, Drewermann applies his findings to the study of moral-theological issues of war and ecological exploitation. He presents an intellectual-historical analysis which finds that the

Early Church, in its struggle for survival, departed more and more
from Jesus' poetic religion, shaped by parables, which integrated feelings and reason, body and spirit, and replaced it with an increasingly
one-sided emphasis on rationality. Hand in hand with this one-sided
rationality emerged a tacit ethical reductionism that culminated in a
secularized version in Kant's view of moral religion. Drewermann's
sociopolitical analysis of the history of Christianity led him to conclude that it inadvertently gave birth to a type of human who creates
objective evil and suffering in the name of subjective good, as exemplified in the follower-mentality of the Christian nation of Germans
during the Nazi regime. At work in this counter-finality of aim and
result is a deep skepticism toward the image-creating layers of the
human psyche, coupled with the human spirit's absolute fears of
meaninglessness which together make human reason itself go mad
and turn it into a henchman of primitive repressed aggressions that
the weak ego now can no longer control. War in the name of peace
and the exploitation of nature in the name of creating a better world
are prime instances in which Drewermann sees the effects of the one-
sidedly rational and anthropocentric heritage of the Judeo-Christian
tradition. In addition, Drewermann argues that this heritage carried
within it unintended seeds of secularization and spawned modern
atheism when its rationality turned against itself. Sociopolitically, the
task of religion is to calm the deep-seated fears of the human spirit
which fuel war and exploitation. Peace and the end of the exploitation
of inner and outer nature are possible when Christianity abandons its
hostility toward the nonrational aspects of the human psyche as has
been attempted, he observes, especially through the work of women
in Christianity. A sacrificial attitude is the result of an experience of
loss of absolute ground after the God-image has been distorted by
fear and an attempt to regain the lost ground through one's own
sacrifices. Following his analysis of the sadomasochistic effects of an
ideology of sacrifice in the Christian tradition that tends to obliterate
the sense of self in the individual, Drewermann proposes a paradoxical reinterpretation of the notion of sacrifice that is in the service of
the individual's spiritual growth and that has truly peaceful social implications: it is a self constructed on the basis of a one-sidedly rational
and anthropocentric perspective due to fear which has to be sacrificed
so that the self as created by God can emerge. It is in this context
that Drewermann sees the idea of sacrifice appropriate. His analysis

of the clergy-ideal exemplifies this critique and reinterpretation of the Christian notion of sacrifice.

Drewermann's analysis of sin in light of human fear goes hand in hand with a recovery of trust as the essential dimension of faith. A central theme of his work is that humans cannot be good if they are under a spell of fear, or, expressed theologically, if they have lost sight of God or the God-image has become distorted by fear. Here is where Drewermann's "Trojan horse" enters into the well-fortified domain of Christian moral theology: if people are not whole [*heil*] then it is inhuman to judge them and punish them as if they were whole; it would amount to a kind of Pelagianism to expect from people who are under the spell of fear, of sin, to live up to God's will through efforts of their own will. Drewermann reproaches moral theology for not taking seriously its own professed doctrine of original sin by assuming that simply by becoming a member of the Church (through infant baptism) humans would be capable of observing "the" moral law. Based on his psychotherapeutic work with clients who struggled at times to the point of becoming suicidal with the moralistic interpretation of the Christian faith, Drewermann presents his plea for a more humane Church and a therapeutic interpretation of the Christian faith that calms rather than heightens psychospiritual fears.

Drewermann's reinterpretation of faith in terms of trust takes its departure from the portrayal of the person of Jesus in the gospels. Employing the depth-psychological paradigms of transference (Freud) and of archetypal psychic structures (Jung), Drewermann reinterprets the central symbol of Christianity, the Cross, in a nonmasochistic way, and recovers a nonviolent God-image which is experienced in concrete history in relationships of profound trust. The conflict which led to Jesus' death is seen not as something confined to the past but as a principal conflict, a perspective which avoids the notorious anti-Jewish tendencies of traditional Christian interpretations of the Cross: Jesus spoke up against a *type* of religion, found universally, in which a violent God-image is used by an elite of religious leaders to control the people in the name of God. Jesus' death was not a sacrifice of self but, to the contrary, was the result of Jesus' living his true self without fear of what humans can do. For that reason Jesus as a person could become such a powerful figure and be connected with the archetypal imagery of the savior of all humanity. By questioning a violent God-image, the Jesus of the gospels came in conflict with both secular and religious leaders whose power was threatened by a nonviolent God-image. According to Drewermann, Jesus faced the Cross not because he wanted to suffer but because he wanted to put into practice to the very end what he had preached and practiced his whole life: that fear will not have the last word, that he would resist a type of piety found in all religions that kills rather than promotes life. Rather than giving in to that inhuman type of religiosity due to fear, Jesus refused to compromise his image of God as unconditionally accepting. That is why the Cross became a symbol of strength. The crucifixion, in itself a horrendous deed, became a symbol for a nonviolent God as it became psychospiritually connected with the deepest human aggressions as well as spiritual longings: God can bear all the worst aggressions which humans would otherwise direct against each other; God does not seek revenge, will not destroy humans; God gives unconditional acceptance, can be trusted, and thus allows the experiential undoing and prevention of the infinitization of human aggression, as symbolically expressed in the eating of the Godhead (e.g., the Eucharist).

In my presentation of major ideas of Eugen Drewermann's work, I have indicated, though without further elaboration, that his revamping of Christian theology in light of psychoanalysis and the human sciences is occasioned both by the experience of the concrete suffering of people under the moralism of church authorities and by the failure of Christianity to prevent the Nazi regime as well as its inadvertent support for the collective ideology of the Third Reich.

At a time when notions of sacrifice in the name of God or the collective are invoked in terrorism and in the fight against terrorism, the work of Drewermann provides us with analytic tools that help us understand from a theological perspective the psychospiritual roots of terrorism and of responses to terrorism that, despite subjectively the best intentions, are often bound, under a spell of fear, to increase rather than reduce the threats and deadly effects of terrorism. Terror and war in the name of God, or of a quasi-divinized collective, is the ultimate result of a God-image distorted by fear: it is the final moral effort to right the world in the name of a God who is reduced to a moral lawgiver and seen as on the side of some humans while against others.

Appendix 1

Drewermann in America

The controversy around Drewermann's silencing and suspension, which received considerable attention in the European mass media and public, did not make many waves in the American media at the time. Somewhat successfully, Rome contained the global waves of the conflict by making it an affair between Drewermann and his direct superior, the archbishop of Paderborn. Some note was taken of it in the English-speaking world despite the Vatican strategy of regionalizing the conflict. *Time International* magazine ran a book review of Drewermann's bestselling book *Kleriker* (8 January 1990). In response to the Church's silencing of Drewermann, an article by Marguerite Johnson appeared in *Time International* on 24 August 1992 presenting Drewermann as a modern Martin Luther (Johnson 1992). The *Boston Globe* printed a Reuters news clip which announced that Drewermann "is the first German theologian ever to have been suspended" as a priest. He was cited as questioning "whether Jesus physically rose from the dead and whether Mary was a virgin" and as "a fierce critic of what he regards as authoritarianism in the Catholic church" (*Boston Globe,* 27 March 1992). An article in the *Los Angeles Times*, 26 December 1996, describing the trend of people leaving the Roman Catholic Church for the "Rome-free" Old Catholic Church, which was founded in 1870 after Pope Pius IX succeeded in making papal infallibility a formal and binding church doctrine, calls Drewermann the "most widely read dissident Catholic theologian in the German language today" and quotes him commenting on the drastic decline in membership in the Roman Catholic Church: "The path of this decline is long, and it appears to be irreversible" (Walsh 1996).

In academic circles in the United States, interest in Drewermann's work has emerged only gradually. The first mention I found was a long and very favorable review of volume 3 of *Strukturen des Bösen* by S. T. Kimbrough, Jr., in the *Journal of Biblical Literature*

(Kimbrough 1982). Why the far-reaching public controversy around Drewermann, which kept the European public and media in suspense from 1989 to 1992, received practically no coverage in the U.S. news media and no response from religious scholars, remains a puzzle. One of the few theological magazines in the United States which noted the official silencing and suspension from priesthood of Drewermann in 1992 was the *Christian Century* (3 June 1992). The first English translation of a Drewermann book was in 1991, titled *Open Heavens: Meditations for Advent and Christmas* (1991g), followed by two books with rather unfortunate English titles: *Discovering the Royal Child Within: A Spiritual Psychology of "The Little Prince"* (1993f), and *Discovering the God Child Within: A Spiritual Psychology of the Infancy of Jesus* (1994b). Though the last two books aim, no doubt, at connecting readers with their own inner world, neither remains "within" but emphasizes the key importance of the interpersonal dimension of love. The first title is a depth-psychological study of the modern tale of the Little Prince, firmly grounded in an analysis of Saint-Exupéry's biography and work and in his particular historical location. The second title is a depth-psychological interpretation of the infancy stories in the Gospel according to Luke, grounded in historical-critical scholarship and tracing the influence of Egyptian mythology on the development of major Christian doctrines. The original German title bespeaks the poetic density of the book: "your name is like the taste of life," a line taken from an ancient Egyptian poem (see Drewermann 1994b, 148). *Dying We Live: Meditations for Lent and Easter* is the fourth and to date last English title published by Drewermann (1994c [original German title: 1991k]). All four titles apply the method of depth-psychological and *daseinsanalytic* interpretation to religious or fairy-tale texts as developed by Drewermann in *Tiefenpsychologie und Exegese* (Depth Psychology and Exegesis) (1984a, 1985b). Sporadic reviews of Drewermann titles have appeared in English language journals in the 1990s (see Carl 1992, 1994; Engelhardt 1994, 1998).

While I inquired into possibilities for the U.S. publication of some of Drewermann's major works, such as *Kleriker* (1990a) or *Tiefenpsychologie und Exegese* (1984a, 1985b), the politically sensitive ramifications his work would have in the Roman Catholic landscape in the United States became evident. An editor from a Catholic publisher wrote to me with respect to *Kleriker:* "[Our publishing house] remains an organization under the control of the clerical *Aparat* [sic!], whose pathologies Drewermann unveils!... Were we to do these books, they would quickly become a matter of major crisis within [our community], and [our publishing house] might well end up a casualty" (pers. communication, 29 Oct. 1996). Fear of a major crisis within American Catholicism is thus one of the factors that has prevented the English publication of *Kleriker*, a book translated into nearly a dozen languages, including Spanish and Portuguese.

Academic conferences in the United States began to recognize Drewermann in 1995 when Dr. Bernhard Lang, professor of religion at the University of Paderborn, presented a paper titled "A New Voice in Psychological Exegesis: Eugen Drewermann" as part of a session of the Psychology and Biblical Studies Group at the Annual Meeting of the Society for Biblical Literature (SBL), the world's largest association of biblical scholars, followed in March 1998 by my paper at the Mid-Atlantic Regional Meeting of the American Academy of Religion (AAR) titled "Embodying Hermeneutics: Eugen Drewermann's Depth Psychological Interpretation of Religious Symbols." The Fourth International Jaspers Conference, in conjunction with the Twentieth World Congress of Philosophy, held in Boston, Massachusetts, August 10–16, 1998, featured a lecture by Hermann-Josef Seideneck titled "Das komplementäre Spannungsgefüge von Wissen und Glaube in konkret-geschichtlicher Perspektive: Bultmann-Jaspers-Drewermann" (The Dynamic Complementary Unit of Knowledge and Faith in Concrete-historical Perspective: Bultmann-Jaspers-Drewermann). Following an online discussion of Drewermann's ideas within the community of the Psychology and Biblical Studies Group of the SBL, its chairperson at the time, Dr. Wayne Rollins, asked me to coordinate a session dedicated to Drewermann's work, titled "Depth Psychology and Exegesis: The Work of Eugen Drewermann," at the Annual Meeting of the SBL in 1998 in Orlando, Florida. Three native Germans familiar with Drewermann's work, Bernhard Lang, Annette Esser (a German doctoral student at Union Theological Seminary at the time), and myself, were invited to present papers. Unfortunately, Esser had to withdraw at the last minute for personal reasons. Her paper was to look at bibliodrama's use of Drewermann's poetic theology. In place of her presentation, I read a translation of one of Drewermann's interpretation of the healing story of the woman with a hemorrhage to illustrate his hermeneutics. Wayne Rollins presided over the session. Respondents were David L. Miller, Margaret G. Alter and R. Todd Wise.

In the fall of 1999 I organized Drewermann's first lectures in the United States. He had previously spoken in Canada at the University of Montreal and to the Goethe-Institute, Montreal, in October 1997. The November 1999 lectures revolved around the theme Biblical Myth and Inner Experience: Why Theology Needs Depth Psychology. Drewermann spoke to audiences at Union Theological Seminary, New York, Drew University, Madison, N.J., Princeton Theological Seminary, Princeton, N.J., and Grace Counseling Center, Madison, N.J. In February 2000, Drewermann gave his first lectures in Mexico City, after recent translations began to stir interest in Spanish- and Portuguese-speaking countries (Drewermann 2001).

Appendix 2

A Note on Translation

All translations of Drewermann's work are by the author unless otherwise indicated. A few words on the translation are necessary.

Translating gendered words from German into English is tricky in many cases, especially generic terms such as *der Mensch* (the human being, m.) or *die Person* (the person, f.). To make the translation as smooth as possible, I have either adopted the plural which does not require an article or alternate between the use of masculine and feminine personal pronouns. Though it may appear at times cumbersome, I have often translated *der Mensch* with "the human being" rather than "a person" and *die Menschen* with "human beings" rather than "people" simply because Drewermann frequently emphasizes the human and individual quality by using these terms ("person," for instance, can also refer to the divine person; "people" has a more collective sense to it than "human beings").

The terms *menschlich* and *Menschlichkeit* are rendered respectively as human or humane and humanity or humaneness. They refer for Drewermann to a way of life characterized by trust and compassion and approximate a sense of peace with self and others in contrast to a way of life under the spell of fear which is compulsively violent to self and others.

Drewermann's writings gain a dynamic aliveness not only through his broad vocabulary and the precision with which he chooses words but also through the use of emphatic words such as *gerade* (precisely, especially...), *durchaus* (by all means, downright...), *geradezu* (downright...). At times an English rendition of the equivalents of these emphatic particles would interrupt the flow of the English text. The translation therefore omits such words where appropriate without indicating so every single time.

Drewermann frequently uses the word *geistig*, which can mean both "intellectual" (as, for instance, in *geistige Arbeit*, i.e., intellectual work) or "spiritual" (as in *geistige Verbindung,* i.e., spiritual connection). He hardly ever uses the word *geistlich,* which shares roots with *geistig* but clearly has religious connotations. The clergy, for instance, are called *Geistliche.* Drewermann's preference for *geistig* is no accident, but an expression of his belief that matters of the spirit find expression far beyond what is commonly known as religious. Since the word *geistig* often connotes both spiritual and intellectual meaning, I will frequently translate it by "intellectual/spiritual" or "spiritual/intellectual."

The word "religious" in English is often clearly differentiated from "spiritual," the former pertaining commonly to *institutional* religion, the latter to an individual's profound subjective experience. In German, the word *religiös* does not necessarily fit this distinction, but can be used in a wider sense as an equivalent for the English "spiritual." Drewermann often uses the word "religious" in a wider sense of the word. He uses the words "religion" and "religious" not only in reference to organized religion. Religion rather is a function of the essential longing for the absolute that springs from the human spirit's characteristic self-awareness with its capacity for infinite regress. Drewermann defines the "essence of religion" as the ability and the process that frees the events and objects of what we commonly call the "real," that is, the physical, material world, from their earthly, finite confinement and transforms them into symbols for the infinite (1994b, 31 [1986c, 26]). His use of the words *religiös* or *Religion* thus are not confined to institutional religion but rather encompasses any concern with ultimate questions. Since the English word "spiritual" does not necessarily have to concern ultimate questions but can equally pertain to relative value questions, I will translate *religiös* with "religious" and ask the reader to bear in mind that in Drewermann's usage it has broader meaning as pertaining to the human spirit's longing for the absolute — however that longing may manifest itself.

Reflecting his attempt to root religious imagery in human evolutionary development, Drewermann uses the terms *Psyche* (psyche) and *Seele* (soul) interchangeably. The common use of the word *seelisch,* for instance in *Seelenkrankheiten* (mental illnesses), often connotes both a psychological and a spiritual element. I thus will translate *seelisch* at times by "mental" or "spiritual" or by "mental/spiritual."

Throughout this book the word *Halt* has been translated with the noun "hold." This important concept in Drewermann's theology seems to connote three aspects emphasizing either the subject or the object involved in the experience described: finding reliable holding in someone ("hold" provided by object); having a firm foothold or ground in contrast to falling (emphasis on subject's passive experience); and having a grip on life, reality, God, person (emphasis on subject's active experience). In the first sense, the word resembles the concept of "holding" in object relations theory. But the word "holding" then mainly refers to the environment or object providing holding rather than to the sense of "hold" which the held person, the subject, experiences. The word *Halt* says something about both the object which provides holding and the subject which feels securely held and holds onto somebody or something.

The word "sin" has pejorative meaning and is commonly associated with doing something wrong. It is frequently understood as a moral category and then associated with moralistic connotations. Drewermann attempts to redefine the term. He wants to free it from its judgmental connotation and use it theologically in order to *understand* the human condition phenomenologically. Without this in mind, we may easily misunderstand Drewermann's use of the term.

Drewermann's use of the word "faith" is not to be confused with belief in a certain set of dogmas. His understanding of faith is radically relational and personal. The essence of faith is an existential experience of trust in the value of one's existence and in the goodness of creation based on a sense of being ultimately wanted by an absolutely good person, God. Faith is the experience of absolute trust: on the one hand, the experience that an absolutely good person, God, puts her trust into our existence, and on the other, the experience evoked by that affirmation of our existence, that is, our trust in the divine. Faith is the experience of the calming of the existential fear of the human spirit in relation to a being who transcends (our) nothingness.

To distinguish between Freudian and Jungian interpretations, Drewermann employs the terms *objektal* and *subjektal*. *Objektal* refers to an object-related perspective, while *subjektal* to an intrapsychic or intraspiritual perspective. I will translate *objektal* in accordance with the terminology used in the English translation of Jung's works as "objective level" and *subjektal* as "subjective level" (Jung 1966b, 84).

When a quotation from one of Drewermann's works contains a reference to a German edition of a work by another author, I have, where available, provided reference to the English edition of the cited author's work. Where no English translation is published, I have provided the translation.

Works Cited

Works by Eugen Drewermann

1971   Gott der Natur — Gott der Offenbarung — Gegensätze?: Zwischen Shiva und Christus. (God of Nature — God of Revelation — Contradictions?: Between Shiva and Christ). *Theologie und Glaube* 61:320–35.

1979   *Die Symbolik von Baum und Kreuz in religionsgeschichtlicher und tiefenpsychologischer Betrachtung (unter besonderer Berücksichtigung der mittelamerikansichen Bilderhandschriften)* (The Symbolism of Tree and Cross from a History of Religions and a Depth Psychological Perspective [With Particular Consideration of Meso-American Iconographic Manuscripts]). Schwerte: Katholische Akademie.

1981   Kirche in der zweiten Hälfte unseres Jahrhunderts: Weitergabe und Probleme religiösen Lebens in Deutschland (The Church in the Second Half of Our Century: Transmission and Problems of Religious Life in Germany). In *Psychoanalyse und Moraltheologie.* Vol. 3, *An den Grenzen des Lebens,* 237–50. 4th ed. Mainz: Matthias-Grünewald.

1984a   *Tiefenpsychologie und Exegese.* Vol. 1, *Die Wahrheit der Formen: Traum, Mythos, Märchen, Sage und Legende* (Depth Psychology and Exegesis. Vol. 1, The Truth of Forms: Dream, Myth, Fairy Tale, Saga, and Legend). Olten: Walter. (1st special ed. 1991).

1984b   *Das Eigentliche ist unsichtbar: Der Kleine Prinz tiefenpsychologisch gedeutet* (English: 1993f) Freiburg I. Br.: Herder.

1985a   [1977] *Strukturen des Bösen.* Vol. 2, *Die jahwistische Urgeschichte in psychoanalytischer Sicht* (Structures of Evil. Vol. 2, The Yahwist Primordial History from a Psychoanalytic Perspective). 5th ed. Paderborn: Schöningh.

English translations of the titles of untranslated German works are given in parentheses following the original German title. Works of Drewermann that have appeared in more than one edition or that were later collated in anthologies — as is the case with many articles — are listed by the edition cited while the year of original publication or presentation (in the case of previously unpublished lectures) is added in brackets [ ].

1985b   *Tiefenpsychologie und Exegese.* Vol. 2, *Die Wahrheit der Werke und
           der Worte: Wunder, Vision, Weissagung, Apokalypse, Geschichte,
           Gleichnis.* (Depth Psychology and Exegesis. Vol. 2, The Truth
           of Deeds and Words: Miracles, Visions, Prophecies, Apocalypses,
           History, Parable). Olten: Walter. (1st special ed. 1991).

1985c   [1981] *Das Mädchen ohne Hände* (The Girl without Hands).
           Illustrated by Ingritt Neuhaus. 6th ed. Olten: Walter.

1986a   [1977] *Strukturen des Bösen.* Vol. 1, *Die jahwistische Urgeschichte in
           exegetischer Sicht* (Structures of Evil. Vol. 1, The Yahwist Primordial
           History from an Exegetical Perspective). 6th ed. Paderborn: Schöningh.

1986b   [1978] *Strukturen des Bösen.* Vol. 3, *Die jahwistische Urgeschichte
           in philosophischer Sicht* (Structures of Evil. Vol. 3, The Yahwist
           Primordial History from a Philosophical Perspective). 5th ed.
           Paderborn: Schöningh.

1986c   *Dein Name ist wie der Geschmack des Lebens: Tiefenpsychologische
           Deutung der Kindheitsgeschichte nach dem Lukasevangelium* (English:
           1994b). Freiburg: Herder.

1986d   "Der Mythos vom Ursprung des Bösen" (The Myth of the Origin of
           Evil). In *Wovon werden wir morgen geistig leben?: Mythos, Religion
           und Wissenschaft in der "Postmoderne": Referate und Diskussionen
           des 13. Salzburger Humanismusgespräch held in Salzburg 28–30.
           September 1986.* Ed. by Oskar Schatz and Hans Spatzenegger,
           155–70. Salzburg: Anton Pustet.

1986e   "Diskussion: Paul Ricoeur, Eugen Drewermann" (Discussion: Paul
           Ricoeur, Eugen Drewermann). In *Wovon werden wir morgen geistig
           leben?: Mythos, Religion und Wissenschaft in der "Postmoderne":
           Referate und Diskussionen des 13. Salzburger Humanismusgespräch
           held in Salzburg 28–30. September 1986.* Ed. by Oskar Schatz and
           Hans Spatzenegger, 171–81. Salzburg: Anton Pustet.

1988   *"An ihren Früchten sollt ihr sie erkennen": Antwort auf Rudolf
           Peschs und Gerhard Lohfinks "Tiefenpsychologie und keine Exegese"*
           ("Know Them by Their Fruits": Reply to Rudolf Pesch's and Gerhard
           Lohfink's "Depth Psychology and No Exegesis"). Olten: Walter.

1989a   *Wort des Heils, Wort der Heilung: Gespräche und Interviews.* Vol. 1,
           Von der befreienden Kraft des Glaubens (Words of Wholeness, Words
           of Healing: Conversations and Interviews. Vol. 1, On the Liberating
           Power of Kaith). Ed. by B. Marz. 4th ed. Düsseldorf: Patmos.

1989b   *Wort des Heils, Wort der Heilung: Gespräche und Interviews.*
           Vol. 2, *Reden von Gott* (Words of Wholeness, Words of Healing:

Conversations and Interviews. Vol. 2, To Speak of God). Ed. by B. Marz. 2nd ed. Düsseldorf: Patmos.

1989c   *Wort des Heils, Wort der Heilung: Gespräche und Interviews.* Vol. 3, *Von der befreienden Kraft des Glaubens* (Words of Wholeness, Words of Healing: Conversations and Interviews. Vol. 3, On the Liberating Power of Faith). Ed. by B. Marz. Düsseldorf: Patmos.

1989d   "Der Herr ist mein Hirte oder: Der Kopf des Orpheus" (The Lord Is My Shepherd, or: The Head of Orpheus) In *Feuer in der Nacht: ein Lesebuch zur Zukunft von Glaube und Kirche.* Ed. by Michael Albus, 36–44. 2nd ed. Düsseldorf: Patmos.

1989e   [1987] "Theologie und Psychologie: Eugen Drewermann im Gespräch mit Michael Albus" (Theology and Psychology: Eugen Drewermann in Conversation with Michael Albus). Interview by Michael Albus. (*Zweites Deutsches Fernsehen,* 14 June 1987). In *Wort des Heils, Wort der Heilung 1,* 120–31.

1989f   [1987] "Geh mit mir diesen Weg: Ein Gespräch zwischen Eugen Drewermann und Bernd Marz" (Share this Path with Me: A Conversation between Eugen Drewermann and Bernd Marz). In *Wort des Heils, Wort der Heilung 1,* 132–68.

1989g   "Das Fremde — In der Natur, in uns selber und als das vollkommen Neue. Dargestellt an einem Märchen" (Strangeness — in Nature, in Ourselves, and as What Is Completely New. Illustrated by a Fairy Tale) In *Wir und das Fremde: Faszination und Bedrohung; Tagungsbericht der 37. Werktagung 1988.* Ed. by Heinz Rothbucher and Franz Wurst, 117–44. Salzburg: Selbstverlag der Pädagogischen Werktagung.

1989h   "Ich lasse mich nicht lebendig begraben" (I Will Not Permit Myself to Be Buried Alive). *Publik-Forum,* 3 November 1989, no. 22:37–45.

1990a   [1989] *Kleriker: Psychogramm eines Ideals* (Clergy: Psychogram of an Ideal). 8th ed. Olten: Walter.

1990b   "Im Ministerium der Wahrheit" (In the Ministry of Truth). In *Der Klerikerstreit: Die Auseinandersetzung um Eugen Drewermann,* 325–57. Ed. by Peter Eicher. Munich: Kösel.

1990c   [1984] *Psychoanalyse und Moraltheologie.* Vol. 3, *An den Grenzen des Lebens* (Psychoanalysis and Moral Theology. Vol. 3, Near the Borders of Life). 4th ed. Mainz: Matthias-Grünewald.

1990d   [1987] *Das Markusevangelium, Part 1: 1:1–9:13* (The Gospel of Mark, Part 1: 1:1–9:13) *Bilder von Erlösung* (Images of Redemption). 6th ed. Olten: Walter.

1990e   [1988] *Das Markusevangelium, Part 2: 9:14–16:20* (The Gospel
             of Mark, Part 2: 9:14–15:20) *Bilder von Erlösung* (Images of
             Redemption). 3rd ed. Olten: Walter.

1990f   *Der offene Himmel: Predigten zum Advent und zur Weihnacht*
             (English: 1991g). Ed. by Bernd Marz. Düsseldorf: Patmos.

1991a   [1982] *Psychoanalyse und Moraltheologie*, Vol. 1, *Angst und Schuld*
             (Psychoanalysis and Moral Theology. Vol. 1, Fear and Guilt). 10th
             ed. Mainz: Matthias-Grünewald.

1991b   [1983] *Psychoanalyse und Moraltheologie*. Vol. 2, *Wege und Umwege
             der Liebe* (Psychoanalysis and Moral Theology. Vol. 2, Ways and
             Detours to Love). 8th ed. Mainz: Matthias-Grünewald.

1991c   *Reden gegen den Krieg* (Speeches against War). Ed. by Bernd Marz.
             Düsseldorf: Patmos.

1991d   [1978] "Sünde und Neurose: Versuch einer Synthese von Dogmatik
             und Psychoanalyse" (Sin and Neurosis: Attempt at a Synthesis of
             Dogmatics and Psychoanalysis). In *Psychoanalyse und Moraltheologie
             1*, 128–62.

1991e   [1981] *Der tödliche Fortschritt: Von der Zerstörung der Erde und
             des Menschen im Erbe des Christentums* (Deadly Progress: The
             Destruction of the Earth and of the Human Being in the Heritage of
             Christianity). 6th enl. ed. Freiburg I. Br.: Herder.

1991f   *Was uns Zukunft gibt: Vom Reichtum des Lebens* (What Gives Us
             Future: On the Wealth of Life). Olten: Walter.

1991g   *Open Heavens: Meditations for Advent and Christmas* (German:
             1990f) Trans. by David J. Krieger. Ed. by Joan Marie Laflamme and
             Bernd Marz. Maryknoll: Orbis.

1991h   [1978] "Von der Unmoral der Psychotherapie — oder von der
             Notwendigkeit einer Suspension des Ethischen im Religiösen" (On the
             Immorality of Psychotherapy — or on the Necessity of a Suspension of
             the Ethical Dimension in the Religion Dimension). In *Psychoanalyse
             und Moraltheologie 1*, 79–104.

1991i   [1981] "Das Tragische und das Christliche" (The Tragic and the
             Christian Dimension). In *Psychoanalyse und Moraltheologie 1*,
             19–78.

1991j   "Jesus wollte diese Kirche nicht": Theologe Eugen Drewermann über
             seinen Streit mit den Bischöfen um Jungfrauengeburt, Priesteramt und
             Abtreibung ("Jesus Did not Want this Church": Theologian Eugen
             Drewermann on His Dispute with the Bishops Concerning Virgin

Birth, Priestly Office, and Abortion). Interview by Werner Harenberg and Manfred Müller. *Der Spiegel,* 23 December, no. 52:61–74.

1991k   *Leben, das dem Tod entwächst: Predigten zur Passions-und Osterzeit* (English: 1994c). Ed. by Bernd Marz. Düsseldorf: Patmos.

1992a   [1982] *Die Spirale der Angst: Der Krieg und das Christentum. Mit vier Reden gegen den Krieg am Golf* (The Spiral of Anxiety: War and Christianity. With Four Speeches against the Gulf War). 3rd ed. Freiburg i. Br.: Herder. [First published as *Der Krieg und das Christentum: Von der Ohnmacht und Notwendigkeit des Religiösen* (War and Christianity: On the Powerlessness and the Necessity of Religion). Regensburg: Pustet, 1982].

1992b   *Giordano Bruno, oder Der Spiegel des Unendlichen* (Giordano Bruno, or: The Mirror of Infinity). Munich: Kösel.

1992c   [1989] "Hoffnung für die leidende Kreatur oder: Das Postulat von der Unsterblichkeit der Tiere" (Hope for a Suffering Creation, or: Postulate of the Immortality of Animals). In *Ich steige hinab in die Barke der Sonne: Meditationen zu Tod und Auferstehung,* 228–47. 5th ed. Olten: Walter.

1992d   *Das Matthäusevangelium, Part 1: 1:1–7:29.* (The Gospel of Matthew, Part 1: 1:1–7:29). *Bilder der Erfüllung* (Images of Fulfillment). Olten: Walter.

1992e   [1984] "Marienkind" (Our Lady's Child) [1st ed.: Olten: Walter, 1984]. In *Lieb Schwesterlein, laß' mich herein,* 43–101.

1992f   *Worum es eigentlich geht: Protokoll einer Verurteilung* (The Real Issues: Report of a Conviction). 2nd ed. Munich: Kösel.

1992g   [1989] *Ich steige hinab in die Barke der Sonne: Meditationen zu Tod und Auferstehung* (I Descend into the Barque of the Sun: Meditations on Death and Resurrection). 5th ed. Olten: Walter.

1992h   *Lieb Schwesterlein, laß' mich herein: Grimms Märchen tiefen-psychologisch gedeutet* (Little Sister Dear, Let Me Enter: Depth-Psychological Interpretations of Grimm's Fairy Tale). Munich: Deutscher Taschenbuch Verlag.

1992i   [1991] "Interview mit Eugen Drewermann im Norddeutschen Rundfunk am 16.3.1991: Im Gespräch mit Peter Hertel" (Interview with Eugen Drewermann on the North German Radio Station, 16 March 1991: In conversation with Peter Hertel). In *Worum es eigentlich geht,* 283–98. (partly overlaps with 1996d)

1993a   *Glauben in Freiheit oder Tiefenpsychologie und Dogmatik*. Vol. 1,
             Dogma, Angst und Symbolismus (Liberating Faith, or: Depth
             Psychology and Dogmatics. Vol. 1, Dogma, Fear, and Symbolism).
             Düsseldorf: Walter.

1993b   "Psyche und Zeit: Zeiterleben und Persönlichkeitsstruktur" (Psyche
             and Time: The Experience of Time and Character Structure). In
             ZEIT-Erleben: Zwischen Hektik und Müßiggang, 12th Goldegger
             Dialoge. Ed. by Cyriak Schaighofer. Goldegg, Austria: Kulturverein
             Schloß Goldegg.

1993c   *Visionen für die Menschen* (Visions for Humanity). Ed. by Felizitas
             von Schönborn. Zurich: Pendo.

1993d   *Wort des Heils, Wort der Heilung: Gespräche und Interviews*. Vol. 4,
             Die Kraft der Bilder (Words of Wholeness, Words of Healing:
             Conversations and Interviews. Vol. 4, The Power of Images). Ed. by
             B. Marz. Düsseldorf: Patmos.

1993e   *Sind Propheten dieser Kirche ein Ärgernis?: Eugen Drewermann im
             Gespräch mit Felizitas von Schönborn* (Are Prophets an Offence to
             this Church?: Eugen Drewermann in Conversation with Felizitas von
             Schönborn). Munich: Piper.

1993f   *Discovering the Royal Child Within: a Spiritual Psychology of "The
             Little Prince"* (German: 1984b). Trans. by P. Heinegg. New York:
             Crossroad.

1994a   *Was ich denke* (What I Think). Quer/Denken. Ed. by H. Herrmann,
             no. 2. Munich: Goldmann.

1994b   *Discovering the God Child Within: A Spiritual Psychology of the
             Infancy of Jesus* (German: 1986c). Trans. by P. Heinegg. New York:
             Crossroad.

1994c   *Dying We Live: Meditations for Lent and Easter* (German: 1993e)
             Trans. by Linda M. Maloney and John Drury. Ed. by Linda M.
             Maloney. Maryknoll: Orbis.

1994d   *Das Matthäusevangelium, Part 2: 8:1–20:19* (The Gospel of Matthew,
             Part 2: 8:1–20:19). *Bilder der Erfüllung* (Images of Fulfillment).
             Düsseldorf: Walter.

1995a   *Das Matthäusevangelium, Part 3: 20:20–28:20* (The Gospel of
             Matthew, Part 3: 20:20–28:20). *Bilder der Erfüllung* (Images of
             Fulfillment). Düsseldorf: Walter.

1995b   *Fonctionnaires de Dieu* (German: 1990a). Paris: Albin Michel.

1995c   *Dieu immédiat: Entretiens avec Gwendoline Jarczyk* (German: 1996b). Paris: Desclée de Brouwer.

1996a   *Jesus von Nazareth: Befreiung zum Frieden* (Jesus of Nazareth: Liberation for Peace). *Glauben in Freiheit,* vol. 2 (Liberating Faith, vol. 2). Walter: Zurich.

1996b   *Näher bei Gott, nah bei den Menschen: Ein Gespräch mit G. Jarczyk.* (Closer to God, Close to Humans: A Conversation with G. Jarczyk) (French: 1995c). Trans. from the French by C. Stüer. Munich: Kösel.

1996c   "Vom Ärgernis Jesu und seiner Notwendigkeit — Eugen Drewermann antwortet Klaus Berger: Das christliche Abendland stellt keine exklusive Form des Menschseins dar" (The Scandal of Jesus and Its Necessity — Eugen Drewermann Replies to Klaus Berger: The Christian West Does Not Represent an Exclusive Form of Being Human). *Weltwoche,* 19 December 1996, no. 51.

1996d   "Durch die Angst hindurchgehen" (To Walk Right Through Fear). In *Mit dem Gesicht zur Welt.* Ed. by Peter Hertel, 119–35. Würzburg: Echter. (partly overlaps with 1992i)

1997a   *Daß alle eins seien. Predigten zwischen Himmelfahrt und Dreifaltigkeitsfest* (That All Can Be One: Sermons between Ascension and the Feast of the Trinity). Ed. by Bernd Marz. Munich: Piper.

1997b   *Hänsel und Gretel* (Hansel and Gretel) Grimms Märchen tiefenpsychologisch gedeutet. (A Depth-Psychological Interpretation of Grimm's Fairy Tales). Zurich: Walter.

1997c   *Und gäbe dir eine Seele...: H. Chr. Andersens "Kleine Meerjungfrau tiefenpsychologisch gedeutet"* (And Gave You a Soul...: A Depth-Psychological Interpretation of H. Chr. Andersen's "Little Mermaid"). Freiburg I. Br.: Herder.

1998a   *Daß auch der Allerniedrigste mein Bruder sei: Dostojewski — Dichter der Menschlichkeit* (So That Even the Least Be My Brother: Dostoevsky — Poet of Humanity). Dusseldorf: Walter.

1998b   *Der sechste Tag: Die Herkunft des Menschen und die Frage nach Gott* (The Sixth Day: The Origin of Humanity and the Question of God). *Glauben in Freiheit,* vol. 3: *Religion und Naturwissenschaft,* Part 1 (Liberating Faith, vol. 3: Religion and Natural Science, part 1). Walter: Zurich.

1998c   "Eine Art elementaren Mitleids — Eugen Drewermann" (A Fundamental Form of Compassion — Eugen Drewermann). In *Paderborner Profile,* interviews by Sibilla Pelke, 29–51. Borchen: Ch. Möllmann.

1999a   *...und es geschah so: Die moderne Biologie und die Frage nach
             Gott* (...And It Was So: Modern Biology and the Question of God).
             Glauben in Freiheit, vol. 3: *Religion und Naturwissenschaft,* Part 2:
             Biologie und Theologie (Liberating Faith, vol. 3: Religion and Natural
             Science, part 2: Biology and Theology). Walter: Zurich.

1999b   Interview by author. 16 November, no. 1, Madison, N.J. Tape
             recording. Author's collection.

1999c   Interview by author. 16 November, no. 2, Car ride from Madison,
             N.J, to New York City. Tape recording. Author's collection.

1999d   Interview by author. 17 November, Madison, N.J. Tape recording.
             Author's collection.

1999e   Interview by author. 18 November, Car ride from Madison, N.J, to
             Princeton, N.J. Tape recording. Author's collection.

1999f   Interview by James Nee. 19 November, Madison, N.J. Tape recording.
             Author's collection.

1999g   Interview by author. 19 November, Car ride from Madison, N.J,
             to Newark International Airport, N.J. Tape recording. Author's
             collection.

2000a   Interview by author. 25 June, by telephone from Sparta, N.J, to
             Paderborn, Germany. Tape recording. Author's collection.

2000b   *Albert Schweitzer-Tatsachen: eine Einführung in Leben und Werk;
             Eugen Drewermann im Gespräch über Albert Schweitzer* (text and
             CD-ROM) (Albert Schweitzer-Facts: An Introduction to His Life
             and work; Eugen Drewermann in dialogue about Albert Schweitzer).
             Leun, Lahn: Edition P12c.

2001   *Diálogo entre razón y fe: Eugen Drewermann en Guadalajara* (Dialog
             between Reason and Faith: Eugen Drewermann in Guadalajara).
             Ed. Lourdes Celina Vázquez Parada. Guadalajara: Universidad de
             Guadalajara.

2002a   *Pädophilie in der katholischen Kirche — Irene Gysel im Gespräch mit
             Eugen Drewermann* (video) (Pedophilia in the Catholic Church —
             Irene Gysel in Conversation with Eugen Drewermann). Sternstunde
             Religion. Schweizer Fernsehen DRS. 26 May 2002.

2002b   *Im Anfang... Die moderne Kosmologie und die Frage nach Gott*
             (In the Beginning... Modern Cosmology and the Question of God).
             Glauben in Freiheit, vol. 3: *Religion und Naturwissenschaft,* Part 3:
             Kosmologie und Theologie (Liberating Faith, vol. 3: Religion and
             Natural Science, part 2: Cosmology and Theology). Walter: Zurich.

2002c   E-mail to author. Ed. by Else and Franz-Josef Schaub, 19 August. Author's collection.

Co-authored by Eugen Drewermann

Dalai Lama and Eugen Drewermann

1993   *Der Weg des Herzens. Gewaltlosigkeit und Dialog zwischen den Religionen* (The Path of the Heart: Nonviolence and the Dialogue between Religions). Ed. by Krieger David. Olten: Walter.

Works on Eugen Drewermann and Other Secondary Literature

Abraham, Karl

1924   "A Short Study of the Development of the Libido, Viewed in the Light of Mental Disorders." In *Selected Papers of Karl Abraham,* with an introductory memoir by Ernest Jones, 418–501. Trans. by Douglas Bryan and Alix Strachey. New York: Basic Books, 1953.

1921–25   "Psycho-Analytical Studies on Character-Formation." In *Selected Papers of Karl Abraham,* with an introductory memoir by Ernest Jones, 370–417. Trans. by Douglas Bryan and Alix Strachey. New York: Basic Books, 1953.

Adler, Alfred

1927   *Understanding Human Nature.* Trans. by Walter Béran Wolfe. New York: Garden City Publishing.

1972   *The Neurotic Constitution: Outlines of a Comparative Individualistic Psychology and Psychotherapy.* Trans. by Bernard Glueck and John E. Lind. Freeport, N.Y: Books for Libraries Press.

Ahrens, Peter

1992   "Religionslehrer zu Streik aufgerufen" (He Called on Religion Teachers to Strike). *Drewermann und die Folgen: Vom Kleriker zum Ketzer? Stationen eines Konflikts.* Ed. by Thomas Schweer, 268–70. Munich: Heine, 1992.

Arendt, Hannah

1965   *Eichmann in Jerusalem: A Report on the Banality of Evil.* Rev. and enl. ed. New York: Penguin.

Aristotle

1966   *Metaphysics.* Trans. with commentaries and glossary by Hippocrates
            G. Apostle. Bloomington: Indiana University Press.

Atwood, Margaret

2000   *The Blind Assassin.* New York: Bantam Doubleday Dell.

Barth, Hans-Martin

1988a   "Gottes Wort ist dreifaltig. Ein Beitrag zur Auseinandersetzung mit
            der 'archetypischen Hermeneutik' Eugen Drewermanns" (God's Word
            Is Trinitarian: A Contribution in the Dispute around the "Archetypal
            Hermeneutics" of Eugen Drewermann). *Theologische Literaturzeitung*
            113, no. 4:241–54.

1988b   "Protestantismuskritik und Ökumeneverständniss bei Eugen
            Drewermann" (Eugen Drewermann's Criticism of Protestant-
            ism and Understanding of Ecumenism). *Materialdienst des
            Konfessionskundlichen Instituts Bensheim* 39, no. 1:3–7.

Benedikt, B. and A. Sobel, eds.

1992   *Der Streit um Drewermann: Was Theolog(inn)en und Psy-
            cholog(inn)en kritisieren. Anfragen von . . .* (The Controversy around
            Drewermann: What Theologians and Psychologists Criticize — In-
            quiries by . . .). With contributions by Hans M. Barth, Dieter Funke,
            Maria Kassel, et al. Wiesbaden: Sobel.

Benz, Helmut

1992   "Drewermann und der Religionsunterricht" (Drewermann and the
            Teaching of Religion). In *Drewermann und die Folgen: Vom Kleriker
            zum Ketzer? Stationen eines Konflikts.* Ed. by Thomas Schweer,
            271–79. Munich: Heine, 1992.

Berger, Klaus

1996   "Priester sind Mörder: Eugen Drewermanns Beitrag zum Unfrieden"
            (Priests Are Murderers: Eugen Drewermann's contribution to Lack of
            Peace). *Weltwoche.* 21 November 1996, no. 48.

Beyer, U.

1995   *"Die Tragik Gottes": ein philosophischer Kommentar zur Theologie
            Eugen Drewermanns* ("The Tragedy of God": A Philosophical
            Commentary on the Theology of Eugen Drewermann). Würzburg:
            Königshausen & Neumann.

Bilz, Rudolf

1971   *Paläoanthropologie: Der neue Mensch in der Sicht einer Ver-
        haltensforschung* (Paleoanthropology: The New Human in Light of
        Behavioral Research). Vol. 1. Frankfurt am Main: Suhrkamp.

Birnstein, Uwe, and Klaus P. Lehmann

1994   *Phänomen Drewermann: Politik und Religion einer Kultfigur*
        (Phenomenon Drewermann: The Politics and Religion of a Cult
        Figure). Frankfurt am Main: Eichborn.

Blank, Josef

1985   "Die Angst vor dem Sturz ins Bodenlose" (The Fear of the Fall into the
        Abyss). Reprinted in *Der Streit um Drewermann*. Ed. by B. Benedikt
        and A. Sobel, 21–27. Wiesbaden: Sobel, 1992.

Böckenförde, Ernst-Wolfgang, and Robert Spaemann

1960   "Die Zerstörung der naturrechtlichen Kriegslehre: Erwiderung an
        P. Gustav Gundlach, S.J." (The Destruction of the Natural Law
        Theory of Just War: Response to P. Gustav Gundlach, S.J.). In
        *Atomare Kampfmittel und Christliche Ethik: Diskussionsbeiträge
        deutscher Katholiken*. Ed. by Franziskus M. Stratmann O.P., 161–96.
        Munich: Kösel.

Boss, Medard

1963   *Psychoanalysis and Daseinsanalysis*. Trans. by Ludwig B. Lefebre.
        New York: Basic Books.

The Boston Globe

1992   "German priest suspended for doubting dogma." 27 March, 2.

Buber, Martin

1976   *Die fünf Bücher der Weisung* (The Five Books of Commandments)
        Heidelberg: Schneider.

Cannon, Walter B.

1932   *The Wisdom of the Body*. New York: Norton.

Carl, William J., III

1992   Review of *Open Heavens*, by Eugen Drewermann. *Homiletic* 17, no.
        1:16–7.

1994   Review of *Dying We Live*, by Eugen Drewermann. *Homiletic* 19,
        no. 1:20.

The Christian Century

1992   "Priest suspended." 3 June 1992. Vol. 109, issue 19, 579, 1/5.

von Clausewitz, Carl

1989   *On War.* Trans. by Michael Howard and Peter Paret. Princeton, N.J.:
            Princeton University Press.

Cocks, Geoffrey

2001   "The Devil and the Details: Psychoanalysis in the Third Reich." *The
            Psychoanalytic Review* 88, no. 2:225–44.

Condrau, Gion

1962   *Angst und Schuld als Grundprobleme der Psychotherapie* (Fear and
            Guilt as Basic Problems in Psychotherapy) Bern: Huber.

1963   *Daseinsanalytische Psychotherapie.* (Daseinanalytic Psychotherapy)
            Bern: Huber.

Denzler, Georg

1973–76   *Das Papsttum und der Amtszölibat* (The Papacy and Official
            Celibacy). Stuttgart: Hiersemann.

1988   *Die verbotene Lust: 2000 Jahre christliche Sexualmoral* (Forbidden
            Desire: 2000 Years of Christian Sexual Morality). Munich: Piper.

Deschner, Karlheinz

1972   *Abermals krähte der Hahn: Eine Demaskierung des Christentums
            von den Evangelisten bis zu den Faschisten* (Again the Cock Crowed:
            A Demasking of Christianity from Gospel Writers to Fascists). 3rd
            edition. Reinbek: Rowohlt.

Dirks, Walter

1958   "Die Gefahr der Gleichschaltung" (The Danger of Uniformity).
            Frankfurter Hefte 13:379–91.

Doering-Manteuffel, Anselm

1981   *Katholizismus und Wiederbewaffnung: Die Haltung der deutschen
            Katholiken gegenüber der Wehrfrage 1948–1955* (Catholicism and
            Rearmament: The Position of German Catholics vis-à-vis the Military
            Question 1948–1955). Mainz: Matthias-Grünewald.

Dostoevsky, Fyodor

1945   *The Double.* In *The Short Novels of Dostoevsky,* with an Introduction
            by Thomas Mann. New York: Dial Press.

1976   *The Brothers Karamazov.* Trans. by Constance Garnett. Ed. and rev. by Ralph E. Matlaw. New York: Norton.

Dührssen, Annemarie

1967   *Psychogene Erkrankungen bei Kindern und Jugendlichen. Eine Ein-führung in die allgemeine und spezielle Neurosenlehre* (Psychogenic Illnesses in Children and Adolescents: An Introduction to the General and Specialist Theory of Neurosis). 6th ed. Göttingen: Verlag für Medizinische Psychologie.

Eibl-Eibesfeldt, I.

1973   *Der vorprogrammierte Mensch: Das Ererbte als bestimmender Faktor im menschlichen Verhalten* (The Preprogrammed Person: Inherited Factors That Determine Human Behavior). Vienna-Zurich-Munich.

Eicher, Peter

1990a   *Der Klerikerstreit: Die Auseinandersetzung um Eugen Drewermann* (The Clergy-Controversy: The Debate around Eugen Drewermann). Ed. by P. Eicher. Munich: Kösel.

1990b   "Der Schuß auf die Kanzel oder von der Freiheit der Theologie: Dem Paderborner Theologen und Tiefenpsychologen Eugen Drewermann droht der Lehramtsentzug" (The Lectern under Fire, or: on the Freedom of Theology: The Paderborn Theologian and Psychoanalyst Eugen Drewermann Is Threatened with Loss of His License to Teach). *Frankfurter Rundschau,* 1 March 1990, no. 51, p. 14.

1992a   "Der Konflikt um die christliche Existenz" (The Struggle for a Christian Existence). In *Worum es eigentlich geht: Protokoll einer Verurteilung,* by Eugen Drewermann, 487–508. Munich: Kösel.

1992b   "Offener Brief von Peter Eicher an Erzbischof Degenhardt vom 1.2.1992" (Open Letter from Peter Eicher to Archbishop Degenhardt). In *Worum es eigentlich geht: Protokoll einer Verurteilung,* by Eugen Drewermann, 508–10. Munich: Kösel.

Engelhardt, Hanns

1994   Review of *Glauben in Freiheit, oder: Tiefenpsychologie und Dogmatik.* Vol. 1: *Dogma, Angst und Symbolismus,* by Eugen Drewermann. *Modern Believing* 35:41–43.

1998   Review of *Glauben in Freiheit, oder Tiefenpsychologie und Dogmatik.* Vol. 2: *Jesus von Nazareth: Befreiung zum Frieden,* by Eugen Drewermann. *Modern Believing* 39:46–47.

Erikson, Erik H.

1958   *Young Man Luther: A Study in Psychoanalysis and History.* New York: Norton.

1966   The Ontogeny of Ritualization in Man. In *Philosophical Transactions of the Royal Society of London,* Series B, no. 772, vol. 251, 337–49

1970   *Gandhi's Truth: On the Origins of Militant Nonviolence.* New York: Norton.

1977   *Toys and Reasons: Stages in the Ritualization of Experience.* New York: Norton.

1993   *Childhood and Society.* New York: Norton.

Evangelische Information

1992   "Unterstützung für Drewermann: Boff sieht Parallele zwischen dem Theologen und seinem Fall" (Support for Drewermann: Boff Sees Parallels between the Theologian and His Own Case). 1992, no. 24:8.

Farine, Marcel

1996   *Das verlorene Paradies des Eugen Drewermann. Antwort eines Laien an einen Theologen* (The Lost Paradise of Eugen Drewermann: Answer of a Lay Person to a Theologian) Foreword by Karl J. Rauber. Trans. from the French by August Berz. Hauteville: Parvis.

Fehrenbacher, G.

1991   *Drewermann verstehen: Eine kritische Hinführung* (Understanding Drewermann: A Critical Introduction). Olten: Walter.

Fenichel, Otto

1945   *The Psychoanalytic Theory of Neurosis.* New York: Norton.

Fest, Joachim C.

1974   *Hitler.* Trans. by Richard and Clara Winston. New York: Harcourt Brace Jovanovich.

Feuerbach, Ludwig

1873   *The Essence of Religion. God the Image of Man. Man's Dependence upon Nature the Last and Only Source of Religion.* Trans. by Alexander Loos. New York: Butts.

1967   *The Essence of Faith According to Luther.* Trans. by Melvin Cherno. New York: Harper & Row.

Foucault, Michel

 1980 *Power/Knowledge: Selected Interviews and Other Writings 1972–1977.* Ed. by Colin Gordon. New York: Pantheon Books

Fox, Matthew

 1998 "Castro Meets the Pope." *Tikkun* 13, no. 3:32.

Frankl, V. E.

 1975 *The Unconscious God: Psychotherapy and Theology.* New York: Simon and Schuster.

 1986 *The Doctor and the Soul: From Psychotherapy to Logotherapy.* Trans. by Richard and Clara Winston. 3rd, expanded ed., with a new Preface, an updated bibliography and an added chapter in English by the author. New York: Vintage Books.

Freud, Anna

 1937 *The Ego and the Mechanisms of Defense.* The Writings of Anna Freud, vol. 2. New York: International Universities Press.

 1965 *Normality and Pathology in Childhood: Assessments of Development.* New York: International Universities Press.

Freud, Sigmund

 1940–68 *Gesammelte Werke.* 18 vols. Ed. by Anna Freud, E. Bibring, W. Hoffer, E. Kris, in collaboration with Marie Bonaparte, Princess George of Greece. Vols. I–XVII, London: Imago Publishing; vol. XVIII, Frankfurt am Main (cited as *GW I–XVIII*).

 1953–74 *The Standard Edition of the Complete Psychological Works of Sigmund Freud.* 24 vols. Trans. from the German under the general editorship of James Strachey, in collaboration with Anna Freud, assisted by Alix Strachey and Alan Tyson. London: Hogarth Press (cited as *SE I–XXIV* [*GW* indicates corresponding pages in the German edition *Gesammelte Werke*]).

 1899 Screen Memories. *SE III,* 301–22 [*GW I,* 529–54].

 1900 The Interpretation of Dreams. *SE IV/V,* 1–627 [*GW II/III,* I–xv, 1–642].

 1905 Three Essays on the Theory of Sexuality. *SE VII,* 123–243 [*GW V,* 29–145].

 1907 Obsessive Actions and Religious Practices. *SE IX:* 115–27 [*GW VII,* 129–39].

1909   Notes upon a Case of Obsessional Neurosis. *SE X*, 155–249 [*GW VII*, 381–463].

1910   Contributions to the Psychology of Love, part 1: A Special Type of Choice of Object Made by Men. *SE XI*, 165–75 [*GW VIII*, 66–77].

1913   Totem and Taboo. *SE XIII*, vii–162 [*GW IX*, 1–205].

1915   Repression. *SE XIV*, 141–58 [*GW X*, 258–61].

1916–17   Introductory Lectures on Psychoanalysis. *SE XV/XVI*, 1–500 [*GW XI*, 1–495].

1917a   On Transformations of Instinct, as Exemplified in Anal Erotism. *SE XVII*, 127–33 [*GW X*, 401–10].

1917b   Mourning and Melancholia. *SE XIV*, 243–58. [*GW X*, 428–46].

1923   The Ego and the Id. *SE XIX*, 1–66 [*GW XIII*, 237–89].

1926   Inhibitions, Symptoms and Anxiety. *SE XX*, 75–175 [*GW XIV*, 113–205].

1927a   The Future of an Illusion. *SE XXI*, 1–56 [*GW XIV*, 325–80].

1927b   Postscript to "The Question of Lay Analysis." *SE XX*, 251–58 [*GW XIV*, 287–96].

1933   New Introductory Lectures. *SE XXII*, 1–182 [*GW XV*, I–iv + 1–207].

1939   Moses and Monotheism: Three Essays. *SE XXIII*, 1–137 [*GW XVI*, 101–246].

1940   An Outline of Psycho-Analysis. *SE XXIII*, 139–207 [*GW XVII*, 63–138].

Frey, Jörg

1995   *Eugen Drewermann und die biblische Exegese: Eine methodisch-kritische Analyse* (Eugen Drewermann and Biblical Exegesis: A Methodological-critical Analysis). Wissenschaftliche Untersuchungen zum Neuen Testament, 2. Reihe, 71. Tübingen: Mohr.

Fromm, Erich

1950   *Psychoanalysis and Religion*. New Haven: Yale University Press.

1973   *The Anatomy of Human Destructiveness*. New York: Holt, Rinehart and Winston.

Fürst, G., ed.

1993   *Brücken zu Eugen Drewermann?: Vom Konflikt zur Sache* (Bridges to
        Eugen Drewermann?: From Conflict to the Issues). With contributions
        by Otto Betz, Gregor Fehrenbacher, Manfred Görg, Ulrich Niemann,
        Heinz Schütte, Josef Sudbrack. Stuttgart: Akademie der Diözese
        Rottenburg-Stuttgart.

Gandhi, Mahatma

1955   *Truth Is God: Gleanings from the Writings of Mahatma Gandhi
        bearing on God, God-Realization and the Godly Way.* Compiled by
        R. K. Prabhu. Ahmedabad: Navajivan Publishing House.

1968   *Freiheit ohne Gewalt.* Trans. and ed. with an Introduction by
        K. Klostermeier. Cologne: Hegner.

Gassmann, Lothar, and Johannes Lange

1993   *Was nun, Herr Drewermann? Anfragen an die tiefenpsychologische
        Bibelauslegung* (What Now, Mr. Drewermann? Questions for a
        Depth-Psychological Interpretation of the Bible). Lahr: Liebenzeller
        Mission.

von Gebsattel, V. E.

1959a   "Die anakastische Fehlhaltung." In *Handbuch der Neurosenlehre und
        Psychotherapie.* Vol. 2, *Spezielle Neurosenlehre.* Ed. by V. E. Frankl,
        V. E. v. Gebsattel, and J. H. Schultz, 125–42. Munich: Urban &
        Schwarzenberg.

1959b   ' "Die depressive Fehlhaltung" (Depressive Disorder). In *Handbuch
        der Neurosenlehre und Psychotherapie.* Vol. 2, *Spezielle Neurosen-
        lehre.* Ed. by V. E. Frankl, V. E. v. Gebsattel, and J. H. Schultz,
        143–56. Munich: Urban & Schwarzenberg.

Geertz, Clifford

1973   *The Interpretation of Cultures.* New York: Basic Books.

Gestrich, Reinhold

1992   *Eugen Drewermann: Glauben aus Leidenschaft. Eine Einführung
        in seine Theologie* (Eugen Drewermann: Passionate Faith — An
        Introduction to His Theology). Stuttgart: Quell-Verlag.

Gibran, Kahlil

1968   *Secrets of the Heart.* New York: Citadel Press.

Glatzel, Hans

1959   "Ernährung" (Eating). In *Handbuch der Neurosenlehre und Psycho-therapie*. Vol. 2, *Spezielle Neurosenlehre*. Ed. by Viktor E. Frankl, Victor E. Freiherr v. Gebsattel, and J. H. Schultz, 429–80. Munich: Urban & Schwarzenberg.

Goggin, James E., and Eileen Brockman Goggin

2001   "Politics, Ideology, and the Psychoanalytic Movement before, during, and after the Third Reich." *The Psychoanalytic Review* 88, no. 2:155–93.

Gundlach S.J., Gustav

1959   "Die Lehre Pius' XII. vom modernen Krieg" (Pius XII's Teaching on Modern War). *Stimmen der Zeit* 164, no. 4:1–14.

Häring, Hermann

1998   *Hans Küng: Breaking Through*. New York: Continuum International.

Hegel, Georg Wilhelm Friedrich

1953   *Reason in History: A General Introduction to the Philosophy of History*. Trans. with an Introduction by Robert S. Hartman. New York: Bobbs-Merrill.

1969   *Science of Logic*. Trans. by A. V. Miller, with a foreword by J. N. Findlay. New York: Humanities Press.

1977   *Phenomenology of Spirit*. Trans. by A. V. Miller, with analysis of the text and Foreword by J. N. Findlay. Oxford: Clarendon Press.

1988   *Lectures on the Philosophy of Religion*. Ed. by Peter C. Hodgson. Trans. by R. F. Brown et al. Berkeley: University of California Press.

Heidegger, Martin

1972   *Sein und Zeit*. 12th ed.Tübingen: Max Niemeyer.

1996   *Being and Time*. Contemporary Continental Philosophy. Trans. by Joan Stambaugh. Albany: State University of New York Press.

Hermann, Imre

1923   "Zur Psychologie der Schimpansen" (On the Psychology of Chimpanzees). *Internationale Zeitschrift für Psycho-Analyse* 9.

1924   *Psychoanalyse und Logik: Individuell-Logische Untersuchungen aus der psychoanalytischen Praxis* (Psychoanalysis and Logic: Individual-logical Investigations from Psychoanalytic Practice). Leipzig: Internationaler Psychoanalytischer Verlag.

1926a "Erscheinungen der Handerotik im Säuglingsalter, ihr Ursprung (Anklammern an die Mutter) und ihr Zusammenhang mit der Oralerotik" (Phenomena of Palmar Eroticism in Early Infancy, Their Origin (Clinging to the Mother) and Their Connection to Oral Eroticism). *Internationale Zeitschrift für Psycho-Analyse* 12.

1926b "Modelle zu den Ödipus- und Kastrationskomplexen bei Affen" (Models for the Oedipus and Castration Complexes among Monkeys). *Imago* 12.

1933 "Zum Triebleben der Primaten" (On the Instinctual Life of Primates). *Imago*. Vol. 19.

Hirschmann, Johannes B.

1984 "Die katholische Lehre über die Wehrdienstpflicht" (The Catholic Teaching on Mandatory Military Service). In *Ja zu Gott im Dienst an der Welt: Vorträge, Aufsätze und Predigten,* with an introduction by Wolfgang Rhein. Ed. by Johannes Beutler, 90–94. Würzburg: Echter.

Hirschmann, Johannes B., et al.

1958 "Christliche Friedenspolitik und atomare Aufrüstung" (Christian Politics of Peace and Nuclear Armament). In *Die Katholiken vor der Politik.* Ed. by Gustav E. Kafka. Freiburg/Brsg.: Herder.

Hofstätter, Peter R.

1957 *Gruppendynamik: Kritik der Massenpsychologie* (Group Dynamics: A Critique of Mass Psychology) Hamburg: Rowohlt.

Homans, George C.

1950 *The Human Group.* New York: Harcourt, Brace.

Homans, Peter

1970 *Theology after Freud: An Interpretive Inquiry.* Indianapolis: Bobbs-Merrill.

Horney, Karen

1937 *The Neurotic Personality of Our Time.* New York: Norton.

Ibsen, Henrik

1962 *Peer Gynt.* In *Masters of Modern Drama.* Ed., with an Introduction, by Haskell M. Block and Robert G. Shedd, 11–66. New York: McGraw-Hill.

Jens, Walter, ed.

1978   *Um nichts als die Wahrheit: Deutsche Bischofskonferenz contra Hans Küng — eine Dokumentation* (Nothing but the Truth: German Bishops Conference contra Hans Küng — a Documentation). Munich: Piper.

Jensen, Adolf E.

1966   *Die getötete Gottheit: Weltbild einer frühen Kultur* (The Killed Godhead: Worldview of an Early Culture). Stuttgart: Kohlhammer.

Jeziorowski, Jürgen

1992   *Eugen Drewermann — der Streit um den Glauben geht weiter* (Eugen Drewermann — The Conflict about Faith Continues). Gütersloh: Gütersloher Verlagshaus.

1993   *Gespräche über die Angst* (Conversations on Fear). 4th expanded ed. Gütersloh: Gütersloher Verlagshaus.

John Paul II (Pope)

1984   *Apostolisches Schreiben im Anschluß an die Bischofssynode "Reconciliatio et paenitentia" an die Bischöfe, Priester und Diakone und an alle Gläubigen über Versöhnung und Buße in der Sendung der Kirche heute*, 12 Dec. 1984 (Apostolic Letter following the Bishop's Synod *"Reconciliatio et paenitentia"* to the Bishops, Priests, Deacons, and to all Believers on the Reconciliation and Repentance in the Mission of the Church Today, 12 December 1984). Verlautbarungen des Apostolischen Stuhls 60. Ed. by the Sekretariat der Deutschen Bischofskonferenz. Bonn: Sekretariat der Deutschen Bischofskonferenz.

Johnson, Marguerite

1992   "Respect for Religious Dissent." *Time International.* 24 August.

Jonas, Hans

1996   [1984] The Concept of God after Auschwitz: A Jewish Voice. In *Mortality and Morality: A Search for the Good after Auschwitz.* Ed. and with an Introduction by Lawrence Vogel, 131–43. Northwestern University Studies in Phenomenology and Existential Philosophy. Evanston, Ill.: Northwestern University Press.

Jung, Carl Gustav

1953–79   *The Collected Works of C. G. Jung.* Ed. by Sir Herbert Read, Michael Fordham, and Gerhard Adler. 20 vols. Princeton: Princeton University Press (cited as *Collected Works* I–XX).

1931	The Spiritual Problem of Modern Man. In *Collected Works* X, 74–94.
1932	Psychotherapists or the Clergy. In *Collected Works* XI, 327–47.
1933	*Modern Man in Search of a Soul*. New York: Harcourt, Brace.
1938	Psychology and Religion. In *Collected Works* XI, 3–105.
1948	A Psychological Approach to the Dogma of the Trinity. In *Collected Works* XI, 107–200.
1952a	Answer to Job. In *Collected Works* XI, 355–470.
1952b	A reply to Martin Buber. In *Collected Works* XVIII, 663–70.
1954	Transformation Symbolism in the Mass. In *Collected Works* XI, 201–96.
1966a	General Problems of Psychotherapy. In *Collected Works* XVI, 3–125.
1966b	On the Psychology of the Unconscious In *Collected Works* VII, 1–119.
1972a	The Structure of the Psyche. In *Collected Works* VIII, 139–58.
1972b	On the Nature of the Psyche In *Collected Works* VIII, 159–234.

Kant, Immanuel

1927	*Critique of Pure Reason*. 2nd ed. Trans. by F. Max Müller. New York: Macmillan.
1963	Conjectural Beginning of Human History. In *On History*. Trans. by Emil L. Fackenheim. Ed. with an Introduction by Lewis White Beck, 53–68. Indianapolis: Bobbs-Merrill.

Kasper, Walter, and Albert Görres, eds.

1988	*Tiefenpsychologische Deutung des Glaubens?: Anfragen an Eugen Drewermann* (Depth-Psychological Interpretation of Faith?: Questions for Eugen Drewermann). *Quaestiones disputatae* 113. Herder: Freiburg I. Br.

Kazantzakis, Nikos

1960	*The Last Temptation of Christ*. Trans. from the Greek by P. A. Bien. New York: Simon and Schuster.

Kierkegaard, Søren

1980a	*The Concept of Anxiety: A Simple Psychologically Orienting Deliberation on the Dogmatic Issue of Hereditary Sin*. Kierkegaard's Writings, vol. 8. Ed. and trans., with an Introduction and notes, by Reidar Thomte and Albert B. Anderson. Princeton: Princeton University Press.

1980b   *The Sickness Unto Death: A Christian Psychological Exposition for Upbuilding and Awakening*. Kierkegaard's Writings, vol. 19. Ed. and trans., with an Introduction and notes, by Howard V. Hong and Edna H. Hong. Princeton: Princeton University Press.

1983   *Fear and Trembling, Repetition*. Kierkegaard's Writings, vol. 6. Ed. and trans., with an Introduction and notes, by Howard V. Hong and Edna H. Hong. Princeton: Princeton University Press.

1991   *Practice in Christianity*. Kierkegaard's Writings, vol. 20. Ed. and trans., with an Introduction and notes, by Howard V. Hong and Edna H. Hong. Princeton: Princeton University Press.

1998   *The Moment, and Late Writings*. Kierkegaard's Writings, vol. 23. Ed. and trans., with an Introduction and notes, by Howard V. Hong and Edna H. Hong. Princeton: Princeton University Press.

Kimbrough, S. T., Jr.

1982   Review of *Strukturen des Bösen. Die jahwistische Urgeschichte in exegetischer, psychoanalytischer und philosophischer Sicht*. Vol. 3: *Die jahwistische Urgeschichte in philosophischer Sicht*, by Eugen Drewermann. *Journal of Biblical Literature* 101, no. 3:423–27

Klein, M.

1975a   [1940] "Mourning and Its Relation to Manic-Depressive States." In *Love, Guilt and Reparation and Other Works*. The Writings of Melanie Klein 1. New York: Free Press.

1975b   [1948] "On the Theory of Anxiety and Guilt." In *Envy and Gratitude and Other Works 1946–1963*. The Writings of Melanie Klein 3. New York: Free Press.

1975c   [1955] "The Psycho-Analytic Play Technique: Its History and Significance." In *Envy and Gratitude and Other Works 1946–1963*. The Writings of Melanie Klein 3. New York: Free Press.

Kohut, Heinz

1971   *The Analysis of the Self: A Systematic Approach to the Psychoanalytic Treatment of Narcissistic Personality Disorders*. The Psychoanalytic Study of the Child, no. 4. New York: International Universities Press.

1977   *The Restoration of the Self*. New York: International Universities Press.

Korherr, Edgar J.

1993   *Von Freud bis Drewermann. Tiefenpsychologie und Religionspädagogik* (From Freud to Drewermann: Depth Psychology and Religious Education) Innsbruck: Tyrolia.

Kott, Jan

1973   *The Eating of the Gods: An Interpretation of Greek Tragedy.* New York: Random House.

Küng, Hans

1979   *Freud and the Problem of God.* Trans. by E. Quinn. New Haven, Conn.: Yale University Press.

Laing, R. D.

1965   *The Divided Self: An Existential Study in Sanity and Madness.* Baltimore: Penguin.

Lang, Bernhard

1995   *Die Bibel neu entdecken: Drewermann als Leser der Bibel* (Rediscovering the Bible: Drewermann as Reader of the Bible). Munich: Kösel.

Langer, William L.

1958   "The Next Assignment." In *Psychoanalysis and History.* Ed. by Bruce Mazlish, 87–107. Englewood Cliffs, N.J.: Prentice-Hall.

Langhans, Daniel, ed.

1994   *Antwort auf den Mythos Drewermann* (Answer to the Drewermann-Myth). Abensberg: Maria Aktuell.

Lauter, Hermann-Josef

1981   *Den Menschen Christus bringen: Theologie für die Verkündigung* (To Bring Christ to People: Theology for Proclamation). Freiburg: Herder.

1986   Tiefenpsychologie und Dogmatik bei Eugen Drewermann (Depth Psychology and Dogmatics in Eugen Drewermann). *Pastoralblatt* 38 (April): 104–8.

1988a   "Um Sündenfall und Erlösung — Zum Gespräch mit Eugen Drewermann" (On the Fall and Redemption — about the Dialogue with Eugen Drewermann). *Pastoralblatt* 40, no. 7:209–12.

1988b   *Theologische Anmerkungen zum Werk Eugen Drewermanns* (Theological Comments on the Work of Eugen Drewermann). Kölner Beiträge — Neue Folge, no. 13. Cologne: Presseamt des Erzbistums Köln.

Lea, H. Ch.

1887   *History of the Inquisition of the Middle Ages.* Vol. 1. New York: Harper & Brothers.

Leach, Maria, and Jerome Fried

1972   *Funk and Wagnalls Standard Dictionary of Folklore, Mythology, and Legend.* New York: Harper & Row.

Leibniz, G. W.

1951   *Theodicy.* Trans. by E. M. Huggard. Ed. by A. Farrer. London: Routledge, Kegan Paul.

Lohfink, G. and R. Pesch

1988   [1987] *Tiefenpsychologie und keine Exegese: Eine Auseinandersetzung mit Eugen Drewermann* (Depth Psychology and No Exegesis: A Debate with Eugen Drewermann). 2nd ed. Stuttgart: Verlag Katholisches Bibelwerk.

Lorenz, Konrad

2002   *On Aggression.* With an Introduction by Julian Huxley. Trans. by Marjorie Latzke. New York: Routledge.

Lothane, Zvi, ed.

2001a   *Psychiatry, Psychotherapy, and Psychoanalysis in the Third Reich.* Special issue of *The Psychoanalytic Review* 88, no. 2.

Lothane, Zvi

2001b   "The Deal with the Devil to 'Save' Psychoanalysis in Nazi Germany." *The Psychoanalytic Review* 88, no. 2:195–224.

Lüdemann, Gerd

1990   "Träume — die vergessene Sprache Gottes? Zur tiefenpsychologischen Exegese Eugen Drewermanns" (Dreams — God's Forgotten Language? About the Depth-Psychological Exegesis of Eugen Drewermann). *Materialdienst des Konfessionskundlichen Institutes Bensheim* 41, no. 4:67–73.

1992   *Texte und Träume: ein Gang durch das Markusevangelium in Auseinandersetzung mit Eugen Drewermann* (Texts and Dreams: A Walk through the Gospel of Mark in Critical Conversation with Eugen Drewermann). Bensheimer Hefte 71. Göttingen: Vandenhoeck und Ruprecht.

Marcheselli-Casale, Cesare

1992   *Von Drewermann lernen: Die Bibel auf der Couch* (Learning from Drewermann: The Bible on the Couch). Foreword by E. Drewermann. Trans. from the Italian by Clemens Locher. Zurich: Benzinger.

Martin, Gerhard Marcel

1990   "Eugen Drewermanns 'Strukturen des Bösen' als Ausgangspunkt eines umstrittenen Denkweges" (Eugen Drewermann's "Strukturen des Bösen" as Point of Departure for His Controversial Way of Thinking). *Theologische Literaturzeitung* 115, no. 5:322–31.

1992   "Neurosen vor Gott. An dem Paderborner Theologen und Psychoanalytiker Eugen Drewermann scheiden sich die Geister" (Neurosis before God: People Disagree on the Paderborn Theologian and Psychoanalyst Eugen Drewermann). *Deutsches Allgemeines Sonntagsblatt,* 6 March 1992, no. 10, p. 23.

McNamara, Robert

1995   *In Retrospect: The Tragedy and Lessons of Vietnam.* New York: Times Books.

Meesmann, H., ed.

1992   *Kirche und Glaube auf der Couch: Eugen Drewermann — ein Theologe im Widerstreit. Texte und Positionen* (Church and Faith on the Couch: Eugen Drewermann — a Theologian in Conflict — Texts and Positions). 2nd rev. and expanded ed. Oberursel: Publik-Forum.

Meissner, W. W.

1984   *Psychoanalysis and Religious Experience.* New Haven, Conn.: Yale University Press.

Merriam-Webster

1986   *Webster's Third New International Dictionary of the English Language Unabridge.* Ed. by Philip Babcock Gove. Springfield, Mass.: Merriam-Webster.

Michel, Peter

1994   *Brücken von Herz zu Herz: Gespräche über die Liebe* (Bridges from Heart to Heart: Conversations on Love). With contributions from the Dalai Lama, Eugen Drewermann, Rita Süssmuth, et al. Grafing: Aquamarin.

Patterson, Charles

   2002   *Eternal Treblinka: Our Treatment of Animals and the Holocaust.*
             New York: Lantern.

Pesch, Rudolf

   1984b   *Das Markusevangelium* (The Gospel of Mark). Vol. 2. 3rd ed.
             Freiburg: Herder.

Pfister, Oskar

   1948   *Christianity and Fear: A Study in History and in the Psychology and
             Hygiene of Religion.* Trans. by W. H. Johnston. London: George Allen
             & Unwin,

Pine, Fred

   1985   *Developmental Theory and Clinical Process.* New Haven: Yale
             University Press.

Pius XII (Pope)

   1956   "Christmas Message, 24 December 1956." *Herder-Korrespondenz*
             11:177–80.

Portmann, A.

   1962   "Zerebralisation und Ontogenese" (Cerebralization and Ontogenesis).
             In *Zoologie aus vier Jahrzehnten: Gesammelte Abhandlungen.*
             Munich: Piper.

   1964   "Die Stellung des Menschen in der Natur" (The Position of Humanity
             within Nature). In *Zoologie aus vier Jahrzehnten: Gesammelte
             Abhandlungen.* Munich: Piper.

   1969   *Biologische Fragmente zu einer Lehre vom Menschen* (Biological
             Fragments for a Theory of Humanity). 3rd enl. ed. Basel: Schwabe.

Pottmeyer, Hermann J., ed.

   1992   *Fragen an Eugen Drewermann: Eine Einladung zum Gespräch* (Ques-
             tions for Eugen Drewermann: An Invitation for Dialogue). Schriften
             der Katholischen Akademie in Bayern, no. 146. With contributions
             from Anton Bucher, Bernhard Fraling, Peter Hünermann, Hermann J.
             Pottmeyer, and Rudolf Schnackenburg. Düsseldorf: Patmos.

Pruyser, P. W.

   1968   *A Dynamic Psychology of Religion.* New York: Harper & Row.

Raguse, H.

1993   *Psychoanalyse und biblische Interpretation: Eine Auseinanders-etzung mit Eugen Drewermanns Auslegung der Johannes-Apokalypse* (Psychoanalysis and Biblical Interpretation: A Discussion of Eugen Drewermann's Reading of the Book of Revelation). Berlin: Kohlhammer.

Rank, Otto

1919   *Psychoanalytische Beiträge zur Mythenforschung: Gesammelte Studien aus den Jahren 1912 bis 1914.* (Psychoanalytic Contributions to Myth-Research: Complete Studies, 1912–14). Internationale Psychoanalytische Bibliothek. Leipzig: Internationaler Psychoanalytischer Verlag.

1952   *The Trauma of Birth.* New York: Robert Brunner.

Ranke-Heinemann, Uta

1990   *Eunuchs for the Kingdom of Heaven: Women, sexuality, and the Catholic Church.* Trans. by Peter Heinegg. New York: Doubleday.

1992   "Maulkorb-Existenz" (Muzzled Existence). In *Drewermann und die Folgen: Vom Kleriker zum Ketzer? Stationen eines Konflikts.* Ed. by Thomas Schweer, 314–15. Munich: Heine, 1992.

Ratzinger, Joseph

1968   *Einführung in das Christentum: Vorlesungen über das Apostolische Glaubensbekenntnis.* Munich: Kösel (English: 1970).

1970   *Introduction to Christianity.* Trans. by J. R. Forster. New York: Herder and Herder (German: 1968).

1996   *Relativism: The Central Problem for Faith Today.* Available from http://www.ratzinger.it/conferenze/crisiteologia_eng.htm, Internet. Accessed 13 August 2002.

Reich, Wilhelm

1970   [1933] *The Mass Psychology of Fascism.* Trans. by Vincent R. Carfagno. New York: Farrar, Straus & Giroux.

1972   *Character Analysis.* 3rd, enl. ed., trans. by Vincent R. Carfagno. New York: Touchstone.

Reik, T.

1951   *Dogma and Compulsion: Psychoanalytic Studies of Myths and Religions.* Trans. by B. Miall. New York: International Universities Press.

Richter, C. P.

1957 "On the Phenomenon of Sudden Death in Animals and Man." *Psychosomatic Medicine* 19:191–8.

Rick, Hermann J, ed.

1991 *Dokumentation zur jüngsten Entwicklung um Dr. Eugen Drewermann* (Documentation of the Latest Developments around Dr. Eugen Drewermann). Paderborn: Bonifatius.

1992 *Dokumentation zur jüngsten Entwicklung um Dr. Eugen Drewermann* (Documentation of the Latest Developments around Dr. Eugen Drewermann). 2nd enl. and rev. ed. Paderborn: Bonifatius.

Ricoeur, Paul

1986 "Diskussion: Paul Ricoeur, Eugen Drewermann" (Discussion: Paul Ricoeur, Eugen Drewermann). In *Wovon werden wir morgen geistig leben?: Mythos, Religion und Wissenschaft in der "Postmoderne": Referate und Diskussionen des 13. Salzburger Humanismusgespräch held in Salzburg 28–30. September 1986.* Ed. by Oskar Schatz and Hans Spatzenegger, 171–81. Salzburg: Anton Pustet.

Riemann, Fritz

1961 *Grundformen der Angst und die Antinomien des Lebens: Eine tiefenpsychologische Studie über die Ängste des Menschen und ihre Überwindung* (The Foundations of *Angst* and Life's Antinomien: A Depth-Psychological Study of Human Anxiety and Its Overcoming). Munich: E. Reinhardt.

Rizzuto, A.-M.

1979 *The Birth of the Living God: A Psychoanalytic Study.* Chicago: University of Chicago Press.

de Rosa, Peter

1988 *Vicars of Christ: The Dark Side of the Papacy.* New York: Crown (German: 1989)

1989 *Gottes erste Diener: Die dunkle Seite des Papsttums.* Munich: Droemer Knaur (English: 1988).

Rosen, Steven

1992 *Die Erde bewirtet euch festlich: Vegetarismus und die Religionen der Welt* (The Earth Hosts a Feast for You: Vegetarianism and World Religions). Foreword by Isaac B. Singer. With an essay by Eugen Drewermann. Trans. from the English by Hank Troemel. Satteldorf: ADYAR.

Rosenblatt, Roger

2001   "God Is Not on My Side. Or Yours." *Time,* 17 December, 92.

Rosenblum, Mort

1996   "Fired French bishop keeps the faith, and faithful Monsignor
            resurfaces on Internet, and e-mail trade is growing brisk." *Boston
            Globe,* 1 September, A18.

Sartre, Jean-Paul

1956   *Being and Nothingness: An Essay on Phenomenological Ontology.*
            Trans. with an Introduction, by Hazel E. Barnes. New York:
            Philosophical Library.

1972   The Childhood of a Leader. In *The Wall: and Other Stories.* Trans. by
            Lloyd Alexander. New York: New Directions.

1991   *Critique of dialectical reason.* New York: Verso.

Schmidt, Kurt Dietrich

1984   *Grundriß der Kirchengeschichte* (A Basic Outline of Church History)
            8th expanded ed. Göttingen: Vandenhoeck & Ruprecht.

Schneider, Reinhold

1949   *Iberisches Erbe: Das Leiden des Camões, Philipp II.* (Iberian Heritage:
            The Suffering of Camões, Philip II). With a new Introduction. Olten:
            Summa-Verlag.

Schönborn, Felizitas von

1993   *Eugen Drewermann. Rebell oder Prophet?* (Eugen Drewermann:
            Rebel or Prophet?). Olten: Walter.

Schoonenberg, Piet

1965   *Man and Sin: A Theological View.* Trans. by Joseph Donceel. Notre
            Dame, Ind.: University of Notre Dame Press.

1967   "Der Mensch in der Sünde" (The Human Being in Sin). In *Mysterium
            Salutis: Grundriß heilsgeschichtlicher Dogmatik.* Vol. 2, *Die Heils-
            geschichte vor Christus.* Ed. by J. Feiner and M. Löhrer, 845–941.
            Einsiedeln: Benzinger.

Schultz, J. H.

1955   "Grundfragen der Neurosenlehre: Propädeutik einer medizinischen
            Psychologie" (Basic Issues in a Theory of Neurosis: Introduction for
            a Medical Psychology). Stuttgart: Thieme.

Schultz-Hencke, Harald

1927   *Einführung in die Psychoanalyse* (Introduction to Psychoanalysis).
        Jena: Fischer.

1940   *Der Gehemmte Mensch: Grundlagen einer Desmologie als Beitrag
        zur Tiefenpsychologie* (The Inhibited Person: Foundations for a
        Desmology as Contribution to Depth Psychology). Leipzig: Thieme.

Schweitzer, Albert

1949   *The Philosophy of Civilization*. New York: Macmillan.

Scorsese, Martin

1988   *The Last Temptation of Christ*. Universal Pictures and Cineplex
        Odeon Films. Directed by Martin Scorsese.

Shakespeare, William

n. d.   *Hamlet, Prince of Denmark*. In *The Complete Works of Shakespeare*.
        With an Introduction by St. John Ervine, 1127-70. London: Collins
        Clear-Type Press.

Sivan, Eyal, and Rony Brauman

1999   *The Specialist*. A film produced entirely from footage recorded in 1961
        in Jerusalem by Leo Hurwitz. Produced and directed by Eyal Sivan.
        Written by Rony Brauman and Eyal Sivan. Original Camera: Leo
        Hurwitz. Film Editor: Audrey Maurion. Executive Producer: Armelle
        Laborie. Inspired by Hannah Arendt's *Eichmann in Jerusalem*.
        Presented by Momento!, France/Israel.

Skinner, B. F.

1948   *Walden Two*. New York: Macmillan.

Sobel, Alfred

1993   *Eugen-Drewermann-Bibliographie* (Eugen Drewermann
        Bibliography). 2nd expanded ed. Wiesbaden: Sobel.

Sölle, Dorothee

1990   Heilung und Befreiung (Healing and Liberation). In *Der Klerikerstreit*,
        27–31.

Speer, Albert

1970   *Inside the Third Reich: Memoirs*. Trans. from the German by Richard
        and Clara Winston. Introduction by Eugene Davidson. New York:
        Macmillan.

Der Spiegel

1992   "Nur noch jeder vierte ein Christ" (Only One Out of Four Are
        Christians). no. 25 (15 June): 36–57.

Spitz, René A.

1955   *The Primal Cavity. The Psychoanalytic Study of the Child.* Vol. 10.
        New York: International Universities Press.

1957   *No and Yes: On the Genesis of Human Communication.* New York:
        International Universities Press.

1965   *The First Year of Life: A Psychoanalytic Study of Normal and
        Deviant Development of Object Relations.* New York: International
        Universities Press.

Stanton, Elizabeth Cady

1972   Womanliness. In *Feminism: The Essential Historical Writings.* Ed.
        Miriam Schneir, New York: Vintage.

Steinbeck, John

1952   *East of Eden.* New York: Viking Press.

Stratmann OP, Franziskus M., et al.

1960   *Atomare Kampfmittel und Christliche Ethik: Diskussionsbeiträge
        deutscher Katholiken* (Nuclear Weapons and Christian Ethics:
        Contributions to the Discussion by German Catholics). Munich:
        Kösel.

Strohmaier, Klaus

1996   *Theologische Anthropologie bei Eugen Drewermann: Von Angst,
        uralten Bildern und befreiender Beziehung* (Eugen Drewermann's
        Theological Anthropology: Fear, Primordial Images and Liberating
        Relationship). Wissenschaftliche Reihe; Theologie, no. 4. Marburg:
        Tectum.

Sudbrack, Josef

1992   *Eugen Drewermann...um die Menschlichkeit des Christentums*
        (Eugen Drewermann...for the Humanity of Christianity). 3rd ed.
        Würzburg: Echter.

Swidler, Leonard, ed.

1981   *Küng in Conflict.* Garden City, New York: Doubleday.

Szondi, L.

1960   *Lehrbuch der experimentellen Triebdiagnostik* (Text Book for an Experimental Diagnostic of Drives). Vol. ', *Text-Band*. 2nd rev. ed. Bern: Huber.

1977   *Triebpathologie* (Pathology of Drives). Vol. 1. Bern: Huber.

Tausch, Reinhard

1970   *Gesprächspsychotherapie* (Dialogical Psychotherapy). 4th enl. ed. Göttingen: Verlag für Psychologie Hogrefe.

Tillich, Paul

1957   *Dynamics of Faith*. New York: Harper & Row.

1958   *The Religious Symbol. Daedalus*. Middletown, Conn.: Wesleyan University Press.

Time International

1990   Book Review of "The Clergy: Psychogram of an Ideal." 8 January.

Tinbergen, N.

1969   "Von Krieg und Frieden bei Tier und Mensch" (Of War and Peace in Animals and Humans). In *Kreatur Mensch: Moderne Wissenschaft auf der Suche nach dem Humanum*. Ed. by G. Altner. Gräfelfing near Munich: Moos.

Tuiavii, Chief, and Scheurmann, Erich

1997   *Tuiavii's Way: A South See Chief's Comments on Western Society*. Adapted and trans. by Peter C. Cavelti. Toronto, Ont.: Legacy Editions.

Ulanov, Ann and Barry Ulanov

1975   *Religion and the Unconscious*. Philadelphia: The Westminster Press

van der Minde, Hans-Jürgen

1994   *Für ein offenes Christentum. Kirche der Zukunft — Zukunft der Kirche* (For an Open Christianity: Church of the Future — Future of the Church) With a contribution by Eugen Drewermann. Munich: Kösel.

Vattimo, Gianni

1992   *The Transparent Society*. Trans. by David Webb. Baltimore: Johns Hopkins University Press.

Venetz, Hermann-Josef

1986   " 'Mit dem Traum, nicht mit dem Wort ist zu beginnen' — Tiefen-
        psychologie als Herausforderung für die Exegese?" ("We Must Begin
        with the Dream, not with the Word" — Depth-Psychology as Chal-
        lenge for Exegesis?). Reprinted in *Der Streit um Drewermann*. Ed. by
        B. Benedikt and A. Sobel, 28–38. Wiesbaden: Sobel, 1992.

Waelder, R.

1936   "The Principal of Multiple Function: Observations on
        Overdetermination." *Psychoanalytic Quarterly* 5:45–62.

Walf, Knut

1990   "Was Eugen Drewermann kirchenrechtlich zu erwarten hat" (What
        Eugen Drewermann Has to Expect in Terms of Church Law). In *Der
        Klerikerstreit*, 317–24.

Walsh, Mary Williams

1996   "Moved by a Different Spirit; Germans who embrace many Catholic
        Church traditions — but not the current pope's conservatism — are
        joining the 'Rome-free' Old Catholic Church, the country's only
        growing denomination." *The Los Angeles Times*, 26 December, 1.

Walter-Verlag

1991   *Der Fall Drewermann: Ausgewählte Pressestimmen* (The Drewermann
        case: Selected News Articles). Jahresgabe des Walter-Verlags für den
        Buchhandel und alle Freunde des Hauses. Olten: Walter.

Weber, Max

1952   *The Protestant Ethic and the Spirit of Capitalism*. Trans. by T. Parsons,
        with a foreword by R. H. Tawney. New York: Ch. Scribner's Sons.

Williams, Tennessee

1964   *The Night of the Iguana*. Screenplay by Anthony Veiller and John
        Huston. Directed by John Huston. Produced by Ray Stark. Metro-
        Goldwyn-Mayer. Based on Tennessee Williams's *The Night of the
        Iguana*. In *The Theatre of Tennessee Williams*. Vol. 4, *Sweet Bird of
        Youth, Period of Adjustment, The Night of the Iguana*, 247ff. New
        York: New Directions, 1961.

Zett, Carl M., and Sabine Brückmann

1992   *Warum ich trotzdem ungern Drewermann lese/Warum ich trotzdem
        ungern die Tagesthemen sehe* (Why I Nonetheless Do Not Like to Read
        Drewermann/Why I Nonetheless Do Not Like to Watch *Tagesthemen* [a
        prime time news program]). Bergisch Gladbach: Editions La Colombe.

Index

abortion, 15, 21, 275, 299–300
Abraham (biblical patriarch), 36, 113, 217n2, 285
Abraham, Karl, 56, 64–65, 68, 79–80, 90, 168, 264
acceptance, unconditional. *See* hold
Adler, Alfred, 49, 88, 89, 105
adolescence, 59
aggression
  absolute character of in human history, 140–41
  against human psyche, 166–85
  caused by alienation from God, 46, 106–8, 328
  hidden, 29
  infinitization of, 142, 186–89, 334
  oral level, 80–87
  and perfectionism, 106–8, 129
  and religious fanaticism, 166–73
  religious resolution of, 147, 191–208, 247–61, 334
  sports as ritualized, 194–95
  suppression vs. working through, 202–3
  war, origins of, 135–45
  see also Genesis 4:1–16; God-image, violent
ahimsa (Jaina prohibition of killing), 10, 81
Albertz, Heinrich, 171
Alexander the Great, 59, 207
Alter, Margaret G., 337
ambivalence. *See* God-image, violent (ambivalent)
anal level
  castration anxiety on, 104–5, 305
  conflicts, resolution of, 252–61
  and evangelical obedience, 300, 304–11
  fear on, 73, 119, 132–33
  sadism and aggression on, 57–58, 89–90, 249
animals, inhumane treatment of, 156–57, 164, 166
anorexia nervosa, 82, 101
Answer to Job (Jung), 216n*

anthropocentrism, 153–57, 160–61, 163–68, 185, 332
anthropodicy, 8, 219
anthropology
  as theological method, 6, 17n11, 22, 33–34, 219, 321, 327–30
  and universal significance of mythic images, 47–51
antisemitism, 167n6, 227–33, 285
anxiety
  castration, 73–74, 82–87, 104–6, 133, 256–57, 303, 305
  and clergy-ideal, 320–23
  and evangelical counsels, 300–320
  existential, 54, 101–3, 95–96, 108–23, 212, 273, 328–29
  five basic paleoanthropological forms, 82–87
  and God-image, 39, 52, 88, 103, 216
  of separation, 73–78, 80–82, 93, 98–99
  and serpent, 68, 70
  "stopping up" as central characteristic of sin, 78, 287–88
  See also fear
Apologeticum (Tertullian), 262
apologists, Christian, 158–59, 161
archetypes. *See* images, psychic
Arendt, Hannah, 23
Aristotle, 97
atheism, 103, 157–66, 332
atonement theories, 217–19, 252
Attila the Hun, 146
Attis (God of grain), 159, 262
Augustine, Saint, 315
axial age, 301, 311, 314
Aztec religion, 200, 223, 251, 261–63, 290, 329

baptism, 196, 266–68, 271
Being and Nothingness (Sartre), 94
being-for-others, 96–106, 292–300, 329
being-like-God, 73–78, 214

being vs. doing, 151, 176–77, 181n10, 182–84, 190–91, 273, 281
Berger, Klaus, 167n6
Bilz, Rudolf, 69, 81, 83–86, 140, 263
Boff, Leonardo, 17
Boss, Medard, 96n15
Boston Globe, 14
Brothers Karamazov (Dostoevsky), 32
Buber, Martin, 35
Buddhism, 176, 201, 312, 324
Bultmann, Rudolf, 237, 242, 322
Bush, George H. W., 169

Cain and Abel, biblical story of. *See* Genesis 4:1–16
Calvinism, 178n*
cannibalism, 79, 137–38, 198–99
Cannon, Walter B., 81, 83, 140
castration anxiety, 59, 73–74, 82–87, 104–6, 133, 256–57, 303, 305
Catholic Church. *See* Roman Catholic Church
Chalcedon, Council of, 311n8
chastity, evangelical, 300, 311–20, 324–25
Childhood and Society (Erikson), 65
"Childhood of a Leader" (Sartre), 280
children, as theological symbol, 126
Christ. *See* Cross; Jesus
Christian Century (journal), 336
Christianity
    ambivalent God-image in, 12–13
    belligerent effects of, 12, 152–85
    exclusiveness of, 286
    fear-based, 12–13
    historicizing interpretations of, 22, 162, 234–35
    impotence of, 23–33, 145–51, 190–91
    neurotic structures in, 122–23
    reason and will emphasis, 162
    secularizing effects of, 157–66
    uniqueness of, 158, 241
    see also Roman Catholic Church
Christianity and Fear (Pfister), 257n20
Christocentrism, 155–56
Christology. *See* Cross; Jesus
church
    impotence of in Nazi Germany, 26–27
    redefinition of role, 20–21, 288, 320–26, 333
    see also Christianity; Roman Catholic Church

"Church in the Second Half of Our Century: Transmission and Problems of Religious Life in Germany" (Drewermann), 25
von Clausewitz, Carl, 145
clergy-ideal, Roman Catholic
    comfort/asceticism dichotomy, 286–87
    diagnosis of the current mentality, 280–92
    etiology of the clerical mind-set, 292–300
    and evangelical counsels, 300–320
    external vs. internal interpretation of, 279
    and fascism, 284–85
    fear and self-sacrifice of, 21–22, 211, 287–300, 331
    and "official" status, 281, 283–84, 287–90
    as promoting psychic and religious alienation, 282–83
    psychological problems associated with, 277
    reform of, 276, 325–26
    and savior mentality, 318–19
    and superego/ego identification, 298
    violence of, 285–86
    vocation as conscious decision *and* divine election, 281–83
collective unconscious. *See* archetypes; images, psychic
collectivism
    and aggression, 190, 195, 199
    and clergy-ideal, 273, 284, 311, 320
    and follower-mentality, 29–33, 128, 233, 305
    liberation from, 14, 208
    origin of in alienation from God, 107–8, 124
    and powerlessness of reason, 184
    as threat to the individual, 20, 25, 30, 50, 57–59, 211, 327–28
commandments, divine, 38–43, 172, 221, 293
Concept of Anxiety (Kierkegaard), 108, 110
"Concept of God after Auschwitz: A Jewish Voice" (Jonas), 9
Condrau, Gion, 96n15
confession, sacrament of, 198
Congregation for the Doctrine of the Faith (Congregation on Faith), 17, 216
"Conjectural Beginning of Human History" (Kant), 92
conscience, primacy of, 17, 19–20
conscientious objection, 19–20, 25, 148, 153
Constantine (Roman emperor), 153

contingency, 96–106
counsels, evangelical
    chastity, 300, 311–20
    and eschatology, 320
    externalization of, 286, 301–2
    internalization of, 280
    obedience, 300, 304–11
    poverty, 300, 302–4
    psychogenesis of, 300–320
    reinterpretation of, 320–26
counter-finality
    of aim and result in fear-based situations,
        21, 29–30, 32, 132, 153–54, 294, 328,
        332
    of reason, 141n4
Cross
    attitude responsible for, 244–45
    as "cipher of redemption," 251, 258–59,
        269
    danger of external-historical
        interpretations of, 255–61
    destructive work of, 188
    as fulfillment of Old Testament prophecies,
        257–58
    history and typology, 226–44
    inner (subjective) importance of, 210–11,
        261–71
    as result of violent God-image, 212–71
    sadomasochistic interpretations of, 21,
        210, 219–26, 250, 333–34
    as symbol of redemption from violent
        God-image, 244–71
    as triumph over fear, 220–26
    in world mythology, 261–63
Cybele (Near Eastern mother goddess), 316,
    329

death
    fear of as basis for war, 189
    fear of mitigated by Eucharist, 203–4
    as punishment, 83, 101
    "sickness unto," 40, 86
    "vagus," 86
death of God theology, 4–5, 165–66
Degenhardt, Archbishop Johannes J., 15, 16,
    17
depression, 114–15, 196–99 (see also oral
    level: guilt)
depth psychology, 14, 19, 236, 247–52, 271,
    275
Deschner, Karlheinz, 311

despair, four types of, 112–19
dictatorships, 128, 139
Dionysus (God of wine), 195
Discovering the God Child Within: A
    Spiritual Psychology of the Infancy of
    Jesus (Drewermann), 336
Discovering the Royal Child Within: A
    Spiritual Psychology of "The Little
    Prince" (Drewermann), 336
docetism, 153
doing vs. being, 151, 176–77, 181n10,
    182–84
Dogma and Compulsion (Reik), 257n20
Dostoevsky, Fyodor, 32, 111
dragon-slaying myths, 57
Drewermann, Eugen
    conflict with hierarchy, 148, 234
    Kleriker, personal reasons for writing,
        274–75
    public figure, 13–18
    priesthood and psychoanalysis, 329–30
    sacrificial mentality, critique of, 121–23
    silencing and suspension from priesthood,
        15–18, 158
    "Trojan horse" metaphor for work, 19–22,
        33, 109–10, 294, 333
duty, 23–25, 55, 127–29, 316–17
Dying We Live: Meditations for Lent and
    Easter (Drewermann), 336

East of Eden (Steinbeck), 88
ecclesiology, 20–21, 288, 320–26, 333
ecology, 21, 131, 157–66, 185, 331
ego, 191–92, 270–71, 311
Eibl-Eibesfeldt, I., 62, 69
Eichmann, Adolf, 23–25, 128
Einstein, Albert, 150
Eleusis, mystery cults of, 196, 201
enemies, inner, 10–13
Enlightenment, Age of, 162, 170, 308
Entwurf ("projection" in Heidegger's sense),
    27, 28, 30–31, 99, 142, 292
Erikson, Erik H., 10, 11n5, 56, 64–65, 79,
    81, 194n14, 199n15, 200n16, 331
eschatology, 312
Esser, Annette, 337
ethical optimism, 171–73, 190
ethics, 28, 32–33, 145–51, 165, 198–99, 332
Eternal Treblinka (Patterson), 156n5

Eucharist
  and aggression, ritualization and subli-
    mation of, 193–94, 199–208, 226,
    334
  feminine appearance of the divine in, 204,
    253
  and fertility religions, 196
  and guilt feelings, resolution of, 194–99
  meal as universal archetype of
    reconciliation, 205–6
  as resolution of psychic conflicts, 252–61
  symbolic understanding of, 192
  as unambivalent God-image, 253
  as unity with God, 271
  and war, solution for, 191–208
evangelical counsels. See counsels, evangelical
evil, 23–33, 91–92, 127–30, 145–51, 165,
  232
evolution, 137–38, 143
externalization
  of clergy-ideal, 279
  of evangelical counsels, 301–2, 320–26
  of historical Jesus, 233–43
  of sacrifice in religion, 200–201
  of symbolism in Christianity, 158–66

fairy tales, 48–49, 60
faith
  guilt revealed by, 120
  as necessary and natural for humans,
    124–27
  as self realization, 270
  as trust, 12–13, 119–23, 333, 341
fall of humanity
  biblical story of (see Genesis 3)
  as universal but not necessary, 91–123,
    331
fanaticism, religious, 169–70
fascism, 8–9, 26, 284–85 (see also Nazi
  Germany)
father-image, 52, 64, 174–75
fear
  and being-like-God, 73–77
  and brain development, 141–42
  calming of with the symbols of religion,
    189–91
  and Christian faith, 12–13
  and counter-finality of actions, 21, 29–30,
    32, 141n4, 328, 332
  and dictatorships, 139
  existential, 28–29, 133–34, 273

fear (continued)
  and individual's disappearance into the
    collective, 327
  as motive for war, 135–45, 173
  as origin of violent God-image in Genesis,
    33–45
  primordial, five types, 82–87
  and reason, affect on, 141–43
  as root of sin and evil, 27–31, 331
  three levels of, 132–34
  vs. trust, 131–35
  unconscious, paralyzing effects of, 330
  see also anxiety
Fear and Trembling (Kierkegaard), 110, 122
feminist theology, 9
fertility religions, 196
Fest, Joachim C., 207, 285n**
Feuerbach, Ludwig, 6, 162, 282, 325
finitude
  and aggression, 189
  and demons in Gospel of Mark, 215
  despair of, 54, 112–19, 175
  and evangelical poverty, 323
  and psychic images, 134
  realization of in axial age, 301
Flood, Great. See Genesis 6–8
follower-mentality, 29–32, 277, 327, 332
Francis of Assisi, Saint, 146, 305–7
Frankl, V. E., 115
Frankfurter Allgemeine Zeitung, 309
freedom
  existential, 91–97, 100, 102–3, 274, 301,
    303, 322
  fear-motivated liquidation of , 29–32,
    109–27, 131–32, 174–75, 288
  in secular culture, 158, 160, 164
Freud, Anna, 71, 75, 77, 259n21
Freud, Sigmund
  ambivalent God-image in patriarchal
    religion, 254
  anal-sadistic rivalry, 89–90
  anxiety, 73–75, 86, 132, 296
  autobiographical character of
    Interpretation of Dreams, 274
  castration complex, 59, 73–74, 82–87,
    104–6, 133, 256–57, 303, 305
  drives, theory of, 99, 193
  on evil, necessity of, 109
  and evangelical counsels, 300–320
  and Gandhi's Satyagraha, 10
  God, human need for, 269–70

Freud, Sigmund (*continued*)
  incest theory, 265
  libido theory, 74, 100
  object-related focus, 341
  Oedipus complex, 72, 78–79, 120, 184n11,
    254–61, 266
  oral stage guilt, 81
  psychical truths as "screen memories,"
    236–37
  psychic imagery (archetypes), 49, 62, 124,
    162, 236–37, 255
  psychic stages, 63, 68
  and religion, critique of, 11, 13, 125,
    221n5, 222, 256, 315, 325
  superego in clergy-ideal, 284, 298, 328
  and transference, 210, 333
  and Yahwist's focus in Genesis, 51–53, 120
Fromm, Erich, 11n5, 207
Future of an Illusion (Freud), 11

Gaillot, Bishop Jacques, 14, 16
Gandhi, Mahatma, 10, 200n16, 206
Gandhi's Truth (Erikson), 10, 194n14
von Gebsattel, V. E., 115
Geertz, Clifford, 174–75
Genesis 2–11 (Yahwist primordial history),
  47–52, 55–59
Genesis 3 (story of the fall)
  God-image alteration in, 76
  exegetical analysis, 33–45
  existential-philosophical perspective,
    96–106
  and hold, loss of, 63–66
  latent sexuality in, 70
  motive for original sin, 38–39, 41–44,
    127–28, 172
  nakedness symbol, 40–41
  and Oedipal stage, 66–73, 179
  and oral stage, 56–57, 179, 196
  punishments as change in human
    experience, 43–44
  psychoanalytic analysis, 59–87
  serpent, 37–39, 49, 66–73, 96–106
  theological interpretation, 108–19
Genesis 4:1–16 (story of Cain and Abel)
  and anal level, 57–58
  as clergy-ideal analogue, 298–99
  existential-philosophical perspective,
    106–8

Genesis 4:1–16 (*continued*)
  psychoanalytic perspective, 87–90
  and sacrificial mentality in fear-based
    religion, 34, 45–47, 128, 172–73,
    212–13, 232
  theological interpretation of, 119
Genesis 6:1–4 (marriage of angels story), 58,
  118
Genesis 6–8 (Great Flood story), 45, 55–56,
  58, 213–14
George, Saint, 318
Gibran, Kahlil, 223n8
Girl Without Hands (fairy tale), 303
Glatzel, Hans, 81
Gnosticism, 93, 97, 234
God
  death of (theological movement), 4–5,
    165–66
  opponent vs. giver of life, 328
  as "Other" only after the fall, 102–6
  proof for existence of, 124–27
God-image
  alienation from the unconscious in
    Christianity, 161–62
  as altered by oral ambivalence, 76–78
  as projection of mother and father image,
    65–66, 252
  as superego, 169
God-image, nonviolent (unambivalent)
  in Garden of Eden, 330
  hold, source of, 46, 211
  as Jesus' source of trust, 21, 334
  and therapeutic theology, 22, 250, 329
God-image, violent (ambivalent)
  and aggression, 22
  church appropriation of, 21, 25
  cleansing of, 330
  development of, 128–30
  fear basis of, 6, 28, 33–45, 76–78
  freedom from, 126
  and freedom, liquidation of, 29–32,
    109–27, 131–32, 174–75, 288
  and guilt, 328
  and infinite justice, 291
  Jesus' opposition to, 209
  and moral prohibitions, 9, 39, 43, 128
  in Nazi Germany, 3–9, 327–28
  and sacrificial religion, 45–47, 212–19
  and war, foundation for, 173
  in Yahwist primordial history, 44

Gollwitzer, Helmut, 171
good and evil, knowledge of, 40–41, 43–44, 75, 92, 98, 101
Good Friday, 220–26, 258–59
Gospels
    typological reading of, 228–29
    see also Matthew, Mark, Luke, or John, Gospels of
grace, 12, 110, 115, 136, 172–73, 186–91, 199, 206, 328
Grand Inquisitor (character in Brothers Karamazov), 32
Greek thought, 36, 154–55, 157–58, 168, 178
Gregory VII (pope), 284
Greinacher, Norbert, 16
group dynamics, three basic laws of, 138–39
guilt
    and clergy-ideal, 292–300
    ecological, 165–66
    existential, 40–41, 43, 82–87, 102–8
    faith-revealed, 120
    and God-image, 328
    inevitability of, 78–82
    in Nazi Germany, 29–31
    oral level origin of, 61, 65, 66–74, 90, 168–73
    origin in hunting prey, 81
    and psychoanalysis, 217–18
    religious dimension of, 33
    resolution of, 191–204, 252–71
    universal yet product of free choice, 91–96, 108–19
Gulf War (1991), 169

Haag, Herbert, 17
Hansel and Gretel (fairy tale), 302–3
happiness, 8–9, 240–41, 256, 298, 314–15
Hebrew thought, 36, 154–55, 157
Hegel, Georg Wilhelm Friedrich, 91, 92–98, 109, 322
Heidegger, Martin, 27, 28, 101, 280
Hermann, Imre, 63
hieros gamos myth, 58
Hinduism, 312, 325
Hiroshima and Nagasaki, 6 (see also nuclear weapons)
historical criticism, 34–35
history
    and Christian myth, 158–59
    and divine revelation, 3

history (continued)
    external vs. internal (anthropological) view of, 4, 22, 226–43
    and Jesus, 226–43
Hitler, Adolf, 4–5, 24, 26n3, 28, 59, 149–50, 184n12, 207–8, 219, 284–85
Höffner, Cardinal Josef, 300
Hofstätter, Peter R., 139
hold (Halt)
    absolute need for, 112, 126–27, 165
    definition of, 341
    drive to cling, 62–64, 204n17
    and Eucharist, 192, 197, 204n17
    and mother archetype, 168–69
    as motive for all human action, 46
    provided only by God, 329
    as theological and depth-psychological goal, 245, 247–52
    and tree symbol, 63–66
Holocaust, Jewish, 3–9, 23–33, 219
Homans, George C., 139
homosexuality, 55, 59, 72n13, 275, 278–79, 317–18
Horney, Karen, 88, 89
"Hostility Against Myths in Christianity, the Contentious Battle among Denominations, and the Inner Disunity of Humans" (excursus in Strukturen des Bösen) (Drewermann), 123, 136, 154, 158
Hussein, Saddam, 169
hysteria, 58, 117–18

Ibsen, Henrik, 136, 179–84
Ignatius of Loyola, Saint, 168, 309
images, psychic (archetypes; symbols)
    ambivalence of, 51, 134–35, 175
    Christian hostility to, 157
    creation of, 331
    Cross, reinterpretation of, 121, 193, 210, 220–26, 244–71, 333
    Godhead, eating of in Eucharist, 191–208, 244, 252–71
    as grace manifestations, 328
    historicization of in Christianity, 162
    as indispensable language of human spirit, 175
    interpretations: philosophical, psychic, theological, 97–98
    mother and father, 174–85, 261–71
    of prohibition, 39
    psychical presuppositions for, 49

images, psychic (*continued*)
  reality and validity of, 124–27, 239
  savior, 233–43
  serpent and tree, 66–73
  therapeutic, 191, 241–43
  tree and fruit, 61–66
  and three dimensions of human existence, correspondence to, 134
  universal significance of in Genesis, 47–51
  see also Jung, Carl Gustav: archetypes
immortality, 313
incest, 55, 71–72, 75, 118, 220n4, 265–66
individual, primacy of, 51, 156, 223, 273
infallibility, papal, 16, 335
infinitization, 133–35, 141–45, 169, 186, 331, 334
infinity, 54, 99–113, 115–19, 215
Inhibitions, Symptoms and Anxiety (Freud), 73
Innocent III (pope), 284–85, 306
inquisitions, religious, 170, 222
internalization, 200–208, 233–43, 280, 320–26
Interpretation of Dreams (Freud), 236, 274
Introduction to Christianity (Ratzinger), 216
Isaiah (biblical prophet), 4–5, 167n7, 301
Islam, 170, 176, 178, 312, 324

Jaspers, Karl, 301
Jensen, Adolph E., 255n19
Jesus
  death of as result of violent God-image, 119–23, 209, 212–71, 333–34
  and fear-based religion, 12–13, 220–26, 250–51
  God-image of, 5–7, 223–24, 233
  historical and transhistorical meaning of, 226–43
  poetic religion of, 332
  therapeutic significance of, 5–7, 241–43, 251, 259
  and trust as historical foundation for Christian faith, 241–42
  uniqueness of, 233–43
  see also Cross
John, Gospel of, 224, 225, 229, 262
John Paul II, 16, 42, 43n*, 311
Johnson, Marguerite, 335
Jonas, Hans, 9
Journal of Biblical Literature, 335
Judas (apostle), 231–32

Jung, Carl Gustav
  and archetypes, 48, 49, 61–62, 87, 124, 163, 210, 255, 333
  and demonizing of God, 216
  on developmental stages of psyche, 33, 55–59, 60
  and evil, necessity of, 109
  and God, human need for, 269–70
  incest theory, 265–66
  persona vs. ego, 284
  subject-related focus, 341
just-war doctrine, 136, 147–49, 150

Kant, Immanuel, 32–33, 91–92, 95, 99, 109, 332
Kasper, Walter, 16
Kierkegaard, Søren
  and Cross, misinterpretation of, 119–23
  despair of resignation, 284
  and ethics, suspension of, 248
  and existential anxiety, 40, 54, 108–19, 124, 133, 175, 185
  religion, critique of, 32–33
Kimbrough, S. T., Jr., 335
kissing, 69–70
Klein, M., 56, 57, 65, 79–80, 168, 180, 248, 264
Kleriker: Psychogramm eines Ideals (Clerics: Psychogram of an Ideal) (Drewermann), 14–15, 273–80, 335, 336
Kohut, Heinz, 20, 259n21
Kott, Jan, 255n19
Krieg und das Christentum (War and Christianity) (Drewermann), 135
Küng, Hans, 16, 17

Laing, R. D., 172n8
Lamech, biblical song of, 58, 129, 143
Lang, Bernhard, 17, 337
Lao-tse, 301
Last Supper. *See* Eucharist
Last Temptation of Christ (Kazantzakis/Scorcese), 316
latency period, 56, 58
Lauter, Hermann-Josef, 13, 217, 234
Leibniz, G. W., 8
liberation, 4, 14–15, 169–70, 212–19, 252–71, 327
liberation theology, 9
Lohfink, Gerhard, 16, 217n2

Luke, Gospel of, 265
Luther, Martin, 17, 321, 335

Manhattan Project, 150–51
Mark, Gospel of, 214–19, 227–29, 232–41,
    251, 253–54, 256, 258, 271
Markusevangelium (Gospel of Mark)
    (Drewermann), 193, 209, 220
Martin Luther. *See* Luther, Martin
Marx, Karl, 325
Mary, Blessed Virgin, 316–17, 335
masculinity, 317–18
Mass, sacrifice of, 194
matriarchy, 67, 71, 143, 177
Matthäusevangelium, Das (Gospel of
    Matthew) (Drewermann), 229
Matthew, Gospel of, 229–33
medical care, 164–66
metaphysicization, 169, 211, 217, 270,
    273–74, 295, 300–321, 327, 330
Metz, J. B., 304n7
Miller, David L., 337
Moment, The (Kierkegaard), 121
monasticism, 301, 311, 312
monophysitism, 311
moralism
    and clergy-ideal, 280–92
    and counter-finality of aim and result, 21,
        29–30, 32, 132, 153–54, 294, 328, 332
    and Cross, theology of, 209–71
    and evangelical counsels, 300–320
    and Gandhi's nonviolence, 10
    inner violence of, 167–68, 170
    and pacifism, 145–51
    and violent God-image, 128, 331
    and war, promotion of, 136, 166–73,
        189–90
morality, and existential evil, 23–33, 91–92,
    127–30, 145–51, 165, 232
mother-image, 61–66, 168–69, 174–75, 178,
    182–83, 319
Mo Ti, 146
mysticism, 170, 177–78
myth, 47–49, 154, 157–66

nakedness, symbol of, 40–41, 82–87,
    96–106
narcissism, 74, 127, 299
National Socialism. *See* Nazi Germany
nature, 36, 154–66

Nazi Germany
    banality of evil in, 23–33, 127–29
    "center of the world" mentality, 239
    Christianity's impotence in, 23–33, 334
    criminal vs. insane nature of, 8
    externalistic reading of religious texts in,
        228
    follower-mentality in, 29–33, 327, 332
    God-human archetype, use of, 124
    Jewish Holocaust, 3–9, 23–33, 135, 139,
        219, 290–91
    propaganda, 142–43
    and reason, powerlessness of, 184
    and sacrifice of the individual, 20, 50
    and violent God-image, 3–9
neolithic revolution, 301, 314
neurosis, 51–55, 114–19
New Introductory Lectures (Freud), 73
Nietzsche, Friedrich, 280, 315, 326
Nimrod complex, 59, 184n12
Noah's Flood. *See* Genesis 6–8
nonviolence, 10–13, 186–208
nuclear weapons, 6, 19, 135, 145, 149,
    150–51, 331

obedience
    evangelical, 300, 304–11, 324
    to God, 268–69
    self-perpetuating in clergy-ideal, 310–11
obsessive-compulsive disorder
    and clergy-ideal, 310
    and Cross, theology of, 251, 256–57
    in Ibsen's *Peer Gynt,* 179, 184
    and moralistic nonviolence, 202
    and sacrificial mentality, 212, 215, 221–22
    theological interpretation of, 54, 114,
        117–19
Oedipal level
    ambivalence toward women, 184
    castration anxiety, 73–74, 82–87, 104–6,
        256–57, 303, 305
    conflict and psychoanalytic transference,
        245–47
    and evangelical chastity, 300, 311–20
    father-image cleansing, 250
    fear on, 133
    in Genesis, 58, 72–73, 104–6, 179
    in Ibsen's *Peer Gynt,* 182
    "madonna and whore" dichotomy, 184
    and "Mother Church," 319
    superego formation, 249

Oedipus complex, 260, 254–61
Old Catholic Church, 335
Olsen, Regine, 121
ontological insecurity, 172n8
Open Heavens: Meditations for Advent and Christmas (Drewermann), 336
"oral conception," 68–69
oral level, 56–57
  ambivalence and tree symbol, 264–65
  conflicts and death of Jesus, 244–71
  conflicts viewed daseinsanalytically, 298
  and Eucharist, 195–99, 252–61
  and evangelical poverty, 300, 302–4
  fear on, 132–33
  guilt (depression), 80–82, 104–5, 196–99
  as regression from Oedipal, 68–71, 75, 303
  sadism and aggression, 22, 57, 65, 81, 168–69, 195–99, 248–49
ordination, of women, 182, 205, 325
original sin, doctrine of, 33, 38–39, 41–44, 136, 172–74, 186, 197, 209, 315, 331–33
Osiris (God of grain), 195, 262

pacifism, 145–51, 171–73, 206–7
parents, 56, 64, 125–27
passion of Christ. *See* Cross; Jesus: death of as result of violent God-image
patriarchy, 52, 67, 71, 72, 174–85, 245, 249–50, 254–57, 265, 316–17
Patterson, Charles, 156n5
Paul, Saint, 188, 198
pedophilia, priesthood, 18, 278–79
Peer Gynt (Ibsen), 136, 179–84
Pelagianism, 171–72, 333
personhood, 159–62
Pesch, Rudolf, 217, 218, 234
Pfister, Oskar, 11, 242n13, 257n20
Phariseeism, 227–33
Pilate, Pontius, 25, 223
Pine, Fred, 50
Pius IX, 335
Pius XII, 19, 153
Pohier, Jacques, 17
Portmann, A., 63
poverty, evangelical, 300, 302–4, 323–24
Practice in Christianity (Kierkegaard), 121

pride
  as insufficient motive for sin, 32, 38, 41, 77, 172, 212
  as motive for war, 146–47
prime matter, 97
principio, a (principally), 36, 249
principio, in (in the beginning), 36, 249
projection (*Entwurf*), 27, 28, 30–31, 99, 142, 292
Protestantism, 121–22, 178, 191, 237, 323
Protestant principle, 321–23
possibility
  despair of, 54, 117–19, 133, 215
  faith as, 119–27
  sin as, 108–19
psyche
  a priori forms in, 49
  Christianity's war against, 157–68
  developmental stages of, 55–59
  feminist aspects of, 174, 177
  and soul, 340
  tabula rasa theories of, 50, 163
  see also images, psychic
psychoanalysis
  as fear resolution, 329
  and "inner enemies," 10–13
  as phenomenology of sin in biblical texts, 51–55
  and transference, 65–66, 244, 245–47, 330–31, 333
psychologization, of the metaphysical, 270, 273
psychotherapy,
  client-centered, 38
  humanity-wide, 205–6
puberty, 59, 299, 309, 317

race wars, 143
Rahner, Karl, 330
Ramakrishna, 206–7
Ranke-Heinemann, Uta, 280, 311
Rank, Otto, 68, 89, 104, 220n4, 265
rationalism, 153–57
Ratzinger, Cardinal Joseph, 17, 216
reason, pathology of, under the spell of fear, 141–43, 193
redemption, as unconditional acceptance, 247–52
regression, from genital to oral level, 66–79, 179
Reich, Wilhelm, 142, 316

Reik, T., 11n5, 231, 257n20
religion
    definition of, 7, 340
    dogmatic deformation of, 7
    as ego vs. superego function, 253–54, 310,
        325–26, 328
    ethical reduction of, 28, 32–33, 145–51,
        165, 198–99, 332
    external and internal views of, 226–71
    impotence of, 145–51, 190–91
    indispensability of in addressing the
        problem of war, 189–91
    and self-realization, 11–12
    and violence, 9
Reply to Martin Buber (Jung), 216n*
repression
    moralistic, 10–11, 168, 171, 177, 179,
        185, 188
    neurotic, 55, 231, 248
    sexual, 175–76, 278, 311, 316, 324
    of unconscious, 57, 161–66, 186, 260,
        273, 275, 281–82, 330
resurrection, 266–68
Richter, C. P., 86
Riemann, Fritz, 115
Rollins, Wayne, 337
Roman Catholic Church
    clergy-ideal, 211, 273–326
    and conscientious objection, prohibition
        of, 19–20, 25, 148, 153
    in Germany, 13–18, 23–33
    historical criticism, dogmatic rejection of,
        236–37
    and images, importance of, 191
    and liturgical postures, 264
    Mass, sacrifice of, 194
    as mother, 182–83
    sexuality, repressive attitude toward, 278
    and syncretism, 178
    and Virgin Mary piety, 316–17, 335
    women in, 182, 184, 205
Rote Armee Fraktion (RAF, Red Army
    Group), 171

sacrifice
    definition of, 45
    external vs. internal meaning of, 213
    paradoxical reinterpretation of, 212–71,
        332
    see also sacrificial mentality

sacrificial mentality
    and aggression, 88–90, 106–8, 128–29
    as being-for-others, 96–106, 292–300, 329
    breaking the cycle of, 199–208
    and clergy-ideal, 211, 280–300
    Cross and baptism as resolution to, 261–71
    and dictatorships, 128
    and duty, 25, 55, 316–17
    Eucharist as resolution to, 252–61
    and evangelical counsels, 303, 320
    and fascism, 8–9, 20, 24–25, 128
    and fear, 34, 35–47
    Kierkegaard and, 121–23
    and salvation, 8–9
    and violent God-image, 45–47, 88–90,
        128, 212–26, 249–50, 328–34
sadomasochism, 21, 210, 219–26, 250,
    333–34
Saint-Exupéry, Antoine de, 336
salvation (*Heil*), 8–9
Sartre, Jean-Paul
    boss mentality, 280, 284
    and evil, inevitability of, 91
    and existential anxiety, 94–106, 109,
        112–19, 120, 189, 323
    and psychic archetypes, 49
Satan, 214–15
Satyagraha (Gandhi's nonviolent resistance),
    10, 206–7
scapegoat, 139, 259
Schillebeeckx, Edward, 17
schizoid disorder, 54, 56, 114, 116–17, 132,
    215
schizoid position, 56, 80n14
schizophrenia, 56, 116, 117
Schoonenberg, Piet, 30
Schopenhauer, Arthur, 165
Schultz, J. H., 115
Schultz-Hencke, Harald, 49, 82
Schweitzer, Albert, 165
science, modern, 157–66, 322
screen memories (inner-historical events),
    236–37
Seideneck, Hermann-Josef, 337
self realization, 270
separation anxiety, 73–78, 80–82, 93, 98–99
Sermon on the Mount, 136, 166–73, 186–90,
    246
serpent, 37–39, 49, 66–73, 96–106
sexual abuse, clergy. *See* pedophilia

sexuality
    and aggression, 143–44, 167–68
    repression of in Christianity, 18, 159,
        175–76, 257
    and Roman Catholic clergy-ideal, 278,
        311–20
    and serpent symbol, 37, 61, 66–73, 97,
        100
    and shame, 82–87
    and suppression of female in Christianity,
        174–85
shamanic religion, 280–81, 288–89
shame
    and abortion, 299
    and anorexia nervosa, 82
    in Genesis, 35, 38–45, 57, 59, 96, 101–2
    existential, 82–87, 102, 104, 107, 113,
        328
    of masculinity, 318
    national, 26, 144, 173, 202
    religious resolution of, 198–99
Sickness Unto Death (Kierkegaard), 110
sin
    as despair, a mis-relation to God, 114
    as disobedience, 32, 42–43, 212
    fear motivation for, 41–42, 108–19,
        131–35, 172
    individual responsibility for, 30–31
    as liquidation of human freedom, 29–32,
        109–27, 131–32, 174–75, 288
    as neurosis before God, 51–55, 92
    nonjudgmental reinterpretation of, 32, 341
    as prior to any act, 43
    as universal and result of free choice,
        91–96
    Yahwist sense of, 36, 172
Skinner, B. F., 51
Socrates, 301
Der Spiegel (magazine), 14
Spirale der Angst (Spiral of Anxiety)
    (Drewermann), 131n1, 135, 136, 154
spirit
    definition of, 110–11, 124–27, 274,
        339–40
    and fear, 172–73
    and infinitization of drives, 133–35,
        141–45, 186, 331, 334
Spitz, René A., 62, 64, 89
sports, 194–95
Steinbeck, John, 88
structuralism, 48

Strukturen des Bösen (Structures of Evil)
    (Drewermann)
    basic thesis, 27, 328, 331
    and contingency of Dasein, 96–106
    evil, interpretation of, 215
    excursus on myth in Christianity, 123, 136,
        154, 158
    freedom, liquidation of, 31–32
    and guilt, necessity of, 91–96
    and "inner enemies," 13
    nature myths analysis, 49
    original sin, doctrine of, 33
    sin, non-moralistic reinterpretation, 32
    theocentric psychology, 54
    theological anthropology of Genesis,
        33–34, 55–59
Sufism, 178n9, 312
superego
    development of, 58, 74, 80, 169
    identified with ego in clerical ideal, 298,
        310–11, 319
    and religion, 253–54, 310, 325–26
symbols. See images, psychic
Szondi, L., 49, 61–63, 87, 88, 204n17,
    263

tabula rasa (theory of psyche), 50, 163
territoriality, principle of, 138
terrorism, 18, 166–73, 334
Tertullian, 262
theodicy, 4, 8, 161, 219
theology
    academic, and obedience to church
        teaching, 308–9
    anthropological/psychological task for
        today, 6, 247–52, 327, 330
    as flight from human responsibility, 6
    moral reduction of, 32–33
    as therapeutic liberation, 4, 327
Third Reich. See Nazi Germany
"thirteenth room" (fairy tale image), 246
Tiefenpsychologie und Exegese (Depth Psy-
    chology and Exegesis) (Drewermann),
    241, 336
Tillich, Paul, 136
Time International (magazine), 15, 335
Tödliche Fortschritt (Deadly Progress)
    (Drewermann), 136, 154, 157
Tolstoy, Leo, 168, 316
Tonatiuh (Aztec god), 251, 290, 329
Totem and Taboo (Freud), 79, 254

totem meals, 78
transference, 65–66, 244, 245–47, 330–31, 333
transfiguration of Jesus, 234, 237–41
tree symbol, 49, 61–79, 85, 98, 100, 127, 210, 220n4, 263–68
"Trojan horse" metaphor, 19, 33, 109–10, 294, 333
trust
    as central dimension of faith, 333
    Cross and Resurrection as symbol of inner, 261–71
    vs. fear, 131–35
    as opposite of sin, 43
    unconditional (see hold)
    theological basis for, 249–50
Tuiavii of Tiavea, 177–78

unconditional acceptance. See hold
unconscious
    collective (see images, psychic)
    denial of in Christianity, 161–66, 186, 273, 281, 330

"vagus death," 86
vampire, as God-image, 290
violence. See aggression; God-image, violent
virgin birth, 268, 335
virginity, 316–17

Waelder, R., 61
Walden Two (Skinner), 51

Wannsee Conference, 24–25
war
    armament as preparation for, 145
    Christian contributions toward, 152–85
    ethical/moralistic approaches to, 145–51
    and Eucharist, 191–208
    depression as root of, 197
    fear motivation for, 135–45
    and final solutions, 140
    in Old Testament, 167
    paleoanthropological roots of, 137–45
    permanence of and theology, 7
    psychological reasons for, 144–45
    religious solution for, 151, 173, 186–208
    tragic inevitability of, 187–89
weaning, 80–82, 196–97
Weber, Max, 149, 279n1
Wise, R. Todd, 337
witch hunts, 176, 222–23
women
    Christianity's suppression of, 136, 175, 179–84
    and evangelical chastity, 313
    as fulfillers of the true task of religion, 332
    ordination of in Roman Catholic Church, 182, 205, 325
World War I, 144
World War II, 144, 151, 207, 296

Yahwist (Pentateuch source), 33–127, 131, 155, 172, 213–15, 244, 249, 294